Teaching Science as
CONTINUOUS INQUIRY

Teaching Science as
CONTINUOUS INQUIRY

MARY BUDD ROWE
Department of Childhood Education
Institute for Development of Human Resources
University of Florida, Gainesville

McGraw-Hill Book Company
New York   St. Louis   San Francisco   Düsseldorf   Johannesburg   Kuala Lumpur   London
Mexico   Montreal   New Delhi   Panama   Rio de Janeiro   Singapore   Sydney   Toronto

This book was set in Primer with Clarendon Bold by Black Dot, Inc.
The editors were Robert C. Morgan, Nancy L. Marcus, and Susan Gamer;
the designer was Barbara Ellwood;
and the production supervisor was Joe Campanella.
The drawings were done by Danmark & Michaels, Inc.
The printer was The Murray Printing Company;
the binder, Rand McNally & Company.

Teaching Science as
CONTINUOUS INQUIRY

234567890MURM79876543

Library of Congress Cataloging in Publication Data

Rowe, Mary Budd.
    Teaching science as continuous inquiry.

    (Curriculum and methods in education)
    Includes bibliographical references.
    1. Science—Study and teaching (Elementary)
I. Title.
LB1585.R57   372.3′5′044   72-13712
ISBN 0-07-054115-9

CONTENTS

PREFACE

An overview
of teaching elementary science
as continuous inquiry

This book has been prepared primarily for use by pre-service and in-service elementary teachers. It has four main objectives: (1) to supply a conceptual system for thinking about physical and biological phenomena that will allow elementary teachers to use any modern elementary science program more effectively; (2) to give teachers the knowledge and skills necessary to actually implement and maintain an inquiry-based science program; (3) to prepare teachers to plan and conduct evaluation activities that will facilitate their students' progress; (4) to provide a basis for adapting curriculum units for use in self-paced and individualized instruction programs.

Each chapter begins with a specification of objectives and concludes with a summary of major ideas presented in the chapter. A set of take-home activities and problems, designed to make the content pertinent to practice, accompanies each chapter. The attainment of the objectives should lead to appreciation, understanding, and enjoyment of inquiry in science.

The book is divided into three parts. Part 1 introduces a core set of basic skills that have applicability to virtually all modern elementary science programs: measurement; design of experiments; graphing; organization and interpretation of data. The content chosen to illustrate these skills includes examples from the physical and life sciences. Special emphasis is placed on the development of a conceptual scheme for thinking about ecological problems.

Thus Part 1 supplies what might be called the scientific framework; Part 2 introduces the pedagogical framework. At the conclusion of Part 2 you will have acquired competence in various areas, which will help you implement a science program focused on continuous inquiry. Topics like pacing of rewards, organization of work groups, development of language, and questioning are illustrated with transcripts of conversations that were tape recorded in classrooms.

Implementing a modern science program also means solving logistical problems, locating human as well as material resources, and adapting the content to various kinds of learners and teaching conditions. Thus we discuss working with handicapped children, organizing work groups, and gathering together supplies and equipment.

The philosophical basis for evaluation in science that is gradually built throughout the book is brought to a focus in Part 3. In Part 3 the emphasis is on diagnosis and decision-making skills. Chapter 16, Task Analysis, presents a procedure for analyzing units of instruction so that one may identify the minimum observations and inferences necessary for progress through a unit to occur. Teachers interested in individualization of instruction should study this chapter carefully.

Curriculum in science is no more a finished or final thing than are theories in scientific research. The final chapter includes a hypothetical symposium in which are discussed the various beliefs, values, and thoughts of people who care about what kind of science children get. If you like social perspective on a problem, you may want to begin this book by reading the last chapter first.

How much this book will help you depends on how actively you become involved as a learner. If you immerse yourself thoroughly in this book and its activities, you will perhaps come to understand why one possible title for it might be "Science and Soul." The margins are wide, to encourage you to write notes and comments at places that seem appropriate to you—that is, to adapt the content to your own needs. There are, as has been mentioned, activities designed to help you achieve the objectives stated at the beginning of each chapter. You may find additional means for achieving the objectives. Your development depends on action as well as thought. It is through action that you make the content relevant for you.

The author's participation in the SCIS, SAPA-AAAS, ESS, and COPES projects as writer, consultant, and program implementer has done much to shape the ideas presented in this book. I saw how valiantly scientists, teachers, psychologists, and science educators struggled to produce teachable units. I saw how difficult it was to implement active, inquiry-based, science programs in the face of fears, overload of work, logistical problems, and the general belief that science is a second- or possibly even a third-priority subject. It is hoped that this book will show the teacher how science can help improve performance in the skill subjects. Science provides such a good vehicle for applying skills in a meaningful context.

I gratefully acknowledge the support and suggestions I have received from colleagues, especially Professor Francis X. Lawlor, who has collaborated with me in research, curriculum development, and teaching activities in elementary schools; Professor Robert Bernoff, chemist, for the questions he pressed me to answer; Professor Emily Girault, who made me aware of how important social-psychological factors are in creating situations where students and teachers can most effectively work together; and Dr. Paul DeHart Hurd, whose constant pursuit of new ways of thought has been much admired. Thanks are due to the many teachers and children who contributed their time and energy in a collaborative effort to find out how to do science better. The willingness of teachers to open their classrooms to new science programs, to share their anxieties and problems, and to try out new ways, no matter how timidly at first, helped me know what to include in this book. The eagerness of children to engage in science and to talk about their ideas and feelings encouraged me to include samples of their discussions in the text.

Without the encouragement and help of Nancy L. Marcus, my editor, this book might not have been completed. There is so much to do in classrooms that one can forget how important it is at times to make the accumulating knowledge available for others to adapt to their own purposes.

To Nancy, Judy, Dennis, Marsha, and their parents, Charles and Nomi Bryant, I owe a special debt, as I do to my brother Jack. They kept me "down to earth" but full of hope.

The patience of McGraw-Hill in waiting for this book to come to fruition has been especially valued. As I lived and worked with teachers and children and thought about what was happening, my ideas about what would really help them grew and changed. At best, I can offer an invitation to inquiry. You may get different answers. You may ask different questions. If you can find a way to share that knowledge with me, I would appreciate it.

MARY BUDD ROWE

Teaching Science as
CONTINUOUS INQUIRY

SCIENCE is a kind of journey into the unknown, with all the uncertainties that new ventures entail. Doing science means using intuition; it means creating abstract ideas out of concrete instances, in order to find out:

1 How things work (description)
2 Why they probably work that way (explanation)
3 What must be done to make them happen in other circumstances (control)

The intent of Part 1 is to provide a kind of conceptual framework for thinking about biological and physical phenomena. Throughout this section there is a focus on certain questions:

1 What do we believe at this point in time?
2 Why do we believe it—
    a What is the evidence?
    b From where did it come?
    c How did we get it?
3 Is there another way to interpret it?

This kind of inquiry takes time, as any researcher will tell you. Everyone engaging in it must give himself license to make mistakes, to retrace steps, to occasionally feel muddled. But when one arrives at an explanation that seems to work—at least for the moment—that is exciting. It feels good. Science is a highly imaginative kind of enterprise. At the same time the product of imagining must bear some correspondence to natural phenomena.

Chapters 1 and 2 are intended to give you some tools for describing phenomena. Chapter 3 views an experiment as a way of asking questions of nature. It uses investigation into food preferences to focus attention on the nature of evidence and its relation to explanation. Chapter 4, War and Peace among the Niches, introduces some fundamental concepts for thinking about ecological problems. Relationships among variables and events are frequently masked because there are so many factors interacting with each other. Chapter 5 discusses some mathematical techniques for exposing patterns of relationships among phenomena. Throughout Part 1 the assumption is made that students would better enjoy both science and mathematics if mathematics were more intimately intertwined with science.

It is exciting when, for example, through the construction of a graph, one suddenly uncovers a trend or a relationship that was not obvious. When a pattern is once discovered, there is an increased potential to have some control of one's future because the pattern provides a basis for making decisions.

Engineering sciences, especially, are interested in analysis of systems, in prediction of the behavior of systems, and in control of phenomena in order to produce a more desirable future. Chapter 6 introduces some of the language of systems. What constitutes a desirable future, however, depends on the cultural context of the times. It depends as well as upon the biological, physical, and social limits of mankind. Chapter 7 examines some of the biological and environmental conditions for learning. It raises the question: How free are we?

CHAPTER 1

First child: *"Well, we put the stuff what's plastic in one corner."*

Second child: *"Yes, then we pacify them."*

Teacher: *"You mean classify them?"*

Second child: *"That's what I mean."*

FIRST-GRADE CONVERSATION

"Now I'll tell you what to do. I'd like you to position that nail or the—I'm using a bobby pin instead of the nail, but it's the right length . . ."   **THIRD-GRADE TEACHER**

"Wow, my system turned blue—no green—no yellow! Its yellow! I just put this like this—only two drops—like this—look, there it goes again. The system is yellow."

SECOND-GRADER IN THE SCIS PROGRAM

FIRST THERE WAS NAMING

OBJECTIVES

When you have completed your study of this chapter and its associated problems, you should be able to do the following:

1 Distinguish between an object, a collection, and a system.

2 Classify objects into groups on the basis of their properties.

3 Use a simple taxonomic key to identify a bird or a tree.

4 Construct a bar graph to describe a collection.

5 Recognize evidence of interaction.

6 State an operational definition for a variable.

7 Serial order a group of objects.

8 Show how the functions an object can serve are related to the properties of the object.

When you have achieved these objectives, you should be able to analyze the activities and experiments intended for the primary grades from any of the current elementary science programs in terms of the concepts and skills discussed in this chapter. You will have begun the process of building your own conceptual map for making your way effectively through any elementary science program.

THE PROBLEM

There are at least twenty-five elementary science programs commercially available. Furthermore, there are many districts which sponsor development of their own programs. In still other schools, there is no defined program, so that science instruction depends on the initiative of individual teachers. All this variety presents a problem for elementary teachers who want to prepare themselves to teach science or to integrate science with other subjects. There is no way of knowing in advance which programs you will encounter in a particular school, at what grade levels you will be expected to teach, and what content should be learned. Is it possible to choose content and approaches that will help teachers to adapt to different programs and to different grade levels? The primary objective of this book and the laboratory activities associated with it is to present a means for developing the reader's competence to cope with the demands of a variety of programs.

SOME COMMON FACTORS IN ELEMENTARY SCIENCE PROGRAMS

Three factors are expressed in some form in all the currently available programs:

1 What scientists do—namely, the processes in which they engage
2 The knowledge that scientists generate and the way in which they organize and use it, i.e., the organized content and applications of science
3 The mental and emotional development of the children, which limits what it is appropriate to do at different stages

According to the psychologist Robert Gagné, the

processes are common to all the various scientific disciplines. Regardless of whether a scientist is a biologist or a chemist or a physicist, he spends much of his time engaging in the processes of inferring, predicting, controlling variables, etc. These processes, Gagné argues, must play an important part in any elementary science program.

Any learner new to a discipline goes through a developmental sequence which begins with the immediately obvious and proceeds past the concrete to a more formal stage in which complex abstract propositions can be thought about. Children usually cannot progress as rapidly as adults to the more abstract operations. They appear to be limited in the kinds of logical operations which they can perform at a given age level. That means that any successful program must place activities intended to develop certain concepts, skills, or both in a sequence that is compatible with what children can reasonably be expected to do.

Fortunately, the early stages in learning any of the scientific disciplines usually can be pursued at the level of common sense and intuition. The child encounters some new phenomena, learns to describe what is most obvious, and acquires new vocabulary to help him organize his experience. Gradually he begins to piece together ideas, and the kinds of logical operations in which he engages become more complex. As he progresses, the problems which arise require that he think more abstractly. At first he uses language mainly to describe phenomena. Later he uses language to express relationships among events and then among variables. The relationships he uncovers become less and less perceptually obvious. He has to organize information and plan experiments based on the logical implications of the knowledge he has acquired. Logical necessity becomes an increasingly strong motivating force. While inconsistencies in results among ideas may not disturb the beginner, they become intolerable to the more advanced learner, who begins to be governed by an accumulated set of relationships which he expects to hold true.

If you ask some seven-year-olds to measure the same object several times, they will often give different reports about how big the object is each time they measure it. The inconsistencies arise when they do not know exactly how to carry out the measurement operation. The fact, however, that the numbers differ does not often disturb them at this stage of mental development.

Cognitive levels describing changes in a child's manner of knowing

Concepts involving space, time, number, quantity, causality, motion, velocity, conservation, etc., are developed.
Initiation takes place; words are tied to actions or needs. Naming begins. Early development of the concept of an object concept probably occurs as memory develops and perceptual-motor coordinations progresses are acquired. Language leads to symbolic processes. The child deals only with appearances. Exploration is unsystematic.

The child begins to believe in a theory. (E.g., in conserving liquids through differently shaped containers, the theory is that physical quantities are invariant under simple changes in shape or location.) A theory has to be discovered all over again in each new context; it cannot be stated explicitly by the child (e.g., the child may conserve the quantity of clay, but not its weight).
The child cannot distinguish between "some" and "all." Time, movement, and speed are confused. Spatial relations are very crude. Dependence on the perceptual field is still high; and the child's own perception is the only reality. The child is strongly dominated by the visual field. Simple systematic exploration (concrete operations) begins. The development of correspondence (1-1) begins. The child learns to do operations. A < B and A > B (composition and decomposition of units) are mastered.

The child conserves weight and can subjugate the visual field to internal clues. He knows more than he understands. Such activities as combining, ordering, and putting objects into correspondence are internalized. Combining, ordering, and qualitative seriation are accomplished.
Classification, grouping, or both allow inclusion of one class within another. Invariance of number emerges. Concepts of space, time, and the material world are formed. Formal operations begin (i.e., the child moves from concrete operations to psychological operations). The child learns how he is going to do an operation before doing it (e.g., he plans simple experiments). The concept of related groupings is formed.

Processes

From sensations to perceptual objects. *Sensory motor period, birth-2; preoperational through (2-4)* *Birth-4*	*Perception to physical objects* *Intuitive thought* I Ages 4-8	*Operations on physical objects* *Concrete operations* II Ages 6-9
Classifying	Similarities and differences; classifications with leaves, shells, animals, aquariums	Purposes; kinds of living things in an aquarium; smoothness (i.e., resistance to sliding); solid, liquid, and gaseous states; key characteristics; color wheel; coding system
Communicating	Using numerals to describe ordered arrangements; communicating with sums. Accuracy; variation within objects of a kind; changes in a plant, balloon; graphing, describing motion of the sun	Describing an experiment. Effect of heat on size of balloon; graphing; motion of a phonograph record; sundial and shadows; motion of bouncing ball; maps; coordinate system; graphing with time variable
Inferring		Characteristics of packaged articles; observations and inferences, displacement of water by a gas; inferring vapor in air; tracks and traces; loss of water from plants
Measuring	Comparing lengths; linear measure; metric; comparison using a balance; volumes; forces (e.g., springs)	Linear; estimations; ordering plane figures by area; forces; volume; liquids; separations of materials from mixtures; rate of change (evaporation); temperature and thermometers; populations
Observing	Perception of color, sound, odor; temperature; weather; solids to liquids; multiple senses; magnets (properties of); rolling balls; collisions	Animal motion; yeast action; bacteria; growth
Predicting		Using graphs; survey; candles
Using Numbers	Order properties; counting and numerals; number line; positive integers (addition); 0-99	Dividing to get rates and means; fractions; decimals
Using Space/Time Relations	Recognizing and using shapes; components of shapes; spacing arrangements; direction; time; angles; distance; symmetry; straight and curved lines and surfaces; shadows	Telling time; rate of change of position; 2-dimensional representation of 3-dimensional figures; relative position and motion

The child conserves volume. Correspondence (one–many; many–one) is mastered. Limitations of concrete operations become apparent when the child tries to deal with three variables.

What is known begins to be understood. The tacit begins to become explicit; this makes knowledge communicable. Relations between propositions begin to develop, and these are imposed upon the physical world. Relations move from arbitrary or accidental; they now appear as logical necessities. Symbolic knowledge allows generalization.

Generalization proceeds to the point where different situations can be recognized as variations on a major thesis. Diversity begins to be reduced in this fashion. The child can begin to deal with generalizations about number that have no concrete application. He can form hypotheses that extend beyond the current task. He makes assumptions and begins to draw conclusions. He tests inferences. He deals with propositions as well as events.

Conceptual symbols lead to →

III   Ages 7–10

Transformations of language and logic
Propositional or formal operations

IV   Ages 8–12

Using punch cards to record a classification; identifying rocks and minerals. Relations; linear relations and slopes	Formulating hypotheses	
Force and motion; coordinates and graphs	Making operational definitions	Density; mass
Inferring patterns through the use of electric currents; inferring composition of materials. Shapes of cut things	Controlling and manipulating variables	Falling objects; candles
Measurement of angles in reflection; measurement involving probability; accuracy and reliability of perceptual judgments		
	Formulating models	
Learning mazes; interpreting field of vision using 1-dimensional and 2-dimensional graphs; various physical systems; continuous movement	Interpreting data	Mass and acceleration; identifying unknowns

FIGURE 1-1

This chart shows the way in which scientific processes and developmental processes together determine the simplicity or complexity of curriculum content.

The processes of science in which the learner must engage grow in complexity, just as the content does.

Figure 1-1 shows a table; along one edge are listed scientific processes and on the other the developmental stages through which children pass. Entered in the body of the grid are examples of content selected at random from several of the programs. While the variety in topics is great, the level of sophistication is reasonable in view of what is known about the logic of children at different stages of maturation. Program demands have to be compatible with the development of certain logical capabilities in the children.

Your own past experience in science will determine the level of confidence that you bring to the teaching of science. Fortunately, being an adult, you can move to advanced levels of reasoning more rapidly than the children; but like any beginner in a new field, you ought not to skip the early concrete stages. This chapter begins at that level. It tries to provide you with a conceptual frame of reference for thinking about how to observe, describe, and classify phenomena. It tells you how to distinguish between *objects*, *collections*, and *systems*. You will be introduced to the concept of a *variable* and to what it means to define a variable *operationally*. These ideas will also be encountered again in succeeding chapters. All the concepts will be discussed in this chapter largely at a concrete level.

You can take some heart from the fact that while the authors of various elementary science programs clearly differ in philosophy, the effect of that difference is not so apparent at the primary levels of the program. An examination of what children are actually asked to *do* in the first two or three years of each shows the programs to be remarkably alike in basic activities, if not in philosophy. These differences in philosophy will be discussed in the last chapter of this book after you have acquired some experiences designed to help you consider whether or not they matter.

OBJECTS, COLLECTIONS, SYSTEMS

The early stages of any science usually involve the beginner in observing, describing, classifying, and measuring objects or phenomena. The child has to acquire some techniques for describing objects, for organizing collections, and for showing the patterns of relationships in systems.

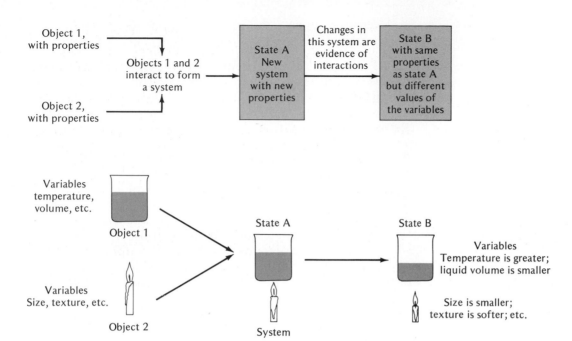

FIGURE 1-2

Objects having unique sets of properties interact to form systems which have other unique sets of properties. One problem of research is to find out what the systems are. This is done by identifying variables whose values *change* as interactions occur. Such variables might be heat, temperature, motion (speed or direction), force, order, hardness, size, volume, number, color, texture, sound, shape, odor, and light.

Charles Darwin, for example, described all the kinds of plants and animals he found in his voyage on the ship *Beagle*. He collected plants and animals, bundled them up, and sent them back to England so that his former professor could develop a plan for classifying them.

A group of objects which bear no relationship to one another other than proximity can be called a *collection*. Within a collection, objects can be classified so that there will be some kind of orderliness. Classification processes can be simple or complex according to the needs of the collector. Classification is done to make some kind of operation or procedure more efficient. A child sorting blocks may sort according to size if he is building something, but only according to color if he is making simple color-based patterns. How complex a category system is depends on the purposes to be served.

Systems involve more than a random collection of objects which can be ordered into groups (Figure 1-2). Unlike the members of a collection, the members of a system have definite relationships among them. The problem is to find out what those relationships are. An investigator infers relationships among the components of a system on the basis of the interactions he observes. In the next sections the distinctions between objects, collections, and systems will be discussed in more detail. There is a unique way to describe each of them. (See Figure 1-10, page 25.)

OBJECTS

Relation of properties to functions of objects

Any object can be described by listing its properties. The set of all properties exhibited by an object may be very large. The problem in description is to decide which of all the properties it will be most useful to list. You make that decision largely on the basis of why you choose to describe the object in the first place. When you ask a child to describe an object, you must listen for the unexpected but appropriate description as well as for the conventional properties because he frequently experiences objects in ways different from adults. Adults usually have reasons for choosing some properties over others. Since the child often does not know why he is asked to describe something, he may choose at random from the potential list.

The functions which an object can serve change easily with the situation, but the properties usually persist. Examine Figure 1-3.

Figure 1-3*a* shows an object. What shall we call it? A table? Perhaps. Now look at Figure 1-3*b*. Will you still call it a table, or would it be more appropriate to call it a platform? Look at Figure 1-3*c*. Now the word *barricade* seems an appropriate label. What function an object serves at one moment may be different in the next, depending on how it is interacting with other objects.

What are the properties that characterize the object? It is long, hard, fairly heavy, inflexible, smooth, slippery, brown; smells like pine; has a thick top, etc. While all those properties and more may describe the object, some of them seem less relevant for some of the functions we want the object to serve than for others. Does it matter, for example, that the table is brown or smells like pine as much as it matters that it is long, hard, and inflexible? Probably not for the functions we chose, but color and smell would matter if our intentions changed and we wanted the object to fit into a particular color scheme in a small room. In that case, some properties that we ignored before would become relevant.

How we choose to describe an object, then, depends upon the function the object must serve. Since, however,

FIGURE 1-3
The properties of an object persist, but its function may change.

(a) Table

(b) Platform

(c) Barricade

the properties partially determine what functions an object may serve, you must focus on defining the properties critical to the function rather than simply focusing on the function. Combinations of properties from the master set of all possible properties make an object potentially suitable for multiple purposes. An object is generally named according to its most common use or function. However, depending on its properties, an object may be put to many different uses. To identify an object suitable for a given purpose, *list the minimum set of properties which will make that function possible and then find (identify) all those objects which exhibit that minimum set of necessary properties*.

By focusing on properties of objects, you increase your freedom to produce innovative solutions to simple problems. Suppose, for example, you wanted children to do a simple experiment and the description of materials called for sixteen beakers. Your school does not have even one beaker. What do you do?

Look at the experiment to see how the beaker is used. What properties must it possess? It has to hold liquid, and the liquid is water at room temperature. Furthermore, the children will have to handle the beakers. This last condition suggests that a beaker probably was a poor suggestion anyhow because a beaker might be dropped and broken. Think of some alternatives. Try milk cartons, frozen orange juice cans, disposable styrofoam or wax cups, etc. *By thinking in terms of the properties that make the particular function or purpose possible, you may increase your alternatives or possibilities;* e.g., "There are no beakers, so there can be no experiment" can be expanded to "There are many containers, so the experiment is possible."

Since the name of an object can change according to its function and since function is tied to properties, it would be unreasonable to emphasize the names of objects. Teachers sometimes hold up objects to be described but begin by asking a student to tell the name of the object. The strategy not only puts the emphasis in the wrong place, it reduces the chance that a child can supply an answer. Either he knows the name of an object or he does not. If, instead, you ask for the *properties* of the object, you put the emphasis in a more appropriate place, namely, on the properties, and you also increase the probability that the child will have something to say. From his observations a child usually can state at least one property or attribute, so not only has he been asked a question he can answer, but the choice of property is left to him. In this way the teacher increases the opportunity to start a conversation, and conversations, as we shall see, are important to the progress of science learning.

The body as the first instrument for exploring objects

Language as a tool. Our experiences are more varied than the language available to describe them. There is an economy in language, but to make that economy work for you means you have to know the context in which words occur. Sometimes we use the same word to describe two different operations. For example, we might describe an object as rough or as hard or as soft or as smooth (Figure 1-4). We could describe it in one of these ways as a result of looking or feeling or both. Rough, hard, soft, smooth do not tell us what *operation* was performed to get the information. In science it is important to specify the operation or procedure used to obtain data. The work of a person can be verified or repeated only if the operations are carefully described. Examine Figure 1-4, for example, to see how students sometimes come to confuse simple concepts like hard, soft, smooth, and rough.

Our bodies store in them all kinds of sensitive and not so sensitive instruments for exploring properties of objects. We can touch things and describe how an object feels when we touch it or rub it or hit it with some part of ourselves. From this we derive *texture terms*, such as rough, smooth, bumpy, velvety, gritty, and *tactile terms*, such as hard, soft, jellylike, bouncy, heavy, light. Children are far more prone to use texture and tactile information than adults are. We can also see things and describe how an object *looks*: We can see its color, grain, and size; whether it is rough, bumpy, glittery, dull, velvety, etc. Notice that some of the same words that describe how an object feels to touch appear in the visual language list. Language is economical. We make the same words apply to different experiences. In teaching, as in science, it is important to verify what operations or procedures a child employs so that he gets the whole range of experiences.

There are also the *shape words*, which put together both our visual and tactile information: square, triangular, spherical, elliptical, circular, rectangular, cubical, curvy, bumpy, elongated, etc.

There are words that describe how an object *sounds*

FIGURE 1-4
The concepts "hard," "soft," "smooth," and "rough" require different types of operations. Failure to make the simple motor discriminations can be misleading.

Operation Outcome

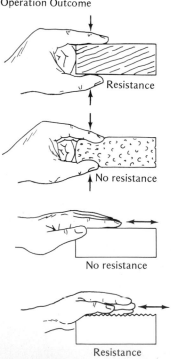

when you knock it against something or drop it—i.e., when you make it interact with another object—clangy, loud, soft, high or low in pitch, like a siren, etc. Children often describe sounds by comparing them with sounds of earlier experiences: "like glass breaking," "like keys rattling," "like wind in the trees," "like whistling," etc. Notice that "soft" appears here in the list of *sound* words as well as in the list of *tactile* words.

Shared Experience and Description

If you look at the lists of words and phrases children and adults use in describing properties, especially the descriptions of odor and sound, you realize how much the communication process depends on a *shared experience*, or at least on experience that can be repeated. If you never have heard keys rattling and someone describes a sound as being like keys rattling, you do not know much more than you did before. One little boy from Georgia looked at some wet brownish-green algae and exclaimed, "It's greens. Can my mama cook those greens?" To him *greens* carried a host of associations. To somebody who knew greens, his communication had a lot of meaning. For somebody unfamiliar with greens, his communication would be puzzling.

It is always possible in science to establish a common base for communication by the "show me" criterion. A description is really only acceptable if the property referred to can be pointed to or the *operation* which led to the description can be repeated: the keys shaken, the wood smelled, or the curved object pointed to.

Early language development in the context of science comes about by the melding of three ingredients: *concrete experiences* combined with *communication* about those experiences in settings *shared* by others so that the common pool of referents will gradually enlarge. There need be no breakdown in the communication process in science if the starting point is a physical object or system which you or the child can point to and manipulate. No matter how abstract the conversation may eventually become, the requirement in science is that you be able to work your way back to the concrete stage when necessary.

Referents

Implicit in almost all property terms is some kind of *referent*. Even if the referent is never made explicit, it is always there. If something is described as long, it is long *in comparison* with some other objects and short in comparison with still other objects. A 32-foot sailboat might be long compared with a dinghy but very short compared with a freighter.

If the referent is not actually physically present, then the speaker must assume the listener is familiar with the referent. If you describe some object as being red, e.g., a lipstick, someone might ask you whether it is red like a tomato or red like an apple. The apple and tomato are the referents. Many odor and sound descriptions depend on referents: it smells like a rose, or it smells like a rotten egg. If you happen not to be familiar with the referent, then the description fails to communicate meaning. Adults frequently use referents without checking to determine whether children are familiar with them. A communication gap develops when there is a missing referent. This kind of communication failure cannot happen in science as long as everyone is careful to show what operation he performed or what referent he used.

COLLECTIONS

Describing Collections

If the list of properties that could characterize a single object is potentially very great, how much more extensive would the list be for a whole collection of objects. A collection of objects might be sorted into any number of categories. For example, round objects in one category and all red objects in another category. If a new object comes along which is both round *and* red, then there may be a subset formed. Biologists use the technique of forming subsets to classify plants and animals into categories and subcategories.

To describe a collection, first classify the objects in the collection into categories. Set up the categories based on properties rather than functions. Choose the categories according to the *purposes* to be served by the sorting and classifying process. Category systems are imposed by man. When his goals change, he may change his categories. In one sense, categories are simply imaginative mental constructions to make life a little less complex.

To see how helpful the process of classifying or sorting objects into classes and applying labels to the classes of objects can be, consider Figure 1-5. Suppose we

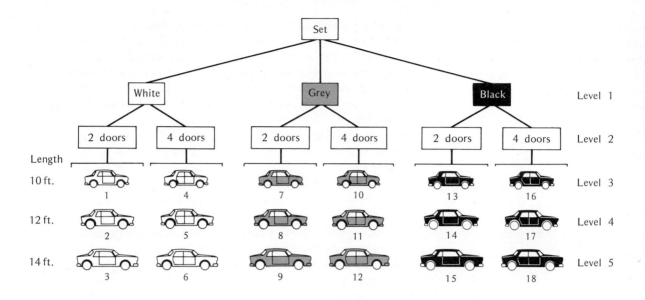

Description of variables and the range values each exhibits

Level	Property	Description of variable	Number of values in the variable
1	Color	Shades of red	3
2	Style	2 and 4 door	2
3	Length	10, 12 and 14 foot wheelbase	3
	Total cars		18

Some classes of cars and the number of members in each class

Classes of cars	Number	Total of class
Light red	6	
Bright red	6	
Dark red	6	18
2-door	9	
4-door	9	18
10′ long	6	
12′ long	6	
14′ long	6	18
Light red 4-door 12′ long	1	1

FIGURE 1-5
Find the dark red, 4-door, 12-foot car. Suppose you saw a car and wanted to classify it. You make a series of stepwise decisions by answering questions at each level. Each level represents the addition of one more variable. Level 1: Which shade of red? Level 2: How many doors? Level 3, 4, 5: How long is it?

look for automobiles that are red, that are longer than 8 feet, and that have two or more doors. Just to make things simple, let's suppose that we had available to us cars that were 10 feet, 12 feet, and 14 feet long and that there are cars with two doors and cars with four doors. How many different models of cars are included in the various categories or classes we can construct from the given properties? We used only three properties: *color, length,* and *number of doors.* Each of the properties has a certain range of values over which it varies. Most properties are like that. They exhibit different values. But our language does not have enough separate labels for each value. It is

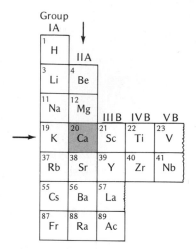

FIGURE 1-6
The periodic chart is a systematic listing of the elements on the basis of their properties. One property of elements is the atomic number. Predict the atomic number of calcium, ca. What is the vertical sequence? What is the horizontal sequence in Group IIA?

often convenient to lump all the various values of a property into one term, such as *red*. If you look at the set of cars in Figure 1-5, you see that they all fit the description of cars longer than 8 feet and with two or more doors. But you see how many different forms there are. No two cars are exactly the same. There are eighteen distinctive vehicles.

A taxonomy of this kind has another use. Suppose one of the cars is missing—for example, number 17. By examining the taxonomy you could say what the properties of the car should be even though you had never seen it. The taxonomy would tell you what to look for if you set out to find the missing car.

Chemists used a similar technique for finding chemical elements that were as yet unknown. They organized a chart of the elements called a *periodic chart*, a portion of which is shown in Figure 1-6. When the known elements were arranged according to their properties, there were "holes," or missing elements. By examining the chart, the chemists could infer what the properties of the missing elements probably were. That gave investigators clues about where and how to look for them.

Biologists organize their information about living organisms into categories. They use key properties to help them classify plants and animals. Students can learn to classify birds, for example, into sets and subsets. Figure 1-7 shows a simple table of decisions that, when followed, will help someone to identify the group to which a bird belongs. Bills and feet are key areas of focus in constructing this taxonomy for birds. If the feet are webbed and the legs are very long, it is probably a water bird and not shown in this taxonomy, which refers only to land birds. In this category system, at level 1 you decide whether the bird is a land bird. At level 2 you answer the question: Is the bill hooked or straight? All the birds of interest in this taxonomy have predominantly straight bills. At level 2, then, you are thinking of birds whose feet are not webbed, who have fairly short legs, and who have little or no hook to their bills. At level 3 you decide which kind of bill best describes the bird you are trying to classify. If it is long and slender, you probably have a hummingbird. If it is long and heavy, you may have a pigeon or a woodpecker. At level 4 you decide which of these possibilities is most probable. With more and more detail added, the taxonomy will finally lead you through successive levels to a partic-

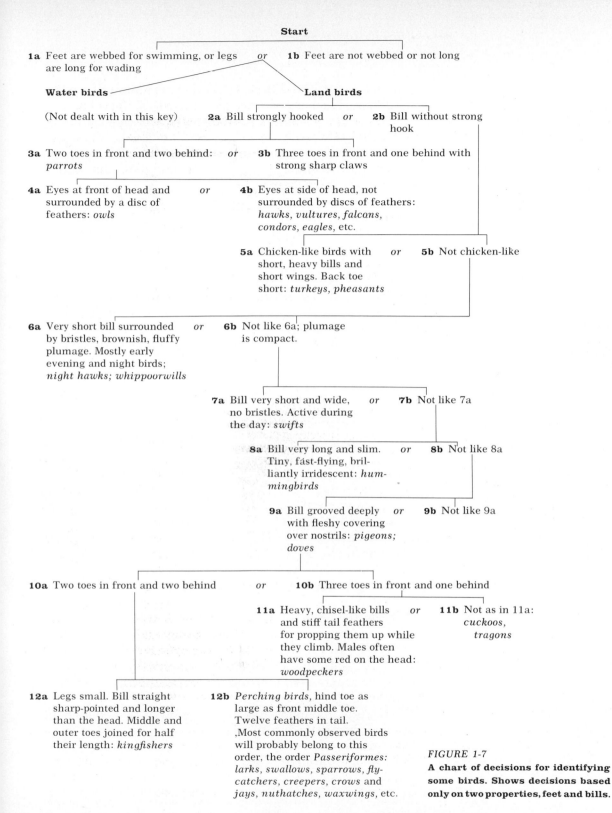

Start

1a Feet are webbed for swimming, or legs   *or*   **1b** Feet are not webbed or not long
are long for wading

Water birds   **Land birds**

(Not dealt with in this key)   **2a** Bill strongly hooked   *or*   **2b** Bill without strong
hook

3a Two toes in front and two behind: *or*   **3b** Three toes in front and one behind with
parrots   strong sharp claws

4a Eyes at front of head and   *or*   **4b** Eyes at side of head, not
surrounded by a disc of   surrounded by discs of feathers:
feathers: *owls*   *hawks, vultures, falcans,*
                                          condors, eagles, etc.

5a Chicken-like birds with   *or*   **5b** Not chicken-like
short, heavy bills and
short wings. Back toe
short: *turkeys, pheasants*

6a Very short bill surrounded   *or*   **6b** Not like 6a; plumage
by bristles, brownish, fluffy   is compact.
plumage. Mostly early
evening and night birds;
night hawks; whippoorwills

7a Bill very short and wide,   *or*   **7b** Not like 7a
no bristles. Active during
the day: *swifts*

8a Bill very long and slim.   *or*   **8b** Not like 8a
Tiny, fast-flying, bril-
liantly irridescent: *hum-*
mingbirds

9a Bill grooved deeply   *or*   **9b** Not like 9a
with fleshy covering
over nostrils: *pigeons;*
doves

10a Two toes in front and two behind   *or*   **10b** Three toes in front and one behind

11a Heavy, chisel-like bills   *or*   **11b** Not as in 11a:
and stiff tail feathers   *cuckoos,*
for propping them up while   *tragons*
they climb. Males often
have some red on the head:
woodpeckers

12a Legs small. Bill straight   **12b** *Perching birds*, hind toe as
sharp-pointed and longer   large as front middle toe.
than the head. Middle and   Twelve feathers in tail.
outer toes joined for half   ,Most commonly observed birds
their length: *kingfishers*   will probably belong to this
                                    order, the order *Passeriformes:*
                                    larks, swallows, sparrows, fly-
                                    catchers, creepers, crows and
                                    jays, nuthatches, waxwings, etc.

FIGURE 1-7

A chart of decisions for identifying
some birds. Shows decisions based
only on two properties, feet and bills.

ular species of bird. Each level adds more details, so that the *categorization becomes increasingly specific*![1]

It should be clear that out of any collection of objects, many different kinds of organizations can be made, depending upon *why* we want to make a categorization. It is important to keep this in mind, especially when one thinks about biological taxonomies. Biologists frequently engage in arguments about how an organism should be classified or what properties it must exhibit to be assigned to a particular class. Children do the same thing, although their logic is less sophisticated. They sometimes group animals together that we do not ordinarily think of as similar. In one first-grade classroom where categorization had been the principal activity for several weeks, the children grouped together pictures of zebras and tigers because both have stripes. Why not?

The formation of a museum by children gives them practice identifying properties and sorting objects into groups based on properties. It illustrates to them how categories change with their purposes, and with added information it informs the teacher. What the children tell you through an activity like this is what properties they are paying attention to when they categorize. They let you know that through their discussions. You also learn through observation how broad class membership is in a particular category. All you have to do is look at the range of objects in each group and *listen* to the arguments. The arguments serve to increase analytical skills since they force attention to key similarities and differences. Every grouping must be justified by a statement of properties.

Bar graphs for describing a collection.   To describe a collection of objects, sort the collection into groups based on properties. Add to this description by constructing a bar graph to show how many objects are in each category. The graph becomes a special kind of picture of the collection which calls attention visually to those categories in which there are many members and those in which there are few members.

Graphs make possible comparison of two collections that are categorized in the same way.

Scientists interested in changes that occur over time keep track of changes with bar graphs constructed at dif-

[1]M. E. Jacques, *How to Know the Land Birds,* Wm. C. Brown Company Publishers, Dubuque, Iowa, 1947, provides a useful and simple taxonomic key for identifying land birds.

ferent points in time. They compare changes in the shape of the graph. These changes in shape, which reflect changes in the numbers of objects in each category, become evidence of changes in the collection. Suppose, for example, you collected litter in a certain area, categorized it, and constructed a bar graph to show what kinds of things people in that area are throwing away. A collection in another area might show a different distribution (Figure 1-8). On the basis of these collections you might make *inferences* about the habits of people and use this knowledge to plan a campaign for reducing litter. Graphs of collections made after the campaign may show changes in the frequency of items in each category as well as a change in the category that is most common. Bar graphs provide a means for comparing collections and for keeping track of changes in collections.

Language for describing a category

Category formation is a fluid, flexible, very dynamic process which goes on in the context of many experiences and which has some arbitrary aspects. There are fewer labels than there are experiences. *It is a social kind of enterprise* because the labels given to the categories not only serve to organize experience but are intended to call up similar experiences in the people with whom we communicate. Mapping experience into language is far from being a well-understood process. In science the operation or rule which is used as the basis for forming each category must be clearly specified so that communication will be unambiguous and so that someone else can repeat the operation with a reasonable expectation of producing the same result.

To *describe a collection* of objects you need:

1 A list of relevant properties, the *categories*
2 *Numbers* which describe how many members of the collection occur in each category
3 A bar graph

To *construct a taxonomy* for classifying objects you need:

1 A list of mutually exclusive categories, with the properties of each specified
2 Subsets of properties

The categories should be chosen in such a way that

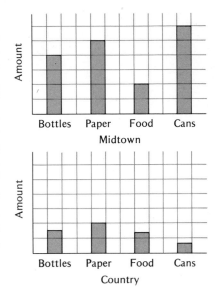

FIGURE 1-8
Two examples of bar graphs used to describe collections of objects. Changing the category system changes the bar graph.

the sequence of decisions one has to make in classifying is very clear.

Notice that we invent categories as we go, according to our needs. They are not "out there" lodged in objects. They are mental constructions that bear some kind of correspondence to what is "out there," but it is not possible to say exactly what the nature of that correspondence is—and we shall not try. The main idea to retain is that you often cannot define a category exactly—it refuses to stay fixed. All you can do is say what *rule* you are using to assign members to a class.

Converting a property into a variable

Within any category there may be objects each of which shows a slightly different value of the property which defines the category. Suppose you sorted leaves into categories on the basis of nice autumn colors (Figure 1-9). In each category you might have several shades of one color. Each property that can appear in different objects, in distinctively different values, is called a *variable*—color is a variable. Each object will exhibit only one particular value of the variable, e.g., each leaf in the category of brown leaves will be some particular shade of brown. Changes in the values of variables may be taken as evidence that some underlying conditions are changing.

Within a category, then, there may be a gradation of values. When a property exhibits a set of values it is called a variable. It is possible to arrange the members of a category in *serial order* from the largest value of the variable to the least or smallest value. (See Transcript 1-1.)

When we speak of the range of a variable, we are generally talking about a class of objects, each of whose members takes on or exhibits one value of that variable. In the example of the cars in Figure 1-5 there were eighteen red cars. But red is a variable with three values in this case—light, medium, and dark. Just as the bar graph provided a way of describing a whole collection, a histogram can be used to show how many members of a category exhibit each value of the variable. A histogram is constructed in much the same way as a bar graph. Instead of listing categories, however, each value of the variable within a category is given, and then the graph shows how many objects exhibit each value.

There are some variables which do not particularly lend themselves to serial order. Take sex, for example. It

FIGURE 1-9

Depending on the variable you choose—*a* color; *b* size—different serial ordering results.

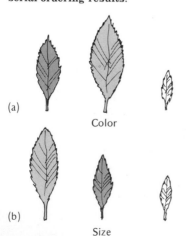

(a)

Color

(b)

Size

has only three possible values: it is male or female, or it can take on a zero value, namely, no sex. It is not possible to order these variables in terms of their magnitude. The same thing can be said about shape. Objects can take on a

Transcript 1-1

	Dialogue	Analysis
Teacher	Okay, now, I'm going to let you do your own collections; but I want to tell you what this is called, what we're doing. It's called *ordering them* . . .	Five-year-olds introduced to the concept of serial order perform the operation on some dowels. But note that the pronunciation of *serial* is the same as the name for something they know well, *cereal*. It is doubtful that their confusion will be solved by teaching them to spell. Instead, they should be given plenty of practice at arranging objects in serial order.
First child	Ordering?	
Teacher	Yes. It's ordering them in a certain way, called *serial ordering.*	
First child	Serial?	
Second child	That what—hey, you have a serial on your stomach and you've . . .	
Teacher	Wait, let me get a pencil so I can write it down for you.	
Second child	Cereal? (Laughs.)	
Teacher	It's a different kind—not what you think it is.	
Second child	You mean is serial right?	
Teacher	Now, this is the way you write it.	
First child	No.	
Teacher	Look—s-e-r-i-a-l.	
Second child	Serial.	
First child	Serial.	
Teacher	Serial ordering. You're ordering it; you're ordering it; you're ordering it in a series. Like I asked you to, from shortest to tallest. Now I'd like you to take the sticks that you have—Martin, you have your sticks, and Cassy, you have your sticks—and I'd like you to do the same thing: order them from shortest to tallest of the sticks you have.	
Second child	Okay, now. Here goes nothing.	

variety of shapes, and we may think of shape as a variable, but it is not possible to serial-order objects according to their shape. Sex and shape are *qualitative variables*. Variables which can be serial-ordered are potentially quantifiable.

SYSTEMS

Scientists try to expose, describe, and explain the mechanisms by which objects and systems change over time. A *system* is *any set of objects or variables among which a relationship is believed to exist*. A system contrasts with a collection, in which there is no necessary relationship among the members. A plant is a system. Try cutting all the leaves off a plant. There will be dramatic changes in other parts of the plant as well as the leaves. These changes are evidence that relationships exist among the parts. One way to expose relationships in systems is to do something to the system and then to look for evidence of change. (See Figure 1-2, page 11.)

Systems, just as property categories, are inventions or mental constructions chosen to fit your intentions. In systems you look for evidence of interaction. The types of evidence are very varied. In systems you infer relationships between or among the components of the system based on the interactions observed. For the distinctions between objects, collections, and systems see Figure 1-10.

Evidence of Interaction

Motion and change of direction.   You can look for motion changes as evidence of interaction. If the speed or direction in which an object moves changes, you infer some force is acting. When such changes occur we are usually prompted to inquire about the cause. Changes in motion and force sometimes go together. A football that is traveling slowly and hits you will hurt less than one that is thrown with greater force.

Order or spatial arrangement.   Another kind of evidence that interaction has occurred lies in the order or arrangement of objects. If you see a whole set of dowels lined up, and later you see them in some different arrangement, you can suspect some interaction has occurred. If you see a building on one day and a few days later you observe a heap of rubble in the same place, you infer what

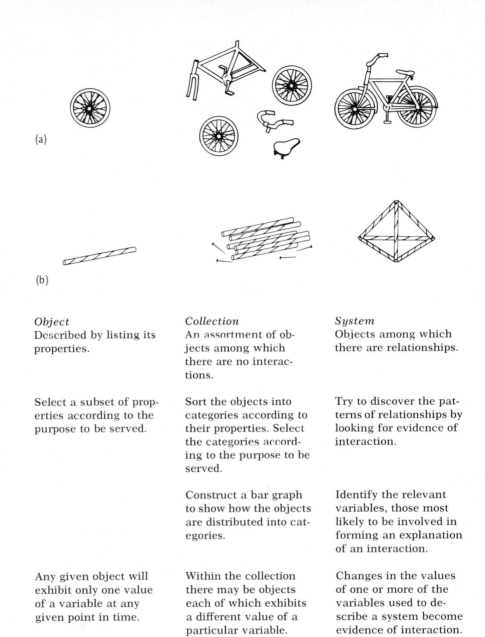

	Object	Collection	System
Definition:	Described by listing its properties.	An assortment of objects among which there are no interactions.	Objects among which there are relationships.
To Describe:	Select a subset of properties according to the purpose to be served.	Sort the objects into categories according to their properties. Select the categories according to the purpose to be served.	Try to discover the patterns of relationships by looking for evidence of interaction.
		Construct a bar graph to show how the objects are distributed into categories.	Identify the relevant variables, those most likely to be involved in forming an explanation of an interaction.
	Any given object will exhibit only one value of a variable at any given point in time.	Within the collection there may be objects each of which exhibits a different value of a particular variable.	Changes in the values of one or more of the variables used to describe a system become evidence of interaction.
			Use measurements to determine the value of the variables. This permits comparing systems and helps in detecting changes in systems that happen slowly.

FIGURE 1-10
The distinction between an object, a collection, and a system is shown here.

has happened, basing your inference on the changes in spatial arrangement of parts.

Texture and consistency.   An increase or decrease in the hardness of some substance can be taken as evidence of changes in relationships within a system. Tar warms up during the day in the hot sun and gets soft. A cake left uncovered for several days gets hard.

Size and number of parts.   Change in size is another indicator of interaction. An object may change its dimensions. A balloon gets bigger when you blow air into it. Another indicator of interaction is change in number of parts. You might start out with a coffee cup, a single object. If you drop it, you may suddenly be confronted with a hundred pieces. The organization of the object is destroyed. The system degenerates into a collection. In a fish tank you may have two guppies. One day when you look you find twenty-five small guppies. That change in number becomes evidence that interaction has occurred.

Color, texture, temperature.   If, for example, you rub sandpaper on a piece of wood, the sandpaper and surface of the wood both become warm. The surfaces that interact become smooth. Changes in color can be taken as evidence of interaction. When people become sunburned, the color change gives evidence of new interactions going on in them. A little lemon juice dropped into tea produces a considerable color change in the tea.

Heat and light are also indicators of interactions. If you put a thermometer into warm water, the water and thermometer interact in such a way that some heat from the water transfers to the thermometer and prompts a change in the liquid in it. The liquid in the thermometer changes its shape and volume as it rises out of the bulb.

Odor.   Odor is another good indicator of interaction. How often have we rushed into a kitchen when some smell gave us evidence that an interaction is going astray?

Sound.   Sound is another indicator of interaction. Changes in loudness, pitch, or both indicate that some relationship in the system is changing. Squealing brakes on a car alert us. Teachers often monitor the volume and quality of sounds in a classroom as indicators of the changing work-play-fight relationships among children.

Using the system concept

The system concept is a device to help you selectively focus on what is interacting in the environment. It is a very powerful kind of bookkeeping device. Changes in the system become tokens or signs that the parts are somehow related or are interacting. While it is common to begin teaching primary school children the concept of systems by having them identify objects which are interacting, it is desirable to move beyond this concrete level as soon as possible to identification of variables which interact.

Using variables to describe systems

Sometimes it is more convenient to describe a system in terms of variables instead of in terms of component parts. Suppose, for example, you have a friend whom you describe according to six variables: weight, height, sex, hair color, waist measurement, and shoe size. You list the values of the variables which describe the system called your friend (Figure 1-11).

One week later you see your friend and note the values of the variables (Figure 1-11). You might begin to suspect that in the interval between the first observation (at time t_1) and the second observation (at time t_2), there must have been interaction between her and some other objects. The change in one property, hair color, and the

FIGURE 1-11
Two states of a system.

Variables	Value at first observation	Value at second observation	Amount of change
Weight	125	135	10lbs. heavier
Height	5'8"	5'8"	0
Sex	♀	♀	0
Hair color	Brown	Blond	Terrific
Shoe size	7	7	0
Waist	34"	35"	1 inch larger

change in the value of the weight variable are evidence of *interaction*. In this case, color and change of weight—and maybe even an alteration of shape—are the evidence by which you *infer* something happened in the interval between observations.

Stop here for a moment and think about what has to happen to you to make you infer anything at all. If you lived in a world in which events seemed to you totally unconnected to each other, then you would not infer anything. You might notice how she looked yesterday. You would find the fact that she looks different today a matter of chance. "That is how the world is," you would say. You would not be provoked to explain the change, because you never assumed any continuity in the flow of events in the first place. If you do not expect a reasonable world then it is not pertinent to inquire. As one fourth-grade ghetto boy said with a shrug, "Yesterday was yesterday and today is today, and they are not the same." The fact that something changed would not send someone of that philosophy in pursuit of an explanation. (This view of the world as being random rather than organized will be discussed in a later chapter when the concept of fate control is introduced.)

The major basis for inferring what patterns of relationships exist in a system lies in being able to connect changes in one variable with changes in another variable. Just as it is important to choose properties of objects that serve particular purposes, so in describing a system it is important to select variables that seem to be relevant to the kinds of questions being asked about the system.

In the case of your friend, there are all kinds of possible variables that you may choose to ignore, e.g., length of fingernails, color of eyes, tone of voice, odor, etc., as well as those you decide to keep in the system. You can be quite flexible with the system notion. To use it requires some degree of creativity because the business of picking relevant variables is something of an art. You choose variables according to what you are trying to accomplish or find out.

Notice in the example of your friend that in order for you to infer that an interaction occurred, you have to be conscious of the state of the system at two points in time. You have to *remember* what variables you focused on and what their values were. You have to check the values of each variable at the second observation and *compare* the second list with the first. With a system as simple as the one described, you do these things almost automatically.

What you may not realize is that the deliberate listing of variables serves to focus attention selectively and increases the probability that you will notice a change if a change occurs. We might call the list of the variables with their values at the first observation, state A. The list of values of the variables at the second observation would be state B of the system.

If a variable takes on a value you do not expect, you usually are prompted to inquire, "Why?" That in turn starts you asking about the interactions, and often you find yourself focusing on some subsystem of the larger system. In our example, you might inquire about the subsystem called *your friend's hair*: "Did you dye your hair, or is that a wig?" Or you might look at her waist and ask whether her new shape is the result of a changed interaction between her and her girdle, i.e., maybe she is not wearing one today. At this point, if she is still talking to you, you might return to the topic of her hair. The facts that you have acquired are that yesterday it was blond and today it is brown. Now you have the task of listing possible explanations. Here are only a few of the possibilities. You should suggest others.

1 She dyed it.
2 She is wearing a wig today.
3 She was wearing a wig yesterday, but her own hair is showing today.
4 She wore wigs both days.
5 She has a twin.

Conflict or differences in interpretation of data come at the stage of constructing explanations. There may be many possible explanations for the observed changes. The problem is to figure out what kind of evidence you would want in order to allow you to infer which one of the alternative explanations is *most likely*. If she will not tell you, there is no way for you to be absolutely certain which alternative is the explanation—or that you have named all the alternatives. Even if she did tell you, you would still ask for evidence and hope that she has the same respect for evidence that you have. In a physical or biological system you ask a question by performing an experiment.

All you simply do, then, in describing a system is a very special kind of bookkeeping. Choose the relevant variables. Let that list represent your system and ignore everything else. Look at the value of the variables in state A. Look at the value of the variables in state B. Compare the values (Figure 1-11). Look for evidence of interaction.

Start making inferences about what might account for changes that occurred. At this point, you may decide to review your idea of the system. You may drop some variables as not relevant and add others. But the trick is to focus on the smallest number of variables necessary to explain what happened. Then you may begin to speculate. Are any of the variables related to one another, that is, if one changes, do the others change in some fashion? Your friend who gained weight might also have changed dimensions. Do you want to keep track of both variables? Will change in one variable correlate closely with change in another? You have to decide what to keep in your system and what to leave out. You might make a list of possible relationships among variables and explanations that could account for changes you noted. Then you could say to yourself, "What evidence would I need in order to make me choose one of these explanations and feel reasonably certain that it will be satisfactory?" *You can rarely be absolutely certain that you have chosen the perfect explanation.* Science is really the business of finding ways to reduce uncertainty—but there is no way to eliminate uncertainly altogether. (We will return to the notion of uncertainty frequently in later chapters.)

The way in which one chooses the components and variables to include in a system depends on the purpose to be served. To illustrate this point, consider how Semmelweiss, a nineteenth-century physician, tried to reduce the high death rate from childbed fever in maternity wards (Figure 1-12). The system consisted of the women and their doctors. In one of two wards he happened to be supervising, Semmelweiss noticed that the death rate was consistently below the death rate in the other. His strategy for attacking the problem might have been to list all the kinds of variables he could think of and see in what ways the women in the two wards were alike and in what ways they were different. He could have chosen any number of variables—average age, weight, state of health, socioeconomic level, number of previous births, etc. Moreover, he observed that the ward for the poor had a better survival rate than the ward for the rich.

He noted another difference besides socioeconomic background: the women on one ward delivered while lying on their sides. The women in the other ward delivered on their backs. Semmelweiss thought that position at birth might be related to death rate. He hypothesized that if all the women in the rich ward delivered on their backs instead of their sides, the death rate would drop in that

Variable	Death rate	Inference

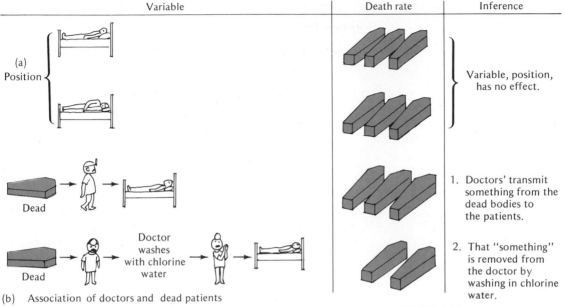

(a) Position — Variable, position, has no effect.

Dead →

Dead → Doctor washes with chlorine water →

(b)   Association of doctors and dead patients

1. Doctors' transmit something from the dead bodies to the patients.

2. That "something" is removed from the doctor by washing in chlorine water.

FIGURE 1-12
Semmelweiss's inquiry

ward. Unfortunately, this first guess at a relationship between two variables proved to be incorrect, so he went back to observing the system again.

This time he noticed something else. Doctors tended to leave autopsies and go directly to the wards, usually to the wards for the rich. Now he expanded his system to include not only the live women and their doctors but the dead women as well. Doctors, he reasoned, were somehow transmitting the disease from the dead to the living. Semmelweiss had also heard that chlorine water had antiseptic properties. He reasoned that if doctors would wash thoroughly in chlorine water after leaving the autopsy area and before visiting the patients, childbed fever would decrease. This supposition turned out to be correct.

It is a shame, in a way, that what finally gets published in scientific reports is just the end product of a whole investigation. It gives a very distorted view of what doing science is really like. The very important "messing about," trial and error phases that usually take up the largest part of the total effort are usually left out. Yet these stages may be more critical for the design of instruction in science than the completed study if for no other reason than they show how important it is to have the freedom to try many alternatives. Many of the alternatives will prove fruitless—in school they might be called errors. At some stages virtually all the modern elementary science programs espouse some inquiry, and inquiry almost always involves some trial and error.

SUMMARY

1 To *describe* a system:

    a Identify its members, either the *objects* or *variables* to receive attention.

    b List the variables.

    c State the value of the variables (measure the variables).

    d State the time of making the observations.

    e State the conditions for making the observations.

2 To *compare* two systems or to compare a system with itself at different points in time to detect changes:

    a Describe each system according to the directions above (1*a* through *e*).

    b Compare each category of variable with the corresponding category from the second system or second set of observations.

    c Calculate differences in the values of the corresponding variables. (Look for gains or losses as evidence of interaction.)

3 Our vocabulary for describing how things feel, sound, and look is rather limited—far more so than our ability to discriminate small differences in those properties. Therefore, we have to make the names stretch over a lot of somewhat different conditions. Learning how to do that in each field of inquiry or in each content area requires that the learner be immersed in the range of experiences from which the language emerges. In that way he comes to learn the *contexts* which convey particular meanings to words. Whenever you encounter confusion in communication, check the context to see whether you and the children are referring to the same referent.

In the next chapter the problem of choosing variables and constructing a procedure for quantifying them will be discussed in more detail. It is only necessary at this point to recognize that measurement is a process for quantifying variables so that objects, collections, and systems can be described more precisely and that without measurement many changes would go undetected.

ACTIVITY 1-1
SHAPES OF LEAVES

OBJECTIVES

1 To discriminate various shapes of leaves
2 To construct bar graphs to describe a collection of leaves
3 To use bar graphs to compare two collections

What to do:

First collect twenty-five different kinds of leaves of various sizes, shapes, and colors. Then sort them into categories based on their properties. For example, you might sort the leaves into groups according to what kinds of margins or edges they have.

1 No teeth or lobes   **2** Gentle wavy margin

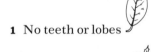

3 Deep undulations   **4** Toothed with the teeth sharp

5 Toothed with the teeth rounded

Alternatively, you might just focus on the tip of the leaf:

a Sharp pointed   **b** Pointed

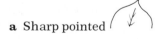

c Rounded   **d** Notched

For whatever categories you choose, construct a *bar graph* to show how many leaves exhibited each property. For example, one sample of twenty-five leaves showed the following numbers of each shape of leaf tip:

Property

Property	1	2	3	4	5	6	7	8	9	10	11	12	13	14	15	16	17	18	19	20	21	22	23	24	25
Sharp pointed	X	X	X	X	X	X	X	X	X	X	X	X	X												
Pointed	X	X	X	X	X	X	X	X																	
Rounded	X	X	X	X																					
Notched	X																								

Frequency

The graph was constructed by marking an X to represent each leaf. The graph permits you to make comparisons between *collections*. For example, if you or someone else collected another sample of twenty-five leaves from a different location and constructed a graph using the same categories, you would know whether the collections were approximately comparable by comparing the lengths of the bars for each category. If the relative proportions of each category are very different, you *infer* the type of plant cover or the conditions for gathering leaves were different. The *shape* of the graph gives a quick idea of relative proportions of each category.

ACTIVITY 1-2
OBSERVING BIRDS

OBJECTIVES

1 To develop skills in observing quickly and accurately properties such as size, shape, color, and motion
2 To learn how to use a taxonomic key for identifying organisms

Background:

Even casual observation of birds will quickly show that they come in all shapes, sizes, and colors. Through observing and describing the characteristics of birds, children develop skill at making quick comparisons of properties. They also learn to observe habits and types of habitats.

Different birds have characteristic behaviors and feeding patterns as well as preferences for association with some kinds of plant communities rather than others.

To identify and categorize birds, biologists have organized data about each species into taxonomic *keys*. According to their properties, birds are generally grouped into approximately twenty different categories called *Orders*. Each Order is then subdivided into *Families*. Each Family is then subdivided into *species*. Rather than to leaf endlessly through books trying to identify a bird, one first tries to identify the Order to which it probably belongs. Then one locates the Family within the Order to which the bird probably belongs.

What to do:

Start a log book in which you record data on five to ten birds. Put data on each bird on a separate page. Collect and organize information in the following categories:

1 *Date* and *time of day* observed.
2 *Number.* Approximately how many individuals were observed? Some birds are solitary while others move in flocks.
3 *Size.* Note its comparative size and choose some well known birds as referents or standards for comparison, e.g., "The bird was larger than a sparrow, but smaller than a robin." Note how long the tail is in relation to the body.
4 *Shape.* Describe the general shape of the body and bill; note the angle of the tail in relation to the body; if in flight observe the general shape of the wings and tail. Example: chunky body with a very short tail and broad, straight bill.
5 *Color.* Note distinctive color markings and their locations, e.g., on head, tail, rump, flank, or belly.
6 *Bill and legs.* These are often major factors in a taxonomic key so note their shape, size, and color.
7 *Behavior.* Note any distinctive behavior, such as bobbing head or tail, undulating flight pattern, feeding habits, nesting behavior, etc.
8 *Biotic community.* "Biotic community" refers to a natural association of plants and animals. Some birds prefer certain communities such as deciduous forests, while others prefer grasslands and still others dwell mostly in marshes.

What is the probable name of the bird?

Note. While it may be nice for your students to learn to recognize and name many birds, that is not the primary objective of this activity. The more important objective concerns the development of skill at observing and describing properties and behaviors quickly and accurately. Many students have never experienced the pleasure that can come from prolonged, careful contemplation of one kind of bird.

Use the simplified key given in this chapter as a first step in trying to identify the order to which each bird belongs.

Plan a series of lessons to teach students how to observe birds.

ACTIVITY 1-3
A CHANGING VIEW

OBJECTIVES

1 To construct bar graphs in order to describe a collection

2 To observe how a bar graph which describes a collection changes in shape when the categories for grouping are changed

Notice that the picture we make of the world depends on the concepts we use to govern our search. When we change the concepts, we get a different picture. In any collection of objects there may be innumerable kinds of relationships. The reality which we perceive is closely tied to and independent on our individual "thought systems." What data make sense at any moment depends on the thought system we happen to be using at the moment. So it is well to be cautious when responding to a youngster for not giving an expected response.

What to do:

1 Construct bar graphs for two properties, shape and pattern.

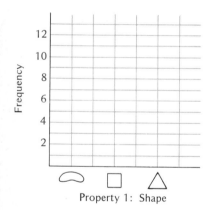

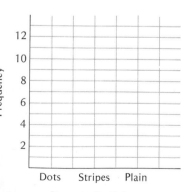

2 Compare the shape of the two graphs, each of which is a description of the collection. Are the shapes the same?

ACTIVITY 1-4
LEFT- AND RIGHT-EYED PEOPLE
AND LEFT- AND RIGHT-HANDED PEOPLE

OBJECTIVES

1 To classify people on the basis of two properties
2 To construct a two-way classification system for organizing data
3 To find out whether there is a relationship between the two properties
4 To construct bar graphs in order to describe a collection

Background:

Most people are either right-handed or left-handed. A few are ambidextrous. Similarly most people are predominantly right-eyed or left-eyed. There may be a few who see equally well out of both eyes. In this activity you will first test yourself and then others to determine how they should be categorized according to the particular combination of properties of eyedness and handedness which they exhibit. The problem of interest is to determine whether there is any relationship between the two sets of properties. For example, is a right-handed person more likely to be right-eyed or left-eyed? If there is no relationship, then you would expect to find that as many left-eyed as right-eyed people are right-handed. You would expect equal numbers of right- and left-eyed people in the left-handed group.

What to do:

1 To determine whether a person is right-eyed or left-eyed, perform the following operations:
  a Punch a round hole in a piece of paper. Make the hole approximately ¼ inch in diameter.

b Hold the paper off at arm's length. Look through the hole at some object with both eyes open. Once the object is sighted, close the right eye and try to sight the same object without moving the paper. Then open the right eye, close the left eye, and sight the object again without moving the paper. Most people will see the object clearly with one eye but not with the other.

2 Construct your own operational definition for distinguishing left-handed from right-handed people.

3 Find twenty to thirty people or more to test. They can be children or adults. For each person, you will have two pieces of information (eyedness and handedness). Design your own form for collecting data on the two variables.

a Organize the data for the whole collection into four categories as shown in the table below:

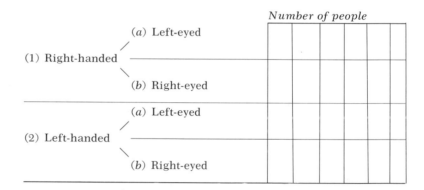

Number of people

(1) Right-handed
  (*a*) Left-eyed
  (*b*) Right-eyed

(2) Left-handed
  (*a*) Left-eyed
  (*b*) Right-eyed

Construct a graph by marking each square on the graph according to the way a person is categorized. For example, one X would be marked according to whether a person is right-handed or left-handed. If there is no association between the variables, then the graphs for right-handed and the graphs for left-handed should be approximately flat. If there is an association, then the graphs for right-hand and left eyes should be relatively bumpy.

b Arrange the data in a two-way table like the one shown below. A two-way table is constructed by putting one of the variables along the top edge of the table and the other along the left edge.

		Eyedness		
		Left-eyed	Right-eyed	
Handedness	Left-handed			How many left-handed? ____
	Right-handed			How many right-handed? ____
		How many left-eyed?	How many right-eyed?	Total

If you know the eyedness of a person, can you predict his handedness?

Optional calculations (especially recommended for people planning to teach at the fourth-grade level or beyond):

1 What proportion of people in your sample are left-handed?

$$\frac{\text{number left-handed}}{\text{total}} \times 100 = \underline{\hspace{1cm}} \text{percent}$$

2 What proportion are right-handed?

$$\frac{\text{number right-handed}}{\text{total}} \times 100 = \underline{\hspace{1cm}} \text{percent}$$

The sum of (1) and (2) should be approximately 100 percent. Try to explain why that should be true.

3 What proportion of people are left-eyed?

$$\frac{\text{number left-eyed}}{\text{total}} \times 100 = \underline{\hspace{1cm}} \text{percent}$$

4 What proportion of people are right-eyed?

$$\frac{\text{number right-eyed}}{\text{total}} \times 100 = \underline{\hspace{1cm}} \text{percent}$$

The sum of (3) and (4) should be approximately 100 percent. Try to explain why that should be true.

5 What proportion of people are both left-eyed and left-handed? ____ percent

6 What proportion are both right-eyed and right-handed? ____ percent

7 What proportion are right-eyed and left-handed? _____percent

8 What proportion are left-eyed and right-handed? _____percent

The sum of (1), (2), (3), and (4) should be approximately 100 percent. Try to explain why that should be true.

You can compare the data from your sample of people with the data from another sample of people by comparing the proportions of people in each category. If the corresponding proportions are about the same, then the two samples are approximately equivalent. What is true of one sample will be likely to be true of the other.

ACTIVITY 1-5

OBJECTIVE

Adapt materials for experiments by focusing on their properties.

What to do:

1 Select any elementary science manual at a grade level that interests you.

2 Pick out an experiment and identify the objects necessary for performing that experiment.

3 By examining the functions of the objects, determine what properties are essential. Then try to think of substitute objects.

REFERENCES

Brockman, C. Frank: *A Field Guide to the Major Native and Introduced Species North of Mexico Trees of North America*, Golden Press, New York, 1968.

Harrington, H. D., and L. W. Durrell: *How to Identify Plants*, Sage Books, Denver, Colorado, 1957.

H. E. Jaques: *How to Know the Land Birds*, Wm. C. Brown Company Publishers, Dubuque, Iowa, 1947.

_____: *How to Know the Trees*, Wm. C. Brown Company Publishers, Dubuque, Iowa, 1946.

————: *Plant Families: How to Know Them*, Wm. C. Brown Company Publishers, Dubuque, Iowa, 1941.

Peterson, Roger Tory: *A Field Guide to the Birds Giving Field Marks of All Species Found East of the Rockies*, Houghton Mifflin Company, Boston, 1947.

————: *A Field Guide to Bird Songs of Eastern and Central North America*, Houghton Mifflin Company, Boston, 19--. Recordings of songs and calls of more than 300 species of land and water birds. Can be used by students to identify songs of birds common in the environment. Also useful for sound discrimination training.

————: *A Field Guide to Western Birds*, Houghton Mifflin Company, Boston, 1941.

Robbins, Chandler S., Bertel Bruun, and Herbert S. Zim: *A Guide to Field Identification Birds of North America*, Golden Press, New York, 1966.

CHAPTER 2

Teacher: *I found all this new science is helping them to learn mathematics. And it fits with math lab, which we're just starting in our school.*

COMMENT AT IN-SERVICE SESSION

"We just measure and measure and never do anything with it —just only write it down."

THIRD-GRADER

Teacher: *Think of something you want to measure.*

Child: *(Puzzled expression.) The clock?*

Teacher: *Why on earth do you want to measure that? Can't you think of something useful?*

Child: *I don't know what you mean. What do you want me to measure?*

DATA AND MEASUREMENT

OBJECTIVES

At the conclusion of this chapter and after the performance of some or all of its associated activities, you should be able to do the following:

1 Construct operational definitions for certain variables and perform the operations for measuring:

    a Length or distance
    b Mass or weight
    c Time
    d Temperature
    e Volume

2 Calibrate devices for measuring length, mass, time, temperature, and volume variables.

3 Use the metric system to measure length, mass, time, temperature, and volume variables.

INTRODUCTION

Counting and measuring are two processes which add to the set of tools a scientist has available for investigating natural phenomena. Description, prediction, control, and explanation of natural phenomena are among the goals of scientific research. Mathematical techniques coupled with measurement operations help in the achievement of these goals. In this chapter the focus is on ways in which variables can be quantified. Measurement is a process which contributes to *prediction* and *control* of interactions in systems. It is a process that helps us determine how much or how little phenomena change over time. It permits us to contrast systems.

The point was made in Chapter 1 that what one chooses to describe depends on the purposes to be served. Similarly in measurement one chooses to count and measure some events and not others, according to whether he thinks the information will help him solve a problem or understand a relationship. This point is particularly important to keep in mind with children, for they sometimes become very skilled at performing measurement operations without having the least idea *why* the operation is supposed to help. We can feel some sympathy for the child in the quotation which introduces this chapter when his teacher asked him to pick some kind of measurement. Without the *context* of a particular problem to help him choose among all the kinds of measurements he might know about, he is at a loss—as any scientist would be. He has no guideline for choosing. The way in which a scientist thinks about a question he is investigating will determine what measurements he elects to perform. Children will willingly measure only when the reasons for doing so are really compelling. If those reasons come from some problem which cannot be solved or understood without measurements, then they are likely to identify variables and try to measure them.

What we choose to measure depends on what we think we will learn about relationships in the system. *How* we choose to collect data partly determines what we can do with them once we get them.

Students can be given many science experiences in which they find it genuinely useful to use measurement and mathematical techniques to help them describe and explain natural phenomena. Since such a substantial portion of a normal school day is usually devoted to mathematics, the tie between science and mathematics should be made very obvious. Science is a place for students to apply mathematical skills.

The focus in this chapter will be on the use of numbers and measurement as the next step in description of phenomena. Prediction and control of phenomena depend in part on the ability of children to make measurements and interpret them.

For each investigation which you encounter in an elementary science program, you should ask yourself the following questions:

1 *Why* do you want to collect a particular category of data; *is it relevant* to the system? What *purpose* is the measurement or the information to serve? "Drill teaching" often helps the children to acquire and practice measurement skills in a way which fails to make the usefulness of the measurement process very convincing to them. When the usefulness of a process escapes them, they are less likely to think of employing a measurement technique when it would be helpful in solving a problem. Knowing how to do something is one thing. Knowing that it is sensible to do it in a particular situation is quite another thing. We will return to this motivational question later.

2 Given that we have reason to measure, what *measurement operations* shall we perform? Which measurements will be most likely to help us understand relationships among parts of a system? These decisions depend on how we specify the system and what questions we are trying to answer.

3 Is there a way to make the measurements of the variables which seem pertinent to the problem? Can the operations or procedures for making the measurement be described well enough that they could be repeated with a reasonable chance of getting the same results under the same conditions? Sometimes there is no way to quantify a variable. This happens when we cannot invent a procedure for measuring it.

4 How can the measurements help us make *inferences* about relationships between variables? In a way, a scientist is a kind of miser. He does not like to lose anything. Perhaps that is one reason why measurement and numbers are such important

facets of science. His ability to explain what is happening in a system depends in part on keeping careful records of both quantitative and qualitative changes.

QUANTIFYING VARIABLES

In this section we will construct *operational definitions* for measuring the variables of length, volume, mass, temperature, time, and force.

Measurement is a process in which there must be

1 A defined *referent unit* which
2 Is *compared* to an unknown (whatever is to be measured)
3 By a well-specified *operation* or procedure
4 In addition there must be a means for *counting* how many of the defined referent units describe the value of the variable in the system being measured.

FIGURE 2-1

Length of distance

Constructing an operational definition for length or distance.   To convey some sense of what is meant by a referent unit and an operational definition, and to show how measurement can help make communication more precise, consider the variable *length*. Most adults know how to measure the length of objects, or the distance around objects, or the height of objects. To analyze what is involved in the construction of devices for measuring length first think about the *units*. Most people are familiar with one or both of two systems: the English system, which employs units called inches, feet, and miles; and the metric system, which uses units called millimeters, centimeters, meters, and kilometers. If you can, for a few moments forget you know about those ways of measuring. Imagine instead that you entered some strange new world and you had to invent a way of measuring length or distance.

When you can measure distances or lengths, you can achieve the following purposes (Figure 2-1):

1 You can describe the dimensions of objects precisely.

2 You can compare corresponding dimensions in two systems.

3 You can detect changes in a system and say something fairly exact about the *magnitude* of the changes.

4 You can measure changes in distance between two objects or systems.

5 Later, when you can also measure time, you can begin to describe the *rate* at which objects move or organisms grow. That is, you can make precise statements about how rapidly or slowly objects or systems move or change.

Such *changes* in systems give evidence that some interactions are going on. It is important to find ways of measuring the amounts of change so that we can begin to make inferences about what is accounting for those changes.

Suppose two people each arbitrarily chose some basic unit of length, and suppose furthermore that the two people did not know each other. They both start out to describe the world. A calls his basic unit the *A unit*. B calls his the *B unit* (see Figure 2-2). Later on both will need some subunits so that they can measure objects and distances that are smaller than the basic units. But at the moment these units are all that each needs, because everything they want to measure is as big as, or bigger than, these units. Now they set out to measure, but first they must describe how they will do the meauring. This is called constructing an operational definition. They develop two rules.

1 Put one end of the referent unit (A unit or B unit) on the object to be measured, being very sure to line up the end of the object with one end of the reference unit.

2 Flip the referent unit end over end until you get to the other side of the object or to the place where you want the measurement to stop.

3 Count the number of flips (called replications).

4 Report the measurement by stating:
   a Its name.
   b How many times the flipping or replicating operation was performed (see Figure 2-2c).

Suppose now that A and B meet. They each have

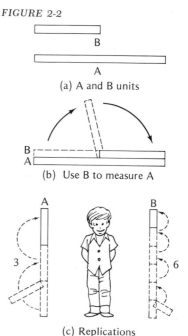

FIGURE 2-2

(a) A and B units

(b) Use B to measure A

(c) Replications

been describing the length of objects, but they have a communication problem because even when they both measure the same object, they get different results. Notice in Figure 2-2*c* that since B is using a smaller referent unit, he needs more of them to measure the length of an object than A does. When A and B compare their reports concerning the length of an object, which they both agree to measure, their results *appear* to differ, but common sense tells them that cannot be so.

Both claim they have a good measurement unit. Neither wishes to change his unit, but both admit they have a communication problem. Something must be done so that they can communicate in the future. There are two possibilities: One of them can give up his basic unit in favor of the unit used by the other—this they cannot agree to do. Alternatively they see whether some regular relationship exists between the two units so that results from one system can be translated into the other system. Since they each have formed strong habits (rather like the people who do not want to change from the English to the metric system), they decide to find a way to translate from one system to the other. When they compare the A and B units, they find that the B unit is half an A unit. It takes two B units to equal the length of one A unit. To communicate in the future:

1 When A sends a measurement to B, B doubles the number of units.
2 When B sends a length measurement to A, A divides the number of units in half.

Next they each decide to invent smaller subunits of the basic referent unit. The smaller units will allow them to be more precise. Big units mean big over- or underestimates of the lengths of objects. To accomplish this purpose they fold their measuring strips in half. When they open the strips, each would be divided into two equal parts—the new subunits. They have each constructed a *scale* consisting of a basic unit and its subunits. A and B can still communicate since the ratio of lengths between these two scales is maintained. Each subunit of the B scale equals two subunits of the A scale.

A and B could, if there were need, proceed to divide their respective referent units into smaller and smaller segments of equal intervals or segments so that they could be increasingly *precise* in their measurements. That is, they could make the error of measurement smaller, although they could never get rid of it entirely.

Sometimes changes in systems are very small. These might go undetected unless the measurement units were sufficiently small. For example, if you want to measure changes in the height of a child over a period of six months, then the units will need to be small. When the errors of measurement are made smaller, then statements about the behavior of systems can be more accurate. In addition someone else can be successful in constructing a piece of equipment to meet certain specifications by using diagrams with precise measurements on them. When the measurements are only approximate, the parts of a system will not fit together very well.

If a student compares measurements made in a system at two points in time and finds differences, he can infer either that some real change has occurred or that his measurement operation was inaccurate.

The metric system.   The metric system for measuring length or distance—which will be the new way—works basically in the way described for constructing an operational definition for length (see Figure 2-3).

1 Choose a basic referent unit and give it a name. In this case the unit is the *meter*. The meter is somewhat longer than a yard.
2 Subdivide the meter into equal-sized, convenient subunits. In this case the subunits are called *centimeters*, and it takes 100 of these subunits to equal the length of one meter.
3 For more precise measurements the centimeter is, in turn, divided into 10 equal-sized subunits called *millimeters*. A ruler has been printed on the inside of the front cover for your use.

It is worth taking some time to learn the metric measurements for the following reasons:

1 Industrial operations in the United States are gradually shifting to metric measures to make trade with other nations easier since most other nations use the metric system. The government has been putting out booklets to help people in business find low-cost ways of switching machinery specifications to metric measures.

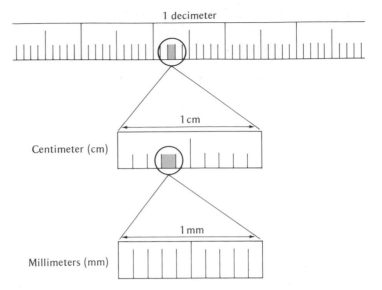

FIGURE 2-3
**The actual length of one centimeter
is _____. One-tenth of a centimeter
is ., one millimeter.**

2 Metric measurement units are used in science. Being literate in science means, for one thing, being
familiar with the metric system.

3 The tens base employed in the metric system fits
in conveniently with many modern mathematics
programs that use the number line to teach the
properties of numbers.

4 They are easy to learn and use—especially if you
do not try to translate metric measures into English measures or vice versa. (If you do try to translate, you can follow the procedure that A and B
used earlier. All you have to know is 1 inch =
2.56 centimeters.)

Recapitulation. Stop for a moment to examine what
you have learned about measurement from this section.
(Refer also to Figures 2-1 through 2-3.)

1 Measurement uses numbers
   a To count the members in a category or class.
This is part of describing a class.
   b To state the value of a variable, e.g., the dowel
is 10 centimeters long.

2 Measurement is a process in which there must be
   a A defined *referent unit* which
   b Can be *compared* with the object to be measured
   c By a well-specified operation

3 Most measurement statements will include two terms:

    a A *number* which states how many of the referent units described the value of the variable

    b A *name* for the referent unit

Knowing what the name stands for means being able to state or demonstrate the operation that was used to produce the number. It is no use, in other words, to report a number without naming a unit, since no one will know to what the number refers.

4 The magnitude of the number depends on the size of the referent unit.

    a The smaller the referent unit or standard unit, the larger will be the number used to describe the object.

    b The larger the referent unit or standard unit, the smaller will be the number used to describe the object.

5 In measurement one specifies the *number* and the *referent unit*. This makes it possible for

    a Others to repeat the work (*replication*)

    b Results to be compared (*comparison*)

6 Measurements can be coarse or refined, according to how precise one needs to be in a particular problem. The size of errors due to measurement can be reduced by using smaller and smaller subunits.

First steps toward prediction and control. In being taught to measure lengths or distances, children need to learn to use some basic referent unit and to move it along from end to end, keeping track of how many times they move the referent unit. But there is something to note about many five- to seven-year-olds and some older children as well: Inconsistencies do not bother them. I have given first and second graders a length-measuring task and discovered that they sometimes slide the referent object along in a haphazard way, meanwhile counting with gusto. That means they get different results each time they measure the same object—a fact which does not disturb some of them at all. The idea that each time they must actually put the measuring instrument at the exact point where the first comparison ended entirely escaped them.

Note that moving the referent along end-to-end and

keeping track of the number of times the operation is repeated involves two steps, the end-to-end step and a step that counts the number of end-to-ends.

We can change the size of the intervals on two adjacent number lines, but we still come up with the report that A is twice as far from the house as B is (see Figure 2-4). That is why, when we construct graphs, we can choose any convenient size for operation *and* the counting. Both are important. Children frequently get the counting idea, but moving the referent object is for many of them a random operation. For such children the whole notion of measurement as a descriptive device in which the fundamental operation involves replicating some basic unit over and over again without overlapping, and keeping count of how many times they replicate the unit, is entirely lost.

The notion that the world should be a predictable place or that there should be some continuity between events has still to develop. The child has not yet seen the necessity for consistency and is unable to relate the results to the means by which the results were produced. Children are capable of imitation. They may imitate what they see the adult doing without grasping *why* the action —in this case, measurement—is done in a strictly prescribed way. Very often the motivation to perform simple measurements in physical systems is low because the shifts or changes in the system are so obvious. Often the changes are so quick and pronounced that children

FIGURE 2-4

If we change the size of intervals on two adjacent number lines, we still report that A is twice as far from the house as B is.

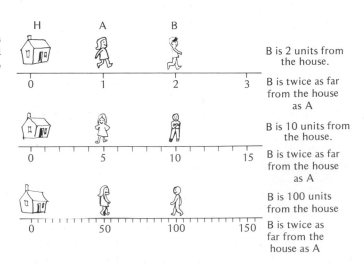

B is 2 units from the house.

B is twice as far from the house as A

B is 10 units from the house.

B is twice as far from the house as A

B is 100 units from the house

B is twice as far from the house as A

feel they do not need to keep track of them. They can "see" the results.

There is little motivation to measure what is already familiar unless you can cast the familiar in a new context. It is sometimes rather useful to employ an unfamiliar system, one which has some degree of novelty to it, to encourage or illustrate the value of making measurements and keeping data.

It is most convenient to think in terms of simple but realizable systems to see how measurement operations go on and what information measurement provides us. With children, and even with ourselves, we need to be sure that the doing of a particular measurement operation is perceived to give useful information. Otherwise it is just another kind of busywork. When an activity in an elementary science program calls for the measurement of a variable, the purpose which the measurement is to serve should be clear. If data are to be organized into tables, students need to see what advantages the organization gives them. Just as organizing a collection of objects helps thinking, so organizing data helps in problem solving.

Making inferences from measurements. Making inferences depends on context and conditions. With measurement data you can *compare* systems. You can also make *inferences* about changes going on in systems.

There is nothing in the measurements in and of themselves, however, that tells you what inferences are reasonable. You must be familiar with the context in which the measurements were made if you are to interpret them correctly. Suppose, for example, you saw data that gave the diameters for three tomatoes as 2.5 centimeters, 6.2 centimeters, and 8.4 centimeters. Figure 2-5 shows that some of the interpretations given to these measurements depend on the context, on what questions the person hopes to answer.

Units of volume

Suppose we need a way for measuring the volume of liquids. Volume is a way of measuring how much space something occupies. If we follow the rules for establishing basic units of measure set down in the previous discussion, the first step in constructing a volume measure

FIGURE 2-5

Interpretations given to measurements depend on the context.

Property change of same tomato over a period of time

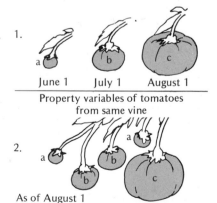

Property variables of tomatoes from same vine

As of August 1

Property variables of different strains of tomatoes

Cherry tomatoes   June pink   Beefsteaks

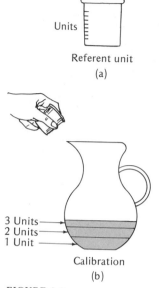

Units

Referent unit
(a)

3 Units
2 Units
1 Unit

Calibration
(b)

FIGURE 2-6
Once a referent unit is chosen, a vessel of any shape can be calibrated.

would be to select some kind of referent unit (Figure 2-6).

Take some container and call it the referent unit for volume. You could, for example, select an empty frozen-orange-juice can as the unit volume, or any other container with straight sides. To find the volume of any other container, you simply count how many times you have to fill and empty the referent container into the container whose volume is to be measured. You then can make statements like the following:

The big pitcher holds 25 unit volumes of liquid. The number reflects the size of the referent unit. Fewer large units will fill a container.

There is a number which described how many times an operation was repeated and a name which implies what the operation was.

If we need to measure the volumes of containers that are smaller than the referent unit, then the referent unit needs to be divided into equal subunits. These smaller volumes can be marked on the container (see Figure 2-6).

By dividing the length of the container into equal distance units, the referent unit for volume can be calibrated, provided the walls of the container are vertical.

In the English system it is customary to use quarts and gallons, and even ounces, to measure volume. In the metric system one of the units of volume is called a *liter*. The referent unit for volume in the metric system is the *milliliter* (abbreviated ml). It takes 1,000 of these referent units to fill up a container which has a volume of 1 liter. Notice also how convenient the dimensions of the referent unit for volume are. It is 1 centimeter $\times$ 1 centimeter $\times$ 1 centimeter. Unlike the cumbersome English system, the measurement of volume in the metric system is logically related to the measurement of length. Any container can be calibrated by taking the referent unit volume and emptying it into the bigger container. (see Figure 2-7.)

Units of mass

So far we can measure how *far* things are from each other and how *big* they are; that is, we can measure length or distance. We can also measure how much *space* things take up by measuring their *volume*. Now we need a way to tell how much matter or material something contains. If,

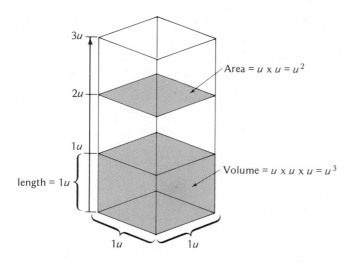

Area $= u \times u = u^2$

$3u$

$2u$

$1u$

length $= 1u$

Volume $= u \times u \times u = u^3$

$1u$ $1u$

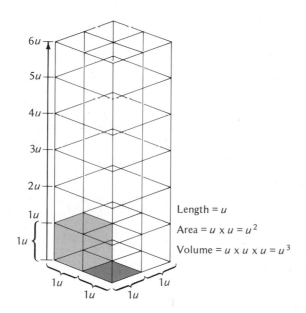

$6u$

$5u$

$4u$

$3u$

$2u$

$1u$

$1u$

Length $= u$

Area $= u \times u = u^2$

Volume $= u \times u \times u = u^3$

$1u$ $1u$

$1u$ $1u$

FIGURE 2-7
Units of length, area, and volume are related.

for example, someone gave you two boxes of the same volume but one felt heavier than the other, you would in-fer that the heavier box had more matter in it. To describe and compare the two boxes with some precision, we need to add to our measures of dimension and volume some new quantity that will allow us to compare the differences in mass more precisely. Applying the rules we have just discussed:

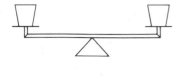

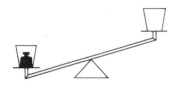

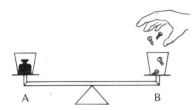

A   B

FIGURE 2-8

1 Select a referent unit

Let us decide to choose a bolt of a particular size.

2 Find out how many referent units equal the mass of the unknown, i.e., the objects whose mass you want to measure.

Here is where a problem develops. How can the comparison between the referent units and the unknown be made? You can hold the unit masses in one hand and the unknown in the other, but your body is not very good at detecting small differences.

3 Specify the operation for finding mass. When the beam or rod is horizontal, the system is in balance. With the unknown on the left and the referent units on the right, the mass of the unknown will be the number of referent units piled on the right.

Take a rigid bar or stick. Balance the whole system. Put the objects to be weighed on the left and the referent units on the right (see Figure 2-8).

The metric system has a convenient referent unit for measuring mass. It is called the *gram*. Just as the bolt was arbitrarily chosen as a mass unit, so is the gram an arbitrarily chosen mass unit. But it was chosen most judiciously. The operation performed to get it was probably approached something like the following:

1 Take the milliliter (ml) unit of volume. It is related to the unit of length since it is exactly 1 centimeter (cm) × 1 centimeter (cm) × 1 centimeter (cm).

2 Fill the milliliter unit of volume with very cold water. Since the volume of water changes with temperature, it is necessary to say what temperature was originally used.

3 That weight is the referent unit for mass. It is called a gram. Anything that will balance this mass on the beam will be equivalent to 1 gram mass.

When weighing in the metric system, the amount of mass in an object being weighed is expressed in grams. Since the gram is so small, the mass of heavy objects is sometimes expressed in kilograms. A kilogram equals 1,000 of the gram masses. If you look on packages and cans of food, you will find that the mass of the contents is often expressed in grams. (To give yourself some sense of how heavy a gram feels, pick up an American nickel. It equals in mass approximately 5 grams.)

Measuring temperature

Measurement of temperature involves some kind of inter-action of the measuring device with the system. The measuring device, when it enters the system, interacts with it. You can detect evidence of that interaction by changes that happen in the measuring device itself. At one level you can get a very concrete sense of what is involved in that interaction. Suppose you put your hands in water of different temperatures and attempt to estimate roughly the degree of hotness or coldness. The water and your hands interact, and a transfer of heat goes from the water to your hands—in which case you perceive the water as warm—or heat goes from your hands into the water—in which case you perceive the water as cold. By means of the heat transfer between the water and the hands, you get the *message* about the relative temperature of the water.

Our own bodies are extremely sensitive but very im-precise kinds of instruments for measuring. It is quite possible to fool the human temperature system. You have perhaps had the experience of sitting on the beach or be-side a pool on a warm day, getting very warm, entering the water, and experiencing a real shock. The water seemed very, very cold to you. After a time the water seemed to warm up. In circumstances like that, there is a rapid transfer of heat from your body to the water and that loss of heat becomes translated by you as *cold*. Had you jumped into the water when you were cooler, you would have called the water relatively warm. Now if you need a precise device for measuring, you do not want it subject to a changeable circumstance like that. You do want the mercury in the thermometer, for example, to contract, but you want it to give the same report about the temperature of the water for each measurement, assuming, of course, that the water temperature remains constant. Receptors in your skin are sensitive to that energy message. They transfer the heat energy into electrical and chemical energy which eventually you translate as "hot enough" or "not hot enough" or "A is warmer than B."

Similarly, when you put a thermometer in a system, it becomes part of the system. Energy flows out of the system into the thermometer. If the system is warmer than the thermometer, the column of liquid expands and rises in the thermometer. If the thermometer is warmer than the system, then energy flows out of the thermometer into the system, and the column of liquid contracts. You will detect evidence of interaction between the thermometer and the system by changes in the length of the mercury or alcohol column or whatever liquid the thermometer contains. If the system is warmer than the thermometer, the column gets longer. If the system is cooler, the column contracts. Any measuring device that interacts with a system changes the system, at least a little, and is in its turn changed by the system. Note that we use change of length of some object—the mercury column in this case—as an indicator of change in a system. In short when we insert one system, a thermometer, into another system to determine how hot or cold that system is, both the system and the thermometer change (Transcript 2-1).

In the measurement of temperature, just as in the measurement of other variables, you need an operational definition of the measurement process. In place of a re-referent object, however, you use two referent points— the boiling and freezing points of water. Developing the basic referent unit for a thermometer involves the following steps:

1 Insert the thermometer in water, which is near to freezing, and mark on the stem the level to which the liquid in the thermometer drops. This is the bottom referent point.
2 Insert the thermometer in boiling water and mark the stem at the level to which the liquid rises. This is the top referent point.
3 Divide the distance between the two referent points into equal intervals. Call these subunits *degrees*.

Transcript 2-1

Dialogue		*Analysis*
Kathy	Want to take my temperature?	Beside distinguishing phenomena from the devices for measuring phenomena, the would-be user must learn to read the device. Here children apparently had the first task in hand— they knew what the device was for. Note how they determine which end should interact with the material whose temperature is to be measured. The numbers cue them. The collection of liquid in the well of the thermometer and the notion of expansion of liquids are not yet a part of their understanding of the way the particular instrument they are using functions, nor should they be at this stage. (One might be tempted to ask the children whether if they turned the thermometer upside down the liquid would run to the opposite end.) Careful attention to short bits of dialogue can furnish the reader or listener with considerable information about the state of children's knowledge and the kind of logic they employ.
David	Now, what do you want me to do?	
Teacher	What does it mean when you say take a temperature of the water? What are you actually doing?	
David	You're seeing how hot the water is and how cold it is.	
Teacher	That's right.	
David	Okay, which is the hot? This is the hot. Am I doing it in the right end?	
Teacher	I don't know.	
Kathy	Looks like the wrong.	
David	Yeah, that's zero up here.	
Teacher	So.	
David	So, I guess we got it in the wrong end.	
Teacher	Do you know how to read this thing?	
David	Yeah. It goes up by twenties, it looks like, on this one. 0-20-40-60-80. Yeah, it goes up by twenties.	
Teacher	All right.	
David	And then when you get to 100, it goes 20-40-60-80 to 200.	
Kathy	And that's a fever!	

If you use big subunits, you will need fewer of them to extend between boiling and freezing than if you use smaller subunits. In the metric system (called the Kelvin, Celsius, or Centigrade scale) there are 100 subunits or degrees between boiling and freezing. In the English system (referred to as the Fahrenheit scale) there are 180° (see laboratory activities on calibration of thermometers). (See Figure 2-9.)

Various factors in systems determine how high or low the temperature will be. Suppose you had two containers of water, one twice as full as the other but both at the same temperature (see Figure 2-10).

If you heated both systems over a hot plate for two

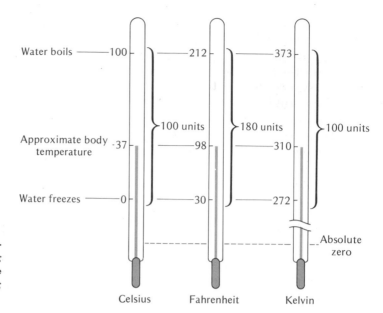

FIGURE 2-9

**Two temperature scales with refer-
ent points at boiling and freezing
water. Note the difference in the
number of units between boiling
and freezing.**

minutes, the temperature in both systems would rise. But
would both thermometers register the same degree of
heat? Probably your intuition or your past experience has
shown you that small volumes of water can be heated to
higher temperatures faster than large volumes of water.
You would predict that the thermometer in the smaller
volume would register a higher temperature. It takes more
heat energy to raise the temperature of the larger volume
to a certain degree than it does to raise the temperature
of the smaller volume to that same degree of heat. It takes
more energy to move a heavy load up a flight of stairs than
to move a light load up the same flight. Similarly, it takes
more heat energy to move a bigger volume of liquid up the
temperature scale than it does to move a small volume of
liquid.

To calibrate a thermometer, simply choose arbitrary
referents, such as the boiling and freezing points of water.
Insert the thermometer in ice and mark the level of the
liquid in it. Do the same for the boiling-water referent
point. Then, on the assumption that the mercury or alcohol or whatever liquid put into the thermometer expands uniformly, divide the distances between the two
referent points into equal intervals of convenient size.
The freezing and boiling points of water are convenient

referent points because the water system visibly changes its state from liquid to solid or from liquid to vapor at those points. Arbitrarily assign a number to the freezing point and another number to the boiling point. Then divide the distance on the thermometer stem into equal intervals. You might decide, as is done with the Fahrenheit scale, to say, "We will call the freezing point of water 32 degrees, and we will call the boiling point of water 212 degrees." Now we will simply divide the distance between 32 and 212 into equal intervals. Or we might, as in the case of the Centigrade or Kelvin scales, call the freezing point zero and the boiling point 100 degrees and divide that interval into equal intervals. On the Fahrenheit scale we get 180 equal intervals. One sees that the size of a degree or interval is larger on the Centigrade than on the Fahrenheit scale. It only takes one hundred equal-size intervals to go from freezing to boiling on the Centigrade scale. The Fahrenheit scale uses smaller divisions, so it takes 180 intervals to go from the 32-degree mark all the way up to the 212-degree mark. It is rather like taking five giant steps to go the same distance it takes nine baby steps to cover. In fact all we are doing is stretching or compressing a number line without changing the relative relations between measures.

Two thermometers constructed of the same materials but calibrated differently will give different readings when inserted in the same system. Nevertheless, in some sense we know that the column of liquid inside each thermometer performed in the same way and that the thermometers are equivalent. A temperature change described in the two systems will be represented by different numbers, *even though it is the same system whose temperature is being monitored* (see Figure 2-9). The number which expresses the temperature in Fahrenheit units will tend to be larger than in Centigrade or Kelvin units because the scale intervals are smaller, and because instead of choosing an arbitrary starting number like zero, the Fahrenheit scale starts at 32 degrees.

In contrast to measuring distances, when we measure temperature with the types of scales described, we really are measuring relative, not absolute, temperature. That fact becomes clear if we recall that objects can get colder than the freezing temperature of water. Objects still have some heat in them. In theory the heat supply

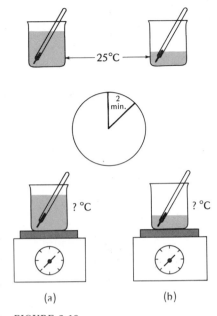

FIGURE 2-10
After two minutes of heating, will the readings on the thermometers be equal?

reaches bottom at about 273°C. This means that the heat energy in a system would be gone absolutely, but at this temperature there would be no interaction between the system and the measuring device, so there would be nothing to measure. The system and the thermometer might

Transcript 2-2

	Dialogue	Analysis
Teacher	OK, now I want you to explain to me what this instrument is. Um, let's see Gloria, why don't you go first? What is the instrument?	Children's conception of what an instrument like a thermometer does and how it functions, to say nothing of what systematic rather than chance instruction. Language associated
First child	A temperature	with phenomena can become well confused in the minds of children. Note the terms that
Teacher	A temperature? OK, a temperature. What is the instrument called?	they confuse—*temperature* and *thermometer*. (That is, they confuse, at least with the labels, the phenomenon "temperature" with
First child	A thermometer.	the device to measure the phenomenon, "thermometer." From an examination of
Teacher	A thermometer. Um, what does a thermometer do?	just this much of the transcript (approximately 100 seconds of dialogue) we can infer
Second child	It tells you how the degrees is.	that the number of different kinds of objects that they had heard called *thermometers*
Teacher	And what is a degree?	or uses to which thermometers had been put could produce some perplexity for them. It
Second child	Its something like—when it's cold, it might be 60 below zero; and when it's hot, it might be 130.	is useful for the teacher to know something about what notions children hold about phenomena and instruments in order to know how to shape the discourse.
Teacher	Very good. OK, so a degree measures what?	
Second child	The temperature?	
Teacher	OK, very good. Do you have one of these at home, Gloria?	
First child	No.	
Teacher	How about you?	
Second child	Yes.	
Teacher	What kind do you have about . . .	
Second child	Uh, it's something like that, but it doesn't have those white things on it.	
Teacher	I see—and where does it hang?	
Second child	It hangs in the wall, and then there's something like a hook around.	
Teacher	OK. And, um, what does it usually register? Do you know what, how much, how hot your room is usually?	
Second child	Yep, it's about 85 degrees.	

Dialogue	*Analysis*

	Dialogue	Analysis
Teacher	85 degrees. That's pretty warm. Good. Do you have one that hangs outside your window at all?	
Second child	Yeah. It's white.	
Teacher	OK. Gloria, does your mother have one that tells some other kind of temperature? When you're sick, for instance?	
First child	No.	
Teacher	Have you ever had your temperature taken?	
First child	My mother has one on the stove . . .	
Teacher	Why don't you say that again? Explain it again.	
First child	She has one in the stove.	
Teacher	And what does it do?	
First child	It tells you how high it is.	
Teacher	OK, good. Um, let's see. What is your normal body temperature? Does your mother ever take your temperature, Armando?	
Second child	Yeah.	
Teacher	What's your normal body temperature—when you're not sick—do you know what that is?	
Second child	Yeah, 95.	
Teacher	95? That's, I think, a little low for normal—is that what your temperature registers, though? The correct temperature is 98.6, I think; but sometimes it's lower than that, even when you're well. Today, I want you to —um, Gloria, will you pour me a half a cup of cold water; put it in this cup.	Nature is never wrong. The temperature is whatever it is. Notice the careless use of the phrase "correct temperature." What is wrong with it?
Second child	I'm thirsty.	
Teacher	That's what water's for. Maybe while Gloria's measuring you can tell me, ah, how you read a thermometer.	
Second child	You read it by numbers, and if this is 70, it's 70 degrees.	
Teacher	OK . . . what's the red stuff in there?	
Second child	It's blood, I think, or ink.	
Teacher	Gloria, do you have any idea what the red, uh, liquid is in there?	
First child	No.	For additional ways of analyzing this transcript, see Chapters 8, 10, and 11.

both disintegrate because there would be no energy to hold the parts together; at least that is one supposition (Transcript 2-2).

Time

Perhaps you have noticed one kind of measure conspicuously absent from our discussions so far. Time, that strange psychological phenomenon that can seem to stretch forever when we are in trouble and pass by in an instant when we are happy, deserves some attention. Like all our other measures in science, we define time by how we measure it, by specifying the operation to be performed. There is something different about time, though, because it is not concrete. When we measured length or mass, we compared some referent object with the thing to be measured. There is no concrete object available as a referent for time.

When we measure time, we compare the beginnings and endings of *two events* rather than comparing some property common to two objects. Measuring time is more like measuring temperature in that you select two referent points instead of a referent object.

We could make a time-measuring device out of anything that exhibits periodic motion, such as a pendulum, or our heartbeat, or water that drips at a regular rate, or anything which vibrates at some steady pace. We could then define the time it took to accomplish a task by simply counting how often the pendulum swung back and forth or some object vibrated, or how many drops of water fell from the start of the event to its conclusion. We could say, for example, that a fly sat on your arm for an interval of three pendulum swings or five heartbeats or four water drops.

A clock operates by ticking at regular intervals, as a wheel full of evenly spaced cogs moves around at a steady speed. The dial preserves information for us. It saves us the trouble of having to sit and keep count. The hands move around a circle so many degrees for each designated time interval like a second or a minute or a day, but why does a clock ordinarily have two or even three hands? What is the relation, if any, among them? A common arrangement shows a sweep hand that moves completely around the dial in sixty seconds. Each time the sweep hand completes one cycle, the *minute* hand jumps one sixtieth of the circle. It moves one sixtieth of

360 degrees, or it changes its direction 6 degrees. Every time the minute hand moves around the circle and completes a cycle, it activates another hand that jumps one-twelfth of the distance around the circle or 30 degrees. Try to figure out what these relationships would be for a 24-hour instead of a 12-hour clock (see Figure 2-11). The hands are the means for subdividing bigger time intervals into smaller subunits.

Of course, units of time are rather arbitrarily chosen. They seem, however, to have historical precedent in the regular occurence and conclusions of some natural events, like the waxing and waning of the moon, which we now call a month; the rotation of the earth on its axis, which we call a day; the time it takes to circle the sun, which we call a year; and possibly even the heartbeat interval, which is approximately a second.

It was only as technology and the necessity for more coordination and communication developed that the drive to refine the ways mankind had of relating events to each

12 – hour clock
60 minutes to the hour
60 seconds to the minute
2 cycles per day

FIGURE 2-11
Twelve-hour and twenty-four-hour clocks. Note how difficult it is to interpret the meaning on a clock which uses units to which you are not accustomed.

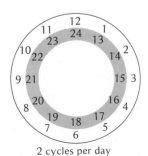

2 cycles per day

1 cycle per day

24 – hour clocks
60 minutes to the hour
60 seconds to the minute

other on some kind of reliable time scale evolved. The unit of time called a second serves as the basic unit of time measure in science.

The relative size of time intervals, say between the beginning and ending of an event, can be measured by any sort of periodic device. If we measure duration of events that are over and done with very quickly, our measuring instrument must be responsive to short time intervals like seconds and fractions of a second. If on the other hand, we are interested in events that take tremendous amounts of time to occur, like geologic changes, then the scale of time may be quite coarse, the units being expressed in years or even in centuries or millennia.

Clocks can be made to run forward or backward, according to our needs. A clock that runs forward tells us how much time has passed since we last looked or how long it took to start a task and complete it. But a clock that runs backward is what we need to catch a plane or launch a rocket. It tells us how much time we have left until a certain event is supposed to occur. Children today are familiar with rocket countdowns where the seconds of the final minute before the launch are called off: 60, 59, 58, etc.

Generally we make a great deal of teaching children in the early grades to read a clock, and we sometimes get impatient when they fail to do it correctly. It is hard, however, for children to know what they are doing when they read a clock—to know what it means. They deserve some sympathy for that. There is, after all, no easy way to define time, because it is not a concrete thing.

Even after we learn to read something, we do not always know what it means. We find ourselves trying to translate the meaning into something we know. Americans, for example, do not ordinarily read a 24-hour clock. They use a 12-hour clock, and separate the day into A.M. and P.M. A day consists of two periods, the A.M. period and the P.M. period. But many European countries, and the military people in this country, employ a 24-hour cycle which equals the A.M. period plus the P.M. period (see Figure 2-11).

Time, then, is just a way for indicating what the duration of an event is from its beginning to its end, or for indicating what interval exists between the starts and ends of two events. We measure the time it takes for a certain event to occur by counting how many of some other kinds of referent event occur from the start to the finish of the event we are interested in measuring. In a way, time is nothing. Nevertheless, we do find it useful to measure.

Force

Like time, force is a factor which you cannot see directly but whose influence you can observe. The dictionary uses phrases like "to press," "to push," "to exert energy on something," to describe the act of applying force. Some of these phrases give a clue to how we might construct an operational definition for force.

Think for a moment what you may have observed when you exerted a force on something. Either the object moved, or it changed its shape. For example, to take off a bottle top that is firmly in place requires some force to be exerted to overcome a resisting force. As long as the resisting force and the force you apply are about equal, nothing happens and you have no visible evidence that force is being applied. When the bottle top finally moves, there is visible evidence that a force is acting.

Forces also change the shape of objects. If you stretch a rubber band or a spring, you exert force on it. The change in shape is evidence that a force is acting (Figure 2-12).

To construct a standard or referent unit of measure for force, we can use the phenomenon of stretching or changing of shape that forces produce to advantage. (When things change shape some part of them moves, so we are really discussing a special kind of motion.) The more something stretches or changes shape, the more force must be involved.

Suspend a spring from which you can hang objects of different weight. The spring will stretch depending on how much force the objects exert on it. Place a card marked off in even intervals, in centimeters for example, behind the spring to measure its stretch. Objects which exert more force will stretch the spring farther than objects which exert little force (see Figure 2-12).

Now you have a force measurer. An object exerts one unit of force when it stretches the spring through a distance of 1 centimeter. An object exerts two force units when it stretches the spring a distance of 2 centimeters on the scale. With the force measurer it is possible to compare the magnitudes of different forces.

In the metric system the unit of force is called a *newton*. To get some feel for how much force a newton repre-

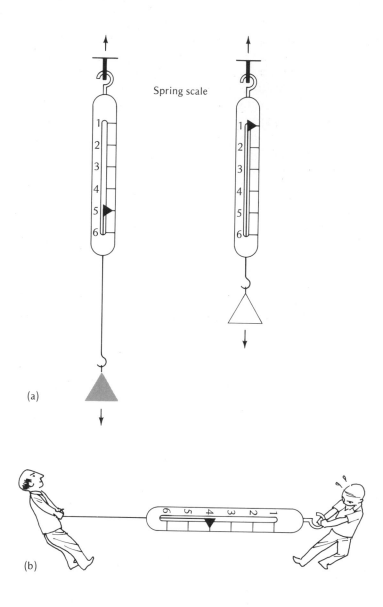

FIGURE 2-12
Force measure.

(b)

sents, pick up some object that weighs approximately 0.2 pounds. Weight is a measure of the force of gravitation. To hold up against the pull of gravity an object that weighs about ²/₁₀ of a pound, you must exert about one newton of force. One kilogram of gravitational force is equivalent to approximately 9.8 newtons of dynamic force. This means you would need to exert 9.8 newtons of force to hold up an object that was being pulled on with a gravitational force of 1 kilogram (1,000 grams), or 2.2 pounds. (One kilogram of gravitational force in the metric system is approximately equal to 2.2 pounds of gravitational force in the English system.)

Forces change the shape of the world. They set things in motion and bring them to a halt.

The analysis of forces and the measurement of their magnitudes are steps toward putting forces to work to help mankind achieve particular goals.

SUMMARY

Measurement is the process of quantifying variables. Some variables cannot be quantified, but with a little ingenuity many variables can be. Measurement is part of the hunt for order. It is one step in the process of making sense out of a natural world that would otherwise seem to behave very erratically. When we try to make judgments in the face of imprecise circumstances, the margin for error and misinterpretation is very great. Measurement helps to bring some precision to investigations of phenomena. Measurement of variables permits us to do the following:

1 Describe systems with precision
2 Determine how much or how little a system changes over time
3 Determine similarities and differences between systems that we want to contrast

Measurement is a process for quantifying variables in which certain conditions must be met:

1 There must be a defined *referent unit*, as in the case of length, mass, and volume, or two *referent* units, as in the case of temperature and time.
2 The referent can be *compared* with whatever is to be measured by a well-specified *operation* or procedure.
3 There must be a means for counting how many of the referent units equal the value of the variable exhibited on the object or in the system being measured.

To state the value of a variable that is quantified, two components are necessary:

1 A *number* which expresses how many of the referent units equal the value of the variable in a particular situation.

2 A *name* for the referent unit. The name implies the *operation* used to produce the number.

In the next chapters we will see that whereas the actual process of making measurements may be relatively easy, the task of deciding what to measure, when to measure, and what to do with the data once you have them requires some intricate thinking.

ACTIVITY 2-1

OBJECTIVE

To demonstrate measurement of length, area, and volume in metric units

Materials:

Metric ruler
Scissors
Paper
Glue or Scotch tape

Length

_____ How long is this line?
_____ centimeters (cm)
_____ millimeters (mm)

Mark off the line in centimeter units. Subdivide the line into millimeter units.

Area

The accompanying figure shows a square which is _____ centimeters long on each side.

1 Find the area of the square by counting how many square centimeters (cm²) it contains.
2 How many square millimeters (mm²) big is the figure? State the operations you would perform to find the area.

Volume

1 Construct a cube which is 2 centimeters long on each side.
   a Construct 6 squares which are 2 centimeters long on each side and arranged as shown in the figure at the top of page 72 (note that this is drawn larger than the dimensions given in the problem).
   b Cut out the figure, fold along the lines, and form into a cube.
2 What is the volume of the cube?
   volume = _____ cm³
   volume = _____ ml

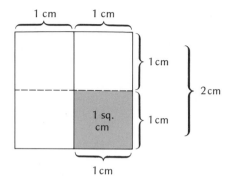

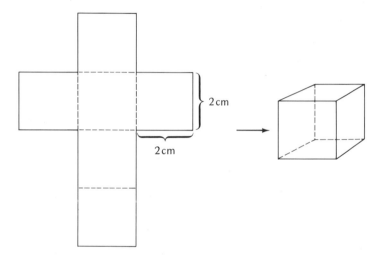

Mass

1 Construct an instrument for measuring the amount of material in an object.

2 Use the device to weigh some objects.

3 Every instrument has its limits. Scales for measuring the mass and weight of objects are meant to operate within certain ranges. Objects which are too light or too heavy will fail to be measured. Objects which are too light will fail to move the system. Objects which are too heavy will exceed the limit of what the system can stand. Locate some scales (e.g., bathroom scales, scales in a supermarket) and try to find out what the limits are.

Temperature

1 Locate some thermometers and note the following:
a In what system each is calibrated

b Over what range each is supposed to operate
2 Note the reading on each thermometer and then find a way to interact with the thermometer so that the reading changes.
3 Read the transcripts on children's conversations while they worked with thermometers. Identify the problems they had.

Measurements

Pick out any elementary science book from a series, preferably material meant to be taught at the fourth-grade level or beyond. Page through it to identify all concepts and operations directly related to measurement.

1 List the kinds of measurements to be made.
2 List all measurement concepts and measurement operations described or which are to be made.

ACTIVITY 2-2

OBJECTIVE

To compare areas and masses of irregular shapes

There are two statements of relationships between A and B shown at the tope of page 74.

1 The area of A is greater than the sum of all the areas in B.
2 The mass of A is greater than the sum of the masses in B.

Problem:

Are the statements true?

Approximately? _____   _____
                      yes   no

Exactly? _____   _____
                yes   no

Not at all? _____

What to do:

Plan and conduct a sequence of operations which will produce evidence to support your answers. Transfer the

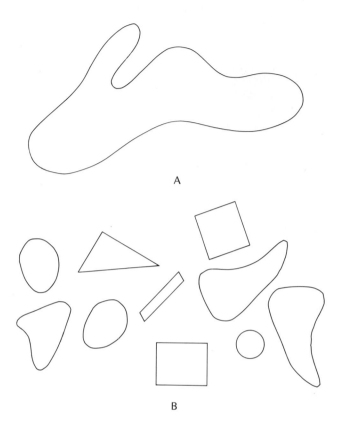

A

B

figures to light-weight cardboard for convenience in weighing.

Hint.   You can make a very sensitive beam balance out of a straw and a straight pin.

CHAPTER 3

First child: *The big ball and the little ball went down the ramp just as fast. That doesn't make sense.*

Second child: *Well, the big ball knocked the box farther, so something is different.*

Third child: *If they went just as fast, I think they should move the box just as far.*

Second child: *Would you rather be tackled by Joe [a small boy] or by George [a big boy]?*

CONVERSATION AFTER AN EXPERIMENT
FROM THE SAPA PROGRAM

Lou: *Oh—the hamster got out, and so did the lizard.*

Betty: *That's OK. We'll just put the food outside the cage and we'll catch them when they come back to eat.*

Tony: *What if it's night?*

FIRST-GRADE PROBLEM

A WAY OF REASONING

OBJECTIVES

In any reasonably well-planned investigation or experiment, or in any modern elementary science program:

1 Identify the variables.

2 Construct operational definitions of the variables.

3 Design a good sampling procedure (this usually gets scant consideration in elementary texts, so you have to make up your own procedures).

4 Collect and organize data in tables.

5 Construct histograms where appropriate.

INTRODUCTION

In this chapter the experiments will be presented in such a way as to focus less on the final outcomes and more on the kind of reasoning that typically must be done when investigating biological phenomena. It is a pity that most published reports of scientific investigations do not describe the long periods of "messing about" that are so much a part of real inquiry. Yet it is this period of mental conflict, of trial and error, and of struggle to find and define variables that is central to inquiry. For the scientist, the period before the production of a definitive experiment is a learning period in which one idea after another competes for attention. Similarly, for students expected to engage in inquiry—and that is a facet of most elementary science programs—there will also be false starts, ideas tried and discarded before something fruitful finally emerges. From an instructional point of view, this phase of inquiry has the advantage of causing students to think about what they already know in many new and different ways. In short, by contrasting ideas, arguing, and designing experiments to check their ideas, the students inadvertently rehearse tremendous amounts of science content as well as the processes of science. Since motivation is high, they are more likely to retain the content, especially when they have finally achieved some tentative answers.

If you achieve the objectives of this chapter, and if you catch the sense of how reasoning may proceed in the course of a biological investigation, you should be able to cope with the great variety of results children will produce when they investigate biological phenomena.

MAKING ORDER OUT OF DISORDER

From an investigative point of view, a biologist's lot is not a simple one. It is difficult for him to repeat an experiment exactly. Most living things change by growing, aging, dying, learning, adapting, and reproducing. In addition, patterns of competition and cooperation change in response to various pressures occurring at the interfaces between groups of organisms. Birth and death rates fluctuate, producing changes in the characteristics of a population. Furthermore, immigrations and emigrations may alternately restore and disrupt the stability of interactions in a particular habitat or site. Patterns of interaction are frequently hidden and must be teased out in order to be recognized.

Physicists and chemists are able to get more reliable experimental results largely for two reasons: They usually can repeat experiments or run hundreds of trials in the time it takes a biologist to coax his organisms through a few trials; in addition, when physicists or chemists repeat trials, they are much more confident than the biologist is that the second batch of materials to be used is identical to the first batch. Quality control is easier to achieve with chemicals, for example, than with seeds or animals. If, for instance, a biologist wishes to investigate the effects of different conditions on seed germination, he must assume that each batch of seeds is exactly like every other batch. Usually this assumption is only approximately true, since there can be so many sources of variation in the seeds. Some seeds will be nonviable. Some will be older than others. Some may be covered by tougher coats. All these sources of variation make it more difficult for the biologist to interpret his results. One of the techniques he uses to help him find relationships when they are masked by all the variation is to construct a histogram, which is a special kind of graph (see Figure 3-1). With the help of histograms, elementary school children can discover all sorts of fascinating things about themselves as well as about other biological phenomena.

CONVERTING A PROBLEM INTO AN EXPERIMENT

Constructing operational definitions for variables

Someone once described an experiment as man's way of asking questions of nature. To ask the questions or to discover the patterns of organization among natural phenomena, there comes a stage when, in order to conduct an experiment that will give meaningful results, the investigator must identify relevant variables. The task, then, is to construct operational definitions for measuring variables that can be quantified. For variables that cannot be quantified, a careful description of how to recognize them must be developed. These descriptions are one way of insuring that when an experiment is to be repeated, it can be performed in the same manner by the same person or by other

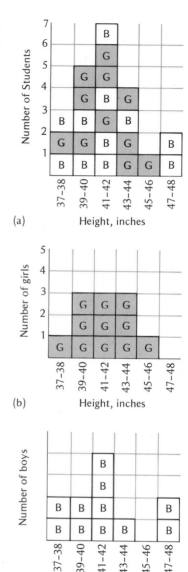

(a)

(b)

(c)

FIGURE 3-1

a **Number of students in each height category in one classroom. There are 22 students. The girls are marked as G, the boys as B.** *b* **Number of girls in each height category. Heights tend to cluster in three categories.** *c* **Number of boys in each height category. There is more variability in the heights of boys in this class. Their heights are more scattered among the categories.**

investigators with reasonable expectation of obtaining similar results.

When we become empirical—that is, when we begin to think of specific operations that we actually need to perform in order to measure a variable—we have to decide what measurement operation will best meet the needs of the situation.

Suppose, for instance, you wished to ask a simple question about a group of plants that have come into your possession: Will the plants grow more rapidly in warm temperatures or in cooler temperatures?

What are the variables?

At first glance the question seems to suggest that a possible relationship exists between temperature and growth rate. But there is still another variable. It is concealed in the phrase *grow more rapidly*. Time is the hidden variable. The question can be rephrased: Which condition, warm or cool temperature, will make the plant grow to a certain stage in the shortest time?

There is still a problem of defining one of the variables operationally. What do you mean operationally by the term *growth*? The answer to that question will depend in part on what is most important to you. You might choose height of the plant, which is a length measurement, or number of branches or size of leaves. The choice will depend on whether good growth in this context means tall spindly, tall bushy, or short bushy, etc. Having made these evaluative decisions, list the variables (see Figure 3-2).

Temperature and time are the variables you can control. You decide what temperatures to use and at what points in time to make observations. Length of the plant and number of branches are the somewhat arbitrarily chosen variables. You do not know, until you conduct the experiment, what values these outcome variables will acquire.

Having decided what variables are relevant, you have to decide *how* to measure them.

You might measure the temperature of the soil in

FIGURE 3-2
Input and outcome variables in the investigation of plant growth. What other variable could have been chosen?

Temperature
Time
} Input variables, also called *independent variables* because they are controlled by the investigator

Length or height of the plant
Number of branches
Size of leaves
} Outcome variables, also called *dependent variables*.

which the plant is growing by inserting a thermometer in the soil and leaving it there. But the temperature of the air around the plant may be a critical factor, so you could measure that too by suspending a thermometer near the plant. The trick of deciding what to measure depends on the problem itself and how you conceptualize it.

You may have found yourself objecting to the choice of height of the plant as an outcome variable because it is quite possible to imagine long, skinny, very unpleasant-looking plants that, while they might be tall, would certainly not represent your idea of satisfactory growth. (For example, if you raise some plants in the dark, they will at first grow faster than those raised in the light, but the plants grown in the dark will tend to be spindly and yellowish, an unacceptable condition esthetically.)

Our motives or special intentions are part and parcel of how we do science. They focus our attention on certain outcomes at the expense of others.

Designing the experiment

(See Activity 3-1, page 94, for steps in converting this experiment into a classroom context.) Having identified the variables and constructed operational definitions for them, we next decide how to conduct the experiment. This means we need to make decisions of the following kind:

1 *Size of the sample.* How many plants will you need to conduct the experiment? To put it another way, if you just put one plant at a low temperature and one plant at a higher temperature, how would you know whether any differences in growth rates came from the difference in temperature? Perhaps there would have been that much individual variation in the height of the plants under normal conditions. You need to select a big enough sample to rule out the effects of individual differences.

2 *When to collect data.* How often or at what points in time would it be well to collect data, that is, to measure the outcome variables? On one hand, the plants under the higher temperature condition might grow rapidly at first and slowly later, while those under the low temperature condition might develop in the opposite manner. On the other hand, the plants in both temperature conditions may grow at uniform rates, but the rate of growth in

one temperature condition would be slower than in the other condition. You need to make some decisions. When you do not know which case probably is true, you need to collect data more frequently in order to expose the pattern of growth. At some point, however, you will decide to stop the experiment. How you decide when to terminate the experiment depends on what you need to know.

3 *Organizing data into tables.* Each plant will be a source of data, so you need a way of keeping track of its growth. You might identify each plant with a number. Then you could record how high it was at the start and at the end of the experiment (see Figure 3-3).

By grouping together the data for the plants grown at each temperature, you can begin to make comparisons of growth rates. Notice in column 4 of the table in Figure 3-3 that to find out how much a plant grew in the time allowed, you have to take into account the fact that not all the plants were exactly the same height at the start of the experiment. To compute growth that occurred during the experiment, you subtract the height at the start from the height at the end of the experiment. Among living things, there is frequently much individual variation that you cannot control experimentally. In such instances, mathematical techniques can help you find the patterns of relationships among the variables. Results might be as shown in the table at the top of page 83.

FIGURE 3-3

Histogram showing growth at one temperature setting; and table for organizing data.

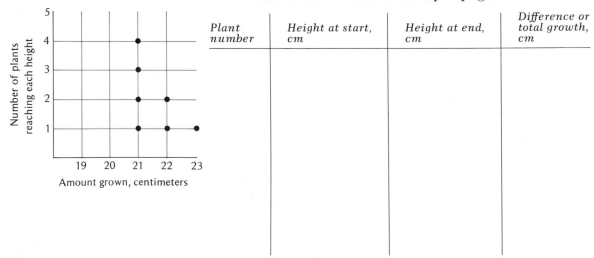

Plant number	Height at start, cm	Height at end, cm	Difference or total growth, cm

Plant number	Starting height, cm	Ending height, cm	Growth, cm
1	3	24	$24 - 3 = 21$
2	5	29	$29 - 5 = 24$
3	4	25	$25 - 4 = 21$
4	5	26	$26 - 5 = 21$
5	4	26	$26 - 4 = 22$
6	5	28	$28 - 5 = 23$
7	3	25	$25 - 3 = 22$
8	4	25	$25 - 4 = 21$

4 *Using histograms to show results.* Histograms are graphs that show how many objects or events (in this case, plants) exhibit some value of a variable (in this case, growth). To construct a histogram for this experiment, you would simply draw a number line and mark it off in equal intervals to show the range of growth. For these four plants, the growth ranged from 21 cm to 24 cm (see Figure 3-3). Next, you would draw a second number line at right angles to the first line. On it, mark off numbers that will show how many plants grew to each particular height. For example, in the data table,

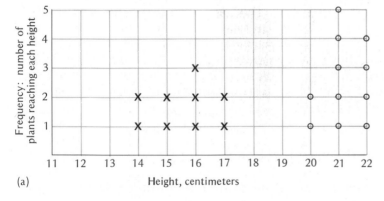

(a)

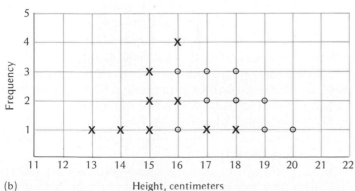

(b)

FIGURE 3-4

a **Histograms comparing two temperature conditions. The lower temperature points are shown as O's and the higher temperature points as X's. One could infer that the higher temperature condition produced more growth in a given period of time.** *b* **Shows a different outcome when a different kind of plant was used. Note the overlap in the histograms for the two temperature conditions. One cannot safely infer that the higher temperature condition influenced growth.**

four plants grew 21 centimeters, so you would mark off three units, as shown. One plant grew 24 centimeters. You would put a mark at the intersection of 1 and 24. After you have entered all the results for one temperature condition, you might construct another histogram to show the results for the second temperature condition. By contrasting the *shapes* of the two histograms, you can make inferences about the influence of temperature on growth rate. Figure 3-4*a* shows a pair of histograms which you might have obtained with a sample size of ten plants at each temperature condition, along with some inferences which could be made by contrasting the histograms.

In this experiment, how safe are we in assuming that temperature accounted for the differences? If the results had been as shown in Figure 3-4*b*, would we have the same confidence?

It is at the point of making inferences from data that arguments lead to new questions and new experiments. Science is a vigorous enterprise where it is legitimate to argue for different interpretations of results and then to design new investigations to see which of the competing explanations lead to correct predictions. Mathematical techniques such as graphing and finding *modes* and *averages* are often helpful. They provide one basis for deciding whether or not a relationship between variables *probably* exists.

SUMMARY OF STEPS

To convert a question or a problem into a state where it can be investigated, you generally engage in the following steps:

1 Identify the variables that seem to be relevant.
2 Construct operational definitions for the variables; that is, specify procedures for measuring them.
3 Classify the variables into those which are the controls and those which are the outcomes.
4 Make decisions about sampling.
  a Sampling population—decide how many measurements will be needed.
  b Sampling the phenomena—decide how often and at what intervals data should be collected.

5 Design tables for recording data.
6 Construct histograms when appropriate.
7 Based on the histograms and calculations made from the data, draw tentative conclusions about probable relationships among variables.

Try recognizing these steps in the next problem, which was chosen for the following reasons:

1 It will lay the groundwork for later introduction of the concept of *ecological niche*. This concept will be fundamental to the eventual analysis of problems concerning population and pollution.
2 It illustrates how histograms can expose patterns of behavior.
3 It illustrates the distinction between specialists and generalists and lays the groundword for relating *survival* to *adaptation*.

Example: Variation in food preference

Suppose a biologist were interested in the *preference* of a group of organisms for different sources of food. (Food preference is the variable.) There are many reasons why he might be interested in food preference. Here are two: First, he might wish to raise a group of animals whose food preferences he did not know, or he might want to find substitutes for what is normally eaten. This is a problem teachers and students frequently face if they wish to keep animals in the classroom. In raising and caring for animals, it is often necessary to find cheap, convenient substitutes for the diets they would normally have in their natural habitats. Second, he might eventually want to test the hypothesis that organisms with broad food preferences would be more likely to adapt successfully to environmental pressures, such as change in the kind, amount, or both of available food, than animals with a narrow band of food preferences. It might also be useful from the biologist's point of view to know the food preferences of pests—certain insects, rodents, etc. Once he knew the range of adaptability of a species to different kinds of food, he could remove the food preferred by pests and thereby increase the chances of diminishing the number of pests in a given area,

Defining the variable food preference. The first task is to find a way to measure the variable called *food pref-*

*erence.*The wider the range of foods an organism will eat, the more likely the organism will be to survive if some of the categories of food are removed. The more narrow the range of foods an organism will choose, the more vulnerable it will be to extinction if conditions change.

Flies, ants, cockroaches, rats, birds—all have food preferences. People, too, have food preferences which limit their adaptability. These preferences are partly governed by beliefs and partly determined by biological restrictions. Some beliefs make potential food sources unavailable even to starving people. During World War II, for example, many Europeans would not eat corn shipped to them from America because all the corn they ever saw was used to feed hogs. Religious beliefs in India make the cattle there unavailable as a food source. As an example of biological limitations, the response of some groups to powdered milk is interesting, and, at the same time, frustrating. Some groups of people who need a good source of protein do not possess sufficient amounts of the enzymes necessary to digest powdered milk. Powdered milk simply produces digestive upset. Although it contains the necessary proteins, milk cannot be used to remedy a protein deficiency for those people who lack the enzymes for digesting it.

Flies, cockroaches, and birds make good subjects for food-preference studies. Suppose we decide to study food preference for flies, ants, or perhaps cockroaches. By setting out a variety of food sources, such as half oranges, potato scraps, syrup, fat scraps, etc., in separate containers, we would be able to discover the food preferences for the subjects we select. (If you were interested in food preferences of seed-eating birds, you might use a great variety of seeds instead of the garbage scraps suggested above. The basic procedures would, however, be the same. You would put each kind of seed into a separate container.)

Decisions. Now that we have a general definition of what food preference means, we have a set of decisions to make if we are to investigate this variable:

1 What do we measure?
2 How shall we measure it?
3 How shall we represent the data to help us discover any relations?
4 What can we infer about species preferences from the data?

What do we measure? What we measure depends on how we decide to operationally define good preferences. Suppose we adopt the view that if any organisms go to a test substance and light on it, the substance may be regarded as a potential food source. Now we can get a lot of argument on that definition. Someone will say that organisms have to rest some place, and they often sit on objects upon which they are not feeding. Someone else will object that just by chance, at any given moment, some organisms might stop at a particular food source in the course of their explorations but fail to eat it.

These are reasonable objections, but we shall cling to the definition anyway. We might decide to modify the definition a little to placate the objectors by saying we will only pay attention to—i.e., count—those organisms that stay on the food source for one second or longer. But another person may object saying that some organisms pick up food quickly and leave the spot immediately. (Scientists often carry on imaginary or real arguments of this sort. Science is, after all, a very social, but not necessarily sociable kind of enterprise. Controversy has the effect of improving the quality of research, if not the disposition of the researcher.)

How shall we measure, and when? In this case we can expect some measurement errors since we can admit that some organisms might be on the food source by chance and would not consume the food if life depended on it. We can reduce the chance of making wrong inferences if we get a large enough sample of the population and if we get measures over a period of time. Then we can construct histograms that will help expose the patterns of preferences.

Suppose we decide to examine our food sources six times a day at equal intervals for five days. Now we still have plenty of problems to face. We made a time-sampling decision. Why aren't we keeping track of the food all the time? What if one species, say the cockroaches, only feed when it is dark and then only for a short time? We might never find them on any food sources. They might appear and leave between observations. Then we might conclude that our test substances were not even chosen from the right food categories when, in fact, they may have been.

If some species operate only at night, how can we see to count how many are at each food source? If we turn on the light they may scurry away, and all we would count would be a few laggards. Cheer up; remember that most measurement operations involve an interaction of the measurement procedure with the system and will usually produce some distortion. We have only to decide whether the distortion is so much that we cannot trust the final results: the point is to try to think of all the possibilities and to make decisions accordingly. If we take enough samples of data, and the patterns that develop are fairly clear, then we may feel confident regarding our inferences about food preferences. We become more uncertain about how to interpret results if we have very little data or if we do not have a reasonable plan for collecting data.

We could take care of some of our measurement problems by putting the food in traps. Then we could count at our leisure how many organisms we find in each trap. Some argumentative person might then say that if you trap the animals, you remove them from the environment, and that might reduce the crowding on one of the food sources. Organisms that occupy less-preferred food simply because they have been crowded out, might leave it and cluster on the highly preferred food. Then they would get caught, too, and the redistribution process would go on. What would that do to the results? One response to this argument might be to provide large containers of each food so that every organism that wished to feed on a particular source could do so without being driven off.

Each decision costs something. There are plenty of counter-responses. We could do away with the trap idea and simply take pictures of the food samples at regular intervals. We could actuate the camera by remote control, and we could use infrared film for nighttime pictures. We would keep track of when each picture was taken; at our leisure we could count the number of individuals on each food source on each picture. Each picture supplies a sample of data. How much detailed planning you do depends partly on how willing you are to risk drawing an incorrect conclusion. There will *always* be some risk.

How shall we represent the data? Look at Figure 3-5. Each row shows how many organisms, of a given kind, gathered on a particular type of food each day. Each population was studied for five days. The blocks show how many organisms were found on each food source during a 24-hour period.

We examine the histograms to see what we can make

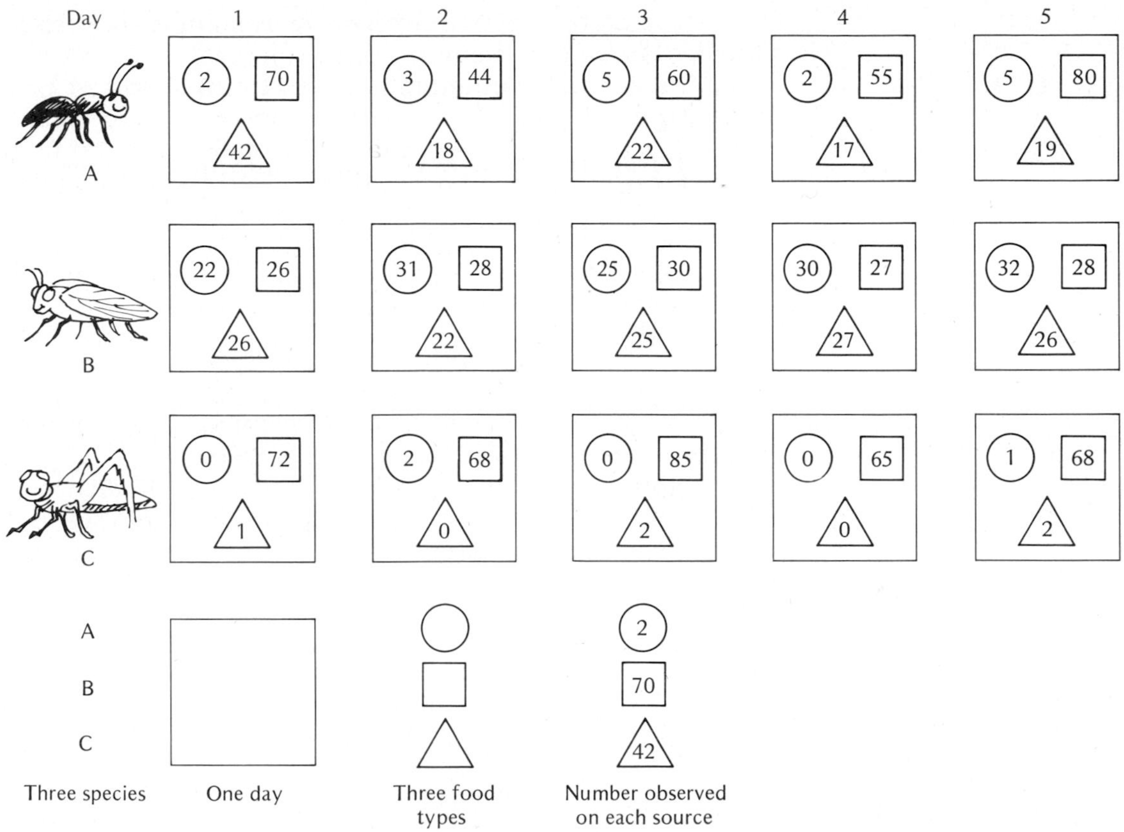

FIGURE 3-5
The number of organisms found on each of three kinds of foods.

of them. For one thing, we suspect that species C is feeding exclusively on the food source represented by the square. While there are a few individuals appearing on the other sources, these strays probably represent examples of the measurement errors discussed earlier. However, one must be cautious. The strays may really be "out" types able to adapt more broadly. We can interpret each result with some probability of being wrong but hopefully with a larger probability of being right. (The part that "out types" or atypical members of a population can play in population survival will be discussed in the next chapter.) For the moment, however, it is probably safe to call species C food specialists.

The food sources were photographed six times in 24 hours. The numbers in each block show the *sum* or total number of organisms found on each kind of food during a 24-hour period. Counts were taken for five days. This seemed like a reasonable sample of behavior since altogether there would be 6×5 or thirty samples of data for each class of organisms.

So far the mathematical operations involved have been the following:

1 Counting how many organisms appeared on each type of food every time a picture was taken
2 Finding the total number of organisms on each type for a day by *adding* the counts from each sample of data

What inferences can we make? Next, we construct histograms as shown in Figure 3-6 to expose the patterns of food preferences and to make comparisons of preferences among the three kinds of organisms.

Notice how the members of species B distribute themselves. They must be the generalists. Notice that they disperse themselves in about equal numbers on each food source. Of course, you cannot be *absolutely* certain that the B organisms could not care less which of the goods they feed on. Another explanation, which you must decide whether you can safely ignore, is that species B really contains three subgroups, each of which is highly selective for *one* of the kinds of food sources. In other

FIGURE 3-6

Histograms provide a basis for inferring food preferences. *a* **Species A;** *b* **species B;** *c* **species C.**

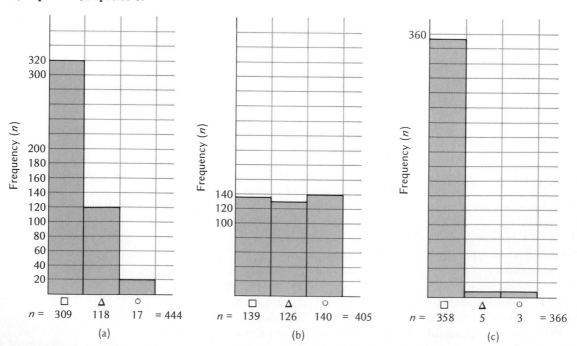

words, instead of being the generalists the data suggest, some of the members of this group might in fact be very specialized in their tastes.

Of course, if you considered this alternative at all possible, you might need to think of some additional data that you could collect to help you decide whether or not you can rule it out. You might, for example, set up a box with only one of the food sources in it and put the B organisms into the box. If the explanation that there might be three subgroups is valid, about two-thirds of the organisms (being so specialized) will die of starvation. If that does not happen, you might feel safer about the generalist notion. If the generalist hypothesis holds up then, in the face of changing food conditions, the B organisms might be more adaptable than the A or C organisms.

We can easily rank-order the preferences of species A. The □ square food source is mose desirable; the △ triangular source is next in preference. The ○ circular food source may not really be a source. The numbers of organisms in the ○ circular food source might just be due to chance, i.e., they are part of the measurement error. When interpreting the results, there are lots of uncertainties since there are so many sources of variation: individual variation, random events, changes over time, sampling problems, etc.. All we can do on the basis of data and our information at any given point of time is to choose the *most likely* explanation or hypothesis. Our judgments in science can never be final or absolute. We have to operate on what seems most *probable*, given the state of our knowledge. New alternatives may come along at any time to disabuse us of our hard-won notions. They start us in pursuit of new factors and force on us new experiments.

It should be clear, however, that histograms do not explain anything. They simply display or represent data in ways that make it easier to discover patterns of relationships hidden away in all the variation. Mathematical techniques are important tools in the search for patterns, but they are useless unless they are employed in a way that makes sense in terms of an investigation.

If, by this time, you have acquired some sense for what a variable is and how data can be represented in a histogram, you should now be prepared to consider the concept of ecological niche to be taken up in the next chapter.

What is important in science is the kind of reasoning one docs. The food-preference experiment illustrates how many different facets one must consider. Answers to questions being investigated can only be stated as probably true. There are so many sources of variation that the risk of drawing incorrect conclusions is always present. For that reason one has to be prepared to hold views in science somewhat tentatively. Among biological phenomena, patterns of relationships are frequently well concealed. When we succeed in exposing them, then we have a basis for making decisions that give us a little more control over our lives. For example, if the food preferences of ants were known, we could design strategies to protect ourselves from ant invasions. If we have knowledge, tentative though it may be, we can plan. If we have none, we must leave our fate to chance. It is worth our while to search for hidden patterns.

SUMMARY

1 Variation in the systems he studies is encountered by the biologist in every direction:

growing	adapting	competition
aging	fluctuating birth and death rates	pollution
dying	immigration	individual variation
learning	emigration	nonequivalence of samples

2 An experiment is man's way of asking a question of nature. To convert a question into an experiment it is necessary to:

a Choose variables that have some relationship to underlying phenomena

b Construct operational definitions for the variables, that is, state the measurement procedures

c Classify the variables into those which are controls (i.e., are independently manipulable) and those which are outcomes

d Make sampling decisions
   (1) About the population—how many do you need?
   (2) About the phenomena—when and how often should you collect data?

e Design tables for recording data

f Construct graphs and histograms where appropriate
g Draw tentative conclusions regarding the most probable answer to the question being investigated

3 Identifying and constructing operational definitions for variables that describe biological events requires considerable ingenuity. Since living systems change, an investigator has to make decisions about *what* data should be collected, *how* they should be collected, *when* they should be collected, and *how often* they should be collected. Some of the investigations described in this chapter and in the associated activities illustrate what is involved in making these decisions. Science is a vigorous enterprise where it is legitimate to argue over interpretations and to design new studies in order to settle differences.

4 When strict experimental control is not possible, mathematical techniques can help find patterns that are masked by all the sources of variation. Graphing is an especially useful technique in such situations.

ACTIVITY 3-1

OBJECTIVES

1 To construct bar graphs
2 To make inferences based on bar graphs

What to do:

1 Examine the data on food preferences in Figure 3-5. Construct a frequency histogram for each day. Record on each histogram how many organisms were observed.
2 Construct bar graphs using proportions rather than frequencies.

One of the first things we notice as we look at the data is that each sample of each species shows different numbers of individuals. That makes the business of comparing samples a little difficult. But all you want to do is find out if, no matter how many individuals appear in the display, a certain proportion of them generally locate on the square food source, another on the round food source, and the remainder on the triangular food source.

To calculate the proportion of each organism on each food source, do the following:

a Find the total number of organisms observed in one day by adding up the numbers that appeared on each food source.

Total for day _____ for organism _____ = _____
           (1–5)   (A,B,C)

b To calculate the proportion of organisms on a food source, divide the total for a day into the number observed on that food source.

$\frac{70}{114} \times 100 = 61.4\%$ on the $\square$ food source.

c To construct a bar graph that shows proportions (percents) of organisms instead of frequencies on each food source, mark the vertical axis in percents instead of frequencies. Draw columns that are as high as the percents calculated on each food source.
3 Although the graphs constructed for this experiment are called bar graphs, they could also be described as histograms provided there was one

change in the conditions. If the three categories of foods represented three values of a variable, such as amount of sugar or amount of acid in the food, the graph would be a histogram.

Design an experiment in which you study your own preference pattern for different concentrations of sweet or sour substances. In this case the variable that you need to regulate in order to study preference is degree of sweetness (or sourness).

a List the variables

b Define the variables operationally

c Design a sampling procedure

d List the arguments for, and against, your various decisions

e Estimate the time it would take to complete the investigation

f List the materials you would need

Note. Frequently the most difficult part of an investigation consists of the first steps in which so much of the thinking must be done. Once the plan is worked out, the actual conduct of the experiment may be relatively simple.

ACTIVITY 3-2

OBJECTIVES

1 To program an experiment for instruction

2 To test a program

Take a food-preference experiment and try to convert it into a series of self-programmed lessons that a fifth- or sixth-grader might reasonably be able to do.

If you possibly can do so, have one or two people try your program. Based on what happens, make changes in it. This kind of process in which one prepares a lesson, tries it, and changes it to improve the conditions for learning is sometimes called *formative evaluation*. In formative evaluation one tries to improve the chances that more students will perform successfully.

ACTIVITY 3-3

OBJECTIVES

1 To detect hidden patterns of taste buds on the tongue

2 To observe the amount of variation in the patterns

Question:

Is the tonque equally sensitive to all tastes on all its parts?

What to do:

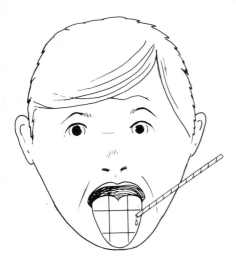

1 Prepare dilute solutions of lemon juice, sugar, and salt.
2 Make a full-page outline drawing of the tongue. Lightly divide the tongue into about seven sections as shown.
3 Select one of the solutions. Put a drop on the tongue in one of the sections. Do you get a taste sensation? Proceed to the next section. Mark in those sections in which there is a relatively strong taste sensation. Mark sections in which there is taste but relatively little. Leave blank sections in which there is no taste sensation for a given solution.
4 Follow this procedure for each solution. Are the taste buds for each flavor distributed uniformly on your tongue?
5 Design an experiment to find out whether the pattern of taste is unique for each individual (as are fingerprints) or whether there is a general trend for particular tastes to be limited to particular sections of the tongue.
6 If possible, conduct your experiment.

Note. One version of this investigation can be found in the second grade of the COPES program. There, a step by step procedure for pursuing the investigation with children is described.

ACTIVITY 3-4

OBJECTIVES

1 To read data presented in a histogram
2 To estimate or calculate a mean

What to do:

1 Examine Figures 3-4*a* and *b*. For each histogram, construct a table of data. For example:

Lower-temperature condition

Height	Number of plants
14 cm	2
15 cm	2
16 cm	3
17 cm	

Complete the table for 17 cm. (You should have an answer of 2.)

2 Try to estimate or actually calculate the average or mean growth for each temperature condition shown in Figure 3-4*a* and *b*. The mean or average is the single number that can best describe the whole distribution of values. (See Chapter 5, where means and graphs are discussed in more detail.)

REFERENCES

Silvan, James: *Raising Laboratory Animals: A Handbook for Biological and Behavioral Research*, The Natural History Press, Doubleday Company, Inc., Garden City, N. Y., 1966. (A publication of The American Museum of Natural History.)

Three major suppliers of animals and biological supplies are also good sources of information regarding care of particular organisms.

Carolina Biological Supply Company
Burlington, North Carolina   East

Powell Laboratories Division
Gladstone, Oregon   West

Ward's Natural Science Establishment
P.O. Box 1712
Rochester, New York 14603   East
    or
P.O. Box 1749
Monterey, California 93942   West

(Ward's puts out a useful newsletter which you can obtain free.)

CHAPTER 4

Don't those gerbils know that if they don't stop it, they are going to have a terrible population problem? —FOURTH-GRADER

My turtle died yesterday, and I didn't know what to do with it. (Pause.) That happens, you know. My mother didn't know what to do with it. I didn't feel so good. —FIRST-GRADER

Well, it's not worth trying, because everything is such a mess. There are too many people, and they're making so much pollution that we'll all be killed. I can't stop it and they don't care. (Begins to cry.) —THIRD-GRADER IN AN UPPER-MIDDLE-CLASS COMMUNITY

WAR AND PEACE AMONG THE NICHES

OBJECTIVES

When you have completed this chapter and its associated activities, you should be able to do the following:

1 Describe a procedure for identifying the ecological niche occupied by a population.

2 State a relation between the concept of population variation and the concept of adaptation.

3 Distinguish among a habitat, a niche, and a territory.

4 Relate environmental deprivation to individual adaptive potential.

5 Define factors that seem to act to limit population density.

INTRODUCTION

This is the age of concern about population and pollution. Unfortunately, people are being alerted to problems, but they are given no conceptual framework that could serve as a basis for finding solutions. All such a situation can do is engender fear. To be constantly bombarded by problems that carry an implicit threat of destruction can lead to abandonment of hope unless people have knowledge that will help them find solutions. Through news media and school, elementary-age students absorb the concerns without acquiring at the same time a productive basis for thinking about how to improve things. We are all being inundated with remedies among which we cannot choose because we often lack knowledge of the fundamental, biological principles involved.

This chapter introduces a conceptual framework that should prove helpful in thinking about population and pollution. Central to this framework is the concept of the *ecological niche*. It provides a perspective within which to discuss population, pollution, and survival in the face of competition for scarce resources. Adaptation to changing conditions will be discussed in two contexts: what it implies in relation to individuals within a population; within the framework of the ecological niche, questions about competition, cooperation, population, pressure, pollution, and the survival value of diversity in behavior will be discussed. It is hoped that the concept of the ecological niche will serve as a device in analyzing conditions for survival. It should provide some help in putting discussions of over-population and pollution in perspective.

In 1934 a scientist named Gauss said that, on the basis of his observations, no two species could occupy the same ecological niche for long. One of them will always be more fit to survive in that niche and eventually will squeeze the other out. The concept of a niche, if it turned out to be substantiated, would serve to organize many separate ideas about the rise and fall of populations. It would be a kind of biological counterpart of the physical principle of exclusion, which says that no two objects can occupy the same space simultaneously. In other words, two species cannot live in an identical niche for very long. One of them will win out. The other will either move away, adapt, or succumb.

All we have to do is figure out what an ecological niche is, namely, decide what variables belong to the concept of a niche. Then we can go about the business of finding out how to recognize niches occupied by different species. Once we get that far we will have built a frame of reference for investigating how organisms respond to competition and what adaptations they make to minimize competitive pressure. We can follow the progress of predator-prey interactions as well as cooperative interactions between organisms; we can begin to identify and investigate the forces that drive organisms to make adaptive and nonadaptive responses to climatic and competitive pressures in the environment. We can distinguish specialists from generalists and determine what circumstances favor the survival of each. With caution we can try to transfer these ideas to the human context.

VARIABLES OR DIMENSIONS OF THE NICHE

Those variables external to a population that are necessary to the maintenance of life and sufficient to allow reproduction to occur, we shall refer to as the *dimensions of the niche*. See Figure 4-1*a* and *b*. External variables are environmental variables, such as temperature, time, light, moisture, space, and food. Each of these variables constitutes one of the dimensions of an ecological niche.

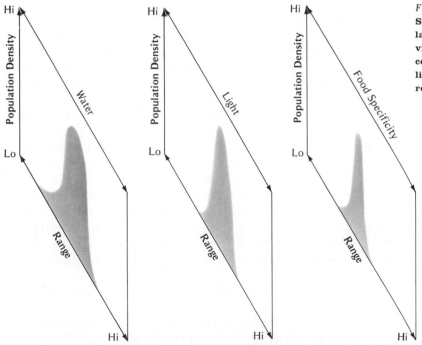

FIGURE 4-1a

Some niche dimensions. A population of organisms that can survive over a wide range of moisture conditions prefers to forage at low light intensity and feeds on a restricted range of food types.

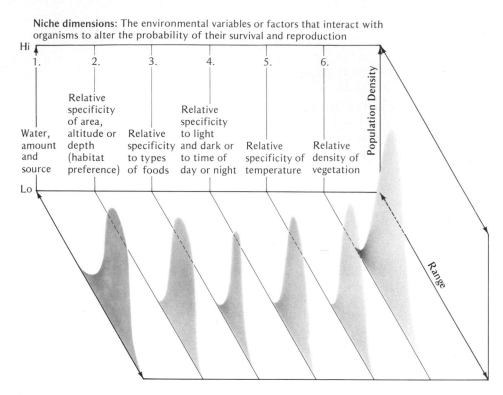

Niche dimensions: The environmental variables or factors that interact with organisms to alter the probability of their survival and reproduction

1. Water, amount and source

2. Relative specificity of area, altitude or depth (habitat preference)

3. Relative specificity to types of foods

4. Relative specificity to light and dark or to time of day or night

5. Relative specificity of temperature

6. Relative density of vegetation

FIGURE 4-1b

Model of an ecological niche. An ecological niche can be thought of as a kind of box within which the members of the population reside. The walls are formed by the niche variables. Each group of organisms is limited by its range of tolerance for each variable. Beyond that range lies the threat of extinction.

Gauss' principle says that no two populations can occupy exactly the same niche. That means no two populations of organisms will exist for long in the same space, at the same time, and under exactly the same conditions of temperature, light, moisture, and food. One population or the other will be more efficient at exploiting the niche. As a result the reproductive potential of one group will improve at the expense of the other. The losing population either leaves, succumbs, or adapts in some way, usually by adjusting to different values of one or more of the dimensions. If two populations of birds, for example, both feed on the same kind of food, they may avoid direct conflict if one group slides its feeding along the time dimension—one group forages early in the morning and the other late in the day. Some adaptation of that sort can happen, provided one or both of two conditions exist:

1 Most of the individuals in the population can adjust to a new time schedule.
2 If most cannot, there must be a few who were already adapted to the new time schedule. These would be variant types.

Before competition started, the histogram that describes the situation might look like Figure 4-2*a*.

In the face of competition from another more efficient population, birds that could not change their habits would eventually die out. Those already feeding late in the day would survive and reproduce. Some generations later, the histogram describing when the population feeds might look like Figure 4-2*b*. The population has adjusted its position on the time dimension and now feeds late in the day.

NICHE REQUIREMENTS: BATTLE OF THE FRUIT FLIES

How similar two species can be in their requirements of a niche and still coexist is an interesting question that can

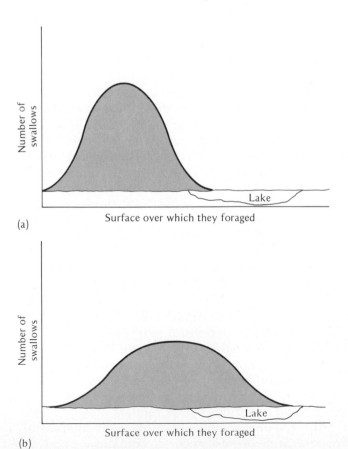

(a)

(b)

FIGURE 4-2
Shows change in where swallows shop for food. Foraging in the air was something like having a whole supermarket to shop in all by yourself. *a* Swallows originally fed on the ground. *b* When swallows could catch insects in the air, all the insects that hovered above water became available to them without competition from ground feeders.

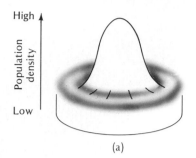

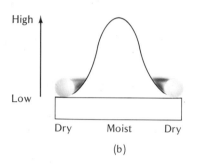

■ Funebris

□ Melanogaster

FIGURE 4-3
Competition between melanogaster and funebris is finally settled when funebris reduces its niche to the dryer area while melanogaster occupies the moist area: *a* **three-dimensional representation;** *b* **two-dimensional representation.**

most easily be answered experimentally. The ubiquitous fruit flies, which produce so many generations in a short time and which have been the subject of so many studies in genetics, make good subjects for studies of the niche in the classroom (the *Populations* unit of the SCIS program is an example).

Drosophila melanogaster and *Drosophila pseudoobscura* have similar food requirements, but a whole cage of *pseudoobscura* will eventually be wiped out if even one gravid *melanogaster* gets into their cage. *Melanogaster* larvae are far more efficient at finding and using food, and their reproduction rate is better.

If the *melanogasters* are now put into a cage of another fruit-fly species, *Drosophila funebris*, the *funebris* population density drops rapidly, but it only drops until it reaches about 5 percent of the total cage population (see Figure 4-3). Then the population of *funebris* holds steady. Now it becomes of interest to know why *melanogaster* can wipe out *pseudoobscura* but not *funebris*.

According to Gauss' principle it must be that in one cage there are really two available ecological niches, but for a long time it was difficult to identify them. Eventually by virtue of patient observation and counts of where the two species occurred in the cage, two niches were in fact identified. It turned out that the food cups are moist in the center and relatively drier on the edges. The two species distributed along the dimension of moisture are shown in Figure 4-3. *Funebris* can survive in the drier zone, which constitutes about 5 percent of the available area of the food cup. Survival and reproduction in the face of such close competition depend on the existence in the population of individuals able to occupy some different portion of one or more dimensions of the niche. In this case *funebris*, unlike *pseudoobscura*, could slide along the moisture dimension to a new position in the niche. If there are no individuals who can adapt, a population may die out in the face of competition for resources.

These laboratory experiments which are closed to immigration and emigration suggest (see Figure 4-4) the possible patterns of interaction that exist between species if they meet in an open system, i.e., in natural settings. Experiments of this type constitute working models of nature, simplified in the number of kinds of interactions in order to make the effects of certain variables more visible. However, good examples of the models may often be found in nature. For example, two different species of aquatic insects may be observed in the same pond. If they both continue to survive and reproduce, study will show that they are occupying different niches. They are adapting to competition by moving to different locations on one or more dimensions of the niche.

OVERLAPPING OF NICHES

Sometimes segments of two niches will overlap. Swallows feed on the same insects that several other species of birds prefer. So there is overlapping of niches on the food dimension. The swallows' adaptation to competitive pressure was to adjust the range of some of the other dimensions of their niche. They specialized on catching insects in the air, and they broadened the area over which they foraged. This adaptation allowed them to catch insects over water and so to expand the range of their foraging to an area unavailable to their more earth-bound competitors. In such cases there is little necessity for overt conflict to break out between the competing populations. From the example of the swallows, we begin to get some idea of what Gauss meant when he said that no two species could occupy exactly the same niche indefinitely. Each niche is unique, a kind of custom-engineered life space.

Now it might be interesting to determine how the swallow managed to contrive such a nice solution to competition (see Figure 4-5). Possibly in the population there were always a few out-types who caught insects on the wing. When the more normal members could not keep up with competitors who invaded their niche, the normals would eventually die of starvation or fail to complete their life cycles. Meanwhile the well-fed flying hunters would multiply. They would become the predominant swallow form.

Admittedly, this explanation involves some speculation. Notice that it begins with the premise that there was variety in the foraging behavior of the swallow population to begin with, and that variety would increase the probability that at least some members of the population could adapt to an environmental change of some kind—in this instance pressure from a more efficient population.

Sometimes the changes that one organism makes in its environment, as a result of its interaction in the niche, convert a particular piece of real estate from hostile to desirable for another organism. In other words, one group of organisms may inadvertently create a niche for another group. Wastes that sometimes accumulate in aquaria

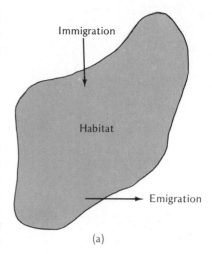

(a)

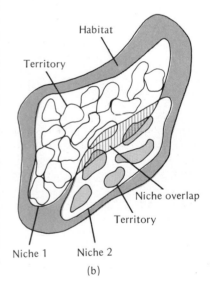

(b)

FIGURE 4-4
a **Organisms may move into a new habitat, immigrate, or leave an old habitat (emigrate) for a variety of reasons.** *b* **A habitat may contain many niches. Inside each niche individuals and pairs often maintain territories which they guard from invasion.**

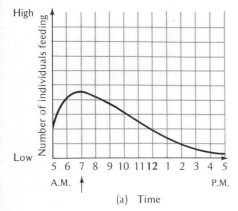

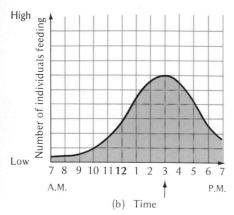

FIGURE 4-5

Customizing the ecological niche. Two species feeding on the same food source may minimize competition by foraging at different times of the day. They each occupy a different part of the time dimension variable: *a* early foragers; *b* late foragers.

from one species often result in a successive appearance of peak populations of different kinds of protozoa and bacteria. What constitutes a toxic compound for one group may be a useful chemical to another. Such organisms may have been existing at very low population levels or sometimes in cysts. When conditions in the aquarium change, certain values of the niche variables favor these organisms. They may multiply at a tremendous rate.

It is possible to keep track of changing distributions of animal populations in an aquarium by withdrawing samples of the aquarium contents, counting with the help of a good magnifier, and making histograms to represent the results. If you performed this experiment, you would be aware that you can only count what you can see. The limit of what you can see is determined by the quality of the magnifier. Instruments extend our senses into areas that would ordinarily contain no interest for us. Without the instruments we would be unlikely to guess that anything was there. On the other hand, you must remember that the range of any instrument is limited, and you may still be missing organisms that are nevertheless there. A low-power magnifier allows you to see so much. A higher-power magnifier, provided it enlarges without losing too much detail, allows you to make finer discriminations. In the aquarium, for example, you could keep track of population changes in species whose members are small in size but not so small that they escape beyond the range of your magnifier.

Of course, it makes a difference how we draw samples from the aquarium. Recall the niche situation of *Drosophila melanogaster* and *D. funebris*. Certain locations in the aquarium may be the ecological niche for one group, while other parts may be preferred by a different species. You may have noticed, for example, that different species of snails prefer different locations, and that some fish tend to be bottom feeders while others prefer to catch floating morsels.

THE FOOD DIMENSION OF AN ECOLOGICAL NICHE (See Figure 4-6)

Coexisting species vary in the way they compete for food resources when the available supply is limited. Successful minimization of conflict depends on what inventions the groups develop to avoid direct encounters. Some groups specialize on certain foods. Others respond to pres-

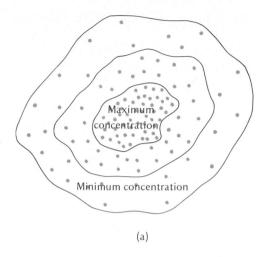

Maximum concentration

Minimum concentration

(a)

Food unit

If k = 5 individuals/gram, then some individuals emigrate or babies get eaten.

(b)

FIGURE 4-6
a **Population densities tend to be highest where food concentrations are high. If maximum food concentration = 1, then each line encloses an area with proportionately less food.** *b* **K-ratio is the number of individuals per unit (e.g., gram) of food. As population density approaches the K ratio, some individuals emigrate or mortality increases from cannibalism and/or starvation.**

sure on a preferred food by foraging on different foods, or at different times of day or night, or at different locations.

Food may become relatively scarce for some of the following reasons:

1 The demands of the population exceed the supply.
  a Predators may overkill their prey, and the prey population dies out. Studies of guppies, whales, and flies among others, indicate that if too many (but not all) of the young are killed (a set proportion, characteristic of each species), the population will usually fail to recover even though members of both sexes are present.
  b The population consumes all that is available. There are too many individuals for the available supply.
  c Pollution poisons the food source.
2 Fire or flood may destroy food sources.

3 Seasonal changes may alter the relative availability of food.

4 Food may not be distributed uniformly in a habitat so overcrowding can occur at some sites while others remain undiscovered.

(Even people may go to special locations called *stores* or *restaurants* to collect their food. We get a small idea of what can happen when many members of the population with slightly different food preferences all converge at the same location: traffic jams, visible irritability, inadequate supplies of preferred items, etc.)

Over short periods of time the size of populations rarely increases without limit, despite the fact that there is a potential to increase exponentially. Before the ratio of animals to available food begins to exceed some limit, the size of the population generally starts to decline (see Figure 4-6*b*). This usually happens through an increase in the mortality rate by starvation, predation, cannibalism, or changed susceptibility to disease. Sometimes emigration begins. Some or all these processes go on in a stable population until the excess disappears, so there is always a kind of fluctuation of the population density as the population interacts with the environment. Population density is higher where food occurs in abundance. This means that relative crowding may mark areas of high food concentrations.

SOCIAL CONTROLS ON POPULATION SIZE

Exactly how reproduction and mortality controls operate to allow the population to reach and maintain some optimum size for a niche is far from clear. When flour beetles are put down in enclosed environments containing different quantities of flour, all environments eventually show a distribution of about 44 beetles per gram of flour. Population density for each enclosure remains high where food is plentiful and low where food is scarce, but the ratio of animals to food arrives at a constant value in each environment (see Figure 4-6*b*).

In the face of unsatisfactory niche conditions, guppies are notorious for cannibalism of their young, as any children who have watched an aquarium for any length of time can tell you. When, however, as much as 60 percent of the new generation is removed, the whole population declines and finally dies out. (Note: This suggests that in maintaining an aquarium the number of guppies that can be removed at any time probably ought not exceed 60 percent of the population.)

Extinction produced by overcropping is somewhat reminiscent of what happened to whale and seal populations earlier in this century and to the beaver in the last century, when beaver hats were in vogue. Human beings apparently overcropped those populations. Some failed to recover. If nonhuman predators overcropped their prey, both species might die because the predator would have destroyed its own source of food.

Example: Norway rats

To isolate the effect social behavior has on regulation of population growth, one researcher, Calhoun, confined a population of wild Norway rats in four connected pens, provided them with all the food and water they required, and removed waste. In other words, he minimized famine, predation, and disease as causes of mortality. He was then in a position to study both the relationship of social behavior to population growth and the effect that the consequent population density had on social behavior. (See Figure 6-3, page 182.)

Some pens were connected by two ramps and others by only one. This would be analogous to setting up some natural barriers to immigration and emigration. In this way he could increase the probability that the number of individuals that would collect in certain pens would be greater than in others. Eating and drinking became social activities, with rats piled up around some feeders while other feeders were rarely visited. Rats that went to a deserted feeder usually left it in search of the popular places. A kind of pathological "togetherness' that tended to interrupt mating, nesting, and infant-nurturing sequences developed.

Eventually most of the population became concentrated in the middle pens, where constant fighting for position in the social hierarchy or peck order went on. In the less-crowded end pens a dominant male established his control of a pen and a harem by driving young males out and preventing their return. He usually tolerated a few subordinate males who spent most of their time hidden in the burrows with the females. In those pens where population density was lowest, mortality rates among infants and females were lower, although the pregnancy rates remained the same as in the crowded pens.

The crowded pens had nothing but trouble. More pregnancies failed to terminate in live births. The crowding aggravated all kinds of pathological behavior. Nest building got disrupted in favor of social encounters; packs of males would pursue a female, and the death rate of pregnant females increased. Females that lived in the low population, protected pens were not subject to such attacks. Females in the crowded pens neglected their maternal functions. Some males would go berserk, attacking females and juveniles and biting tails of other rats; some males failed to contend for status, instead they spent time trying to mount other males. Another identifiable group emerged that Calhoun called the *probers*. Probers always ran away from a dominant rat, but they were the most active in investigating the pens and also in following females into burrows where they sometimes cannibalized the young. Probers never wanted to wait for anything, either sex or food.

As population density increased, so did the incidence of social pathology. With immigration and emigration within the whole enclosure controlled and with sufficient food, some factors other than just the K-ratio seemed to be at work. Rats collected where other rats were. Some were driven into the center pens and kept there by the dominant rats. As the population in the center pens built up, the dominant rats in the end pens prevented emigration. Beside the K-ratio and the niche dimension, some other kind of territorial and social factors within the population came into play. Crowding reached a limit; then social pathology developed until the population density dropped back down to some acceptable level.

Example: community birds

Starlings and other birds that roost as a community may also be using the social interaction occasioned by their congregation to test for the K-ratio, the numbers of birds to food available. Through the gathering and chattering, they "measure" their population density. When the population reaches its critical ratio, the members somehow respond to that fact and some individuals, usually the young, emigrate. Birds that sing in the morning and evening may be communicating and receiving information about population density in relation to food density. If emigration must occur, the newer or younger or immature adults get the "message" to leave.

Territoriality

Within a population of animals, individuals, pairs, or other subgroups may set up foraging territories that they protect from invasion by other members of the same population. These individuals or pairs act as though they had marked out an area within which to forage and perhaps to raise young, the boundaries of which must be defended from all interlopers. In times of plenty these territories seem to be smaller than when the food supply is poor. Within each niche, then, individuals and pairs frequently maintain private foraging territories (see Figure 4-4). While the concept of territoriality is intuitively appealing, it is nevertheless necessary to identify the behaviors that could be interpreted as suggesting that an animal has established a territory. Birds and people make good subjects for study. When another member of the population invades a territory, we may observe threat behavior in the form of loud noises, much motion, and occasional fighting involving direct contact, etc. Once the invader moves back some distance, the furor dies down.

THE CASE OF THE MANCHESTER PEPPERED MOTHS – A STUDY IN POPULATION ADAPTATION TO POLLUTION

There is no way to guarantee survival of a population, short of maintaining all relevant variables in their niche at some fixed optimum level. Since that is nearly impossible, heterogeneity in the population increases the probability that some variants or out-types will be adequately fitted to respond to the changed conditions. We shall see in the case of the peppered moths a relatively rapid progression of a population from a predominantly light-colored mode to a dark mode in a period of about eighty years. Successful adaptation by a population builds to some extent on features that were once novel, or out of vogue, if you like.

Consider now a well-documented example of an adaptation to an alteration of the environment produced by the intrusion of waste from man's technology upon the countryside. It illustrates how variety in a population can save the population from extinction. This could be called the case of the ugly ducklings that saved the peppered-moth population from probable extinction when the land around Manchester, England, became polluted. In 1850 someone caught and preserved a relatively rare, dark form of this moth that contained an unusual amount of a dark pigment called melanin. The normal color of the moth at that time was quite light. In other words, color did vary in the population of moths, but the majority of members had very little of the melanin pigment that is present in large amounts in dark forms. In the 1850s industrial soot had not yet covered the land. The dark moths were very visible to predators against the normally light background colors of the foliage and tree trunks. The color of the light moths, on the other hand, helped them blend with the background, and hid them from predators. The dark moths, those containing more melanin, so the reasoning goes, had a higher probability of being seen and caught by bird predators than the normals. Consequently relatively few melanics lived long enough to complete life cycles. As a result, fewer of them reproduced; consequently, dark forms were rare (see Figure 4-7a).

Then the environment began to change. Manchester industrialized. Gradually soot accumulated on the tree trunks and foliage, and the general background or strata on which the moths found themselves darkened greatly. Eventually the background got dark enough so that the normal light-colored moths began to stand out like beacons beckoning to the predators. The melanics, on the other hand, as soot increased, began to blend into the

FIGURE 4-7
Relative frequency of dark and light moths: *a* **before soot;** *b* **after soot.**

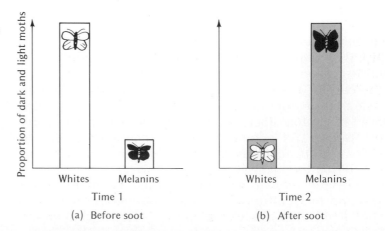

(a) Before soot

(b) After soot

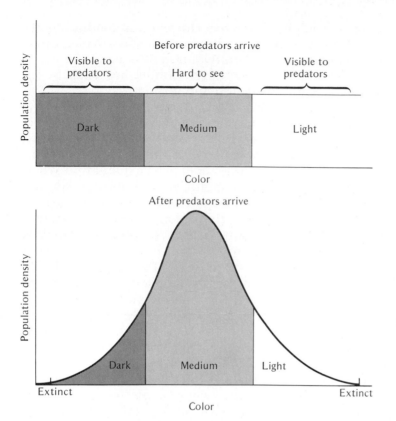

FIGURE 4-8
The peppered moths—how they might have changed. *a* Assume that in early times the peppered moths came in a variety of shades from very dark to very light. Assume approximately the same proportions of each category. *b* Assume predators entered the habitat. The very dark and the very light forms would be easily visible so they gradually are eliminated. The medium browns would live to multiply.

background and became, as a result, less detectable to their enemies. When that happened, predators began to catch larger proportions of the light-colored moths. As a result fewer of them lived long enough to reproduce. Proportionately more melanics completed life cycles and passed the dark color on to the next generation. After a time the "normal" or predominant color of peppered moths in industrial areas became melanic (see Figure 4-7b). Thus, over an eighty-year period the population gradually adapted and survived a change in the color of the environment by trading on the variability in the distribution of color among its members.

In the peppered-moth case, the population adapted to a gradual change in an environmental variable, color, by virtue of the fact that not all its members were homogeneous on color. Selective pressure produced by technological soot shifted the sharpness of the color interface between the organisms and the environment. Variation on the color variable made adaptation of the population to a sooty background possible. In this case, individual members of the population could not adapt when the environment was unfavorable. Individual moths were not capable of changing their color. The solution had to lie in the population. (See Figure 4-8a and b.)

How about that for a story? Notice the smooth way it slipped from facts to an explanation of what happened. If you have begun to acquire the "doubting Thomas" attitude of science, you should have found yourself objecting —why did we settle on this nice, neat explanation when some other explanations might be possible? After all, maybe the reproduction rate of melanic moths increased from other causes, or the light moths' reproduction rate decreased for some reason, or both. Or possibly the birds that fed on the moths changed their habits. Anyway birds might not be color sensitive at all. Possibly they detect moths by mere shape or motion, so the color change was just incidental. Or it might be that melanics and normals did more mating. Since the genetic code for melanin is dominant, more offspring of normals would also be dark. Who said birds even feed on peppered moths in the first place?

Arguments like this are what really give science its impetus. Dr. H. B. D. Kettlewell took up the challenge to the hypothesis of camouflage or background-blending. First he documented through frequent field observations that birds do eat peppered moths. If he had found that moths had no predators, he could have excluded the camouflage explanation right away.

Next he trapped a large number of melanics and normals and later released equal numbers of each in polluted and unpolluted areas of England. He watched where the moths came to rest. After a certain period he again counted the moths in the soot-covered area and found that many more melanics remained alive than normals. When he recounted the moths in the clean, lighter-colored area, he found far more normals than melanics alive. He offered these results as evidence in support of the camouflage hypothesis. Since the proportion of darks and lights changed rather sharply in a relatively short time, he could rule out some of the other arguments of differential fertility rates and cross-mating as explanations.

Notice, however, that while the experimental data support one explanation at the expense of others, the hypothesis is never really absolutely proved beyond a shadow of a doubt. Science is like that. We have to be able to rule out alternative explanations by producing data that fit one pattern of ideas better than another. In that way one hypothesis becomes increasingly plausible.

In the case of the moths, we saw that individuals could not, or at least did not, modify their behavior to solve the problem presented by soot. The population, however, did adapt. The genetic code passed on to some individuals contained the melanin factor, which provided a solution to the problem of adapting to a changed environment.

In one sense the predator in a predator-prey relation, as long as it does not get too rapacious, does the prey a favor by keeping it from multiplying to such an extent that it exceeds its own available food supply. Conservation experts know what a tremendous problem develops for a population when it exceeds it characteristic ratio of organisms to food. The animals keep on multiplying and more and more of them die by starvation. By overgrazing they literally destroy their own niches. That is why "harvesting" protected herds such as deer amounts to a kind of "service" by the predator to the prey.

RATS AND MEN—A PROBLEM IN OVERLAPPING NICHES AND INDIVIDUAL ADAPTATION

Hans Zinsser wrote a book called *Rats, Lice and History* in which he told how whole armies were laid low by virtue of their encounters with rats and lice.

There is a long history of association between men and rats. (Figure 4-9.) Rats can consume all sorts of human garbage. They have a remarkable reproduction rate as well as dispersal rate. They can range widely and live

FIGURE 4-9
Overcrowding in a niche can lead to invasion of other niches. Rats are a major problem for man since they frequently occupy the same habitat. The niches of men and rats sometimes overlap. To control rats, man must learn about their patterns of behavior.

2. He has millions of close relatives in town. All hungry.

1. He's 18 inches of grease and other assorted filth. (9 inches of tail, 9 inches of rest of rat).

3. He raises a family every 30 days. With a half-dozen new garbage eaters in every litter.

4. He can swim the East River. Climb a brick wall. Jump 8 feet from one rooftop to another.

5. He devours 17 pounds of garbage a year. Rotting grapefruit rinds. Old coffee grounds. Stuff no human could stomach.

6. He's a living flea flophouse. He carries enough germs on his hide to destroy an army.

7. He can gnaw through stuff you wouldn't believe. Cement. Oak planks. Telephone cables. (But not galvanized steel). That's why your best defense against rats is a garbage can. With the lid on. Tight. **Starve a rat today.**

well on all sorts of food. Rats are true generalists. As long as the garbage supports the rat population, the rats will not try to take food from the humans or attack them directly. But once the available garbage and food drop below the requirements of the rat population, rats will begin to attack humans, as happened recently in a town in southwestern Texas. The usual human response to an invasion of niche by rats is to close up garbage and food in containers that rats cannot get into and thus produce starvation. Poisoning is another technique man's technology makes available to him. Man tries with varying degrees of success to use his knowledge to beat the competition when the outcomes seem unfavorable to him. Where much garbage accumulates and disposal arrangements are inadequate, as sometimes happens in big cities, rats are sure to come. But the rat has a certain advantage because man in order to protect himself usually has to activate dormant social interaction patterns involving complex political, economic, and communication systems. These systems tend to be relatively inert until the threat posed by the invaders reaches some critical level. Usually that occurs when the rats start attacking the more vulnerable human beings—babies and old people.

Among rats every individual is capable of ranging widely over the dimensions of the niche; some insect populations, in contrast, adapt in quite another way: that is, each individual becomes highly specialized. Individual bees, ants, and termites, for example, are adapted to perform only certain tasks and no others. Some gather food, others protect the colony, and some are specialized for reproduction. Thus each individual loses some degree of freedom to range relatively broadly in exchange for the acquisition of a specialized function performed for the population, which as a whole, then, has more adaptive potential.

The more specialized or adapted a group becomes to restricted values of particular dimensions of the niche, the more efficient or fit it becomes at exploiting the niche to its own advantage. As long as conditions in the niche remain relatively constant such a population of organisms, by its adaptation to a very particularized band of each variable, minimizes competition with other populations. In so doing it increases the likelihood that occasional invasions by would-be competitors will fail to displace the group from the niche. For one thing, the probability that another kind of organism would occupy exactly the same

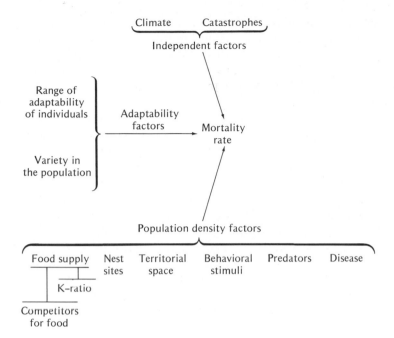

FIGURE 4-10
**Some factors which influence the
mortality rate in a population.**

niche—that is, function best at the same values of the variables—is somewhat small.

Specialization to very restricted ranges on each dimension of a niche, however, has its hazards.

Intuitively one senses that organisms, either individually or collectively, that can range broadly over important factors or variables in their environment may not be so efficienct in exploiting each factor but also that those organisms have a better chance of surviving if the environment should change, as it is prone to do. Food sources are notoriously unevenly distributed in the environment, and being able to adapt to alternative forms, for example, would be a useful attribute. Climatic changes in some parts of the world vary rapidly; even in places where conditions are stable for long periods, the average values of temperatures or humidities may gradually shift. Highly specialized species have less chance of competing in the same habitat with species that are more broadly adapted, if the environment changes (Figure 4-10).

COOPERATIVE ASSOCIATIONS

So far we have used examples of competitive relationships in which one competitor either adapts or dies. There are other kinds of relationships that can develop in which both sets of organisms benefit by association with one another. They help create or maintain niches for each other. The fact that species that share some part of a habitat may change that habitat can form the basis for a mutual relationship to develop.

The relationship between termites and the small protozoa that reside in termite digestive tracts represents an example of a mutual association. The termite chews up but cannot digest cellulose in wood. The protozoa feed on the cellulose, and the by-products of that metabolism can, in turn, be used by the termite. If we experimentally kill the protozoa in termites with antibiotics or by exposure to heat, the termites starve to death *even though they go on chewing up cellulose.* But if the protozoa are set out on wood to shift for themselves, they, too, die. What a succession of adjustments of the niche must have occurred for so subtle and complex a pattern of interaction to develop between the two species!

Another benign form of association exists between cattle and grass egrets, benign for the cattle and egrets but bad for grasshoppers, which egrets like to eat. Grass egrets, which are beautiful white birds from Africa, tend to collect in fields where there are cattle. Presumably the cattle stir up the grasshoppers, and this increases the likelihood of the grasshoppers' being seen and caught by the egrets—a condition that the humans who keep the cattle often find most acceptable, unless they, too, happen to be grasshopper eaters. The cattle-egret association is largely a one-way benefit system. The egret benefits, although according to some accounts the egrets ride around on the backs of the cattle and pick lice off them.

No organism lives in an environment without changing it. Interaction implies that both objects change in some fashion. We have seen that organisms can change the environment for each other by preempting food sources, by dumping waste, by population explosions, or by entering into cooperative associations.

EFFECTS OF SENSORY DEPRIVATION ON INDIVIDUAL ADAPTABILITY

As the nervous systems of organisms become more complex, more of their behavior moves out from under direct control of the genetic code. The preset behavior of bees and termites, for example, disappears among higher vertebrates such as rats, monkeys, and man. Provided there has been no fundamental deprivation, individuals within advanced vertebrate populations gain some freedom to respond to a wider range of environmental contingencies. That is, they can expand the range of individual adaptation along the various dimensions of the ecological niche. The more independently responsive individuals in a population become by virtue of the complexity of their nervous systems, however, the more severe will be the effect of early deprivation on individual adaptability.

Rats, dogs, and monkeys raised in social isolation in soundproof rooms where the walls of each cage are all uniformly the same never develop normal behavior patterns. Even when returned to the main group of animals, they will not defend themselves if attacked. They usually will not mate even though they are sexually mature. Animals so deprived never learn to play, and they perform badly in comparison with their normal counterparts on problem-solving tasks set for them by investigators.

Probably the most comprehensive long-term studies of social deprivation on primates is the work done by Harry and Margaret Harlow at the University of Wisconsin. Their studies arose out of an unexpected result occasioned by their attempts to raise disease-free, strong monkeys by separating them from their mothers shortly after birth, maintaining them in hygienic environments, and feeding them on an enriched formula by remote control. The monkeys developed into beautiful physical specimens but could not learn to play or defend themselves when returned to cages with other monkeys. They could not solve problems, and they failed to mate.

The Harlows suggest, on the basis of their experiments, that deprivation of physical contact accounts for much of the retardation they observed.

Aberrant human mothers sometimes force equivalent isolation experiments on children by closing them up for years in a room, in large boxes, in attics, or in cellars. Such children interact with another human being only when someone comes to feed them. They, like the organisms in other studies, generally turn out to be unable to respond to social stimulation. Of course, they do not develop recognizable speech. (We cannot attribute their failure to develop totally to deprivation, however, since the genetic code of such children may have been subnormal in the first place.)

A better indicator of the effect of interaction between the organism and its environment on development of human beings with normal genetic codes is the historic work of R. A. Spitz in which he compared development of children being raised in a foundling home with those raised in a nursing home. In the foundling home, all the children were efficiently and well fed by six nurses, and maintained in a hygienic setting. Each crib was surrounded by sheets, thus effectively blocking off the view of the staff and other babies. In the nursing home, by contrast, the children's mothers fed them; they received more fondling, and their view of the nursery was not blocked. Spitz found that whereas the developmental index of infants entering the foundling home was slightly higher than the index of those in the nursing home, at the end of one year of hygienic but sensorily deprived care, the foundlings' development was well behind development of those in the nursing home. What is more, their susceptibility to infection and their mortality rate were higher. At the end of three years, whereas the nursing home children could walk and talk like normal children of their age, only two of the foundling children could walk and their vocabularies were much more limited. Spitz' study indicates the *importance of sufficient environmental interaction to normal development.*

Vision in primates develops by interaction of the visual system with light. If light is prevented from entering the infant eye for a sufficient period of time, say for reasons of trauma, the retina will not develop completely. If light is allowed to enter the eye after several years, the probability that the organism will be able to learn to see is very small and depends on how early and for how long the infant was deprived of visual interaction.

Language development among human beings depends on the early availability of appropriate models in the environment, on a sensory apparatus that can detect sounds, and possibly on the ability to manufacture sounds. Deaf children constitute another inadvertent deprivation experiment. In contrast to normals, they ordinarily do not receive language training until near the end of the primary formative period for language development, age four or five. Failure of the hearing mode reduces the richness of contact with language samples; consequently language does not develop to any great extent unless the children are taught to process language through visual modes.

It follows, then, that although all the conditions for normal development and adaptation may be present, if some situation prevents organisms from interacting totally, their potential will usually never be completely realized. A partially deprived individual has less adaptive potential in the face of changing conditions than does a nondeprived individual.

BIOLOGICAL AND SOCIAL LIMITS ON HUMAN BEINGS

How free are we?

Among more advanced vertebrates there are biological, physical, and social-psychological limits on the adaptive capacity of individuals, and on the adaptive capacity of groups like populations or communities. Those limits vary from individual to individual and from group to group. It remains an interesting but unanswered question as to whether man with his knowledge, technology, and individual differences in variability can successfully confront the problems presented by his own population and pollution pressures. We do not know if he is really that free.

Most of us like to think of ourselves as free. We think we should be free to choose what we do and when we do it. But we know that we can never be completely free. We are not free, for example, to live without oxygen or without water or without food. We are not free to jump 40 feet into the air or go three weeks without sleeping. We know, in short, that there are many biological and physical limits to our freedom.

We cannot escape from the effect of social-psychological variables upon freedom any more than can other advanced vertebrates. Some of these factors increase our freedom but others limit it. Families, communities, teams, or certain other groups in which we hold membership determine, in large measure, how we act or what we think about. We may believe that we are entirely free to decide what we shall think, or whom we shall believe. We are not that free. Instead we usually hate and fear the same things that the people around us hate and fear. We may think we are free to change our ideas and our feelings whenever we want to or whenever it is expedient to do so, but we are not that free. Instead we are socially adapted to respond somewhat synchronously.

If we want to remain a member of a social unit, we may have to give up some of our freedom once in a while in favor of improved outcomes for the group. We respond to pressures of acting the way the team or group wants us to, often without even being aware that any pressures have been actively exerted. Sometimes we have to choose between what we want to do and what the group wants us to do. When we want to do something different from what the group wants us to do, we may feel unhappy or even like fighting. Most of the time we want to do what the group wishes. In general we have learned to want what the group wants, and to know that sometimes interaction of collections of individuals in an organized pattern produces better returns for each member of the group.

While the group may limit or cut down our personal freedom without our even knowing it, it is sometimes an agent to give us more freedom then we could get by ourselves. By virtue of specialization of labor, not all of us have to perform all the necessary functions of the population. Some poeple produce food, others carry away waste.

Within the biological, physical, and social-psychological constraints that the environment puts on us, each individual has some range of adaptability—some capacity to stand considerable changes in the environment and to adapt to those changes as necessary. Some individuals can adapt to a high level of uncertainty in their environment. Other individuals, however, exhibit a remarkably small capacity to respond adaptively to even small alterations in the environment. Groups, like individuals, vary in their capacity to adapt to changes in the niche. Groups, populations, and communities regarded as organized systems of associations acquire properties of their own that are different in kind and degree from the properties of the constituent members.

Another way in which we are not free may surprise you. The expectations of the groups to which we have belonged from the beginning of life have some degree of effect on our behavior. In some communitites and tribes those expectations are well defined, and their transmission to the young often begins at birth. Such expectations may govern what we are free to learn. (We will return to this topic later in the book.)

It is worth mentioning factors from the human domain simply to suggest that the ideas touched on in this chapter may have some application to human beings as well as to other kinds of organisms. Despite the fact that

FIGURE 4-11
Overcrowding produces many anti-social tendencies. (Planned Parenthood World Population.)

human beings have great technological facility to increase their freedom to range broadly over their ecological niche, they sometimes cannot activate the necessary social mechanisms fast enough to respond appropriately to incipient problems, such as pollution and population, stemming from their own actions (Figure 4-11). Figure 4-12 shows the kind of population balance man tries to maintain.

Future revisions of existing elementary science programs will probably reflect the growing concern of society over the population explosion with its attendant competition for scarce resources. The incipient fears that accompany these concerns burden the people of this era. In other periods there were different fears. Unless we want to be driven into a frenzy of blind attempts to find solutions we must try to discover the science of the situation.

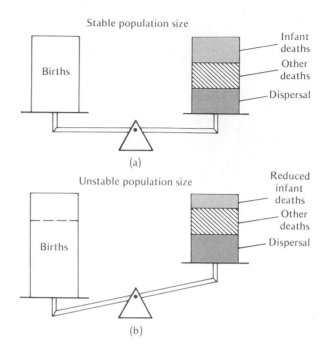

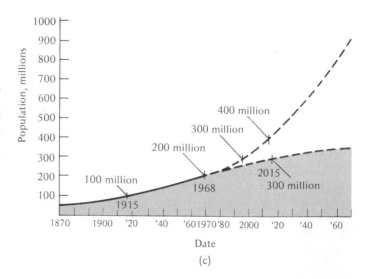

FIGURE 4-12

a **Model I. Most animals do not use this model. Man is trying to attain a balance between the birth rate plus infant survival rate and the adult death rate.** *b* **Model II. The way most populations, including man, have operated.** *c* **Changes in the population of the United States between now and the year 2070 for a two- versus a three-child family.**

The conceptual ideas and skills developed in this chapter were chosen with the idea that they might be generally useful in helping you organize and think about problems such as population and pollution, should you encounter these topics.

It must be stressed, however, that in transferring

biological ideas to human affairs, a great many other disciplines besides biology become involved—sociology, eco-
nomics, and politics, to name a few.

SUMMARY

1 According to Gauss' exclusion principle, no two
   populations can occupy the same niche for long.
   One group will die out, emigrate, or adapt to a
   new niche.
2 Adaptation to changing niche conditions can occur provided:
   a There are individuals already operating at the
      new values of the niche variables. Out-types or
      variants may contain the population's solution
      to the problem.
   b There is enough adaptability within individ-
      uals so that most of them can adjust to the new
      values. (This would be more likely in higher-
      order vertebrates.)
   c High variety increases the probability that
      some segment of the population will emerge
      with a solution.
3 If one population destroys another, we can infer
   that they both occupied the same niche.
4 If two populations exist within a habitat, then
   there must be two niches.
5 Sometimes wastes from one population create a
   desirable niche for another. Sometimes two populations enter into a mutually beneficial association.
6 Scientists frequently use laboratory experiments
   as models of what goes on in nature.
7 Overlapping of niches may be responded to by adjusting the range of foraging, as in the case of
   swallows and fruit flies; the time of foraging, as
   in the case of some birds; or by predation, as
   when rats attack men. Populations rarely increase without limit despite the fact they have
   the potential to do so. Either of the following may
   occur:
   a The mortality rate may increase through star-
      vation, disease, or cannibalism.
   b Predation may increase.
   c Emigration may take place.

8 For some populations there seems to be an optimum K-ratio, that is, an optimum number of individuals per unit of food. If the number of individuals per food unit either exceeds or drops very far beyond the K-ratio, the population will tend to die out. Extinction can be produced by overcropping of a prey by a predator.

9 Social-psychological factors may play a part in limiting growth of a population, especially in advanced vertebrates.

10 The effect of early sensory deprivation is to cut down the adaptive capacity of individual organisms, especially among advanced vertebrates.

11 In general, the more variety that a population exhibits in its exploitation of its niche, the more likely the population is to be able to adapt to changing conditions. However, highly specialized populations exploit their niches more efficiently. There are times when it is better to be a specialist and times when it is better to be a generalist.

ACTIVITY 4-1

The case of the Norway rats described in this chapter has attracted a good deal of attention because people think something like it might happen in human populations. Consider the Norway rat case as an analogy. What are its strengths and its limitations?

ACTIVITY 4-2

Competition and cooperation can both be discussed using the concept of ecological niche. Distinguish between them. Find some examples of each kind of interaction.

ACTIVITY 4-3

Immigration and emigration arc two processes populations sometimes use to regulate their size. Describe some of the circumstances that prompt human beings to use these processes.

ACTIVITY 4-4

"The greater the variety in a population, the better are the chances that the population will survive." Explain this statement and cite two examples.

ACTIVITY 4-5

In big cities the number of people per unit of land is very high. Along what dimensions of the niche do people adapt to make this high density possible?

ACTIVITY 4-6

Design a population study of your own. (Crickets, aphids, or guppies; also, snails make good organisms for study.)

ACTIVITY 4-7

As a part of his effort to increase the space and food dimensions of his niche, man is beginning to move into and beneath the ocean. Collect articles on these efforts and note the following:

1 What kinds of adaptations must be made for survival?
2 What objectives may eventually be achieved?

ACTIVITY 4-8 (See Figure 4-12*a*, *b*, and *c*)

OBJECTIVES

1 To compare the slopes of two graphs
2 To distinguish between outcomes based on different assumptions
3 To state the use of graphs in making predictions
4 To construct data tables from information in a graph.

What to do:

1 Complete the table below by reading the graph in Figure 4-12*c*.

Date	Estimate of population, millions
1870	
1900	
1930	
1960	

Construct a bar graph to show the results.
2 Complete the table at the top of page 129 for the two- and three-child conditions shown in Figure 4-12*c*.

Date	2-child	3-child
2000		
2020		
2040		
2060		

3 Find a way to illustrate why the population increases so much more rapidly (steep slope on the graph) for the three-child than for the two-child family.

4 Imagine life in the year 2000, barely a generation from now. What political, economic, social, nutritional, and pollution conditions would be different if we are averaging three-child instead of two-child families?

REFERENCES

Calhoun, J. B.: "Population Density and Social Pathology," *Scientific American*, vol. 206, February 1962, pp. 139–150.

Harlow, H. F., and Margaret Harlow: "Social Deprivation in Monkeys," *Scientific American*, vol. 207, no. 5, 1962, pp. 136–146. In this article the authors relate how one batch of young monkeys that was being raised in isolation showed normal social and psychological development. This fact puzzled the authors for some time until they discovered that a young laboratory assistant was taking the babies out of the cages each evening, fondling and playing with them.

Kettlewell, H. B. D.: *Heredity*, vol. 9, 1956, pp. 323–342; vol. 10, 1956, pp. 287–301. Also in **E. B. Ford**, *Moths*, Collins Press, London, 1955.

Silliman, R. P., and J. S. Gutsell: *Experimental Exploitation of Fish Populations*, U.S. Fish and Wildlife Service Fishery Bulletin, vol. 58, no. 133, 1958, pp. 214–252

Zinsser, Hans: *Rats, Lice and History*, Bantam Paperbacks, 1971

CHAPTER 5

Teacher: *What shape produced that shadow?*

Student: *A cube.*

Teacher: *Are you absolutely certain?*

Student: *I'd bet a thousand dollars on it.*

Teacher: *Get out the money in your pocket.*

Student: *(Puts money on desk and waits.)*

Teacher: *How much of that will you bet?*

Student: *(Long pause.) Well, I need money for lunch. (Another long pause.) I guess I wouldn't bet any of it. I guess I'm not that certain.*

—THIS CONVERSATION OCCURRED BETWEEN TWO SCIENTISTS, ONE OF WHOM WAS LEARNING ABOUT THE SAPA PROGRAM THROUGH DOING A LESSON IN WHICH SHAPES OF SOLIDS ARE TO BE INFERRED FROM THE SHADOWS THEY CAST.

IN SEARCH OF A HIDDEN WORLD

OBJECTIVES

At the conclusion of this chapter and its associated activities you should be able to do the following:

1 Recognize when a graph would be a useful way to describe a collection.

2 Recognize when a graph would be a useful way to describe the relation between two variables.

3 Construct and interpret histograms.

4 Construct and interpret graphs of two variables.

5 Compute two measures of central tendency, the *mode* and the *mean,* or the average.

6 Recognize that while data may tend to cluster around some point, such as the mean or the mode, there is almost always some variability.

7 Compute a *measure of spread or variability* in the data.

8 Given a histogram, distinguish relatively certain outcomes from relatively uncertain or unlikely outcomes.

9 State a relationship between predictability and variability.

10 Recognize that because objects can combine in different ways, many different systems can be formed from relatively few different kinds of objects or elements.

INTRODUCTION

Probably one of the most difficult but important ideas for children of the twentieth century to grasp concerns the existence of a whole world of interactions which go on, even though they cannot see them, touch them, or hear them directly. This world can be discovered by extending the range of human senses with instruments and through the conduct of experiments. On the basis of data obtained from experiments, children can begin to infer what is going on in the invisible world and how it affects them.

Recall how Semmelweiss "invented" the idea of invisible objects, germs, that produced childbed fever. Once he imagined such things, he began to act *as if* they actually existed. He tried to kill the imagined objects or at least stop them from reaching women. When his efforts were successful, the results lent support to his idea that invisible but powerful germs carried the disease. The explanation was not proven; it just became more probable when action based on the explanation produced the predicted results.

Experiments provide a way of discovering how the invisible as well as the visible world is organized. In an age where both invisible and visible pollutants pour into air and water, the children of a modern technological society must learn about the existence of systems and interactions not directly observable. Survival probably depends on it. To discover relationships between themselves and phenomena that may ultimately affect them, they must come to believe that there are things going on which they cannot see but which nevertheless may be brought under their control.

This chapter illustrates some techniques for finding patterns of change when they are concealed. It focuses on making decisions in the face of uncertainty, which is what most of us have to do even in the course of ordinary living. With all the combinations of ways events can happen, we come to expect some unlikely as well as likely outcomes. There is always some uncertainty. Some events have a high probability of happening, given past experience, but few events can be counted on to occur with absolute certainty. When an underdog football team triumphs, people in our culture get excited—it was an unexpected event. Then, after the fact, they try to explain how it happened—what made the initial predictions go wrong. *Generally we are prompted to inquire or to investigate when the unexpected or novel event intrudes.* There is little motivation to inquire about what is familiar or highly predictable. It is well to remember this in choosing phenomena for children to investigate—either they should be exposed to unfamiliar phenomena or they should be prompted to see some unexpected or unnoticed feature of familiar situations. *Uncertainty prompts inquiry.*

As the quotation which opens the chapter shows, some professional scientists may go about their business reasonably successfully without being conscious of the fact that they are operating under conditions of uncertainty virtually all the time. Students need to learn that most explanations and decisions in science are made in the face of some uncertainty about their essential correctness. Nature is so complex that its organization is difficult to uncover. Men have worked at it for hundreds of years. They learn to live with the *most probable* explanations. If new evidence arises, the belief in an explanation will be either strengthened or weakened—depending on whether or not it seems to be consistent with the most probable explanation.

Many modern elementary science programs present experiences from which students are expected to construct and test their own explanations. Finding patterns of relationships or detecting patterns of change can be a frustrating process, for both scientists and students. Both have to survive the periods of confusion which mark any genuine problem-solving experience. Teachers can help develop a spirit of intellectual adventure in their students by making the students safe from reproof when they fail to produce the most-expected explanations. Since all explanations can be held only tentatively, although some are more probable than others, students and teachers accustomed to operating as if there is always one right way may feel uncomfortable for a while in a modern elementary science program.

We live in a complex world marked by more interactions than we can begin to grasp; virtually all explanations are simplifications of that world. When an explanation "works,"—that is, yields predictions that are verified by experience—we gain confidence in it. New evidence or more data can increase our confidence in an explanation and can also lead to the invention of new explanations. This point of view—that we are more likely to get a better picture of relationships by collecting and organizing data from more than just a single event—applies to the social sciences as well as the natural sciences. Kenneth Boulding, the economist, remarked that if we were less prone to make important judgments and to form attitudes just on the basis of idiosyncratic experience, we could make better political, economic, and social decisions. We would have given ourselves time to evaluate evidence and to think about the connections between events. Many of the modes of reasoning introduced in this chapter apply to the social sciences as well as the natural sciences.

THE LANGUAGE OF UNCERTAINTY

The kind of vocabulary that is appropriate when making decisions in the face of uncertainty is *nouns* such as *chance, probability, confidence, uncertainty, risk, odds, likelihood, approximation, expectation, variety, combinations*, and *assumptions; adverbs* such as *probably, likely, relatively*, and *possibly*; and *adjectives* such as *random, probable*, and *statistical*. Although the examples in the chapter illustrate how the union of mathematics with science improves the quality of inquiry, you will need to keep in mind the warning that *good mathematics cannot make up for science which is badly done or illogically conceived*. If the science is bad, the fact that the mathematics is good provides little solace. Mathematical procedures are meant to describe data, not to explain; consequently, the procedures are never in and of themselves a source of knowledge. Statistical techniques such as graphing or computing averages simply help inquirers extract information from complex situations. Once phenomena are described, someone has to make the inferences, someone has to make decisions and furnish explanations. On the basis of data and accumulated knowledge, some explanations will become more probable than others.

THE SEARCH FOR PATTERNS

"The world is so full of a number of things . . ." So the child's verse begins. What the world is full of is variety, not as much as there might be, but more than enough to keep us busy trying to cope with it. If we paid attention to every detail, no two events would ever seem to be alike; learning would be useless, since nothing would be exactly like anything else—there would be no patterns or trends that we could count on to guide our decision making. Our poor nervous systems, being overloaded with details, would soon short-circuit. Fortunately, man is a pattern-seeking being. He simplifies life by treating objects and phenomena that are approximately the same *as if* they were exactly the same. He has a memory which stores information from his past experience. When he encounters a new situation, he tries to find out in what ways it resembles something he already knows—he searches for the same or a similar pattern of relationships.

To expose relationships among variables, when nature camouflages those relationships with all kinds of random events, requires imagination, ingenuity, a great deal of patience, confidence in the face of uncertainty, and some experimental and mathematical techniques for dealing with variety. Making decisions in the face of necessary uncertainty characterizes modern science as well as modern business. Each event is connected to a set of other events. A change in a system can set off a whole chain of interactions.

This chapter deals with some of the ideas associated with what might be called a statistical view of nature or making decisions in the face of uncertainty about the outcomes. Statistics is the art of dealing with vagueness through analyses of the sources of variety. Its motto might be, "Learn to live with uncertainty—but no more than necessary." The techniques introduced provide a means for reducing uncertainty, or upping the odds in favor of people.

In science, phenomena always have some Alice-in-Wonderland quality. Things generally do not happen in *exactly* the same way every time. Predictions or expectations frequently fail to be fulfilled; uncertainty about outcomes and explanations is a daily condition. Each investigation is a little like taking a trip down the rabbit hole—looking for the combinations that unlock nature's secrets. Some words that describe feelings during these trips are *exciting, scary, fun, frustrating, puzzling, steadying, hopeful, certain, fulfilling,* and *"messing around."* These words came from two groups: ten scientists, and two classes of fifth-graders in their second year of engaging in a modern elementary science program that involved them in a great deal of experimenting. Knowing that there can be frustrating moments in the search for patterns, teachers can develop intellectual venturesomeness in their students by encouraging them to develop and test their own explanations, requiring only that the explanations exhibit some logical relationship to the evidence.

Once down the rabbit hole, Alice acted like a child who might have emerged from a modern elementary science program. When things behaved too erratically, she stopped to observe carefully and sometimes to experiment bravely, if cautiously. She hunted for outcomes she could depend on to happen again. To find patterns of relationships, she had to see some events happen on more than one occasion. In a sense, she had to sample the strange new world to find out what the possibilities were. She used the information to guide her behavior, but she had to tolerate a great deal more uncertainty about outcomes than she ordinarily did.

Science is an enterprise in which people believe, as Alice did, that there are fundamental relationships which, when they can be found, make the world more predictable. When people believe in magic, they live more as if in a perpetual Alice-in-Wonderland world. They do not think there are fundamental patterns or relationships among phenomena which they can discover and eventually control. For believers in magic, the world is governed by powerful forces over which they have no control except, perhaps, through placating or cajoling demons with incantations or complex ritual.

PREDICTION, CONTROL, AND EXPLANATION

When Alice discovered that she could achieve her objective of changing her size by eating pieces of toadstool, she did not much care about why eating the toadstool could change her size—at least, not while she was in trouble. Later, once she had her world more in control, she might turn her attention to explanation. *Control* and *explanation* are two goals of science and engineering. Control and explanation depend on the discovery of predictable patterns of relationships among objects, among events, and among variables. To find those patterns, many of which are well concealed and must be inferred, is the immediate objective of most experimentation. Mathematical techniques, as you have already seen, become increasingly important as a way of exposing patterns in the data produced by experimentation. *Finding patterns usually comes first. Explaining them generally comes later.*

Prediction, control, and explanation of natural phenomena are complementary goals of science.

Measurement and statistical techniques, furthermore, provide a means for keeping track of how the odds are developing in favor of different hypotheses, theories, or explanations.

If you feel uncomfortable about using mathematical techniques to extract information from data, it may be that you had little satisfying experience doing that when you attended school. Most of us spend years in elementary school "doing" mathematics but rarely *using* it to help untangle knotty situations. Science can be a vehicle for bringing mathematics into the world of objects and phenomena.

REDUCING VARIETY TO SOMETHING MANAGEABLE

How does an inquirer reduce the variety that confronts him to something manageable? What techniques he employs depends on what he knows and knows how to do.

Quality is vague, but quantity is precise. As was pointed out in earlier chapters, quantity is not inherent in the thing quantified, but lies instead in the *operations* performed to convert quality to quantity. Volume, mass, time, length, etc., have operational definitions that permit investigators to describe, evaluate, and compare systems with great precision instead of magnificent vagueness. To convert qualities to quantities, we choose operations out of which some kind of measurement procedure can be constructed. According to the kind of scale evolved, various standard mathematical procedures become available for processing data—addition, subtraction, multiplication, and division. You may recall the famous story of how Archimedes converted a qualitative question about the purity of a gold crown into a mathematical format in order to arrive at a convincing answer without doing any damage to the crown. He used ideas of mass and volume to construct a new index of purity, called *density*. This combination of scientific logic supported by mathematical operations can be very exciting.

IDEALIZED WORLDS

As scientists worked to enlarge the world that could be objectively measured, they began to form models of a

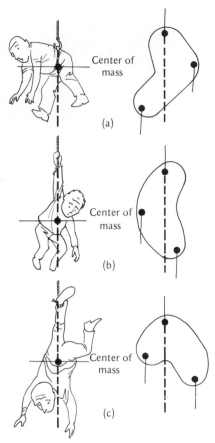

FIGURE 5-1
Locate the center of mass of an object by suspending the object from three different points.

world not immediately available to the senses. They started with a directly perceived world but became preoccupied with idealized worlds. Some people believe that the early development of mathematics and geometry, with the beauty and perfection of its logic, led men to the notion of a different world, one not immediately available to the senses, a world that conformed to perfect patterns of geometrical and mathematical relationships. Quantitative science describes ideal rather than actual situations, yet those idealizations have proven remarkably helpful in dealing with real situations. Nature seems to have been on the side of the mathematician.

As an example of an idealization that makes the life of a physicist much simpler, consider the simple but profound decision to act *as if* all the mass of an object were concentrated at a point. There is even a way to find this hypothetical point. To locate your center of mass, for example, we could hang you up first by one arm, then by the other, and finally by a leg. By extending an imaginary line through you each time, we would eventually find one point where the three lines converge. That point is the center of mass (Figure 5-1). It is as though all your mass were concentrated at that point. It is not, of course, but the fiction makes some nice predictions possible. Such apparently diverse questions as which of two objects will be more stable when the location of their centers of mass is known, what will happen in collisions of different kinds, and what must be compensated for in a rocket as it consumes fuel in order to prevent it from tumbling out of a predicted orbit, can be answered using the point-mass concept. Mathematical equations describing the orbits of moving objects assume the point-mass situation to be true. Predictions based on those equations are remarkably accurate. Common sense tells us that the mass of an object is not located in one point but is in fact spread out. Abstractions in science often go beyond common sense—a fact that you may have suspected for some time. You will encounter more idealizations in the rest of this chapter. They are a means for cutting through the screen of variation to expose hidden patterns. As paradoxical as it may seem, idealizations are frequently practical.

VARIETY AND UNCERTAINTY

When you read a published report of some investigation, you see only the end product of the research. You learn very little of all the harassments nature visited upon the poor researcher. In a way, that is too bad, because you may fail to grasp what the process of abstracting from all the variety and complexities might have been like. You could get a false idea of what it means to do a piece of research.

To discover relationships when so many extraneous or random variables intervene requires some imagination in conceptualizing what might be going on, and some ingenuity in designing experiments that will show how well the facts conform to the imagining. With all the fluctuations in conditions under which experiments may be performed, with the normal variability within and between measuring instruments, some variety in the outcomes of two equivalent experiments cannot be avoided. The kind of variety you get, when *ideally* you expect all the different repetitions of an experiment or repeated trials to give the same results and they do not, is called *error*. Error gets in the way of what you want to accomplish, but it is inescapable. You may reduce it to some acceptable level by refining and coordinating your instruments and by careful control of extraneous variables, but *you cannot eliminate error entirely*. It is called *error* simply because it is unwanted deviation from expected values, arising from our inability to control exactly all the sources of variation.

Just as in a dart game some of the darts will fall on the right of the bullseye and others will fall on the left or above it or below it, you *assume* that the errors in repeated trials of an experiment will tend to be distributed randomly around some central point. The task is to find that central point. It is called the *mean*. You also assume that no systematic bias has crept into the experiment. In the dart game, if most of the darts persisted in landing on the right side of the target point, you would look for some factor that produced this nonrandom result (Figure 5-2).

It is not always so easy to tell in an experiment when bias creeps in. Once, for example, some professors at the University of California gave their psychology students some rats and directed them to study the ability of the animals to run through mazes. They told the students that some of the rats came from a stock of very intelligent animals and that others came from a stock of relatively unintelligent animals. Each student was told whether he had a dull rat or a bright rat. Next the students submitted the rats to "objective" maze tests and confirmed that the bright rats performed much better than the dull rats. After everyone reported how his rat performed, the professors

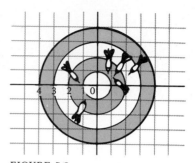

FIGURE 5-2
The darts are clustered, but to the right of the bullseye.

told the students that all the rats had in fact come from the same stock and that each group of rats was genetically like every other group used in the experiment. All rats were equally intelligent. Bias can creep into an experiment so subtly that the best-intentioned person may not recognize it. Normally, however, errors will fluctuate back and forth on either side of some theoretical midpoint—at least, that is the theory on which one usually operates. *The mean or average is the best estimate of that theoretical midpoint.* Just as the center of mass is the single point best able to represent an object, so the mean is the single point which can represent all the data.

Just as with the dart throwing, when you throw more darts you are more likely to get better and better at hitting the target, so repetitions of an experiment increase your confidence that you can locate what the mean or center of mass of the distribution would be if random factors did not interfere with these outcomes.

To illustrate more concretely the ideas discussed so far, consider next in some detail an investigation into the influence of activities in your day on pulse rate. You will encounter the average or mean in a number of different contexts. Remember, however, that the average is simply the single number which best represents a collection of data.

The *mean* or *average* is that single number which, if you had to choose one point from a collection of data, would best represent the collection. It corresponds, in a way, to the center of mass. The whole system, or collection of values, will balance itself out at that point. Finding that point is analogous to finding the balance point of a seesaw loaded with children. It is the least tipsy location.

YOUR PULSE RATE

Some natural processes slow down or speed up under different conditions. Pulse rate is one of these processes. During the day, there is some variation in pulse rate. Exercise produces changes in the pulse rate. Normally the pulse will speed up and then gradually drop back down to some base rate. How much it speeds up and how long it takes to return to its basic rate after exercise varies to some extent from person to person as well as with the strenuousness and duration of the exercise. The problem is to find out whether the pulse responds in a totally random way or whether there is a pattern to the way it responds to changes in your activities.

Your mean pulse rate

In this section you will try to determine how to answer the following questions:

1 What is your average (mean) pulse rate on an average day?

2 How much does your pulse rate change during an average day?

3 Is your pulse rate cyclic—that is, does it increase and decrease in some predictable pattern on an average day?

4 What is the pattern of change in the pulse rate like during and after exercise?

5 Does your pulse rate change when you laugh hard or when you are anxious?

6 How does your average pulse rate on an average day compare with the average pulse rate of your friends?

To answer these questions, you will need to make a series of decisions about how to collect, organize, and interpret data. You will learn to compute averages and to find the range over which pulse rate fluctuates under different conditions. The major variable is pulse rate, but time is also a variable. *Pulse rate* refers to the number of pulse beats you detect in a given unit of time. You have to decide what the unit of time will be—a second, a minute, and an hour are all possibilities. It will also be necessary to decide what *an average day* means.

Consider now how you might obtain answers to the first three questions. A set of decisions must be made.

1 Decide what an average day is for you—one in which you are likely to eat and move about at your normal pace and which is not likely to be more than normally stressful. Since pulse rate partially reflects heartbeat rate, and since heart rate is known to change under stress, a stressful day might produce an elevated average pulse rate. At least that is a hypothesis you could test.

2 Make the following decisions about measuring pulse rate:

   a *Size of sample*—Since it is impractical to count the pulse continuously for a day, it is necessary to select a sample of pulse rates at intervals. Decide how many times it would be advisable as well as practical to measure the pulse rate in one day. The task is to find the average pulse rate. Each measurement is an estimate of what the average really would be if you could have measured continually all day long. Your risk of making a mis-estimate is big if you just sample once in the day. The more times you sample, the more likely you are to approach the correct value.

b *Error of measurement*—Each time you collect a sample, you may find it useful to repeat the measurement several times so that errors of overcounting, undercounting, or missed beats can be averaged out to find the most representative measure for the sample.

c *Duration of measurement*—Decide for how long you will count pulse beats each time you collect a sample. A minute is a good period. Each decision has gains and costs attached to it. If the time is made shorter, the data may be collected more rapidly but may be less representative of the true pulse rate since the rate may fluctuate slightly. If the time is lengthened to an hour, there is likely to be error because of boredom or fatigue. However, the number of beats recorded will be much larger and therefore more representative of the true pulse rate.

d *Conditions for measuring pulse rate*—According to how big the sample is meant to be, decide how many intervals the day should be broken into. If, for example, you decide to sample your pulse rate once an hour, you will take measures at the start and end of the day, and at other times spaced uniformly throughout the day.

Let us say you have made the following set of decisions:

1 The pulse rate will be sampled at equal intervals during the day from 7:00 A.M. to 7:00 P.M., once each hour.

2 The unit of time for counting the pulse will be one minute. Pulse rate will be expressed in beats per minute.

3 Each time you collect a sample, you will measure three times and use the average of these three as

Decision: Take pulse every hour.

the best estimate for the interval. These measurements are called *trials*. Out of each set of three trials, one number—the average or mean—will be obtained. This number will be plotted on a graph.

Decision: Measure pulse for 1 minute.
Repeat three times per hour.
Data: 68, 67, 70

Decision: Take the average.
Data: $\dfrac{68 + 67 + 70}{3} = 68$ beats/minute

Figure 5-3 shows pulse beats per minute for three trials for each of four samples.

The mean or average for each set of three trials is found by adding up the total beats for three minutes, and then dividing by three to find out what number is most representative of the collection. Notice that at 7:00 A.M., three trials gave the following measures:

64 beats per minute
66 beats per minute
65 beats per minute

We do not know whether these differences come about because there is natural variation of that kind in the heartbeat or because we cannot be sufficiently accurate in our counting to get constant results. Both possibilities may be true. If we could represent each of the numbers with a block, and balance the blocks on a rod as shown in Figure 5-4, we would find the center of balance for the

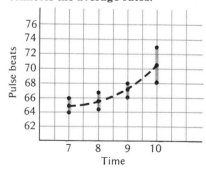

FIGURE 5-3

This graph shows all three measurements made each hour. The line connects the average rates.

	Time of day												
	7AM	8	9	10	11	12	1PM	2	3	4	5	6	7
Trial 1	64	64	66	68									
Trial 2	66	66	68	68									
Trial 3	65	66	67	72									
Total	195	196	201	208									
To compute the average	$\dfrac{195}{3}$	$\dfrac{196}{3}$	$\dfrac{201}{3}$	$\dfrac{208}{3}$									
	↓	↓	↓	↓									
Average pulse beats per minute	65	65.3	67	69.6									
Range	66-64 = 2	66-64 = 2	68-66 = 2	72-68 = 4									

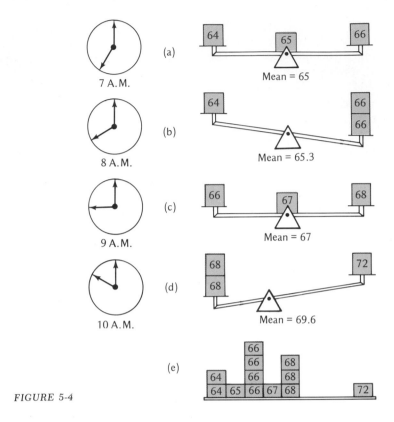

FIGURE 5-4

system to be right under the block representing 65 beats per second. Finding an average is like finding the center of balance for all the data. You accomplish the same thing arithmetically by adding up the number of beats for three trials and then dividing by three, the number of trials. This will give the average pulse per trial.

Notice that at 8:00 A.M. the blocks would be piled differently. Now the center of balance would need to be moved slightly to the right. The mean pulse would be 65.3 beats per minute instead of 65 beats per minute as shown in Figure 5-4.

At the 7:00 A.M. readings the beats *ranged* from a low of 64 to a high of 66. *To compute* the range, subtract 66 from 64. The fluctuation is 2 beats per minute. The range indicates how much fluctuation there is in the data. At 8:00 A.M. the pulse again ranged from 64 to 66 beats per minute, despite the fact that the mean pulse rate was somewhat higher. Notice that at 9:00 A.M., pulse beat ranges from 66 to 68, again a fluctuation of 2 beats per minute. However, the mean pulse rate is now up to 67 beats per minute. The blocks representing beats would be piled in still a different location on the rod.

Suppose for a moment that we are interested in examining the whole collection of measures obtained from 7:00 A.M. to 10:00 A.M. in order to find out what pulse beat occurs most frequently and how much fluctuation there is. What we are trying to do is find the mode, or most frequent value, and the range that indicates the fluctuation. We can stack all the blocks representing pulse beat on an imaginary rod as shown in Figure 5-4*e*.

Figure 5-5 shows the mode to be 66 beats per minute. The range for the whole collection extends from 64 to 72; that is, the pulse shows a fluctuation of 8 beats per minute. Where would the center of balance, the mean, be? If you looked at the way the blocks are stacked, you might guess that the mean or center of balance for the distribution probably would be located between 66 and 68 beats per minute. You can find that value by adding together the four averages obtained and then dividing by four to find the average for all four samples.

$$
\begin{array}{r}
65.0 \\
65.3 \\
67.0 \\
\underline{69.6} \\
\text{Sum } 266.9
\end{array}
$$

$$\text{Mean} = \frac{266.9}{4} = 66.7 \text{ beats per minute}$$

Finding the center of balance of the distribution is like trying to find the center of mass or center of gravity of some object or system. If you have ever played on a seesaw, or helped children to play, you probably found the

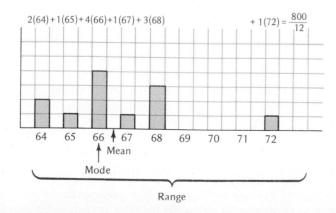

$$2(64)+1(65)+4(66)+1(67)+3(68) \qquad\qquad +1(72)=\frac{800}{12}$$

64 65 66 ↑ 67 68 69 70 71 72
        ↑ Mean
      Mode

Range

FIGURE 5-5

Distribution of all measurements taken from 7 A.M. to 10 A.M. The mode (most frequently occurring rate) = 66 beats per minute. The mean (the sum of all beats divided by number of measurements) = 800/12 = 66.6 beats per minute. The range (the difference between the highest and lowest measurements) = 72 minus 64 = 8 beats per minute fluctuation (or variation) over the four-hour period.

center of mass or balance almost automatically. You just slide the board along until the system of board and children comes into balance.

With the data acquired so far, if someone asked you to estimate the most likely pulse beat that you would expect to find on other mornings, what number would you choose? You would be wise to select the mean as the most likely outcome; otherwise, choose the mode.

If we examine what is happening to the averages for each set of trials, we might begin to suspect that, on the whole, pulse beat is rising as the day progresses. If we plot the averages for the first four hours on a graph, we see that the line which shows pulse beat plotted against time is rising, as shown in Figure 5-3.

Some observations about deviation.   The mean has a kind of everyman character to it. A particular mean could be produced in almost an infinite number of ways. Think of all the combinations of children you might arrange on a seesaw and have it always balance at the same point. The mean is like the seesaw system: it could be produced by closely clustered points or by points scattered all over the place. So if you want to know how much scatter a mean hides away under its skirt, you could compute an average deviation or average scatter for the distribution. To do that, you would simply find out how far above or below the mean each value is. For example, in Figure 5-7, the average for the 7:00 A.M. reading is 65 beats. The deviations from the mean are $65 - 66 = -1$, and $65 - 64 = +1$, and $65 - 65 = 0$. You could find the average deviation by summing up the individual deviations, paying no attention to whether they are above or below the mean (drop the signs), and dividing them by the number of readings.

$$\text{Average deviation} = \frac{\text{Absolute deviations}}{\text{Number of readings}} = \frac{1 + 1 + 0}{3} = \frac{2}{3} = .66 \text{ beats per minute}$$

Average deviation is a way of measuring how closely the points are clustered around the fluctuation you could expect between successive measures.

Reading data from a graph (interpolating)

If someone asked you to estimate what your pulse rate probably was at 8:30 A.M., you could use the graph to help you decide, even though you did not actually take measurements at 8:30. The graph line will help. Locate 8:30 on the horizontal axis of Figure 5-3. Move your finger or a pencil vertically upward until it meets the graph line. Mark a point on the graph line and look to the left on the vertical axis to see what number is opposite that point. The number on the vertical scale will be a good estimate of what the pulse-beat rate probably was at 8:30 A.M. It is approximately 66.3 beats per minute.

Graphs of two variables are called *bivariate* graphs. The one just discussed shows the relation of the variable pulse rate to the variable time. Graphs make it possible to estimate values of variables not actually measured. The process of using a graph to estimate values between measures is called *interpolation.*

By studying the trend of the graph line, you could try to predict what the next average pulse rate would be for 11:00 A.M. Just extend the line lightly in the direction it seems to be going in. Prediction of points beyond the graph is more risky, because the trend could change abruptly. Nevertheless, if you have to make an estimate of the average, that would be a good way to make a prediction—provided that conditions do not change. The process of estimating which values will occur beyond those actually measured is called *extrapolation.* Extrapolation is much more risky than interpolation because there is less information to go on.

Suppose we constructed a bar graph to show all the pulse rates measured during the first four hours. We would be making a graph of one variable, pulse rate. It would be like a histogram that shows the frequency with which each value of the pulse-rate variable occurred (see Figure 5-5).

Two people might produce graphs like those in Figure 5-6. A shows much more variability or fluctuation in pulse than B does. When the graph is spread out and "fat," there is a lot more variability than when the graph is tall and "thin." *Univariate* distributions describe the collection of data for a single variable. Bivariate graphs show the relation between two variables. Both kinds of graphs constitute a kind of scientific snapshot of nature. Like x-rays, graphs expose underlying patterns. Graphs do not explain anything; they simply portray nature so that the investigator can see what needs explanation.

Do a pulse-rate study on yourself. Plot the points and find out what happens to your mean pulse rate over the course of a twelve-hour day.

FIGURE 5-6

Frequency distribution of pulse rate for two people. All measurements of pulse rate over a period of five days were plotted. Which person shows greater variability?

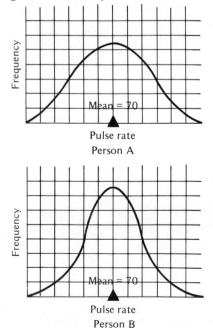

Pulse rate
Person A

Pulse rate
Person B

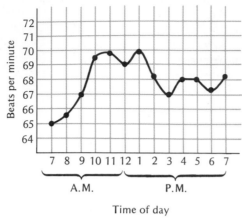

Average pulse rate for three trials	
Time	*Rate*
7AM	65.0
8	65.3
9	67.0
10	69.6
11	69.8
12PM	69.0
1	70.0
2	68.1
3	67.0
4	68.0
5	68.0
6	67.2
7	68.1
Grand average for the day	67.8 beats/minute

FIGURE 5-7

Average pulse rates for one person from 7 A.M. to 7 P.M.

Figure 5-7 shows the averages plotted by one person from 7:00 A.M. to 7:00 P.M. It shows that the pulse rate ranged from a low of 65 beats per minute to a high of 70 beats, a fluctuation of 5 beats per minute. The mean pulse rate for the day was approximately 67.8 beats per minute.

The mean is a number which represents a whole collection of data. Statements that are true about the collection may not be true of any individual event. In the example the mean pulse rate is 67.8 beats per minute, but we did not measure any fractional pulse beats. We got numbers like 67 and 68. Pulse beat is really a discrete variable. There are no in-between values. *The collection of events, however, is a new entity with its own properties,* of which one is the *mean,* another the *range,* and still another the *mode.* Means, modes, and ranges are mathematical descriptions of collections of data. Computing a mean is one step in the process of reducing the variety with which we must deal, since one value can represent the collection. The collection is the referent for the mean, the mode, and the range.

INTERPRETING GRAPHS

Univariate graphs

Graphs are mathematical models or snapshots. It does not matter to a graph what content it is representing. Graphs are mathematical forms or structures into which all kinds of content can be dropped. The content can come from physical, biological, or social science.

Consider some graphs that show how the variable of age is distributed in some human populations. (See Figure 5-8.) Among human beings, as well as among other organisms, the age variable has an important influence on the properties of the population. Among humans the age variable has political, economic, and cultural—as well as biological—importance. The five graphs shown in Figure 5-9*a* through *e* are all univariate; that is, the frequency of only one variable is involved—age. The graphs

FIGURE 5-8

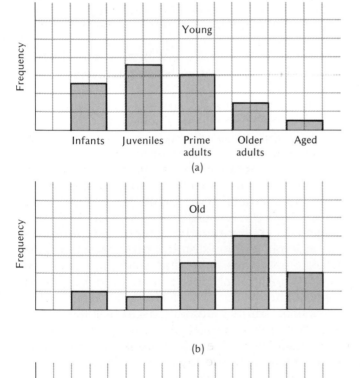

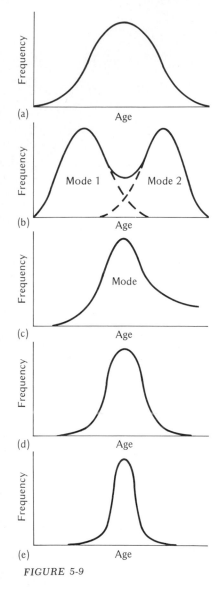

(a)

(b)

Mode 1   Mode 2

(c)

Mode

(d)

(e)

FIGURE 5-9

show age distributions in different groups. Try to think of populations you know or have read about that might be described with frequency distributions or histograms similar to these.

Consider Figure 5-9a, d, and e. The difference in the shape of the graph tells you how much variability there is. Figure 5-9a and b could be graphs of the same population at different points in its history. For example, Figure 5-9b could turn into e, if some bronchial infection caused high mortality rates among babies and elderly people. The transition from graph d to e could also be produced if some part of the population left the area. There is a tendency, for example, for old people to collect in communities designed especially for them. Figure 5-9b could describe either the young suburban group left behind or the community of the elderly. The effect of the separation is to reduce the range of ages in each group. Much of the valuable information in a graph lies in its shape. But the same shape can describe many phenomena, so you must consider the content.

Sometimes a population might show a bimodal distribution like that in Figure 5-9b. There may have been a period of war, famine, or disease that had the net effect of producing a population with a large number of very young people and a large number of very old people. Bimodal distributions lead one to suspect that there is a tendency for two populations to develop. That suspicion should prompt inquiry into the reasons. It is common to assume that the normal, approximately bell-shaped, unimodal distribution is what we would find if only chance factors were at work. Departures from that shape are cause for inquiry.

A graph of the distribution of the age variable in an elementary school, adults included, might look like Figure 5-9c. The mode is skewed to the left. Most of the population is bunched in the early ages. Teachers, at their relatively advanced age, are out in the tail of the distribution.

Bivariate graphs

Bivariate graphs have to be interpreted in much the same fashion as univariate graphs; however, in this case two variables are being related. Figure 5-10a through h is a series of graphs showing possible relationships between two variables. In Activity 5-4 you will be asked to interpret these graphs. Remember, however, that graphs do not explain anything. They simply describe relationships. Explanation must be furnished by the investigator.

MATHEMATICAL MODELS

The remarkable agreement between actual experimental outcomes and outcomes predicted from strictly mathematical considerations could lead a person to suspect that nature is on the side of the mathematician. In spite of the idealizations necessary to make situations sufficiently simple for mathematical treatment, the comparisons and predictions that the models make possible are remarkable. The equations and procedures are entirely indifferent to the particular contents dumped into them. Often phenomena that seem perceptually and cognitively different conform to the same equations. It is as though the equations and graphs float above the plane of our perceptions, simplifying and ordering what comes from the tremendous milieu of possibilities. Thus the use of mathematical techniques releases us somewhat from the perceptual binding in which the rich variety of stimuli enshrouds us. If you have not yet found mathematics a palatable subject, you might at least comfort yourself with the fact that when mathematics is applied to complex situations, it can frequently help you extract order from what might otherwise be a morass of facts.

What we are doing by using collections rather than individual events to make predictions is accepting a kind of statistical view of nature. We give up the hunt for strict determinism in favor of what we can in fact find from a probabilistic approach. We learn to live with uncertainty and to seek techniques that reduce uncertainty to the lowest possible limits. In short, we aim toward a kind of statistical determinism.

For an example of how accurate prediction can be, consider a statistical model of the world in the field of genetics. Ordinarily in sexual reproduction the offspring receives from each parent one gene, or piece of genetic information, for each trait. The offspring carries around two pieces of code that signal to the developing system how the trait is to be displayed. Suppose that two hybrid red flowers cross and produce offspring. The hybrid parents each contain genetic information for red and for white flowers. However, red being dominant, the parents appear as red. But what can we expect of the offspring? If

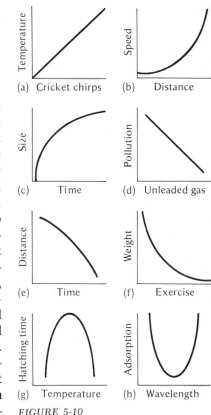

(a) Cricket chirps
(b) Distance
(c) Time
(d) Unleaded gas
(e) Time
(f) Exercise
(g) Temperature
(h) Wavelength

FIGURE 5-10

we collect and plant the seeds, we might find it very difficult to predict with certainty how any individual seed will turn out with respect to color. Perhaps, however, we could look at all the possible combinations and construct a mathematical model of how the colors are likely to be distributed in the collection of offspring.

Three possible gene combinations might occur as a result of the kind of gene each offspring might get from parent number one (P_1) and from parent number two (P_2), each of which has information for red and white. See Figure 5-11 for a genetic model.

Code from hybrid P_1 P_2 *Red White Red White* *Offspring would get*	*Properties of the offspring*	*Probability model predicts*
1. Red Red Red from each parent	Offspring would be true red. It would look red and would produce reds. **Pure red.**	25%
2. White White White from each parent	Offspring would be true white. It would look white and, bred with whites, would continue to produce whites. **Pure white.**	25%
3. Red White 4. White Red A red from one parent and a white from the other parent	Offspring would appear red but contain codes for both red and white. **Hybrid red.** Crossed with other hybrids or with pure reds or pure whites, it will produce a mix of types. Both red-white and white-red are listed to show that possible contribution from each parent.	25% 25%

The mathematical model *assumes* that only chance operates to determine which of the two messages that each parent carries the offspring will get. Three possible combinations might be present among the offspring: pure red, pure white, and hybrid red. What are the probabilities attached to each alternative? Each offspring has a 50 percent chance of getting the red message from P_1 and a 50 percent chance of getting the white from P_2—at least, that is what we assume in the ideal world. Each combination should show up about 25 percent of the time. Given that all combinations are equally likely, 25 percent are predicted to be pure white, 25 percent pure red, and 25 percent plus 25 percent or 50 percent hybrid red. Whether the hybrid offspring is a red-white or a white-red is a mat-

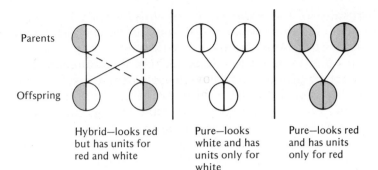

Parents

Offspring

Hybrid—looks red
but has units for
red and white

Pure—looks
white and has
units only for
white

Pure—looks red
and has units
only for red

FIGURE 5-11
Possible gene combinations.

ter of indifference, since there would be no way to distinguish these two types from each other. Thus we can add the probabilities for each of those alternatives together. Now we can study the offspring to see how well they conform to the expectations of the model. Our model says that 25 percent of the offspring will be white and 25 percent will be red. But the reds will be of two kinds, hybrid and pure. Of the next generation, 25 percent will be pure red but 50 percent will be hybrid red. Hybrids contain codes for both red and white.

The only way to distinguish the pure reds among the offspring from the hybrid reds is to cross each one with a pure white when it reaches maturity. Hybrid reds will produce some white offspring, whereas pure reds will produce all red hybrids.

By examining and recording the colors and results of crossing, we can see how well nature conforms to the expectations of the model.

Some of the outcomes will approximate the model fairly closely, while others will seem not to be conforming to it. Over many such samples, if the model is correct, the average relative frequency for each combination will approach some constant, and you hope that the constant will match well with the expected probabilities given by the model. If the probabilities do not turn out approximately as expected, you start looking for reasons. Not only does a probability model provide a way of thinking about outcomes of an experiment, but when its predictions are not confirmed empirically, that fact impels you to look for the reason why. *The probability model, then, is a tremendous stimulus to inquiry as well as an organizer of information.*

Because the union between mathematics and science can be so fruitful for the would-be inquirer, the opportunity to use mathematical operations while children conduct simple investigations ought to be exploited. The combining of mathematics with science can begin as soon as children learn to count. If from that time on, they get as much practice as possible at turning meaningful science content into arithmetical and mathematical expressions, it may be more likely that mathematics will function as a kind of universal language for them. That is at least one hypothesis worth trying out. It seems to me somewhat immoral to put children through arithmetic and mathematics lessons day after day and year after year with the promise that it will all turn out to be useful to them some day, when you know that the day will never come for most of them.

If you can use mathematical as well as experimental techniques for exposing relationships among variables or for exhibiting the properties of systems, you greatly strengthen your ability to design good experiments as well as to extract the most information possible from the data produced.

Skill, insight, and ingenuity are required on the part of an investigator to conceive systems that are defined by variables whose interactions depend on a relatively narrow set of reproducible conditions. If the sources of variety in the situation are too numerous, then the results will not be reliable and reproducing the results of such experiments will become nearly impossible.

A FEW COMMENTS ON TESTING HYPOTHESES

Robert Hogland at the University of California exposed rats to 300 parts per million of carbon monoxide fumes from highway pollution. He wished to study their drinking behavior. Water, glucose, saccharin, and alcohol were equally available to all rats in the study. His intent was to find out whether drinking habits and exposure to carbon monoxide were related. He provided four kinds of liquids and asked what was the probability that the pattern of preference, or the amount of liquid consumed, or both, would be influenced by the monoxide intake.

Suppose we examine the set of expectations Dr. Hogland might have had. If he had little evidence to cause him to expect the normal preference for water to change, then he might expect the rats to do at least 90 percent of their drinking from the water container and distribute 10 percent to the remaining alternatives. If, on the other hand, he had reason to think the preferences would change as a result of exposure to carbon monoxide, but was not certain how, he might have adopted a noncommittal strategy by dividing his expectations equally among the alternatives, 25 percent to each liquid. These predictions would become his model for testing. He would start with a hypothesis of no difference; that is, he would expect the rats to sample all the liquids in about equal amounts. The means for the amount of each liquid consumed would be predicted to be the same. He would assume a difference between means of zero and then look to see how well his expectation was met. If the carbon monoxide had no influence, all liquids would be consumed equally. If more of some liquids were consumed, then he might be able to infer that carbon monoxide influenced drinking habits. First, however, Dr. Hogland would have to determine whether observed differences in the liquid consumed could have occurred by chance alone on account of the random factors at work in the situation. After all, data always involve some variability or randomness that must be seen through. A common research strategy is to begin with a hypothesis of no difference among the alternatives and then to find out how far apart the means are. In this case, Hogland found that the rats became avid alcoholics. When he added cigarette smoke to the carbon monoxide, the rats became positively addicted to alcohol. He therefore discarded his null hypothesis, his hypothesis of no difference. Proceeding in somewhat the same manner, he found that as little as 200 parts per million of carbon monoxide stunted the growth of young rats.

In making statistical inferences, you can follow a logic which assumes that the probabilities would be distributed evenly among the possible alternatives. Expect no difference between means other than what might occur by chance. Find the means and the average deviation to get some idea of how much scatter there is, and decide how likely it is the differences came about by chance. If you rule out chance fluctuations, then the probability that the independent variable played a part in what happened increases. In that case you reject the hypothesis of no difference for a hypothesis that favors one of the alternatives. Of course, if you find a difference, you cannot reject altogether the possibility that it came about by chance. Each time you repeat the experiment, the results will change the probabilities assigned to each alternative. After repeated trials, the probabilities tend to favor one alternative and to approach a constant value. Then you come to have more confidence in one alternative.

Mathematical models make certain assumptions about the "state of nature." On the basis of those assumptions, the construction of graphs and equations follows from logical considerations only. Observational techniques make a pool of data available from which models can be inferred, or, once some model is postulated, its conformity with reality can be checked by gathering more data.

SPEED OF ANTS

Consider what seems to be a simple descriptive question: How fast, *on the average,* do ants move per minute? You might be interested in that question just out of curiosity, or you might be trying to find a speed variable for ants so that later you can relate it to energy expenditure or to food consumption. What could you do to get an answer? To show you something not only of the measuring, but also of the sampling and statistical implications of the question, let us go through this problem briefly. Children usually like to do the investigation.

First, remind yourself that speed is a derived variable made up of distance and time. You can do the same investigation with children who have not yet learned division; instead of asking them how fast an ant moves, you can have them try to find out, on the average, how far ants move in a fixed amount of time, such as a minute. In general, however, the investigation is more fruitful for fourth-graders or older children who can measure, do division, and construct histograms.

Next, you need to find some way of keeping track of how far an ant moves in the selected time period, say one minute. One way to do that might be to pick out an ant, put it on a sheet of paper, put your pencil down behind the ant, and make a track of the ant's path. You will introduce some error at this point because sometimes you will not be able to track an ant exactly. Try it. Remember that some error is inevitable.

Now you need to find some way of measuring the length of a track that might look like the one in Figure 5-12, which was made by tracking five ants in Santa

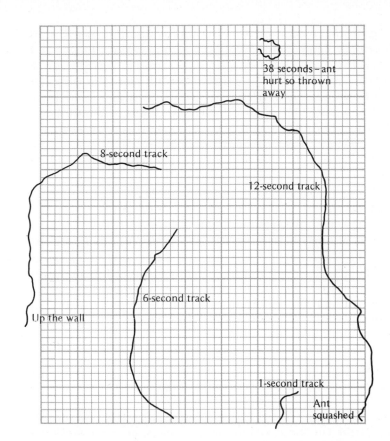

Time, sec	Distance, cm	Speed, cm/sec
1		
6		
8		
12		

FIGURE 5-12
Ant tracks.

Barbara, California. One way to do that might be to take a piece of heavy thread and lay it out along parts of the trail, then pick it up, straighten it out, and compare it with a ruler. Another technique might be to thrust some straight pins through a piece of cork or a pencil eraser and use the interval between the pins as a unit measure. Compare that interval with a ruler. Move the divider along the track, and add up the distance. You might use both the string method and the divider method to see whether they yield equivalent results.

Given that the basic methodological questions are solved, you now have several kinds of sampling problems facing you. How reliably can you measure the track? If you repeat the measurements of the same track, how closely do they agree?

Having found a reasonably reliable way to measure the track, you still face the question whether or not the one-minute sample that you took was fairly representative of the ant's speed. Or perhaps you found you could not get a one-minute continuous sample. You cannot compute an average from just one track. You need more ant tracks. How many? Well, that depends on how much confidence you have that however many you decide to collect, they will be representative of the true case. In short, you have *sampling* decisions to make. You must decide for how long a period to track an ant and how many ants you should track to get a fair representation of the rate at which ants in general move.

Of course, it makes a difference whether you try to find the average speed of a particular ant or whether the question you really want to answer is: What is the average speed of ants in a certain population of ants? If you are interested in one particular ant, then you might take a number of one- or two-minute samples from it. If you are interested in generalizing your findings to a whole population of ants, then you might collect the sample from many different ants. The latter procedure, giving as it does a potentially more general answer, usually would be the one of interest. If you were doing this investigation with a class of children, then each child might measure a number of tracks and compute the average speed for one or two ants. Then you could combine the average track length for each child's measures to make a big histogram which would portray the distance covered per minute by the entire sample from the population of ants. The sample represents the population. If the sample is sufficiently large, then the results should predict fairly well what would have been obtained if the speed of every ant in the population had been measured.

Before leaving the problem of the speed of ants, it may be well to remind you that finding ways to organize data or observations in convenient tabular forms will help you locate patterns and make comparisons. Take the small amount of data in Figure 5-12 and try putting it into the accompanying table. Try arranging it in different ways. What you do in forming tables or in collecting results into categories that can be graphed is exactly analogous to the sorting and grouping activities described in Chapter 1.

CONTROLLING VARIABILITY EXPERIMENTALLY AND MATHEMATICALLY

In designing an experiment, you may be aware of many variables which you did not choose to include in the system but which may create trouble for you. You can make a variety of kinds of decisions about how to accommodate these variables so that you can rule them out as major factors in the experimental outcomes.

1 You can choose to *ignore* some of the variables on a number of grounds: they are irrelevant; they are so small in comparison to the main effects that they can be neglected; other, similar, experiments show nothing is gained by including them.

2 You can arrange the conditions of the experiment so that the variables in question are held constant during the course of the experiment. You "fix" the variables at some level and maintain them at a constant value throughout the experiment. This is commonly known as *experimental control*. For example, in a study of the effectiveness of toothpastes in preventing the formation of plaque, one group might brush just with water. All groups might be directed to brush for two minutes.

3 You can randomize variables. You *assume the average* value for each of the experimental conditions will be the same, since you distributed the objects or events to be experimented on to each treatment condition in some random fashion. That is, each object has as much chance to fall into one treatment condition as another. Suppose, for example, you wanted to study the influence of three kinds of toothpaste on some property of teeth, such as the number of cavities that develop. You would have to find a way to assign people to each kind of toothpaste and to the control (the no-toothpaste condition) in some way so that whatever individual variations exist from one person to another will be distributed in about the same amount to each treatment condition; e.g., people prone to getting cavities will be as likely to appear in one treatment condition as another. One way to obtain statistical balance or randomization might be to throw a die and assign each person in turn to a treatment according to the number that appears. If a 1 shows, assign the person to the control; if a 2 appears, assign the person to the toothpaste A group, etc. This method of randomization assumes that variations in people will be distributed uniformly among the treatment conditions and so will have no net effect on the experimental outcomes. Randomization is a way of controlling for the effects of

previous history. The average value of whatever variables people might exhibit at the beginning of the investigation will be the same for each condition. This is what is meant by fixing or controlling variables statistically. Under this reasoning, then, each treatment group will be assumed to be equivalent to all the others at the start of the experiment, so that any differences which develop in the growth of cavities can be reasonably attributed to the influence of the toothpastes. If no differences develop, then the toothpastes are said to have no influence.

4 Often experiments conducted in the early stages of an investigation teach the investigator what he does not have to pay attention to. When that is the case, he simply reports the evidence for believing that certain variables do not matter or remain fixed. For example, you may find in the toothpaste study that sex does not matter. Cavities are just as frequent in females as males. You might discover, however, that age is a factor—namely, that people in certain age brackets are more prone to develop cavities than people in other age brackets.

ORGANIZING AND GRAPHING DATA

As the investigations of pulse rate and ant speeds show, even the most simple experiments can produce a snowstorm of data. Just as in a snowstorm, where the world of forms disappears for a time in a "white-out," the relationships you seek to expose through an experiment will disappear from view in flurries of data. All the randomness will bury any relationships unless you develop techniques for managing data and displaying them in some fashion. Arranging data in different ways in tables can help bring some order out of confusion. Graphing data can also help.

Graphs of the distribution of a single variable, univariate graphs, describe how that variable is distributed among the members of some population of events. The frequency with which each value of the variable occurs is indicated along the vertical axis, or y-axis (also called the *ordinate*), while the possible values of the variable are marked along the horizontal axis, or x-axis, of the graph (sometimes called the *abscissa*).

Constructing graphs is one kind of skill, but learning to read them is another. Much of the useful information in a graph lies in its shape. Reexamine the univariate frequency distributions in Figures 5-8 and 5-9. These distributions purport to show how the variable of age is distributed in some hypothetical human groups. Many variables could produce graphs with these forms. Try to imagine other variables that might be distributed in some way that resembles one or more of the graphs shown. Figure 5-9*a* is the so-called *normal* curve. Its misuse is sometimes a matter for some amusement as well as frustration in regard to educational matters. Many teachers use this curve as a guide for giving grades. In doing so, they either deliberately or inadvertently assume that no learning will result from their teaching. Perhaps in making that assumption they are correct. If the teaching were having any effect, the curve would be skewed.

The shape of the distribution can prompt you to start looking for factors that make the shapes appear skewed or bimodal. When the shapes are distorted away from the normal-curve distribution, you begin to suspect that some kind of constraint must be operating, and that suspicion, in turn, starts you looking for the cause of the constraint.

Bivariate graphs are used to expose relationships between two variables. These graphs show how the systematic manipulation of one variable, usually called the *independent variable*, affects another variable, the *dependent variable*. Sometimes the independent variable is called the *input variable,* and the results of the interactions in the system are referred to as the *output variables*. The language does not matter so long as you understand that whatever variable you call input and whatever output, or independent and dependent, hangs not on the variables in question but rather on your intentions. If you have sufficient control over one variable whose value you can change as you wish, it is customary to call that the independent or input variable and place it on the horizontal axis (x-axis) of the graph. The variable which changes as a consequence of the actions of the input variable is placed on the y-axis and is called the outcome or dependent variable. By plotting the two variables together on one graph, you may expose a relationship or dependency between them. Such a *bivariate* graph will show how changes in one of the variables are associated with changes in the other variable.

Bivariate graphs can depict relationships, but they

cannot explain what accounts for the relationship. That responsibility belongs to the investigator. Some samples of bivariate distributions appear in Figure 5-10*a* through *h*. Again note how shape gives information, in this case about the dynamics of the relationship between two variables.

COMBINATIONS AS A SOURCE OF VARIETY

If someone gave heaps of fifty distinctive objects to each of a thousand people with directions to build something using all the pieces, the chances are good that no two people would produce identical structures. From fifty different objects it is possible to construct many more than one thousand unique combinations and arrangements of parts. All the variability of materials and complexity of organization that surrounds us results largely from the fact that basic components can be put together in nature or by man in a potentially infinite number of combinations and patterns.

All the tremendous variety in materials which we encounter each day can be shown to result from combinations of only approximately 100 distinctive basic elements. Each system formed by a combination of elements acquires its own unique properties. Sulfur, iron, copper, carbon, oxygen, nitrogen, sodium, chlorine, silicon, and lead are ten examples of about a hundred elements out of which all other matter that we know about is compounded. Protoplasm, hair dyes, plastics, detergents, chlorophyl, skin, and millions of other materials which either occur naturally or which man has learned to produce all exhibit some combination of two or more of the basic 100 elements. Each material, by virtue of the ways in which the elements are arranged and the ratios of different components present, has its own unique characteristics.

To get some feel for how so much variety could arise from so few basic elements, imagine that you had only three different kinds of elements. Let the atom be the basic unit; that is, you have three distinct kinds of atoms, represented as follows:

□ △ ○

How many different two-atom molecules can you form from three different atoms, given that you ignore order (for the time being, that is) and you treat □△ and △□ as equivalent?

□△
□○
△○

Answer = three combinations of two-atom molecules

Suppose you added one more element to the last, so that there are four:

□ △ ○ □

How many distinctive two-atom molecules can you form from four different atoms?

□△   △○
□○   △□
□□   △□

Answer = six combinations of two-atom molecules

How many three-atom molecules can you form from four elements?

□△○
□△□

Answer = four combinations of three-atom molecules

Draw the remaining combinations.

So far in the four-element world there are six two-atom combinations plus four three-atom combinations plus, of course, one four-atom combination, making a total of eleven combinations if order does not matter. As you will see shortly, however, order does matter so the possibilities are actually greater.

Ordered arrangements increase the possible variety

In the examples above we ignored the sequence in which the elements occurred. That means we only looked at how many distinct *combinations* could be formed from a given set of elements. We ignored the possibility that the *order* in which the elements were arranged in relation to each other might also make a difference in the way molecules interact. As it happens the order or pattern of arrangement often does make a difference. So, for example, whereas the table summarizing the results of our combination experiment reports that there is only *one* possible combination of three-atom molecules in a three-element world, it happens that those three elements can occur in six different sequences. (See Figure 5-13.)

□△○   ○△□
□○△   △○□
△□○   △○□

A world with this number of elements	Can produce this number of distinct two-atom molecules	And this number of distinct three-atom molecules	Total different combinations of two- and three-atom molecules
3 □△○	3	1	3 + 4 = 4
4 □△○□	6	4	6 + 4 = 10
5 □△○□◇	10	10	10 + 10 = 20
6 □△○□◇⬚	15	20	15 + 20 = 35
7 □△○□◇⬚	(predict)	(predict)	

Note: Try to draw the possibilities for a seven-atom world.

FIGURE 5-13

The number of two-atom and three-atom molecules that can be formed from different numbers of elements. When data are arranged in a table, trends in the data may become apparent. What, for example, would seem to be a likely prediction for the number of two-atom combinations that could be formed from a set consisting of seven elements?

If order matters, and it usually does, then these six arrangements (sometimes called *permutations*) may each exhibit different physical and chemical properties. When order enters the picture, the number of possibilities increases greatly. In this case the possibilities have increased from *one* to *six*. From three elements six different three-atom molecules could emerge. Imagine how great the possibilities for combinations are in our 100-element world. We tend to take particular arrangements of components for granted until something happens to make us aware of them. A whole line of traffic on a highway, for example, may move along a defined path in a reliable, patterned flow until some condition changes. In heavy rain or snow it is more probable that a car will go out of control, spinning out of the pattern and setting off a chain of accidents. Accidents are disruptions of a pattern. In fact, when there is an accident, our attention becomes focused on the normal interactions that maintained the pattern. When the pattern of events is disrupted, prediction and control of outcomes become very uncertain. New combinations and permutations make successful prediction of outcomes less likely until the new arrangements are found to occur often enough to show a new pattern. In chemical reactions, elements come together in different combinations and orders. The new compounds that are formed all have their own unique sets of properties.

SUMMARY

1 Objects and events can occur together in potentially many combinations and arrangements. This makes it possible for an almost infinite variety of systems and materials to be formed from relatively few components. (See Figure 5-13.)

2 Mathematical models are based on deliberate simplifications of situations. Thus, for example, it is convenient to speak of point masses, and to assume that genes passed from adults to offspring sort on an equally probable model. Mathematical models predict the distribution of events that will be found in nature. If observations approximately agree with the expectations of the model, belief in the correctness of the model is strengthened. When observations do not conform to expectations, then inquiry into the reasons begins.

3 Graphs are a useful way of depicting data.

   a Univariate graphs show the frequency distributions of values of single variables.

   b Bivariate graphs show the relation between two variables.

4 The mean, mode, and range are statistical statements about collections of data.

   a The *mode* is the most frequently occurring value of a variable in a univariate distribution. Some distributions have two modes. Bimodal distributions lead one to suspect that two distinct populations or sets of conditions are probably involved, and a search for them should be started.

   b The *range* is a measure of scatter or variability in the data. It is the difference between the maximum and the minimum values of a variable.

   c The *average deviation* is another measure of scatter or variability. It tells how much the data deviate from the mean.

   d The *mean* is a single number that can be used to represent a whole collection of data about a variable. It is found by adding together all the values of the variable and dividing the sum by the total number of data points collected.

   $$\text{Mean} = \frac{\Sigma \text{ of values of the variable}}{\text{Number of measures taken}}$$

   Σ is a symbol that means add up all the values.

5 To pick out most likely events in a distribution, choose the mean; otherwise, choose the mode. The more spread or variability there is in the data, the less likely you will be to make an accurate prediction. When variability is small, predictions based

on graphs are more likely to agree with outcomes.

6 By constructing bivariate graphs, it is often possible to determine values of variables that were not actually measured. Thus the graphs can save considerable experimental time.

7 Most bivariate graphs show a kind of idealized relation.

8 Science is a place to put mathematics to work. Mathematical techniques, especially statistical techniques like graphing and computing means, can help to uncover patterns of relationships among variables.

ACTIVITY 5-1
OUR CHANGING VIEW

OBJECTIVES

1 To construct three bar graphs of a collection
2 To compare three bar graphs in order to observe how changes in categories change their shapes

Field of observation

Background:

The picture we make of the world depends on the concepts we use to govern our search. When we change the concepts, we produce a different picture. In any collection of objects, there may be innumerable kinds of relationships. The reality that we perceive is closely tied to and dependent on our individual "thought systems." What data make sense at any moment depends on the thought system we happen to be using. In the collection below are objects of different shapes and markings.

What to do:

1 Construct a bar graph for the shapes.
2 Construct a bar graph for the markings (see the accompanying figures).
3 Fill in this table. The first box is already entered.

	Bean	**Triangle**	**Square**	**Sum**
Dots	4			
Stripes				
Plain				
Sum				= **Total**

a Using the data in the table, make some statements about the association between shape and markings.
b The sum of column 1 should equal: _____
The sum of column 2 should equal: _____
The sum of column 3 should equal: _____
The sum of row 1 should equal: _____
The sum of row 2 should equal: _____
The sum of row 3 should equal: _____
The total of rows and columns is: _____
Why are the sum of the rows and the sum of the columns equal?

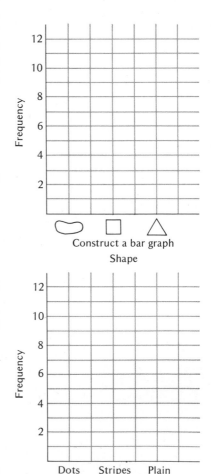

Construct a bar graph
Shape

Pattern of markings

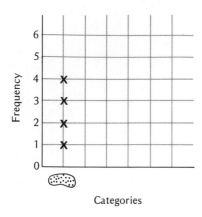

Categories

c Construct a bar graph using the nine categories shown in the table. The first category is drawn in for you (see the accompanying figure). Notice that by using *combinations* of properties the number of categories is increased. The shape of the bar graph changes again.

ACTIVITY 5-2
YOUR BEATING HEART

OBJECTIVE

To construct a bivariate graph, showing the relation of exercise to heartbeat rate

Background:

During exercise heartbeat increases and so does pulse rate. Blood circulates more rapidly carrying oxygen and removing waste. Depending on the kind of physical condition a person is in, a specified amount of exercise will produce a pulse speedup which is less abrupt and which returns to normal more rapidly.

Problem:

Find out whether there is a relationship between rate of exercise, heartbeat rate, and time needed for heartbeat to return to normal.

What to do:

1 Design and conduct an experiment to compare the influence of moderate and rapid exercise on heartbeat.
   a What are the variables?
   b State operational definitions for each variable.
   c Perform the experiment.
   d Construct a bivariate graph to show the results.
   e What inferences are reasonable concerning the relation of exercise and heartbeat rate?
2 Design a series of lessons that an individual student might follow in order to do a similar study.

ACTIVITY 5-3
QUALITY CONTROL

OBJECTIVES

1 To use data as a basis for redesign in order to improve the performance of a product
2 To distinguish between relatively reliable and relatively unreliable results

Background:

Doing science is a little like playing darts in a windstorm with the dartboard some goodly distance from you. You are more likely to score if you make the target area big rather than small. But to get two darts in succession to do exactly the same thing, i.e., to follow the same path—hit the same point at the same angle—borders on the impossible. Certainly it falls in the class of events called improbable. You might increase your chances of getting one dart to hit exactly where another did if you just threw enough darts. There are so many randomly acting factors at work on the dart that an exact repetition of any particular event may be hoped for but not expected.

If they wish to repeat experiments, scientists and engineers face the same problem. The world in which they work is very complex and being so it is nearly impossible to exactly duplicate a result. Just as the darts may fall first on one side of the target point and then on another, so the results of a series of repeated experiments will show some kind of scatter. In industrial production, quality control depends on the success with which engineers can get the products of a manufacturing process to be as nearly identical as possible. Periodically they pull items off the production line to test them.

Scientists have to agree, just as dart players do, on what they will accept as the limits within which performance is acceptable. Once they make that agreement with respect to a particular experiment or production process, all repetitions of the experiment or the process whose results fall within some acceptable area will be taken as an indication that the process is going as expected. The outcomes could be considered equivalent, if not identical. The more closely the results are required to

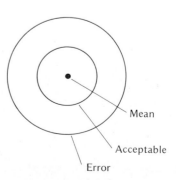

agree, the more stringent must be the control of the factors that produce deviations. An experiment that yields one result in one place, and very different outcomes in another part of the world or in a different era, makes men distrust the relationships that it purports to expose. Only stable relationships or regularities make prediction possible. How big the target area can be and how much uncertainty can be tolerated must be decided in each experiment.

The problem:

You are a maker of paper airplanes. The problem is to design a plane with the best performance characteristics. (Elementary school students enjoy this activity enormously, and they can learn a great deal of science in the bargain.)

What to do:

1 Decide what variables make up good performance, e.g., height which a plane reaches, distance it flies or time which it stays in the air or both; accuracy in hitting a target; etc.
2 Decide how to measure the variables. (In doing this activity with students, take them to a gymnasium or to the lunchroom, or out into the schoolyard if it is not a windy day.)
3 Construct two planes and fly them. Collect data. Fly each plane at least ten times. How much variability is there in the outcomes? Use a histogram to show the results.
4 Modify the planes and launching procedures to see if you can get more reliable or consistent results.
5 Modify the planes to see whether you can produce better performance.
6 A final product. Give all the performance data on the best model you achieved. Note the following points:
    a Wide scatter = unreliable.
    b Close scatter = reliable.
    c Off to one side = bias.
    d Little target, big target = acceptable risk.
      (1) If too big—takes no skill. Random factors can operate freely.
      (2) If small target—need to try to control more of the conditions.

ACTIVITY 5-4

OBJECTIVE

To interpret graphs

What to do:

Examine the graphs in Figure 5-10*a* through *h*. Try to suggest other phenomena that would be described by graphs of those shapes.

ACTIVITY 5-5

OBJECTIVE

To distinguish between young, prime, and old populations

What to do:

1 Examine Figure 5-8*a*, *b*, and *c*. How are young, prime, and old populations distinguished from each other?
2 The three figures could represent three different populations, or they could represent the same population at different points in its history.
   a Try to list some conditions which might produce a shift from a prime to an old population.
   b Try to list some conditions which might produce a shift from a prime to a young population.
3 What differences do you think there would be in political, educational, medical, and advertising efforts according to whether the census showed the country to be occupied by a young, prime, or old generation?

CHAPTER 6

First child: *"Systems! What is that? You mean like the bus system?"*

Second child: *"She means like the system. You gotta know the system, or you get in trouble."*

Third child: *"The horse system. You bet, and if you have a system you might win."*

Fourth child: *"I think it means Mr. Fox and Mrs. Powers. In his class there is a system, and you know it. But her class is wild. Like anything goes. She has no system."*

—COLLAGE OF COMMENTS MADE DURING VARIOUS INTRODUCTIONS OF THE CONCEPT OF SYSTEMS IN THE "SYSTEMS AND SUBSYSTEMS" UNIT OF THE SCIENCE CURRICULUM IMPROVEMENT STUDY.

SYSTEMS AND SEARCH STRATEGIES

OBJECTIVES

At the conclusion of this chapter and after completion of the associated activities, you should be able to do the following:

1 Identify the properties of four types of experiments:
   a Methodological
   b Explanatory and exploratory (discovery)
   c Fact-finding
   d Boundary-setting

2 Classify experiments in any elementary science book according to their type.

3 State the function of black boxes in an investigation.

INTRODUCTION

As the quotations suggest, *system* is a word children frequently have heard used in a variety of everyday contexts. In general, the everyday use fits fairly well with the way the concept of system is used in science and engineering. In Chapter 1 a system was distinguished from heaps and collections by virtue of the fact that there is a kind of *interdependence* of the parts in a system. If something happens to one part of a system, there are related and consequent changes in other parts of the system. That the children somehow already have acquired an intuitive feeling for this relatedness can be inferred from their statements: ". . . the bus system," "The horse system. . . . ," and the observation that where a teacher had no system things were "wild." When things are related to each other, they are not so free to go off in all directions, that is, there is less chaos, less chance for the parts to go "wild." They are under constraint. Outcomes are more predictable.

Because the importation of system concepts into modern science programs probably represents one of the major content innovations, it deserves special attention, especially by people who want students to be able to do practical things as well as to talk theory.

Engineering groups, the scientific doers of our society, employ systems strategies extensively. Certainly where control of outcomes is desirable—and that is generally the case in engineering—systems analysis and systems strategies for describing phenomena have proven very useful. Since so much of human striving is goal-oriented, at least when it comes to the application of ideas in practical contexts, systems thinking in science instruction merits extra consideration.

If engineers find systems strategies helpful in applying knowledge to achieve practical ends, then it is not unreasonable to suppose that something of the same approach could help children make the most of what they learn.

The activities that accompany this chapter should serve both to enhance your own understanding of systems philosophy and to help you translate systems strategies into an instructional program. Activity 6-1 employs straws and pins to teach some properties of systems. It may be well to begin as soon as possible so that you will have a concrete example.

FIGURE 6-1
**Students construct straw systems.
In the process, they learn how different shapes are related to properties of the system such as flexibility
and strength. (Courtesy of Dixon
Ericson, Xerox Corporation.)**

SOME RECENT HISTORY

In the period following Sputnik, the American government made a substantial effort at reform of elementary
school science programs by supporting independent

groups of people to prepare new materials for instruction. (The effort began with a focus on secondary school mathematics and science. Soon afterwards, it expanded to include elementary science and mathematics. Finally, social studies groups also received support for production of new materials.)

Teams of people gathered in different locations around the country to begin the task of preparing new curriculums. Scientists, science educators, a few engineers, psychologists, and mathematicians sat down together with some classroom teachers to distill from their collective knowledge and wisdom what they thought would be most beneficial for the rising generation to acquire. They tried to translate these ideas into lessons that children and teachers could reasonably be expected to do together with profit and enthusiasm. Soon after a unit was completed, a package consisting of materials for experiments along with printed instructions for teachers, students, or both was sent to a group of teachers who had agreed to try out the units. These trial teachers, in turn, made suggestions for changes and additions—in some cases they recommended excluding units that seemed unteachable. On the basis of this exchange between classroom and writers, units were revised and retested until some satisfactory version was achieved. It follows, then, that at least in those programs which went through trials, such applications of system thinking as have survived the trial period are reasonably well conceived.

One of the major curriculum groups originally funded by the National Science Foundation, the Science Curriculum Improvement Study (SCIS), based its program on the idea that systems concepts give a person tools that will serve him well in any kind of investigation in the physical and biological sciences, and possibly in the social sciences as well. The SCIS people even went so far as to name one of its units "Interaction in Systems and Subsystems."

Another group funded by the National Science Foundation, under the acronym of SAPA—for Science A Process Approach—employed systems thinking in the layout of its entire program. Guided in part by the psychologist Robert Gagné, who had done research on man-machine systems, and in part by the fact that unlike most of the other writing groups this team included some engineers among its members, the SAPA people incorporated systems thinking into their instructional materials. They did this by emphasizing analysis of problems beginning with identification of input and output variables and by introducing the concept of a *black box* as a useful tool in problem solving. Black boxes will be discussed and illustrated in some detail later in this chapter.

At New York University, the Conceptually Oriented Program in Elementary Science (COPES), which was organized considerably later, incorporated the concept of system within what it called the "great ideas of science" approach to curriculum construction. According to the COPES group, whose support came primarily from the United States Department of Education, science does not consist of just detailed descriptions of phenomena. Its vigor comes from the invention by men of highly prized and imaginative models or theories that form the bases for explanation of phenomena. The germ theory of disease, kinetic molecular theory, conservation of mass and energy, gene theory of heredity, and a statistical view of nature are a few examples of great schemes of explanation. While these great ideas are not directly subject to empirical verification, they nevertheless have a unifying effect because they put events into perspective. Conceptual schemes help men to account for what they observe in nature, and they are what scientists turn to when faced with particular problems.

THE SYSTEMS APPROACH TO STATING AND SOLVING PROBLEMS

Scientists and engineers often describe their work differently. Scientists spend more of their time trying to explain how things work. They develop and test theories about how variables of one kind or another are related. Engineers, on the other hand, usually take as given the relationships that scientists discover and concern themselves more with the application of the knowledge. They devote more of their effort to designing, building, and testing systems that have desirable properties. Engineers take theories and convert them into operating systems of all kinds. As J. Robert Oppenheimer once put it, the theoretical and the applied sciences are like the two sides of a coin. One cannot exist for long without the other. Engineers are problem solvers. They find systems thinking useful. Students, too, are problem solvers who will find systems thinking useful.

Choosing the variables in a system

The question of relevance depends on what you already know or believe. What facts interest people and what experiments they undertake depend on what they believe about a situation. Every experiment is conducted in a psychological milieu of some kind. That milieu can function favorably for an investigator, or it can make his work exceedingly difficult.

Recall the efforts of the physician Semmelweis in trying to stop women from dying of childbed fever following pregnancy. One conjecture held by some of the physicians was that the priest and bells going through the wards scared the women to death. Semmelweis did not care for that hypothesis, nor did the data support it. He worked instead on a contamination hypothesis. He *imagined* some invisible organism or agency that was transferred from doctors to the women. He reasoned that the doctors carried the contaminating factor on their hands (see Figure 6-2). They had probably picked it up at autopsies. Semmelweis argued that only by thorough scrubbing with chlorinated compounds could this agent be removed. He then had to test the hypothesis that washing with chlorinated water would reduce childbed fever. It was no simple matter to obtain the cooperation of other doctors for what was regarded as such a fanciful notion. Note that *once Semmelweis formed this imaginative conception of some invisible agent which he could not see, but which he could kill, a whole set of procedures for testing the idea naturally followed.* The input variables changed from priests and bells to washing hands with chlorinated compounds to "remove" or "kill" the imagined agent. The decline of childbed fever was still the desired output variable.

Experiments provide data on which to base arguments about the performance and structure of some bit of nature. Logical arguments and imaginative leaps of the kind Semmelweiss made form a bridge across the facts. Unless the explanations can be turned into *testable* propositions, unless they suggest what data would be pertinent, and unless they imply what outcomes one should expect if nature were organized as the idea pro-

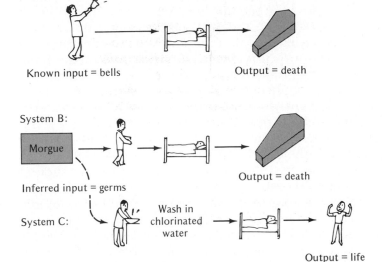

System A:

Known input = bells   Output = death

System B:

Morgue

Output = death

Inferred input = germs

System C: Wash in
chlorinated
water

Output = life

FIGURE 6-2
Three systems; three procedures.

poses, they are of little value to science. Until someone conducts experiments to verify the predictions implicit in the arguments, there will be no evidence on which to base a preference for one explanation over another.

Imagining richly

The systems approach to problem statement and to finding solutions invites creative imagining. In any situation, you try to conceive of all possible alternatives without bothering at first to appraise their plausibility. Just think them out. Imagine as richly as you can. Then start trying to order the ideas, so that you can convert them into experiments that will produce some evidence. You will want that evidence to be strong, because there is no privacy in science. Everything is open for inspection and contention. The ingenuity with which you design the way you will get data is limited only by the power of your imagination—and the size of your purse. The two constraints go together. You have to be more imaginative when you have fewer resources.

When confronted with a difficult problem, industries and governments sometimes do something that at first glance looks unreasonable. They bring in people from different disciplines, which may appear to have no connection with the problem, to listen to what the investigators think the problem is and then to suggest solutions. This technique is especially useful where some kind of invention is required, but it also has been employed in thinking about biological problems. The outsiders have a certain freedom to imagine that the people in the field from which the problem emerged may not have, because their previous knowledge, habits of thought, and disciplinary traditions smother imagination. The outsiders, unencumbered by professional paraphernalia, may innocently suggest solutions that would at first seem scandalous to the original investigators, who could never forget what their fellow researchers would say should they pose such seemingly naive solutions. Interdisciplinary visitors introduce variety into the field by removing some of the psychological constraints. Once the outsiders have done their work, then the knowledge and the experience of the original proposers of the problem will be usefully focused on trying out and evaluating some of the proposed solutions. (See the Beveridge reference.)

At the free-wheeling, richly imagining stage, anything goes. After that, however, the proposed solutions must submit to rigorous testing. At that stage all the knowledge and techniques one can possibly muster will serve him well. The period of wild imagining, however, gets too little recognition, especially since it rarely appears in the literature of science. This period in which one gives free reign to his imagination is faintly reminiscent of Alice's conversation with the queen in *Through the Looking Glass*.

> "I can't believe **that**! said Alice.
> "Can't you?" the Queen said in a pitying tone. "Try again: draw a long breath and shut your eyes."
> Alice laughed. "There's no use trying," she said; "One **can't** believe impossible things."
> "I daresay you haven't had much practice," said the Queen. "When I was your age, I always did it for half-an-hour a day. Why sometimes I've believed as many as six impossible things before breakfast."

To dream impossible things and then to realize the dream—that is what science is all about. Tragedy consists in knowing the future from the evidence of the past and still being unable to do anything about it. That kills the dream or leaves it stillborn in the dreamer.

A taxonomy of types of experiments

Different experiments accomplish different things. It may be useful in thinking about design of experiments and intentions of an experimenter to keep a simple taxonomy in mind. The taxonomy will help you to decide what sort of experiment a child is trying to do at any given time, or what kind of experiment a curriculum calls for at some point. You may be in a better position to give children guidance if you can diagnose the experimental requirements of their problems. The kind of experiments they will be trying will depend on what they are attempting to accomplish. No experiment is ever conducted in a psychological vacuum unless, in the case of children, the experiment is forced on them and they find no purpose in it. In that event the activity still does not qualify for any label better than "drill."

The taxonomy will assist you to identify the emphases or intents of different investigations given in the various elementary programs you might encounter. Roughly speaking, experiments fall into one of four categories.

Methodological experiments.   These serve the purpose of improving some *technique* or procedure. Often they are experiments that must be done in order to allow you to progress toward some other goal. Suppose, for example, you are studying various factors that govern the growth of amoebae. You are interested in how heavy an amoeba can become. How will you weigh it? These small one-celled organisms must be maintained in a liquid medium. They weigh so little that even a sensitive micro-balance cannot respond to what would be for the amoeba substantial changes in the weight or mass of the amoebae. Before you can continue to investigate the relation of mass to various input factors, such as food and temperature, you must first develop a technique for weighing an amoeba. Presumably the methodology that you develop would be of interest to other researchers as well as to instrument makers. Often it takes more effort and time, and means more frustration, to invent and evaluate a technique that you need than is required to perform the basic experiment itself. The experimentation that went into the invention and calibration of a new device, such as the one to weigh amoebae, sometimes will be published separately from

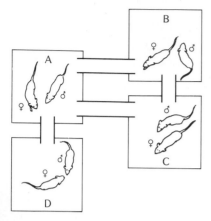

FIGURE 6-3
One arrangement of cages.

the main experiment. It will be described only briefly in the main research paper.

Methodological experiments normally use known principles organized in some novel fashion to achieve some kind of end. For example, a group of students who were doing a population study had gerbils in cages connected to each other by ramps (see Figure 6-3). They wanted to invent a way to keep track of the number of times gerbils moved from cage to cage. In this way they could study territoriality, immigration, emigration, and traffic flow. What they had to do was invent a method for detecting and recording movement on the ramps. It took them two weeks to invent a system. In order to investigate the main problem, they first had to engage in a methodological study.

When children invent their own devices to accomplish some measurement or when they materially improve the equipment for an investigation in the classroom, they are conducting methodological experiments. When they try to calibrate some piece of apparatus such as a thermometer, they are performing a methodological experiment.

While you may know perfectly well what data you want to collect once you have stated your hypotheses or framed your questions very precisely, you may have to try many methods for collecting data before finding one that is satisfactory. Sometimes a theory has to wait for evidence until the technology develops that makes its testing possible. Einstein predicted that light would bend when it entered a gravitational field. A definitive verification of the hypothesis had to wait four decades, until 1970, for the technology to develop that made a test of the hypothesis possible.

The trouble, of course, with most published accounts of an investigation is that they convey false images about how easily investigators developed their equipment and arrived at their final results. All you read about is the finished product and its performance. What is usually published omits all the mistakes, all the ideas that failed, all the frustrations, and all the doubts the investigator endured in the course of the inquiry. Convention does not permit him to say something like the following: "Halfway through the experiment, the apparatus broke down. Then I started getting anomalous data. It didn't make sense. Nothing fitted into the patterns I expected. I felt awful and very muddled. What was the matter with me that I couldn't come up with an answer?" You have to wait for

memoirs to read about those feelings and to get some
sense of what reality was for the man or woman involved.
Ghiselin has collected a number of these descriptions,
given by some of the great scientists and mathematicians
of the past, in a fascinating little book called *The Creative
Process*. It is very reassuring to read it when you are in the
throes of inquiry.

Explanatory or heuristic experiments.   These include
a subclass called *exploratory experiments*, and are designed to expose relationships among variables. They
provide the data on which to base explanations of phenomena and to generate laws.

In a very remote sense, all things on the earth interact with all other things and so may be regarded as related. If you make the chain of interactions sufficiently
weak, then you can say that everything is related to everything else. We still experience great difficulty understanding relatively simple systems where the effects of
interactions are pronounced. While science has progressed
very far toward explaining natural phenomena, it has
accomplished its progress by deliberately *ignoring* most
relationships in order to focus on those which seem most
salient or pressing. Choosing variables and interactions
on which to focus is rather like having a bevy of relatives:
some are close to you physically and psychologically, and
what they do and say in relation to you makes a difference;
others could vanish forever, and you might even be un-
aware of the fact since they have so little immediate effect
upon you. Discovery of relationships that have some
importance is one of the goals of explanatory or heuristic
experiments.

Often experiments in this classification are frankly a
matter of "finding out what is out there." Such exploratory
experiments are not to be construed as blind probes, which
Paul Weiss, a respected biologist, warns us are coming to
be too common in the biological community. Weiss tells
us that while a blind chicken may still discover a few
grains of corn, the sighted chicken will do better. "But the
major class of experiments is that which boldly tosses
questions back at nature and tricks nature into answering
them by confronting her with combinations and constella-
tions of conditions unprecedented in her standard reper-
tory" (1962, p. 469). Weiss cites as examples tissue culture, surgical removal of portions of rat cortex, and
injection of foreign molecules into a rabbit—in each case,

departure from the ordinary led to some considerable strides in biology. Each of the investigators connected with the studies anticipated the outcomes they got in much the same sense that Semmelweiss did. They were not experimenting haphazardly.

When he is in pursuit of relationships hidden away in nature, the inquirer must expect to explore some by-ways that will not prove productive. Unfortunately, he cannot tell in advance which ventures will be most likely to pay off. But through intuition informed by his accumulated knowledge plus his past experience, he will rapidly come to prefer some alternatives, and the deductions that stem from them, to other alternatives.

One thing seems clear: the scientist conducting heuristic or explanatory experiments *must reserve to himself the right to be wrong, to venture down blind alleys and come back, and to say that he does not know something with absolute certainty. He has to tolerate high uncertainty long enough to give himself a decent amount of time for his search.* If two alternatives in ten pay off in this category of experiments, he has a remarkably good success rate. It is tempting to ask why children should be denied similar rights as they try to learn science.

Serendipitous discoveries are more likely to happen to the prepared mind. Reading broadly is one very effective way to condition the mind. An investigator may make discoveries he did not expect along the way. If he has some knowledge—that is, if he is not a blind chicken—he is more likely to recognize a good thing when it comes along than if he has no knowledge. The informed observer will be more susceptible to the unanticipated, anomalous, strategic data that could become the occasion for developing a new theory or for extending an existing theory to a new area.

Frequently in heuristic or in exploratory investigations, events happen that fall outside of one's expectations. New questions arise that must be answered. When that happens, the investigation proceeds in stages, guided by what one sees along the way. This sort of thing is sometimes referred to as *discovery research.* Frequently educators and scientists, too, speak about the *discovery approach* to learning science. In some respects this is the most sophisticated kind of venture imaginable. This exploratory kind of investigation may move in any direction, according to the ideas of the inquirer and the results he gets from the system. We must be mindful, however, of Weiss's admonition against blind probing.

Heuristic experiments are usually succeeded by *fact-gathering* and *boundary-determination* experiments. Once the mental "messing about" stage is over, once the free reign of imagination has had its chance, then comes the careful, arduous, but exciting work of finding out whether the facts fit the reasoning. One science curriculum group, the Elementary Science Study (ESS), organizes its instruction into units of highly motivating materials intended to provoke questions and exploratory ventures. ESS people reason that if several scientists began independently to study some topic, they would shortly be off in different directions. Given the same materials to start, children too, they maintain, would soon be pursuing different tasks—provided that teachers did not constrain them to fit one pattern. In relation to the children, the teachers in their turn maintain an exploratory stance, guiding themselves in making decisions by what they see the children do and what they hear them say.

When the children arrive at the stage of doing the fact-finding experiments that give their ideas some concrete substance, methodological questions arise. They cannot penetrate the content to any depth without receiving explicit training in the appropriate procedures for making measurements—for forming testable hypotheses. That is the charge that critics level at free exploratory approaches to doing science. The proponents of discovery and exploratory learning respond by saying that children will do what scientists do: when they need a skill or a technique, they develop it. The motivation to learn is greater when a need exists.

Fact-finding experiments. These are designed to transform the data that are relevant to specific hypotheses or questions. They are also intended to collect data on the performance of systems under a greater variety of operating conditions than those obtained during the exploratory or explanatory phase.

All experiments produce facts, but some investigations have fact-gathering or "what is the case?" inquiries as their primary objective. The world is full of facts, enough to saturate us all. The trick is to *ignore* most of them, to decide what you want to know relative to the system you are studying, and to choose a judicious way of finding out. The great bulk of all experimentation probably falls into the fact-finding category. Because such experiments are usually conducted within a framework of some previous knowledge and because there is consequently less "messing about," there is generally less frustration and uncertainty about what one is looking for and what will turn up; there is less, but not none.

A great many of the experiments appearing in elementary science programs fall into the class of fact gathering and verification of previous information. Since children are notoriously avid information seekers, fact-finding experiments suit their wants. *It takes considerable encouragement from the teacher to focus them on interpreting and explaining their findings.*

Boundary-setting experiments. These are a special version of fact-gathering experiments. They seek to uncover the range of application of some idea or theory or the range of conditions under which a hypothesized relationship continues to be detectable. Boundary experiments usually follow after a hypothesis has been established. The limitations of the conditions under which the relationships can be expected to occur will be exposed by boundary studies. Normative studies, designed to find out what values the variables usually attain in nature, belong to this category. Boundary experiments try to expose parameter values. Suppose, for example, you wanted to bake a big cake, could you quadruple the recipe and expect to produce a successful product? That is a question for experiment. Sometimes processes that go on well in small quantities do not when they must be mass-produced.

In an explanatory study—in contrast to a boundary experiment—the size of the samples can be small, the number of replications of the experiment can be few (but the controls that determine how free the variables are to vary are very strict), and the number of extraneous variables will usually be reduced to a minimum. In fact, the whole experiment may be performed under very unnatural, artificial conditions. That is often the only way that nature can be coerced into exposing herself. Thus some new medicines may be tested with a small number of carefully selected people. If the outcomes are successful, then the size of the sample may be increased and a wider variety of people admitted to the study.

This is part of the process of finding how generally applicable the treatment is. Boundary-seeking experiments come closer to studying a system under natural conditions. For example, studies on the relation of cigarette smoking to cancer began by investigating whether coal-tar residues would induce cancer in mice and rats. Once that was established, the next step was to find out whether there was any relationship between the presence of cancer and heavy smoking. That relationship had to be inferred, on the basis of statistical analysis. Many sources of variation enter the experiment when many different people, with unique histories and combinations of maladies, become part of the investigation.

Example: Blood-sugar levels.   To clarify the relationship between *methodological, heuristic, boundary,* and *fact-finding experiments,* consider a problem having to do with blood-sugar concentrations in human beings. Once many people died of a malady called *diabetes.* A person suffering from diabetes cannot metabolize sugar for its energy. Instead, in an untreated diabetic the blood-sugar levels remain well above normal. Eventually researchers connected an endocrine, insulin, to diabetes. Insulin, which is produced in the pancreas, was necessary to the sugar-breakdown process. Diabetics, it was discovered, do not produce enough insulin to accomplish sufficient breakdown or metabolism of the sugar to release energy to carry on other functions of the body. The brain, which has one of the highest energy requirements of any organ in the body, is the first part to suffer in an untreated diabetic.

Consider now how the taxonomy of experiments draws attention to the stages of an investigation.

1 Methodological—a way to measure blood-sugar levels had to be developed. Later a way to extract insulin for use in experiments had to be devised.
2 Boundary seeking—enough studies of blood-sugar levels in all kinds of people had to be done to find out what was normal. Diabetics could then be recognized as exhibiting higher than normal blood sugars.
3 Heuristic/explanatory—a connection between blood-sugar levels and the presence or absence of insulin had to be made.
4 Fact-gathering—studies had to be conducted in which the hypothesis was tested that if insulin were present in sufficient amounts, blood-sugar levels in diabetics would drop to normal levels, and a normal supply of energy would be released. It was also necessary to find out whether insulin

extracted from animals other than man would function in the way expected in man.

5 Methodological—a way to extract insulin or to synthesize it for large-scale use by diabetics had to be found.

Once the basic relation of food to sugar levels and of sugar levels to insulin, and of their interaction to the maintainance of life functions is established, the arduous boundary experiments begin. Their objective is to determine critical thresholds for the production of insulin. They also expose how the sugar level and insulin production are phased, and what constitutes normal fluctuations of these relationships. To conduct such a study, researchers needed many blood samples and cooperation from many different kinds of people. In this phase they collected a great many related facts. They had people ingest sizable amounts of sugar on fixed schedules. They did a good deal of graphing to expose patterns of relationships. In the heuristic stage, researchers worked with large amounts of blood taken from relatively few subjects. In the boundary-setting phase, however, they worked with smaller samples of blood but took them from more subjects. By increasing the variety of samples studied, they were able to produce a family of graphs that depicted the relationship between normal blood-sugar levels, insulin production, and food-type intake. They were then able to distinguish individuals whose patterns deviate very far from the normal.

Example: A boundary experiment. American and Russian researchers who are interested in the possibility of long space flights wished to find out, among other things, what prolonged exposure to a gravity-free environment would do to the human cardiovascular system. The cardiovascular system appeared to be designed to function by pumping blood uphill against the force of gravity. There had been no way to remove the effects of the gravity force field in order to see how the system functioned without it, so all hypotheses related to the question had to be held in abeyance. The question was whether the cardiovascular system would suffer any permanent damage when it was removed for a long period from that force field, as would be the case in space flights beyond the earth's orbit. What functions might be disturbed? Those questions are now being answered because the technology finally exists to get the data: just send some people out into space and let them stay awhile. If any functioning is disturbed, then it becomes important to know how long the system can operate in a gravity-free world without permanent damage. That is a boundary investigation, and the strategy for such a costly experiment is to overstay the projected boundary or time parameter, which the Soviets did. What they found does not augur well for prolonged trips into space, since at least one of the cosmonauts suffered permanent cardiovascular impairment. To offset these negative effects of a gravity-free world, man may need to engage in some methodological experiments to find means of preventing the damage.

Determining appropriate types of experiments

If you read an elementary science unit that calls for students to do some investigating of phenomena, you should be able to identify which kinds and combinations of experiments are called for: methodological; explanatory or heuristic; fact-gathering, hypothesis testing, or both; or boundary-setting. One group of fourth-grade students in a big city took an interest in cockroaches—where they lived, what they ate, how they grew and multiplied. The questions investigated arose at different stages.

Among the *methodogical problems* faced by the students were the following: (1) how to trap cockroaches; (2) how to set up a combination of magnifiers so that they could watch growth of the embryos in the eggs; and (3) how to measure growth, when cockroaches are prone to keep moving.

Among the *fact-getting* problems the students tried to solve were the following: (1) Will eggs hatch faster in darkness or light, at low temperatures or at relatively higher temperatures? (2) Could birth (hatching) be helped by splitting the egg case with a razor?

Among the *boundary-setting* problems they had to solve were the following: (1) What is the normal rate of growth? (2) What proportion of embryos do not hatch?

While there were some exploratory probes, there were no experiments that would qualify as explanatory or heuristic.

What kinds of experiments will be involved in an investigation depends in part on how a problem is set up for students. In a study of the life cycle of mealworms, for example, you might simply give children mealworms to maintain for a few weeks without telling them that the mealworms go through dramatic transformations to emerge eventually as beetles. After some time, beetles begin to appear in the system, which started out consisting only of food, moisture, and mealworms. The children's observations at different points in the history of the system might resemble the following:

System at the beginning	System at a later time	System still later
Food	Food	Food
Moisture	Moisture	Moisture
Mealworms (mature)	Mealworms	Mealworms
	Beetles	*a.* mature
		b. new
	Oddly shaped white objects	Beetles

The students unfamiliar with the transformation must make a giant, imaginative leap—they must somehow connect the mealworms with the beetles. As imaginative as children are, they nevertheless more frequently choose first another eminently reasonable alternative, namely, that the beetles somehow "got in" from the outside. Later, the children perform a *fact-gathering experiment* in which they close the system off to entry by outside organisms. In this way they rule out the hypothesis that the beetles got in from outside.

If, on the basis of their studies, they guess that mature (large) mealworms, crystalis (nonmoving white object), beetles, and new mealworms are somehow connected, then they begin to design fact-gathering experiments to find out if the cycle of relationships is as they supposed. Alternatively, the teacher may suggest that such transformations occur. If the teacher makes the connections, then students try to verify the relationships. In that case, there is no heuristic or explanatory stage to the experimentation.

In a systems approach, it is customary to list the variables each time the system is observed and then to compare the lists to see what has changed. Careful record keeping is very important. With good records one does not have to rely so heavily on memory, which can be notoriously unreliable.

Black boxes

For students unfamiliar with the transformation of meal-worms (or even of butterflies and moths), the connections or relationships between the successive forms is an unknown. All that they can say for certain is that if you put mealworms in an environment with food and a little moisture, you end up with some beetles. Whatever happens in between, which has not yet been explained, is referred to by scientists and engineers as a *black box* (Figure 6-4). Once the set of internal connections has been identified or inferred with reasonable certainty, then that part of the system is no longer a black box. When it is possible to draw in or write in the details, the black box disappears. In the mealworm's life cycle, there might be two black boxes, depending on what the students already know about the cycle (Figure 6-4).

Engineers, particularly, find the black-box way of thinking about systems useful. Sometimes they just need to know that given a particular input, a system can be counted on to produce a particular output. Then that output can become an input to another part of the system. How the black boxes work is sometimes immaterial in view of the larger objective of making a whole system operate according to specifications, At some point, however, the connections or relationships inside a black box (which, as you can see, is just a metaphor, not a physical

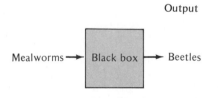

Output

Mealworms → | Black box | → Beetles

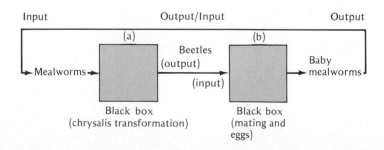

Input   Output/Input   Output

Mealworms → Black box Beetles (output) → Black box → Baby mealworms
             (chrysalis   (input)   (mating and
             transformation)   eggs)

FIGURE 6-4
The chrysalis is a black box.

object) need to be explained. Often there is more than one way to explain them, more than one model or theory that makes sense. But gradually, through fact-gathering experiments, alternative models and theories are eliminated.

Many of the modern elementary science programs give students so-called black-box investigations to perform. Sometimes students receive sealed boxes inside of which various objects have been placed, some fastened to the sides and others loose in the bottom. The task given to the students is to infer from evidence they collect what is probably inside the box and, possibly, how it is arranged. (See Transcript 6-1.) In these black-box investigations, the program writers are trying to simulate for students the problems faced by researchers who cannot really open a box. Chemists, for example, cannot open an atom and look at its parts in any conventional sense. Instead, they make models of what the parts might be and how they are probably related. With experience and new data, those models change.

Transcript 6-1. Black-box problem.

	Dialogue	Analysis
		Students have a box which tilts strangely when it is picked up but there is no sound. They propose three possible models. In this portion of the transcript they have not found a way to decide which alternative is most likely.
Teacher	Try to figure out what is in the box and tell us how you know.	**Model 1:** A round thing.
Belinda	It's heavy. I'm going to rock it. It's one of those round things.	
Ricardo	It goes up and down, up and down. It's a slinky.	**Model 2:** A slinky thing.
Teacher	What makes you think it's a slinky?	
Peggy	It's a bottle with something in it. Right?	**Model 3:** A bottle with something in it. Shifts from model 1 to 2.
Belinda	It's a slinky. It's all wires. It's a spring thing.	
Oliva	It goes up and down.	
Ricardo	It's heavier than a slinky. If you feel it, it's like a jar with something in it.	Shifts from model 2 to 3.
Peggy	Well, it's a bottle flat up and down.	Sticks to model 3.
Ricardo	It's not glass. It could be a plastic jar with something in it.	Modifies model 3.
Karen	I give up.	
Ricardo	I don't.	

It is rather problematical whether elementary students see the parallels between their artificial black boxes and those that appear in a real investigation (as, for example, with the mealworm). Another favorite black-box experiment for students, which appears in some version in a number of elementary programs, concerns circuit boards or boxes. Once students have learned something of electrical circuits, they receive boxes or boards in which wires have been connected in different patterns, as shown in Figure 6-5. On the basis of the kinds and combinations of interactions they get, they try to draw a model of how they think the boxes are wired. Often it is possible to draw

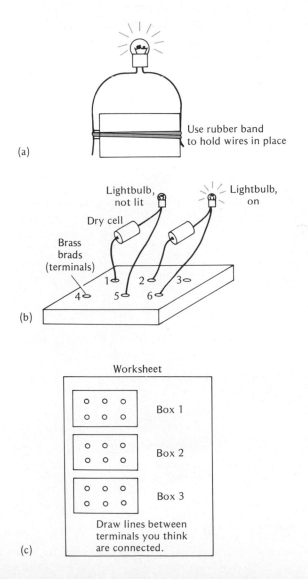

(a)

(b)

(c)

FIGURE 6-5
a **Basic circuit used to test for the presence of a conductor.** *b* **Box with connections hidden from view. The problem is to infer where the connections are. If the bulb lights, there is a connection. Which terminals are probably connected?** *c* **A sample student worksheet for recording data.**

more than one model to fit the facts. Then the students, like any researchers, must live with the uncertainty that comes with having more than one alternative explanation.

SOME FURTHER COMMENTS ON THE SYSTEMS APPROACH

Systems strategies, because they bring about simplicity in what would otherwise be complex situations, deserve attention. Any set of techniques that reduces the variety in the environment to a more manageable level, that helps students focus attention selectively, and that facilitates clear communication has instructional potential.

As was indicated several times in earlier chapters, different investigators engaging in the same kinds of study may state their problems differently, may think up different hypotheses, may disagree heartily on what constitutes relevant data, may choose different measurement techniques, and may interpret data in different ways. How they each specify their systems depends on

FIGURE 6-6
Two parents learn about electric circuits as part of an orientation program. (SCIS Curriculum.)

how they think and feel about the decisions they make. The choice of systems is rather like the choice of weapons for a duel. It depends on personal preference. People generally choose first from the arsenal of familiar weapons. Previous knowledge, theory, skill, experience, and intuition all play a part in the early stages of an investigation (Figure 6-6).

When someone with a system orientation tries to explain how a system functions, anyone else can check his inferences by looking at the properties of the system that he describes, especially the inputs and the outputs. By specifying the variables of the system, he furnishes for himself and others a means of reminding himself that all those members must be taken into account in the explanation. When he finds some members not necessary to his explanation or to the functioning of the system, he drops them from the list. In this way he gradually weeds out the unnecessary factors and achieves, thereby, a conceptual economy. That is, he tries to get the description and explanation to the greatest possible state of simplicity.

For teaching, the special kind of "bookkeeping" that is part of the system technique has particular pertinence to the development of *communication skills*. Once students approach investigations by listing system members, describing system variables, and recording data in such a way that the input and output relations are exposed, the teacher as well as other students can quickly determine exactly what was done and what happened (Figure 6-7). By this means, students establish a good base of evidence upon which to build explanations, and teachers gain access to valuable diagnostic information about the state of the students' thinking. A student trained to diagnose a problem using systems techniques will be able to state what he considers to be part of his system, and what happened when he did something to the system. That is, he will describe the system by relating the inputs to the outputs. For the teacher, who usually must be the onlooker for many different systems developing simultaneously around the class, the diagnostic information which the student furnishes through this description has high value. A teacher can always find out to what stage an inquiry has progressed by listening to or reading these descriptions. In addition, students can compare evidence (outcomes) when they develop competing explanations. The systems strategy for describing interactions furnishes to the student and the teacher a neat conceptual technique for

FIGURE 6-7
Students investigate interactions in systems which they construct using pulleys and rubber bands. (SCIS Curriculum.)

selectively focusing attention by separating, from the too busy environment of things and events, some piece of the action for intensive consideration. It ensures that everyone knows which phenomena are being talked about and which are being deliberately ignored. It does not matter which explanation is true as long as they both give the same results. The trick is to finally design an experiment such that one model would predict one outcome and the other model would predict a different outcome. In this way the model whose prediction was not fulfilled would be eliminated.

Of course, students know that they could look inside the electric black boxes teachers give them if they were allowed. A scientist cannot do that. In each box he "opens," there are other boxes, more processes to understand. Teachers should make it clear in a black-box study that the students are to act *as if* they could not look inside. While students as young as eight may do the electric puzzles successfully, their ability to appreciate the import of a metaphor like the black box depends on their having reached the stage of formal thinking which normally does not happen until about the age of eleven. As puzzles, such activities may provide them with practice at making inferences and learning to live with their inferences.

SUMMARY

Explicit instruction in systems concepts is a new innovation in elementary science. At least three of the programs whose development was funded by the United States government incorporate the language and procedures of systems: Science Curriculum Improvement Study (SCIS), Conceptually Oriented Program in Elementary Science (COPES), and Science—A Process Approach (SAPA).

Investigations or experiments can be classified into a four-part taxonomy:

1 Methodological experiments, which serve the purpose of improving a technique or procedure.
2 Explanatory or heuristic investigations, which uncover basic relationships.
   a Exploratory ventures to discover "what is out there"
   b Discovery of new questions
   c Experiments that throw questions back at nature
3 Fact-gathering and hypothesis-testing experiments conducted to verify and make precise relationships between variables. They are designed to obtain the data relevant to specific hypotheses.
4 Boundary-setting experiments which seek to uncover the range of application of a relationship or theory. Many so-called discovery experiments in elementary science fall into this category since they call for application of ideas to different settings.

Black boxes are metaphors that scientists and engineers use to tag a part of a system whose inputs and outputs are known but the explanation for which is unknown. What is a black box for one person may not be for another. *The state of knowledge of the inquirer about the system determines what components in the system will be labeled as black boxes.*

ACTIVITY 6-1
STRUCTURES, STRENGTH, AND RIGIDITY

This is a series of tasks that require only straws and straight pins. While you will be expected to perform the tasks, they have been written so that you could use them directly with students. To make that possible, a brief teacher's guide is included. Each of your students would get an activity sheet plus a set of straws and straight pins. Each student works at his own pace. On completion of an activity sheet, a student picks up the next sheet and continues to the next set of tasks. The student's knowledge of the correctness of what he has done comes from simple tests he makes on the systems themselves. There is some advantage in having your students work in pairs, since this encourages conversation and argument—both of which make students think about more possibilities. This series of lesson is adapted from the African Primary Science (APSP) unit "Construction With Grass." You are encouraged to find some children who will try out the lessons with you.

OBJECTIVES

1 To determine what patterns of angles make the most *rigid* structure
2 To distinguish rigid from nonrigid frames
3 To test a structure for strength by hanging weights on it

Vocabulary:

> Rigid
> Nonrigid
> Flexible
> Angles
> Free-standing
> Frame
> Self-supporting
> Specifications
> Strength
> Safety factor

Materials:

>   24 straws per student
>   14 straight pins per student

Keep the straight pins together by sticking them on masking tape or into a piece of styrofoam from a hot cup.

Introduction:

Angles have much to do with strength and rigidity of structures. Strength of a structure refers to how much weight it can hold without collapsing. When engineers plan and build structures, they estimate how much weight the object must withstand. Then they build the structure to hold up under three or five or even ten times that weight. This is called the safety factor.

In many structures the weight moves around; if the structure were not rigid, it might begin to tilt. That would be too bad for everybody. So an engineer must not only plan how to put the building elements together to produce a strong structure, he usually must also plan what to do to make the building rigid.

Different geometric shapes have different effects on the rigidity and strength of a structure. The structures must be built to meet certain *specifications*.

In this unit we control one variable, the building materials. The children work only with straws and pins. That way they can concentrate on the geometric properties that give strength and rigidity to a structure that must meet certain specifications.

The "experiments" in this unit on structures require children to use both concrete and abstract mental operations. To perceive geometric shapes in nonsolid structures forces children to pay attention to the structural properties of different shapes. It is the shape itself which conveys relative strength to structures. To "see" triangles embedded in more complex structures is abstract. At some point near the end of the series of lessons, there is an experiment for you and the class to do together. If several children (not more than three) finish ahead of the others, have them build a tall, strong, rigid structure by combining all their straws and pins. Once the structure is complete, here is what you do: Form two building groups of three students each.

Ask the class whether there is any straw on the structure that can be cut without making the structure collapse. When the class makes a decision, *cut* the straw in half. If the building holds up, ask if there is another straw that could be cut. Continue this process. In this way the children test the interactions in the system.

The objective is to find the least number of straws that would be necessary to make the structure stand up. Have the children *predict* how many straws can be cut before the building collapses.

Note: You are urged to resist the temptation to teach vocabulary before the start of the lessons. Try to teach the language of science in the *context* of experience.

Print in small letters, possibly on green background.

Straws: Lesson 1

Name _____ *Grade* _____

You have twenty-four straws and fourteen pins.

1 Build the shapes shown here and show where you would add straws to make each shape *rigid*.

   a Triangle

   b Rectangle

   c Pentagon

2 Which shape is the most rigid?

3 What is the *least* number of straws you need to add to make the rectangle rigid?

4 What is the least number of straws you need to add to make the pentagon rigid?

5 When you try to make rigid structures, what shape is best to use?

6 Take the triangle, square, and pentagon apart. Build the *largest* structure you can with the twenty-four straws. The structure must be rigid. Draw the picture of the structure you built.

7 Put your straws and pins away. Ask for the next experiment.

Straws: Lesson 2

Name _____ *Grade* _____

You have twenty-four straws and fourteen pins.

1 Build the *tallest* structure you can that is rigid. Use all twenty-four straws.

   a How many centimeters high is your structure? It is _____ centimeters high.

   b How many triangles do you have in your structure? My structure has _____ triangles.

(a) Triangle

(b) Rectangle

(c) Pentagon

c Draw a picture of your structure if you can.

2 Hang a weight on different parts of your structure to see if it is rigid. What happened?

3 Can you pick up your structure?
Yes _____ No _____
If your structure is not very rigid, you cannot pick it up very well. If your structure was not easy to pick up, what changes can you make?

4 Take the structure apart. Put your straws and pins away. Ask for the next experiment.

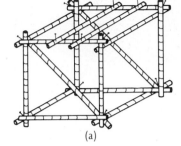

(a)

Straws: Lesson 3

Name _____ *Grade* _____

You have twenty-four straws and fourteen pins.

1 Build a house with sixteen straws. Make the house as strong as you can. Test the *strength* of your house by hanging weights on it.

2 Add straws to the house to make it stronger. How many straws did you use? How many triangles do you have in your house?

3 Here are pictures of three houses (*a*, *b*, and *c*). Each is made with sixteen straws. Which one is strongest?

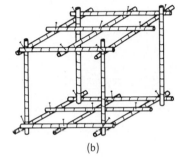

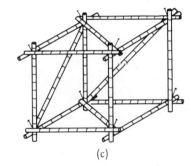

(b)

4 Give your operational definition of "strong." Build the structure you think (you predict) is strongest. Hang a plastic cup from the roof and add weights to the cup. How many weights can you add before the structure starts to bend?

5 Take the structure apart. Put away your straws and pins. Ask for the next experiment.

Straws: Lesson 4

Name _____ *Grade* _____

You have twenty-four straws and fourteen pins.

1 Support one straw between some books or between two desks.

2 Hang a plastic cup from the straw. Place the cup in the middle of the straw. Add weights to the cup until the straw bends. How many weights made the straw bend? Now slide the cup along the straw to different positions. Does the straw bend as much? What made the difference?

3 Put two straws in the system. How many weights make the two straws bend?

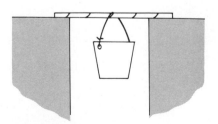

(c)

4 Build the strongest chair you can with your straws. Test the *strength* and *rigidness* of the chair.
a How did you test for rigidness?
b How did you test for strength?

5 Draw a picture of your chair.

6 Take the structure apart. Put your straws and pins away. Ask for the next experiment.

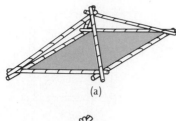

(a)

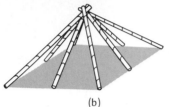

(b)

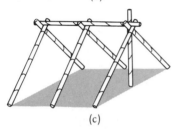

(c)

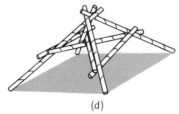

(d)

Straws: Lesson 5

Name _____   *Grade* _____

1 Build the strongest, most rigid bridge possible. The bridge must be at least 16 inches long.

2 How many triangles does your bridge have?

3 Draw a picture of your bridge.

4 Can you pick your bridge up?

5 Take the bridge apart. Put away your straws and pins. Ask for the next experiment.

Straws: Lesson 6

Name _____   *Grade* _____

You have twenty-four straws and fourteen pins.

1 Find three other partners. Each group will need one pair of scissors.

2 Build the tallest, free-standing, rigid structure you can using all the straws and pins.

3 How tall is your structure?

4 Look at the structure. Is there one straw you could cut out and still have the structure stand up? (*Predict*.) Cut out that straw? Find another straw you think you could cut out without causing collapse or loss of rigidness. (*Predict*.) Continue finding and cutting out straws. How many straws did you take out before the building became wobbly?

5 Why do you think it is possible to take out straws and still have a rigid structure?

Appraisal measure:
Here are some roofs all built on the same base and all using eight straws (*a, b*, and *c*). Make the following predictions:

a If you used the same amount of materials for these roofs, eight straws, which one would be stronger? State your reasons. Tell how you would test your prediction.

b Which one would be more rigid? State your reasons. Tell how you would test your prediction.

REFERENCES

Beveridge, W. I. B.: *The Art of Scientific Investigation*, Vintage Books, Random House, New York, 1950.

Ghiselin, Brewster: *The Creative Process*, A Mentor Book, The New York American Library, New York, 1952.

Oppenheimer, J. Robert: *Science and the Common Understanding*, Simon and Schuster, New York, 1954.

Weiss, Paul: *"Experience and Experiment in Biology,"* *Science*, vol. 136, May 11, 1962, pp. 468–471.

CHAPTER 7

Richard: *Well, I think the more time you have it under the light, the darker the part that isn't under the light gets.*

Kathy: *I disagree with you because . . . uh . . . it's the side that is in the light that gets darkest.*

Henry: *I agree with Kathy, because how could anything happen to the part that, like, just isn't in the light?*

—FOURTH-GRADE DISCUSSION OF
WHAT HAPPENED TO BLUEPRINT
PAPER EXPOSED TO LIGHT (AAAS
LESSON)

"Well, God made all these things; so how come we have to worry about them?"   —THIRD-GRADER

CONFLICT AND INQUIRY

OBJECTIVES

On completion of this chapter and its associated activities, you should be able to do the following:

1 State three conditions which produce the kind of conceptual conflict which is likely to induce productive inquiry behavior.

2 Demonstrate how a piece of content from any of the modern programs might be presented in order to induce inquiry.

3 Recognize that physiological interactions seem to underlie thinking and learning and that these interactions take time to occur.

4 Recognize that novelty usually prompts exploratory behavior.

5 Recognize that highly repetitive or very familiar situations produce boredom or fail to capture attention.

INTRODUCTION

Ordinarily the human nervous system completes its maturation in fourteen to sixteen years, *provided it receives sufficient amounts of the correct kinds of stimuli.* While there is little evidence that an environment rich in all kinds of relevant stimuli can substantially speed up the maturation process, there exists a great deal of evidence that, deprived of appropriate stimulation, maturation can be prevented from proceeding normally or even be permanently arrested. The body acts as though its development runs according to a kind of biological clock that has been set for things to happen in sequence at certain intervals. But the clock needs winding. Environmental stimulation seems to supply that need.

If through accident or parental dereliction an infant born with a normal set of eyes is kept in the dark for the first seven years or so of its life, the probability that it will develop normal vision on exposure to light is small. Each year that light fails to reach the eyes, the chances of normal development become smaller. There exist, in other words, periods of time in the course of maturation when sufficient amounts of appropriate stimuli must be present in order for the potential of a system to be realized. Deprived of the appropriate stimuli, the new connections will not form. Even though the organ systems may still be present in a basic form—e.g., rods and cones in the retina still remain—the system is no longer biochemically capable of interacting with light stimuli. Consequently, the potential of the system cannot be realized.

If a child is deprived of speech in early years, his cognitive development may be permanently blocked. Children, for example, need to be exposed to a great deal of human speech and verbal interaction with adults or older normally developed peers in the period of life from two months until seven or eight years of age if their cognitive development is to proceed normally. Adults have a remarkable capacity to perceive patterns in the sounds children make and to feed back to them corrected versions of the patterns. Thus the properties of speech are learned almost as a gestalt, and a network of mental connections is built simultaneously. Deaf children who fail to receive some kind of equivalent speech training early enough in their development often never recover from an early language deficit. The apparatus for speech or speech-equivalent communication may be there, but it must be stimulated if it is to develop normally.

This chapter is meant to give the reader some understanding of those biological aspects of learning and thinking which seem to be especially relevant to the modes of inquiry which modern elementary science programs advocate. It will show how the blend of emotion with intellect through the mediating effect of a section of the brain called the reticular formation probably occurs. Like a cake that can fall flat when the ingredients are not properly blended, so successful mental functioning depends on achieving optimal mixes of signals from different parts of the brain. If emotions run at too low or at too high a level, the cake will fall—the learner fails to get involved with the problem, or he gets so excited or so anxious that he cannot function. Somewhere in between the extremes lies the proper blend of mind and emotion to drive the investigative spirit on.

There is a central coordinator in the nervous system called the *reticular formation* (see Figure 7-1), which lies in the brain stem. We rarely hear about this small organ buried deep in the brain, yet it appears to serve as a kind of managing editor for the brain. As teachers, we all need to know something about how this editor operates and what it takes to get his cooperation. The function of the reticular formation in problem solving will be discussed, especially its role as a mediating agent between the cortical, limbic, and hypothalamic portions of the brain. Sometimes the cortex is described as the seat of thought, while the limbic and hypothalamic sybsystems

FIGURE 7-1

a **The reticular formation is the area which is shaded. When a stimulus enters along some neural pathway, it passes through the reticular formation, which may "wake up" the entire cortex. See** *Scientific American,* **May 1957, p. 238.** *b* **This portion of the cortex plays a central role in the analysis, coding, and storing of information. See** *Scientific American,* **March 1970, p. 67.** *c* **This portion plays a major role in the formation of intentions and plans. See** *Scientific American,* **March 1970, p. 67.**

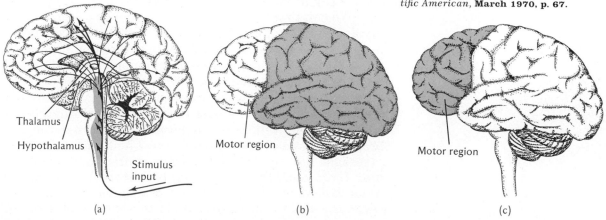

Thalamus

Hypothalamus

Stimulus input

(a)

Motor region

(b)

Motor region

(c)

are characterized as the center of emotion. Apparently, the reticular formation edits the flow of messages to and from both locations. It decides which messages coming from the outside world should be responded to as "news." As teachers, we need to know how to get the reticular formation turned on for purposes of instruction. We also need to know how to carry on instruction in such a way that the coordinating, integrating, and synthesizing functions of the brain, which are necessary to effective operation in our complex society, can develop. The research suggests that without models, without opportunities to practice, and without feedback, the mental and emotional development of children will be stunted. Mental starvation, as well as physical, can produce permanent retardation.

THE RETICULAR FORMATION—MANAGING EDITOR FOR THE BRAIN

The level of complexity at which the nervous system will operate depends in part on what connections already exist in it, on its capacity to form new connections, and on its ability to integrate messages from several sources. Most of the cognitively complex processes occur in the cerebral cortex. But the cerebral cortex will be almost totally unresponsive unless a small organ much deeper in the brain "wakes up the cortex." This small organ, the ascending reticular formation, alerts the cortex for business and apparently maintains it in an "on" condition for a period of time. When the activity of the reticular formation is depressed by drugs, excessive fatigue, or sleep, the cortex ceases cognitive activity. (Figure 7-1*a*.)

We can think of learning as a sequence of events that involves interactions of various organ systems of the brain in definite sequences. Messages generated by the receptors that pick up information from outside the body move toward the brain through the afferent or incoming nervous system up into the lower part of the brain. Branches from the main sensory tracts pass to the reticular formation as well as to the limbic and hypothalamic portions of the brain, the areas most closely associated with emotions. Messages flow out of the affective centers into the reticular formation. This small organ collects direct sensory input from the environment and corresponding input from the limbic and hypothalamic regions as well. All the major nerve trunks, while they go directly to the cortex, also branch into the reticular formation. Apparently it is the job of the reticular formation to keep a person conscious.

While it may at times be convenient for psychologists and educators to speak about three domains—the cognitive, affective, and motor—as though they were separately manipulatable entities, the research suggests it is the nature of the *interaction* between parts of the brain that matters. The reticular formation receives information from the limbic, hypothalamic, afferent, and cortical areas. In turn it sprays out messages, some back to the cortex and others out over the efferent paths to the muscles.

The reticular formation seems to serve a kind of gatekeeping function. When sensory inputs, such as sound, arrive at the reticular formation, it apparently "decides" to which sounds to give attention. Based on its evaluation of the input, the recticular formation either wakes up or leaves the cortex in peace.

Arousing the reticular formation

The role the reticular formation plays in selective listening is not clear but has to be of great interest to teachers. If a whole array of sounds arrive at the ear, a human being can select from the array what he wishes to attend to and disregard the rest. In a classroom, for example, through all the clutter of voices that can happen at any instant, a child may be able to follow one conversation and ignore another. Both sets of sounds enter the ears but one is suppressed and treated as noise while the other passes through and is interpreted as meaningful. In addition, if several conversations go on around him at one time and he is fairly familiar with the content, a student will be able to report what transpired in more than one of the conversations. In other words, as long as there is no substantial amount of new learning that must occur, the reticular formation will apparently let both sets of messages through to the cortex. That the limbic system is also involved is illustrated by the fact that if one of the messages is emotionally fraught for the listener, e.g., some kind of murder story, then only that message will be heard. If the listener's name is mentioned in one of the conversations, his attention will be drawn to that discussion. A person's name arouses some emotion—signaling him to go on "alert" status.

As the English researcher Donald Broadbent has shown, verbal *instructions* can have an effect on the way

Subject can pay attention selectively.

If content of both messages is familiar, he picks up both.

If a message is emotionally "hot," it grabs his attention.

FIGURE 7-2

Dichotic listening experiments raise interesting questions concerning what a student can absorb when working under a variety of conditions in the classroom. Frequently, many sounds impinge on him simultaneously.

the reticular formation functions (Figure 7-2). Instructions can dispose a person to hear one message rather than another. In experiments on dichotic hearing, different messages are sent through each earphone. A person may be instructed to pay attention to the message coming in through the left phone. Normally, people can *ignore* the message coming into the right phone. If, however, something comes through that phone which has some emotional value for them, they are likely to pick it up. For example, attention will be distracted from the left phone if a person hears his own name coming in through the right phone.[1]

Messages that have the potential for arousal get through the reticular gate and reach the cortex. The cortex "wakes up," does something to the information, and fires a message back to the reticular body. The reticular formation apparently evaluates the state of things and determines whether to maintain alert or to return the cortex to a lower level of activity. If it makes the latter decision, then the muscles get a signal to relax and even the size of the pupillary opening in the eye may change. The reticular formation permits the body generally, as well as the cortex, to fall back to a relatively lower level of activity.

EMOTIONS

Conceptual conflict

The evidence indicates that emotional states can prepare the brain for learning and maintain it in an alert condition. Of course it is possible to imagine emotional overloading of a nervous system such that the reticular formation could not function to integrate the interactions between the cortex (center of thinking) and limbic (center of feeling) systems. When the reticular formation fails to function properly as happens upon exposure to certain drugs, then the unchecked, unintegrated firing of messages into the cortex and the miscoordination of the cortical output can set off rebounding cycles of messages that produce hallucinations as well as barrages of pulses that disrupt previously formed connections.

[1]D. E. Broadbent, "Attention and the Perception of Speech," *Scientific American,* April 1962, pp. 143–151.

As we shall see a little later, conceptual conflict has high arousal potential. When two ideas do not seem to be compatible, when information does not seem to fit with what one already knows, a state of mental conflict exists. The cortex is maintained by the reticular formation in an "on" condition as long as ideas fail to be integrated. The fuel that drives inquiry along seems to come from intense interactions among the hypothalamic, limbic, reticular formation, and cortical portions of the brain. If teachers can produce situations in which, for example, there exists room for differences of interpretation, students will attempt to resolve those differences. Cognitive conflict is part of inquiry. As long as it exists, the emotional investment that accompanies it maintains the student in an alert condition. Arguments between students, e.g., discussions in which students express differences of opinion or report experimental results that do not match expectations, tend to maintain the reticular formation in the "on" condition. This, in turn, keeps the cortex working on the problem until the conceptual conflict is resolved.

There is some evidence from the research of Berlyne[2] that conceptual conflict in small doses may actually be rewarding, provided the individual has a history of past successes at resolving such conflicts. In problem-solving situations, for example, mental conflict or tension is created when a student thinks of a number of possible solutions or explanations. As long as the student has no basis for preferring one of the solutions, a state of mental conflict potentially exists. If he chooses one solution as most likely and still is not certain whether it is correct, he will suffer some doubt. *Doubt* is a form of conceptual conflict. In an effort to reduce the doubt—to get rid of it—the student may search for all kinds of support for the solution he chose. These two different kinds of conceptual conflict, perplexity and doubt, drive inquiry along.

Incompatible ideas which a student may have in his head will not produce any mental conflict until some situation arises which forces him to have to make choices between competing possibilities. The whole body is somehow involved when a person's attention is focused during problem solving. Galvanometers attached to the surface show changes in the electric potential of the skin. The

[2]D. E. Berlyne, "Uncertainty and Conflict: A Point of Contact Between Information-Theory and Behavior-Theory Concepts," *Psychological Review,* vol. 64, 1957, pp. 329–339.

papillary openings may also change in response to the degree of conceptual conflict that a person experiences. Thrust into a condition of conceptual conflict, either as a result of something that happens during instruction or as a consequence of his own thought processes, a student either struggles with it or flees from it. On the one hand he may exhibit flight behavior—all kinds of avoidance moves ranging from simple refusal to have anything to do with the situation to becoming ill. On the other hand he may try to resolve the conflict by seeking new knowledge or trying to reorganize the ideas he already has. In teaching it is a delicate matter to so select and present problems that they provoke enough arousal to sustain inquiry but do not induce excessive mental conflict leading to flight behavior. Apparently, relief from conceptual conflict and doubt is sufficiently rewarding to promote those inquiry behaviors that are seen as a means of alleviating the situation.

Curiosity

Human beings, like other vertebrates, frequently engage in spontaneous exploratory behavior. Novelty prompts spontaneous exploratory behavior. Large, bright, or shiny objects, for example, have been known to attract fish, birds, and men. On encountering something never experienced before or never experienced in a particular context, people usually explore it. Human beings ask questions—they may directly probe the object or situation (i.e., experiment) or they may process information already stored in the brain. Information stored in the form of language or in other abstract forms permits the human being to seek to satisfy his curiosity by thinking and questioning as well as by securing information directly through acting on the environment. Novelty arouses emotions, usually emotions that are regarded as pleasant. It stimulates exploratory behaviors that can be interpreted as indicators of curiosity.

Attention

Thinking, reasoning, and problem definition do not start until something captures our attention, i.e., until the reticular formation sends messages to the cortex. *Large, bright, contrasting, or other predominant attributes of the environment* compete strongly for our attention, provided they are somewhat novel, i.e., we have not become habituated to them. We also pay attention to *systems that change with time,* especially if they change rapidly or unexpectedly. In the course of experimenting, students become excited when things change suddenly or in ways they did not expect. That is why it is often a useful teaching device to ask them to predict results and to elicit an explanation for the prediction prior to doing the experiment. If events go as predicted, the outcome is rewarding. If events do not go as predicted, then attention is focused on finding out why. Reward comes from settling the conceptual conflict. Note that both kinds of reward, those arising from confirmed expectations and those from reducing conceptual conflict, stem from the relationship that the student has to the situation rather than the relationship he has to the teacher. Reward potential that lies in the situation is more likely to induce sustained inquiry than is some pattern of overt verbal rewards administered by the teacher. Overt verbal sanctions and other kinds of tangible rewards and punishments may be useful in concept learning, in drill situations, or in inhibiting undesirable behavior. Where there must be sufficient repetition to ensure that the information gets "wired in" to the brain, some external incentive may be necessary. In problem-solving situations, overt verbal rewards probably get in the way. They may block productive conceptual conflict.

In an experiment, then, *if the results do not correspond to our expectations,* to our stored impressions, we are especially likely to find our attention captured. When the *difference between a pattern observed in the environment and a recollected pattern* exceeds some tolerance level, we have conflicting information. That captures our attention. If the new pattern does not "fit" the old one, the resulting conceptual conflict must somehow be eliminated.

If, on the other hand, some pattern begins repeating itself and keeps on doing so, the reticular formation finally represses the signal or filters it out in some way so that it no longer is presented to the cortex. Thus excessive drill may encourage shutdown of the attention mechanism, as might continual shouting for order. Stimuli that are no longer novel tend to be ignored. Patterns of behavior that are so well rehearsed they fall into the category of habits no longer receive attention.

CONCEPTUAL CONFLICT AND PROBLEM SOLVING

Cognitive or conceptual conflict, which is pertinent to problem solving and investigation, is likely to be produced under the following circumstances:

1 Information coming to the person from outside or as a result of internal thought processes fails to "fit" with his *expectations*.

2 A set of possible solutions or alternative decisions is made. If more than one of them seems reasonable, the person is confronted with a need to make and justify a *choice*.

3 Given that a person has made a decision or a choice or drawn a conclusion, he may be uncertain that it is the most probable conclusion or the best choice. He is in *doubt*.

4 A person encounters some entirely new event or object. *Novelty* prompts exploratory behavior that is likely to persist until he has found a way to incorporate the new experience.

Conceptual or cognitive conflict probably represents one of the best means for stimulating learning and problem solving, since as long as a state of mental conflict exists, the reticular formation will keep the cortex at work. *Novelty* generally turns on the reticular formation. Boredom leads to its shutdown. From a teaching point of view, if you wish the learner to remain in a state of active cortical stimulation for a sustained period, you must confront the student regularly with new or unexpected events and ideas. Alternatively you present familiar events in a novel context. If these ideas upset his existing beliefs at least a little, if they run counter to his expectations, then the probability is high that he will engage in exploratory and investigative activities that lead to reduction of the conceptual conflict.

No one will be provoked to inquire or to learn or study what he already knows, or thinks he knows, or what he considers at the moment to be irrelevant. He either has to encounter the material in some novel way that produces conflict with what he currently believes or he has to see phenomena in some entirely new set of relationships. The old adage "Start with what the pupil knows" runs exactly counter to what we would do if we took seriously the description of how the parts of the brain probably function together. Familiar events do not provoke inquiry unless they are seen in some new context. On the other hand, familiar events, experiences, and ideas may serve as useful analogies once the learner or researcher starts to work on a problem. They may suggest how to solve a problem.

In some stages thinking hurts. When a problem genuinely bothers someone enough so that the reticular formation alerts the cortex, the emotions rise and prevent the cortex from turning off until it has discovered, tried out, and evaluated some possible solutions. During that period before a solution emerges, older memory traces that might be relevant or provide a hint about its solution are probably called up or selected out and compared with the new information and ideas. These traces suggest new questions which mean getting new information or thinking about existing information differently. During this period in problem solving, a person generally feels some anxiety. He often suffers from feelings of inadequacy. He alternately gets angry, confused, frustrated, and excited in a way that will not let him turn away from the problem. Often he works toward a solution in little bits, solving simpler problems until something in the conglomerate suggests the direction he should take.[3]

Once possible solutions emerge, the person begins to evaluate them mentally. In this stage he processes ideas very rapidly and often feels intensely exhilarated. He may work long hours without rest. Indeed, measurements of muscle tone, tension, and speed of work in this period suggest that all parts of his body are functioning at higher levels. Once the cortex arrives at an acceptable solution, it signals the reticular formation which in turn slows down its rate of firing back to the cortex and signals the motor system to relax. At this stage, problem solvers usually report a sense of fatigue coupled with relief and, after a time, a desire to sleep. Thinking, or problem solving, while it has its pleasurable moments, certainly is a turbulent process. This latter phase is intrinsically rewarding for many individuals. Brewster Ghiselin[4] has collected de-

[3]George Polya's highly interesting and very readable paperback *How to Solve It* suggests that a person adopt this as a deliberate procedure. When unable to solve a particular problem, try to find some simpler problem which resembles it that you know how to solve and see whether, by analogy, a solution occurs to you. Princeton University Press. 1945.
[4]Brewster Ghiselin, *The Creative Process,* A Mentor Book, The New American Library, New York, 1955. Also see Anne Roe, *The Making of a Scientist,* Dodd, Mead and Co., New York, 1952.

scriptions of these feelings as given by thirty-eight famous people.

The brain and its subsidiary neural organs have to arrange the stimuli gathered; i.e., the data and ideas produced in an experiment must be arranged into *patterns*. The brain has to select relevant stimuli from the great barrage of stimuli it receives. It has to *compare* the patterns it forms with what it already has in storage in the form of *memory traces*. It is important that a person stay alert and interested until he can unscramble the variables and put them into some sensible relation to each other.

This process probably involves sequencing messages, or converting them into spatially arranged patterns; checking to see whether the pattern compares with anything already stored; and deciding on some action. If one of the suggested actions seems likely to produce a solution, the cortex signals the reticular formation to turn down the "juice." *It is at this turning-off point in the operation that a teacher may be especially interested in intervening.* The student may treat a problem at too low a level of complexity. He may be satisfied before its ramifications are sufficiently explored. That can happen when the problem produces too little arousal initially, or when it exceeds the capacity of the brain to handle it at that point in its development. If there do not exist sufficient relevant memory traces that might be confronted by the input, then arousal may not occur in the first place. What we focus on depends in part on what we already have in our heads.

Previous experience governs to some extent the kinds of data and events that capture attention. A person whose background is relatively rich in experiences is more vulnerable to conceptual conflict than is the person whose experiences have been extremely limited.

Whether a given situation or some particular piece of information creates a problem for a person depends on how well it fits his previous knowledge or on whether the flow of events somehow makes sense to him. Consider the short piece of conversation that introduced this chapter as an example of a situation in which there is cognitive conflict for one student but not for another. In this short burst of conversation, we can observe some of the kinds of learning and thinking problems that the study of physical phenomena presents and which can produce arousal.

First there is the matter of making observations, choosing relevant properties to pay attention to. Then there is the task of associating or correlating events with each other, establishing relations between input and output.

What is supposed to happen in the lesson is that the blueprint paper, which is white to begin with, turns dark where it is exposed to light and remains white where it is kept from light. All three children correctly observe that one part of the paper is dark and the other part is white, but Richard is confused about how this happened. There are several possible explanations for his confusion any or all of which might be involved. He may have paid no attention to which part of the paper was in the light and which was in the dark at the start of the experiment. On the other hand, he might have paid attention to that but could not remember which end of the paper was which. Not having any idea that light would be relevant to any outcome of the experiment, he may have simply failed to think it important to note which part of the paper had been kept covered and which part had been exposed to light. Of course he might have forgotten what the paper looked like to begin with, i.e., he might have lost the referent from out of his active memory.

Kathy has no problem. Her ideas fit together. Part of the paper was white. Later it turned dark. She treated the two parts differently. The section kept out of the light did not change. The section left in the light did change: Kathy (1) made a correct association of input variables (light or no light) with outcome variables (dark or light ends of the paper) and (2) correctly stored in memory or on a sheet of paper (record keeping) the sequence of events. The problem for her is solved.

Such detailed analysis of approximately 45 seconds of dialogue about blueprint paper is justified if it points out how complicated learning and thinking processes are and how highly individualistic in their expression they can be. Ultimately, students may arrive at the same solution to a problem, but the routes they take to get there differ in their properties. From the point of view of the teacher interested in improving the inquiry skills of students, the most useful diagnostic data come from analyses which focus more on the process than on the product of inquiry. From many such observations and analyses of a wide variety of situations, we may eventually learn how to get the reticular formation into action so that it will

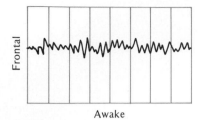

FIGURE 7-3
Alpha rhythm brain wave. See *Scientific American,* **November 1960, p. 226.**

maintain the cortex in the "on" condition long enough to engage in increasingly sophisticated problem-solving ventures.

In any case, by encouraging exchange of information and ideas among students, there is a better chance to maintain a state of conceptual conflict long enough for two things to happen. First, the students will persist in their investigations long enough to arrive at sufficiently good solutions in the eyes of the teacher as well as their own. Second, in their attempts to reduce the conceptual conflict, students will be forced to think about the information in so many different ways that it will be likely to be remembered.

Wiring concepts and generalizations into the brain often requires more than one trial. A state of conceptual conflict tends to force rehearsal of information as well as frequent appraisal of relationships between variables.

The reticular formation has much to do with the *focus* and *maintenance of attention* as well as with the general integration of sensory and motor messages. There is a developmental facet to the functioning of the reticular formation as well as to other brain functions. Infants up to the age of three or four months are normally incapable of manifesting integrated attention. Instead they exhibit undifferentiated, unselective responses to stimuli. After the onset of the alpha rhythm, which is visible in an electroencephalographic picture of the brain waves, infants manifest a higher degree of consciousness (Figure 7-3).

Brain function generally will be impaired if children fail to receive sufficient environmental stimulation. The potential for development may exist, but the necessary biochemical changes that must occur in order for the potential to be realized depend on all kinds of stimulation. Just as malnutrition can stunt brain development, an environment that is educationally impoverished can stunt mental development. Each year that a child is deprived of appropriate adult models and feedback, the chances that the deficiency can eventually be overcome seem to grow smaller.

STEREOTYPIC RESPONSES

As man broke free from stereotypic responses, he broadened the environmental niches to which he could adapt. The ability to adjust responses to the environment on the basis of internally created symbolic structures conferred a remarkable degree of adaptive potential on man.

All the flexibility that man has available to him comes about as he frees himself from dependence on perceptual or literal input and as he gains facility in symbolically representing the world to himself. As he reduces his stereotypic responses, he increases his options. He also becomes less subject to superstitious fears.

By way of contrast, consider for a moment some instances of genetically controlled, stereotypic patterns that are so rigidly enforced that the adaptive potential of an organism remains very limited. Dilger studied the nesting behavior of different kinds of lovebirds. The basic routines for building nests come "wired in" at birth. A young bird requires only a brief period to learn them. Different species have characteristic patterns. The peach-faced lovebird builds its nest by tearing up small strips, tucking some of them into its wings and carrying *several strips at once* to the nest site. On the other hand, the Fischer lovebird always works with *one strip* at a time. What would happen, Dilger wondered, if these two different kinds of patterns occurred in the same bird. What happens if a Fischer mates with a peach-faced lovebird? Would the hybrid inherit two competitive patterns for carrying strips. How would it act?

According to Dilger, when the hybrid offspring starts nest building, it acts completely confused. Instead of the brief time its parents needed to learn to build nests, the hybrid offspring needs three years to perfect its bill-carrying behavior. It finally ends up carrying just one piece at a time, but even after three years of trial and error, it still tries to tuck extra strips in among its feathers in the manner of its peach-faced parent.[5] Here the organism clearly has no ability to represent its problem symbolically and then to compound a solution. The lovebird is tied to *what is*, not to *what could be*.

A young human starts out in life tied to what is. Given appropriate environmental stimuli with which to interact, and a language system for encoding and storing his experiences, he is free to focus more and more on *what could be*. Thus, gradually, he wins from the environment some control over his own fate. He accomplishes this by increasing his ability to represent situations and

[5]William C. Dilger, "The Behavior of Lovebirds," *Psychobiology, The Biological Bases of Behavior,* readings from *Scientific American,* W. H. Freeman and Company, San Francisco, 1967.

problems symbolically, to abstract their salient properties and to manipulate internally, as well as externally, generated patterns. It is a primary function of education to help him learn to represent problems symbolically.

ADAPTIVE POTENTIAL AND INTELLIGENCE

The adaptive potential of an organism depends in part on how free an organism can become of stereotypic or rigid responding when necessity requires it to do so. African bushmen, Eskimos, and big city dwellers all require particular sets of aptitudes and knowledge if they are to function adaptively in their cultural and environmental contexts. Confronted with problems, each must be able to invent solutions. Different cultural contexts call for different sets of aptitudes to be realized if an individual is to function adaptively. Halstead developed a concept of biological intelligence that relates to adaptive potential.[6] Halstead searched for some fundamental indicators of adaptive potential that might be applicable in all kinds of cultural contexts and ecological niches. By studying normal people as well as those who had suffered brain damage through accidents or drugs, Halstead was able to localize where certain kinds of brain activity probably occur. This work suggested that the brain is highly differentiated. From a study of people with brain lesions in a given location, for example, it was possible to show that speech production could be damaged while speech interpretation remained unimpaired.

Halstead measured fifteen variables using 5,000 stimulus materials of different levels of complexity directed to the eye, ear, and sense of touch. All responses were nonverbal in character. Out of the fifteen variables, he extracted four mental factors. He labeled the factors as follows: *judgment,* or the ability to organize repetitive or recurrent elements into principles or categories; *power,* the arousal potential of the cortex (through the reticular formation); *memory,* for organization and form as well as for details of spatial relationships; *modality,* or the availability of organized routes for inputs and outputs of different kinds. The battery of tests have been administered to all kinds of normal groups as well as to groups damaged cerebrally, metabolically, and by drugs, and

[6]W. C. Halstead, *Brain and Intelligence,* University of Chicago Press, 1947.

have proven to be very sensitive to different kinds of impairments. Interestingly, the battery is proving to be relatively "culture free," a fact that one would hope for if the tests do assess overall biological adaptive potential.

To illustrate what consequence this multiple-aptitude conception of the brain has for education in general and for science in particular, consider an interesting investigation made by Susan S. Stodolsky and Gerald Lesser of Harvard University. They selected four aptitudes that seemed to be closely related to school success: verbal aptitude, reasoning aptitude, number facility, and space conceptualization. *Verbal aptitude* is the single best predictor of academic success particularly in the social sciences. The most commonly used intelligence tests in public schools are primarily verbal facility tests. The instrument used by Stodolsky and Lesser simply provided a measure of the extent of recognition vocabulary that the children in their study exhibited. The *reasoning-aptitude* measure assessed the ability to weave together ideas and to draw inferences from them. The *number-facility* test assessed skill in addition, subtraction, multiplication, and division. The aptitude tapped by the forth measure is of special interest in science, engineering, and architecture —and as will be suggested later, may be involved in certain kinds of reading problems. The *space-conceptualization* measure gives some indication of the skill a student has for recognizing and using spatial relations between objects, visualizing movements of objects, and imagining their appearance under different rotations. This aptitude correlates well with success in mechanics, drafting, and art as well as engineering.

In one of their studies Stodolsky and Lesser gave these four aptitude tests to children from two socioeconomic levels in Boston and New York.[7] Their intent was to study the influence that various *patterns* of scores are likely to have on the quality of school performance. They asked the following question: Is there some benefit to be derived from matching instructional strategies to patterns of mental ability? (See Figure 7-4.)

Right now in curriculum writing, at least in science, little or no attention goes to adjusting the formats in which content is presented to make some units available in alternative forms. The two investigators tried an experiment. They planned some lessons designed to capitalize

[7]Susan S. Stodolsky and Gerald Lesser, "Learning Patterns in the Disadvantaged," *Harvard Educational Review*, vol. 37, no. 4, Fall 1967, pp. 546–593.

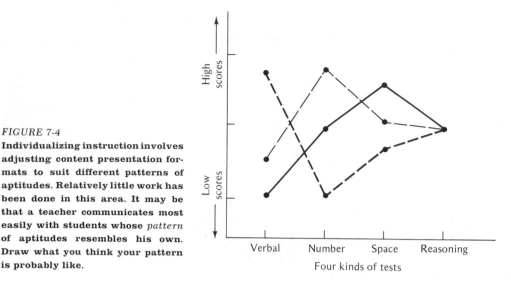

FIGURE 7-4
Individualizing instruction involves adjusting content presentation formats to suit different patterns of aptitudes. Relatively little work has been done in this area. It may be that a teacher communicates most easily with students whose *pattern* **of aptitudes resembles his own. Draw what you think your pattern is probably like.**

on a child's strengths and to minimize the load on less-strong aptitudes. "For example, in teaching mathematical functions to children strong in Space Conceptualization but weak in Numerical Facility, we use graphical presentation; in teaching the same concept to a child strong in Number Facility but weak in Space Conceptualization, we rely on the manipulation of numbers in tabular form."[8]

The two investigators did not try to diminish the conceptual complexity of the content. All they did was to alter the format for presentation to conform to particular *patterns* of aptitudes. They then presented the various formats to children according to the following plan: Some of the children received presentations that were compatible with their patterns and some received presentations that were definitely not compatible. Stodolsky and Lesser measured the time it took for learning as well as the amount of learning that took place. They found that correct matching of format with mental profile produced variation in gains, but net gains were substantial. *Incorrect matching, however, produced insignificant gains.* In fact the investigators reported that it was somewhat easier to produce destructive mismatches than uniformly good matches.

Careful analysis of curriculum, e.g., by means of the technique of task analysis (see Chapter 16), would show

[8]Ibid., pp. 580–581.

the extent to which particular sets of lessons make demands on each of these four abilities. With a child's profile in mind, as well as his or her own, a teacher might find alternative ways of communicating comparable information.

Recently investigators working on reading problems under a grant from the National Institute of Health found that children who are high on the space conceptualization factor are likely to have reading problems. Dr. Jean Symmes of the National Institute of Child Health and Human Development and Dr. Judith L. Rapoport of the Georgetown University School of Medicine found that boys who excel in building models and who can remember and produce patterns better than their peers tend to be poor readers. This ability, which is useful in the sciences, namely, three-dimensional spatial visualization, may make these children mistake certain letters for others. For example, with a high facility to imagine in three-dimensional space, letters in two-dimensional space, such as *b, p, q,* and *d,* which are all the same form simply reversed or inverted or both, could easily be mistaken; a *b* could be an upside-down *p* or a *d* viewed from in back. Such children might profit from a study of science and geometry before studying reading, and arithmetic.

In any event, the existence of different patterns of mental aptitudes leads to the inference that instructional practices could produce better effects if they were adapted accordingly. A child receiving content in an incompatible format needs more time in order to break the material up into segments and to convert it into a format he can understand. Since the teacher also has a profile to live with, it will be necessary to work especially carefully with children whose profiles are markedly different, since he will tend to transmit information with strategies that match his own pattern.

Probably the great contribution that new science programs make to an eventual solution of the problems presented by the presence of so many distinctive mental patterns concerns the direct access of the children to phenomena. If the classroom situation is such that students can do a great deal of talking with each other as they work on gathering, organizing, and drawing inferences from data, a natural accommodation process will take place. Each individual begins with data of direct experience, clarifies it through talk (argument), hears how people with different aptitude profiles interpret the system, and thus has access to a wide variety of models and a great deal of information.

TIME AND LEARNING

While the exact nature of the electrochemical interactions that must occur to establish a new pattern or to activate an old one is not even now entirely understood, the fact remains that it takes time for pathways to form, for integration to occur, and for sufficient rehearsals to be carried out to get some stabilization of the learning. Certain biochemical processes apparently need to take place when an organism is learning. For example, Hyden and Egyhazi[9] studied changes in the amount of RNA (ribonucleic acids) in cells of the cortex of right-handed rats who were being taught to use the left hand to collect food from a tube. The areas of the sensory-motor cortex that control which hand will be used were identified. There is one such area in the left hemisphere and one in the right hemisphere. The investigators found a significant increase in the amount of nuclear RNA on the side of the cortex that was involved in learning. Nerve cells and glial cells removed in the early stages of learning showed much less of an increase in RNA than in later stages. There are a complex set of specific chemical changes that seem to occur as part of the process in which an organism encodes information. The research suggests that one trial learning is usually not sufficient to produce biochemical action for learning to occur.

Brain proteins carry information. They seem to be the vehicle for storing specific information. After a time they break down. It is an interesting and fascinating question for research to find out how long-term memory is maintained.

Some of learning probably involves the synthesis and transport of compounds across cell membranes. When children try to map experience into language, the encoding and decoding processes take time, especially as the children probably suffer from a version of the "lovebird syndrome." At certain stages their intellectual systems cannot easily resolve the conflict between literal input

[9] M. Hyden and E. Egyhazi, "Changes in RNA Content and Base Composition in Cortical Neurons of Rats in a Learning Experiment Involving Transfer of Handedness," *Proceedings of the National Academy of Science,* vol. 52, 1964, pp. 1030–1035.

and symbolic messages. They will tend to be bound or constrained by the appearances of things (perceptual binding) and that binding will limit the level of problem solving in which they can engage. The process of consolidation of previous learnings into a new pattern takes time and engenders considerable emotional heat, which keeps the cortex working. To receive, recognize, and respond adaptively to stimuli from the environment requires the human being to engage in a multistaged process, each stage of which consists of subprocesses or subroutines. The time necessary for processing depends on how complex the task or problem that confronts the person is, on what he has in storage, and on the speed at which appropriate biochemical processes can occur.

In reaction-time experiments, Sternberg studied the memory-scanning times that subjects required to produce appropriate responses.[10] He found, as we might expect, that subjects responded to item-recognition tasks more rapidly than to context-recall tasks. In an item-recognition tasks, the subject only has to recognize whether a certain word is on a list presented to him. In a context-recall task, he has to remember its exact location, i.e., he has to store positional information about the word. In the item-recognition task, the subject always has only two response alternatives no matter how long the list is—either the word is on the list or it is not. But in the context-recall task the number of alternatives to which he must respond increases as the list increases, since the number of places where the word could appear also increases. Since most of the learning which one does in science is essentially contextual in nature and calls for far more complex operations than Sternberg's subjects had to employ, the additional processing time which a learner requires must be taken into account in instruction. This last caution must be taken seriously since research that I have done in classrooms shows that teachers frequently give students an average of only 1 second to begin an answer to a question. If the student pauses for longer than 0.9 seconds in the course of giving an answer, the teacher is likely to interject a comment or another question. These findings will be discussed in Chapter 8.

Cerebral processes seem to be biochemical or electrochemical in nature. What is puzzling about these proces-

[10]Saul Sternberg, "Memory-Scanning; Mental Processes Revealed by Reaction-Time Experiments," *American Scientist*, Winter 1969, vol. 57, no. 4, pp. 257–421.

ses, however, is the dramatic speed at which they do occur —more rapidly than one would predict from knowledge of the chemistry of the situation. Nevertheless, they do not go on so fast or with so few rehearsals or opportunities to evaluate alternatives that students can be expected to learn under such short wait-times. Sternberg's work suggests recognition learning may go on under such conditions, but context learning probably will not.

SUMMARY

1 The reticular formation, a small organ buried deep in the brain, seems to be responsible for arousing attention and for keeping the cortex working on a problem.

2 Conceptual conflict has high arousal value. It induces sustained inquiry behavior in many people.

3 Conceptual conflict which leads to investigative behavior by a student may be produced in the following ways:

a Information coming to the person from an outside source or as a result of his own internal thought *fails to fit his expectations*.

b A *choice* must be made among alternative decisions.

c *Doubt* or uncertainty exists concerning the correctness of a decision or a conclusion.

d Curiosity is aroused by objects and events which are entirely *novel* or which appear in novel contexts, also by novel ideas which arise as a result of thought. ("Aha! experiences" may fall into this category.)

4 Exploratory or investigative behavior will fail to be aroused if the stimulus has the following properties:

a Is very familiar

b Is highly repetitious

c Is perceived to be irrelevant

What is familiar and boring to one person on account of his prior experience may not be to another.

5 Familiar experiences and knowledge of past procedures for solving problems can suggest how to proceed in new situations. Past experience can serve as a guide or as a basic metaphor. Given a complex problem, try to find a simpler one that

resembles it. Solve that. It may suggest how to proceed.

6 During learning, electrochemical changes go on in the brain. Studies of rat brains made before, in the course of, and at the conclusion of learning experiments show changes in brain proteins in specific sections of the cortex. Mental processing of information involves many complicated operations.

7 During inquiry, a person may alternately pass through stages of excitement, anxiety, depression, and elation. Emotions, provided they are not excessive, drive the brain and the rest of the body to work.

ACTIVITY 7-1
A CASE STUDY: ENVIRONMENT, TECHNOLOGY,
AND TRAINING—OR, WHAT IT TAKES TO BE AN
ALEUTIAN ESKIMO

The case study below is introduced to illustrate the inter-
connectedness of environment, technology, and education. As you read, do the following:

1 Identify the environmental variables the Eskimo
must face.
2 Identify the technological inventions he has made
for solving problems presented by the environment.
3 Identify the skills he must acquire in order to
survive.
4 Describe how the society teaches those skills.
5 Identify the people in the society who teach him.

K is a young Eskimo man who lives in the Aleutian
Islands. He and his Eskimo friends can do something that
no European or non-Eskimo can do. They can hunt from a
kayak. People who are not Eskimos can learn to paddle a
kayak with great skill. In fact, kayaking is now one of the
sports in the Olympic Games. People who are not Eskimos
can also learn to hunt very well if they do not use a kayak.
But only Eskimos can learn to hunt with a kayak. Why is
it that K and Eskimos like him can learn to hunt with a
kayak and no one else can?

Stop here: Try to explain what accounts for the fact
that non-Eskimos cannot hunt successfully from a kayak.

To obtain an answer to this question, you must learn
something about the kind of world in which Eskimo men
and women live. You must know something of how Eskimo adults train their children. This case will tell you about
a group of men and women who live in one of the coldest,
foggiest parts of the earth. It will tell you about how K
learns to paddle far out into the sea to hunt. It will try to
explain how K finds his way home even when the fog is
very heavy. It will describe the problem that faces K when
he hunts for and catches a humpback whale and tries to
tow him home in a kayak that weighs only thirty-five or
forty pounds. K's kayak is so light that he can pick it up
and carry it on land or across ice floes.

To understand how difficult and dangerous kayak
hunting is, you must know something about the Bering
Sea and the Aleutian waters. The water of the Bering Sea

is cold. American aviators whose planes sometimes crash into the sea will die of the cold if they are not pulled out of the water within 10 minutes. So if K makes a mistake and his boat turns over, he must be able to set it right side up again very fast. He can do that. It is one of the lessons he learned when he was very young. In fact, young Eskimos sometimes have contests to see who can do more kayak rolls the fastest. The better an Eskimo is at righting his boat, the better are his chances for survival while out hunting.

Even if K sets his boat upright, he still could have another problem. Suppose he got wet? The air is so cold that he would soon freeze. There is no way to get dry on an ice floe. If K turns over in his boat, he must not only right the boat, he must do it without getting wet. The way he keeps from getting wet is to wear special waterproof clothes, which his wife makes for him from the intestines or the tongue of a whale. Whale intestines and tongue may seem like unusual materials to use for clothing, but the women make them into excellent waterproof, windproof parkas for the kayak hunters.

Another problem K and his friends face is glare. Sunlight reflected off the ice and water is very bright. The bright light could damage K's eyes, even blind them. A blind Eskimo is useless in a community where every member must work to survive. The Eskimos wear goggles or more often a long wooden visor. They pull the visor down low over their foreheads. When the visor is pulled low, it cuts out glare and keeps dry, flying snow out of the Eskimo's eyes. In heavy fog, moisture drips off the end of the visor and does not get in the eyes.

What is it like to hunt in a kayak? Well, one thing is certain: A kayak hunter like K can never relax. Balancing a kayak is almost like riding a surfboard. The rider is always on a moving surface. He must continually change and adjust his position in the boat as he paddles up one wave and slides down another. If he throws a spear or harpoon, he must do it without capsizing his boat. Non-Eskimos cannot seem to learn the trick of harpooning without capsizing. That is one reason why they cannot be kayak hunters. K must also be a good judge of his own strength. He has to save energy to get himself and his catch home.

The Aleutian area where K lives may be foggy all day, every day, for weeks. But K goes off to hunt in this fog.

The land disappears from his sight very soon. If he catches sight of a humpback whale or a sea lion, he will start to follow the animal. He may stalk his prey for many hours through the fog. *When K or other Eskimos get far from home in the fog, how do they find their way back home?* He carries no navigation instrument. Even if he did, the navigation equipment would not help him in fog. If you have ever seen a heavy fog, you know how difficult it is to find your way from place to place even when you have streets and buildings to give you clues. Of course there are no obvious street signs on the water. People who are not Eskimos do not seem able to learn to kayak hunt in the fog. They get lost. That is another reason why Eskimos can hunt with a kayak and non-Eskimos must stay home in the fog.

The special training of Eskimo children must be very thorough and very rigorous. A child must learn and re-member all his lessons well because each time he goes out to hunt is like taking a final exam. If he flunks the test, it may cost him his life. In general, only Eskimos who pass the test every time they hunt live in the community, have children of their own, and pass on their knowledge to the next generation through special very tough mental and physical training.

What does K need to know to be a successful hunter? For one thing, he must learn to see accurately and do it quickly. For example, when he goes out to hunt, he may paddle along a shoreline that has many bays or inlets. He cannot waste time in a place that has no animals. His kayak sits very low in the water. He waits until a wave lifts it high and looks quickly around the bay. He tries to detect movement on or near shore that gives away the presence of an animal. His boat drops down into the trough of the next wave, and he must wait for another quick glance. He must also learn to hear at long distances and to figure out where a sound is coming from in the fog and what it means. One of the things he listens for is the breathing of a seal. Seals breathe air, and when they blow out the gases in their lungs, the sound can be heard for more than a mile. Another sound that K learns to listen for in the fog is the sound of surf against the land or ice. He must judge from the sound how close he is to land when visibility is poor.

Whenever he can, K tries to find an animal that is asleep. He has a good chance to sneak up on such an animal. Since his kayak moves through the water quickly and quietly, and since it is constantly washed by water and thus has no odor, the animal may not hear or smell K. Since K and his kayak sit low in the water and their color is dark like the water, K has a good chance to come upon an animal napping. For these reasons it is most practical for K to pursue an animal by sea. Sometimes his prey lies sleeping on an ice floe, often far from the edge of the ice. Now K has a problem. He must kill the animal eventually, but he would rather wound it enough to immobilize it, that is, to stop it from struggling, but not enough to kill it. His reasoning is that a dead animal is difficult to move, and some of the animals he will catch weigh a half ton or more. K would rather kill a bear, for example, over near the edge of the ice where it can be towed home through the water. It is easier to tow a big animal than to drag it across ice. Getting big animals like that to the edge of the ice floe is no easy matter. When he catches animals like the sea lion or the humpback whale, he wants to tow them home, but to do that he must keep the animal from sinking. An animal which still keeps air in its body is not so likely to sink. Clearly K cannot load 1,000 pounds of animal on a kayak which is only 13 or 14 feet long and weighs less than 40 pounds. Thus he uses, for example, a toggle-head harpoon which, if it lands right, will not kill the animal but will make it possible for K to tow the animal home.

If K finds birds, he tries to catch and strangle them so as not to ruin their skins, which his wife uses to make the family clothing.

So kayak hunting means that a man like K must learn to control his boat while throwing a harpoon. He must learn to move quietly and quickly. He must learn to find his way in the fog. He must learn to see and hear accurately. He must learn to hunt without killing until he has gotten his prey home or near the edge of land.

How did K and other Eskimos learn all these skills, and why cannot other people learn them? K's training began when he was one year old. He had to develop strong hands and arms in order to manage the paddling of his kayak, expecially when he throws a harpoon. For this reason Eskimo grandparents, who usually take care of the training while the parents work, play games with the young. The games teach him what he needs to know. In one of the games, the baby Eskimo takes hold of a bar near the ceiling of his dwelling and hangs by the hands until he cannot hold on any longer. Then he drops. At first his grandparents catch him, but after a while he must learn to land on his own feet quickly and gracefully. Thus, in time, he not only develops strength in his hands and arms but learns to fall through space and land right side up.

Another game that the grandparents play with the baby Eskimo strengthens and lengthens the muscles along the back of his shoulders and legs. While the grandparents sing to make the game more fun, they stand the young Eskimo up and put his arms straight over his head, pulling back on them as far as they can until the boy loses his balance. Someone catches him, and the game goes on. He tries to last longer and longer before he falls. The grandparents play the same game when the young Eskimo sits on a table. Someone holds his knees and someone else pulls back on his arms. He tries to resist the pulling and to sit up as long as he can. After a while he gets less and less help from the person holding his legs. In this way arm and leg muscles of a young Eskimo become elongated and strong. That means that when he hunts, he will be able to sit in the kayak and throw his harpoon without tipping his kayak. If you ever tried to sit on the floor and throw something very hard or far, you know it is not easy. The Eskimo's arm works like a catapult: the special training makes it possible for him to take a harpoon or spear, swing it straight back over his shoulder, and throw with great force and speed. No other group of human beings has developed this skill. No other group of human beings receives this kind of training or starts such rigorous training at so young an age.

Young Eskimos must learn to see and throw quickly with great speed because when they hunt they may need to hit an animal at a distance of as much as 120 feet. This is no simple task when you consider that the seal or sea otter, for example, may be going down in the trough of one wave, while the kayak hunter is rising upon the crest of another wave. So his target, as well as he himself, is moving. Clearly hunting on land is very simple compared to hunting with a kayak on water.

We have still not described how K and his friends find their way home in the fog. Apparently their ability to do this rests on their ability to remember very long chains of events. For example, K might start out with the wind blowing over his left shoulder coming from the southwest. He may begin to paddle, and as he moves through the water he must remember when his kayak changes direction. When he paddles in a new direction, the wind seems to come from another direction, perhaps over his right shoulder or perhaps in his face. As he stalks the animal, K must store in his mind the memory of every change in direction that he made in his boat in order to be able to retrace his way home. Not only must he remember what changes in direction he took, he must remember about how long he moved in each direction and judge about how fast he was paddling. Since he may be away on a hunt for as many as 15 hours and in that time he may stalk an animal for 4 or 5 hours, he must remember a great deal of detail about his movements.

Now of course sometimes the wind itself either dies or changes direction. What does an Eskimo do then? That is a question that apparently still has no answer. He does find his way home, but scientists who study Eskimos do not know for sure what clues Eskimos use to get home. Water currents may be the answer. Water currents do not change as fast as wind currents.

What happens to an Eskimo who is too old to hunt? Among the Aleutian Eskimos these people still are valuable members of the community. They not only train the young, but in summer they also bring in food that they collect in the intertidal zone. That is, along the coast as the tide comes and goes the aged, the women, and the children all collect seafood from tidal pools. They also fish for halibut close to land. The Aleutian Eskimos live in an area that is very rich in animal life. Of course the summer is very short; when the winter comes and brings the winter ice, only those who can travel far out on the ice to the edge of the water can bring in food. The community must depend on stored-up food in the winter and on what the strong, active hunters can catch by traveling far from home. In the summer everybody can and does help collect food in some way. That means that the size of the Eskimo population which lives along the coast can be much larger than the size of Eskimo populations which live way inland on the ice in North Central Canada. In that area there is no use for the aged since they cannot help with the hunt, nor are they so important for training the young. Generally Eskimos living inland do not live to become very old. When they can no longer help, they are left on the ice to die. Among the people in K's group, however, people may live very long. It is not uncommon for some people to reach one hundred years of age, and many live to be at least eighty. So if an Aleutian Eskimo does not fail his hunting tests, and if he does not contract a disease, he may expect to have a long life. Old, experienced hunters will teach him his trade. When K, in his turn, finishes his career as hunter, he will still be important to his family as a teacher of the new generation. How well the new generation survives depends, at least in part, on how well he trains the new young Eskimos.

Note: Concepts from Chapter 4 are especially applicable when considering differences in population characteristics of coastal and inland Eskimos.

REFERENCES

Lockard, J. David (ed.): *Seventh Report of the International Clearinghouse on Science and Mathematics Curricular Development, 1970,* a joint project of the American Association for the Advancement of Science and the Science Teaching Center, University of Maryland, College Park, Md., 1970. This is the seventh report in a series first issued in 1963. It summarizes on-going activities in the development of curricular materials in science and mathematics. Descriptions of projects in America and abroad are given. For each project the following information is supplied: project director; project address, staff; source of support; project history; commercial affiliations, if any; project objectives; methods of instruction used; specific subject, grade, age, and ability levels; materials produced; materials available for purchase; language(s) in which available; teacher preparation; project evaluation; and plans for the future. The zip code is 20742. Telephone area code 301, 454-4028.

Toffler, Alvin: *Future Shock*, Bantam Books, Inc., paperback, New York, 1970. Provides a turbulant but insightful description of factors with which education and curriculum must contend. Chapter 18 discusses education in the future tense.

A CLASSROOM may be regarded profitably as a system without doing too much violence to the idea of system, subsystem, and interaction developed earlier.

Recall that in a physical system if one component changes, some or all the other components may also change by virtue of the fact that the parts interact. We learn to search for those interactions. Similarly, interactions occur between teachers and children and among children, but we have not been as systematic in our study of those interactions. Just as in a physical system we can find evidence of interaction, so for the system called the *classroom,* evidence of interaction comes in detectable behavior, in words, and in noise.

A physical system becomes conceptually interesting to us when we begin to discover some regularities in its behavior; i.e., when its interactions are not totally random, the system begins to "make sense." If we regard the classroom as a dynamic system composed of many possible subsystems, we can borrow some of the strategies of science to help us discover useful patterns of relationships among its components. We can experiment on the system to discover patterns of inter-action. In short, we can invent concepts to help us make sense of data we already have, and we can develop theories that provide parsimonious guides for decision making. We may take the view, then, that the teacher can interact blindly in the system, but the payoffs will be greater for the teacher who experiments with a purpose.

As we go about the process of developing explanatory systems for classroom phenomena, we will do well to remember that the leap from evidence to inference is great. What makes one inference more desirable than another, given that both are reasonable? Usually we choose the one that explains the greater variety of data more economically. Theories based on data serve to reduce the apparent complexity of phenomena, and thereby make the systems of interest potentially controllable.

What evidence and what inferences we attend to depends on our intent, our knowledge at the time, and the particular "thought system" we employ. If, for example, a biologist, a geologist, a housing contractor, and a child cross a field together, it is unlikely that they will report the same observations when they reach the other side. Their various thought systems and interests cause them to focus selectively on some interactions and to ignore others. So, too, alternative ideas or theories regarding teaching and learning can be examined to see which are most helpful.

Consider the classroom to be like the field, full of complex interactions in need of simplification if we are to form any sound basis for making decisions. Imagine three adults—a teacher, a principal, a visiting parent—and *a child* barraged with those interactions. At the end of a science lesson, what will they report? What will they make of what they have observed? What mental organizers or constructs might they profitably employ to examine the classroom as a system? We shall proceed by reviewing some data we already have, adding new data at points, and then suggesting ways of thinking about the data. Once we evolve the ingredients of a thought system, we will use them to guide our inquiry even further. That inquiry will turn up at least as many questions as answers, which is a common experience in science, anyway, and ensures that the inquiry-minded person can stay in business for as long as he likes.

If you are in the classroom for any reason, whether as teacher, principal, parent, aide, or supervisor, your job is inquiry. The stuff of your inquiry lies in the system compounded of children, adults, and materials. The business of the children is to experiment with natural phenomena. Your business, on the other hand, is to experiment with instruction. Now, that turns out to be difficult because the minute you interact in the system, you become a part of it. You get involved. If you are not careful, you somehow come to think that everything that happens there, good or bad, stems from you alone; however, you—like any of the children—are only one ingredient, powerful, but nevertheless still only a part of a complex system of interactions.

To be inquiry oriented about a system in which you are also a dynamic component presents problems. No observer is outside the system he observes. The act of observing couples him to the system. Whether he will experiment on the system blindly or with purpose depends on whether he has any idea of how it functions.

To begin to understand interactions in the classroom, we must act on the faith any scientist employs, namely, that the behavior of the system is not entirely whimsical. There are regularities to be discovered in it, in spite of its complexities. Neither are we in a totally ignorant state about what might be important variables to explore. Just as in science, theory sometimes guides the pattern of exploration; here our view of science, and what it means to learn science, determines what data in the complex system of the classroom we will focus on, and what we shall ignore.

First, we examine briefly how three factors—*silence, sanctions,* and the form of *asking questions*—seem to be involved in successful teaching of current elementary science programs which emphasize inquiry. We consider findings of investigations in which these three factors played a part, and what payoffs might result from the classroom teacher's deliberate changing of these variables during science instruction. Next we consider some management and control aspects of science teaching.

In science programs which actually give children access to materials, and which can be even remotely characterized as oriented toward inquiry, ideas are supposed to grow out of that inquiry. Information that cues students regarding next steps is supposed to lie in the system of materials and in the conversations about outcomes of experiments. As we have already suggested in Part 1, one can form any heap of objects into many different arrangements or patterns. In any such heap lies more than one kind of experiment, more than one kind of result. In science as in law, any set of events or data may be subject to a variety of interpretations. Children need to learn that pertinent information lies in the interaction between them and the materials. What counts is what happens in the system of materials, and *what they make of it.*

Authority in science rests on evidence and on ideas that "work." Therefore, no particular point of view in the class is more sacred than another—not even the teacher's. In principle, the view that prevails is the one best supported by the evidence available at that moment. As knowledge about a phenomenon or problem accumulates, students have the right, indeed the obligation, to change their views, to try out new explanations, and so do teachers. It is hoped that you will pursue Part 2 in a spirit of inquiry.

CHAPTER 8

"I am afraid that if I wait longer, the class will get out of control. Everyone wants to talk. There is no time to wait."

—CLASSROOM TEACHER

Student: I thought as fast as I could, but he didn't let me finish. I needed to do one more thing to be sure.

—FIFTH-GRADER

"I don't know how to react any more. I thought I knew, but now I can't be sure. I can't wait all the time. Sometimes something really good happens, and sometimes they just sit and look at me. I think they have to learn to listen to each other too. I tried to stop repeating, but I am still afraid they might miss the point. (Pause.) Well, I'll keep trying but it isn't so easy."

—TEACHER IN THE SECOND WEEK OF CHANGING
TO LONGER WAIT TIMES

SCIENCE, SILENCE, AND SANCTIONS

OBJECTIVES

On completion of this chapter and its associated activities, you should be able to do the following:

1 State probable relationships between wait time and ten outcome variables.

2 Demonstrate an average acceptable wait time during a teaching session.

3 Design an experiment to study the influence of wait time on one or more outcome variables.

4 State a possible relationship between the variables of wait time and rewards, and the development of a sense of fate control.

INTRODUCTION

Suppose you had to sit all day every day answering questions. Suppose those questions were fired at you very rapidly, possibly at the rate of two or three questions per minute. Suppose you had to try to start an answer within one second. Suppose that when you did give an answer, the person asking the questions either reacted to the answer or asked another question within nine-tenths of a second. How do you think you would feel? Probably you would begin to suffer from what we might call "question shock."

Analysis of more than 800 tape recordings of science lessons taught by teachers in city, suburban, and rural schools indicates that the average teacher asks questions at the rate of two or three per minute. A student must start a reply on the average within one second. If he does not, the question will be repeated or rephrased, or someone else will respond. Once an answer is given, teachers react on the average within nine-tenths of a second by asking another question, or by commenting on the answer. Under this rapid regimen students rarely ask questions—even though modern science programs are meant to provoke questions, and to provide time to think about possible answers. It takes time to interpret experience, and it takes time to express complete thoughts. When wait times are so short, the students' answers tend to be fragmentary, and their thoughts have a corresponding tendency to be incomplete.

While a pattern of rapid questions and replies may be suited for instruction in some subjects, it seems to present some special problems for teachers who are trying to conduct inquiry-oriented science lessons. The basic notion that underlies all new science programs is the belief that in inquiry the information or relevant cues lie hidden in the materials and not in the head of the teacher. On the basis of evidence, students make inferences about how variables are probably related. Ideas can be modified or even discarded if the evidence requires. No particular point of view in the class is more sacred than another. What counts is what happens in the system of materials. Authority rests with the idea that "works." Evidence must support arguments. Teachers and students need time to think and to evaluate results and ideas. One second is hardly long enough.

WAIT TIME IN MODERN SCIENCE PROGRAMS

Current science programs depend heavily on an *intrinsic* rather than an extrinsic motivation model. Conceptual conflict is meant to drive inquiry along just as it does in the scientific enterprise. Conversation marked by the free flow of ideas is supposed to be a mark of an inquiry-centered program in science. When wait times are short and reward schedules are high, payoff for students comes in doing only one thing—focusing totally on the wants of the teacher. Modern science programs simply do not thrive under those circumstances. These programs seek to develop self-confidence in students by encouraging them to work out their ideas in experiments. Children judge the validity of their ideas by appraising the results. When predictions no longer work or when new information makes a point of view untenable, then pupils should be free to change their views.

It is in preserving for ourselves the *right to be wrong* that we gain courage to try out new ideas, to explore more alternatives, to objectively evaluate our own work as well as that of others. The authority for changing ideas comes from the results of experiments. Students have to learn to trust their ability to find answers. They have to feel safe in asking questions. They need time to think and a safe environment in which to speculate. It is doubtful that such short wait times and high reward schedules will foster a healthy climate for inquiry.

Analysis of tape recordings made while teachers conducted discussions with small groups or with a whole class showed that not only were wait times short, but as much as 20 percent of the talk of some teachers consisted of evaluative responses, such as "Good," "Fine," "OK," "Very nice," "All right," and "You know better." It may be that a high rate of overt verbal rewards in addition to short wait times tends to steal student attention away from the phenomena. Rather than evaluating their results on the basis of how well ideas fit together with data, students focus on trying to deliver behaviors that will please the teacher. To do that, they need to spend more of their time monitoring the teacher than the materials.

During problem solving, high rates of overt verbal reward may have negative effects by doing the following things:

1 Undermining confidence.
2 Acting as distractors.
3 Prompting premature termination of search.
4 Disposing a student to choose the first explanation that comes to mind rather than to seek alternatives.
5 Discouraging sharing of ideas. Students guard information until they can "dump it" on the teacher and collect praise.
6 Disposing a student to suppress innovative ideas for fear of being wrong.

EXPERIMENTING WITH INCREASED WAIT TIME

The focus in this chapter is on wait time as a variable. Later chapters will treat rewards, questioning, and fate control in more detail. It is a matter of some interest to know what would be the effect on the quality of inquiry if teachers experimented by increasing the average wait time. If average wait time were increased, what would be the influence, if any, on language and logic? There are two wait times to which one must give attention (Figure 8-1).

1 The pause that follows a question by a teacher. Here the teacher tries to wait before framing a second question. The students may answer quickly, but if they do not, the teacher tries to wait.
2 The pause that follows a burst of talk by students. The teacher tries to wait before responding, reacting, or asking another question. When a pause occurs here, the probability is higher that talk by students will be continued.

FIGURE 8-1
Wait time 1 and wait time 2 are potential pauses which may occur after a question (1) and after a response (2). When students are involved in explanation their thoughts are frequently expressed in bursts separated by pauses.

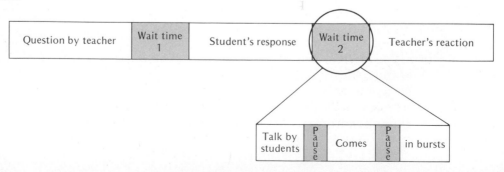

Groups of teachers agreed to work with me to explore what happens when average wait times are increased to 3 seconds or longer. We began to experiment to test the effect of the following factors on the verbal behavior of children:

1 Increasing the period of time that a teacher waits for students to construct a response to a question.
2 Increasing the period of time that a teacher waits before replying to a student's statement.
3 Decreasing the amount of reward and punishment delivered to students during discussions in which they are attempting to draw inferences from evidence or to explain phenomena.

A game model of instruction

To begin, we used small groups of students. Earlier work showed that a group of four or more students makes a satisfactory model of the speech patterns to be expected of whole classes. To make comparisons, instruction was conceptualized as a game in which there are two players. The teacher is one player and the set of students constitutes the other player. There are four kinds of moves that each player can make.

1 Structuring—in which a player gives directions, states procedures, and suggests changes. E.g., "Put the thermometer into the ice water."
2 Soliciting—in which a player asks a question. E.g., "Why do you think that happened?"
3 Responding—in which a player answers a solicitation, expands on a structuring move, reports data, or continues a line of reasoning. E.g., "I put the thermometer into ice water, and it went down to 4°C."
4 Reacting—in which a player evaluates statements made by the other player. It includes verbal rewards and punishments—e.g., "Good," "Fine," "OK," "I don't think that's right," and "That doesn't work the way you said, because this light is on."

In theory both players have equal access to all four moves. In practice the recordings show that the teacher monopolizes three of the moves: structuring, soliciting, and reacting. Students have a corner on responding. Yet modern science programs, properly done, should give the student player more access to the other moves. By categorizing the moves and plotting them approximately on a time line, which is based on which player makes the moves, the patterns of interaction can be clearly displayed. Figure 8-2*a*, for example, shows what the "inquisition" looks like. It is characterized by a rapid question-answer sequence with the solicitations coming

FIGURE 8-2

a **The "inquisition." Note: The heavy line separates the two players. The moves, soliciting (Sol), structuring (Str), reacting (Rea), and responding (Rsp), are listed above and below the line according to their relative frequency of occurrence in the usual classroom pattern. Teachers do most of the structuring and soliciting and the students do the responding.** *b* **The "conversation." In this pattern both players engage in all of the kinds of moves. Students begin to suggest experiments (structuring) or they converse and react to each other's statements (responding and reacting). In contrast to the inquisition pattern, more of the weight of the moves falls below the center line and the overall pattern exhibits more variety.**

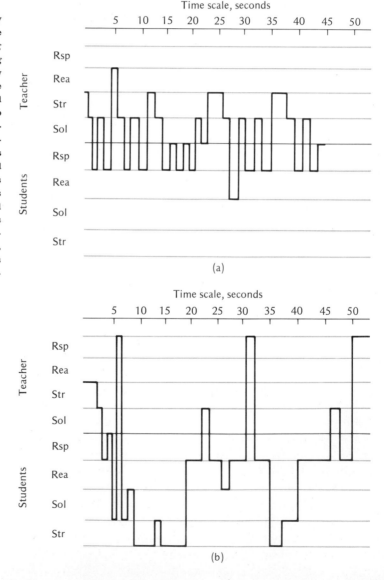

(a)

(b)

usually from the teacher. Figure 8-2*b*, on the other hand, shows what an inquiry pattern or a conversational pattern looks like. More of the kinds of moves are shared between the players. Students do more questioning, reacting, and structuring.

Measuring wait time

To measure wait time was a problem. By the time a stop-watch was punched for each pause, the discourse had moved on. We needed to find another way to measure wait time that would not be hampered by the fact that the time necessary to actuate the clock was very slow in comparison with the rate at which interactions occurred.

This measurement problem was partially solved by delivering the sound into a servo-chart plotter and making a kind of picture of the discourse. The plotter pen was adjusted to move horizontally when there were pauses and vertically when there was sound. As Figure 8-3 shows, the incidence of pauses as long as one second in a classroom where the teacher is not alerted to wait time is very small. (The height of the peaks simply indicates the amplitude of sound generated.) The chart plots also showed that children generate speech at a slower rate, on the average, than teachers do. This was reflected in the plots by the width of the peaks as well as by pauses in the body of their talk.

Initial observations

Servo-chart plot of talk as it came from students who had enough time to express themselves as fully as they wished showed something interesting. When a student is trying to explain or interpret some event, his speech does not flow smoothly (Figure 8-4). Instead it comes in bursts, separated by pauses of as much as 3 to 5 seconds. Mapping experience into language is an arduous process. When teachers react to one of the speech bursts without waiting for at least 3 seconds, the effect is to cut off the remainder of the student's thought. Apparently the reason for the high incidence of fragmented or phraselike, rather than propositional, responding that marks classrooms with short average wait times is brought about by the intervention of the teacher between the speech bursts. A teacher hears a phrase, does not realize more is probably coming and intervenes in the pause to react or to ask an-

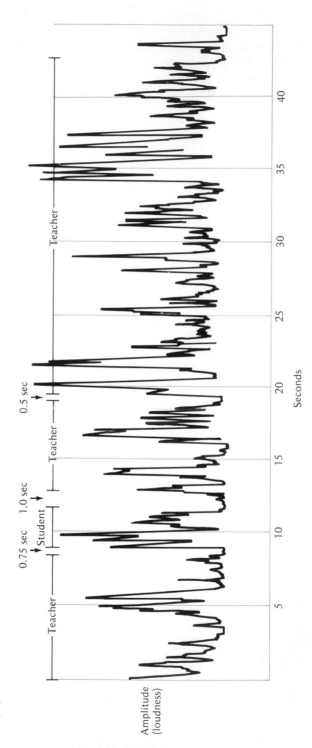

FIGURE 8-3

Servo-chart plot of discourse in an average classroom shows how rapid exchanges are. The needle tracks horizontally when there are pauses.

other question. Before the use of the servo-chart plotter, we had paid most attention to what was called the *first* wait time—the amount of time teachers gave to students to begin an answer. The chart plots showed us that the *second* wait time—the one which is potentially available *after* a student starts a response or after a student concludes a response—might be equally important. By holding on to that wait time, the teacher increases the probability that a student will improve his response or that another student will build on an idea initiated by the first student.

When the wait times are very short, teachers exhibit little flexibility in the responses they allow. Contests for control of the metaphors (e.g., steps versus xylophone) are common, and the teacher usually prevails. Examine, for example, the transcript on serial ordering in which students observed a teacher arrange a group of wooden dowels in a sequence from longest and thickest to shortest and thinnest (illustration, page 250; and Transcript 8-1). The teacher shows no more flexibility than a teaching machine. When the student says the display looks like a xylophone, the teacher who was "programmed" by the teacher's manual to think of "steps" simply could not use the xylophone response. A computer teacher would usually cycle back and repeat the question, possibly with more cues—which is what the human teacher did. A human

FIGURE 8-4

Servo-chart plot of student's speech when an explanation is being attempted. Notice the pauses in the body of the discourse. When the teacher reacts too quickly one only hears a fragment of an idea.

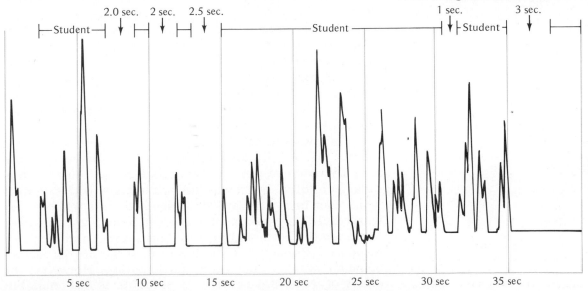

teacher who took *time to think* would be curious to know what properties of the dowel system prompted the "xylophone" response. Similarly, when one student says "It looks like train tracks," the teacher does not use this new metaphor. In such cases a teaching machine either goes on with whatever is next in its program, or it cycles back and asks the question again and again until the student gives the "right" answer—"steps." When the teacher's response is that rigid, students might as well be taught by a machine. As teachers succeed in increasing their average wait times to 3 seconds or more, they become better at using student responses—possibly because they are giving themselves more time to hear what each student says.

Effects of the teacher's expectations

A clear pattern of the teacher's expectations develops early in the history of each classroom. Differences in the wait time and reward patterns administered to children ranked at the top, as compared with those at the bottom, suggest that teachers unconsciously act in such a way as to confirm their expectations. Thirty-six teachers were asked to tell who, in their judgments, were their five best and five worst students. When we examined the amount of wait times given, on the average, to each group, we found that the top five received nearly 2 seconds to answer while the bottom five received slightly less than 1 second (0.9 seconds) to respond. That is, students rated as slow or less apt by teachers had to try to answer questions more rapidly than students rated as bright or fast. This result apparently surprised the teachers. As one of them said, "I guess we just don't expect an answer, so we go to someone else." This group of teachers then began to experiment deliberately with increasing wait times for poorer students. Response by "slow" students increased gradually, at first, and then rapidly.

The amount of sanctioning behavior directed toward the two groups also differed. The bottom-ranked children actually received more overt verbal praise than the top-ranked children, but it was difficult to know with certainty what was being rewarded. It seemed that teachers rewarded the top groups for correct responses, but they rewarded the bottom groups for both correct and incorrect responses. Presumably the intent of some of this reward behavior was to encourage participation. However, the effect of reward behavior on students is questionable.

Serial ordering, Transcript 8-1.

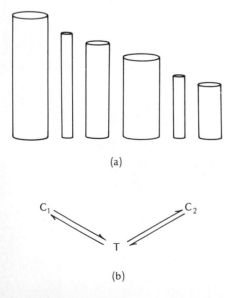

(a)

(b)

Transcript 8-1

Commentary		Moves	Actor		Time elapsed
	1	Reacts	*First child*	I know what.	
	2	Sol/Str/Sol	*Teacher*	I want you to . . . Can you see, Gail? All right, I'll turn it around this way so you can both see. Now just take a look and . . . look at them and see what you can tell me about them. [15-sec interval]	15 sec
3 Child opens with a metaphor: xylophone	**3**	Responds	*First child*	It's a xylophone.	
4 Teacher rejects metaphor and says try again. (Objects in front of the child described *as he saw them,* but description not accepted.)	**4**	Reacts/Sol	*Teacher*	Well, it's not really a xylophone. What does it look like?	
5 Child qualifies his metaphor. He is not willing to give it up. (Teacher missed chance to find out how the children saw the system by not asking in what way the arrangement looked like a xylophone.)	**5**	Responds	*First child*	You can make a xylo— xylophone.	
	6	Sol	*Teacher*	How did I arrange these? [30 sec]	30
7 Children at this age answer questions literally. Here the sequence of the teacher's moves is exactly described. Note child's emphasis on thickness.	**7**	Responds	*First child*	You sort of . . . you put one here, and you put the medium there, and you put the skinny one there, and then you put the other medium there, and then you put the fatso there, and you put the skinny one there.	
	8	Str	*Second child*	When you listen on there you'll see what we said.	
9 Teacher asks, "Why did I . . . ?" I.e., she asks children to guess her motives rather than getting more description of the dowels. This trains children to monitor the teacher more closely than the materials.	**9**	Reacts/Str/Sol	*Teacher*	That's right. [45 sec] But let's look at these sticks again. Why did I put them this way?	45
10 Child 2 knows the metaphor the teacher had in mind: Steps-metaphor 2.	**10**	Responds	*Second child*	Because you made a design full of steps.	

Commentary	Moves	Actor		Time elapsed
11 Teacher immediately rewards for correct response, then asks how they know they should say "steps." Note the teacher's focus on length.	**11** Reacts/Sol	*Teacher*	Steps, that's right. How can you tell they're steps? [60 sec]	1 min.
12 Child 1 returns to thickness property and gets strong cuing from teacher to forget thickness and pay attention to length: "Just look at the tops."	**12** Responds	*First child*	Because one is medium, then the other one's skinnier, then it gets medium again, then it gets fatter, and then it gets skinnier.	
	13 Responds/Str	*Teacher*	Well, there are other types of steps, too. Just look at the tops.	
14 Child 1 holds on to thickness idea: "fatter." Contest for control of the metaphor goes on. Teacher directs child to look at the tops four times [13, 15, 17 (twice)].	**14** Responds	*First child*	It gets fatter.	
	15 Structure	*Teacher*	Just a minute, Steven. Just look at the tops of these sticks.	
	16 Reacts	*First child*	But . . .	
	17 Str/Sol	*Teacher*	Just look at the very top. [15 sec] What can you tell me about the very top?	1:15
18 In spite of this repetitive cuing, Child 2 replies with a new metaphor: train tracks-metaphor 3.	**18** Responds	*Second child*	Looks like train tracks.	
19 Child 1 rescues teacher by naming teacher's metaphor, "steps," and is immediately rewarded. Note the "but . . .". It signals that the teacher is not yet satisfied. She asks them about the step idea.	**19** Responds	*First child*	They look like steps on the ends.	
	20 Reacts/Sol	*Teacher*	Very good, like steps; but what can you . . . [15 sec] How can you tell they're like steps? One is . . .	1:30
	21 Responds	*Second child*	One is high.	

Commentary		*Moves*		*Actor*		*Time elapsed*
22 to 23	As Child 2 and Child 1 respond, she hears a comparison word. "higher," repeats it to reinforce it, and asks the children if they agree. It would be difficult to disagree.	**22**	Responds	*First child*	Up. It goes higher.	
		23	Reacts/Sol	*Teacher*	Higher than the other, right?	
		24	Reacts	*First child*	It goes up, up, and then up and up and up and up.	
25	Once teacher seems satisfied, Child 2 returns to *his* metaphor, "trains."	**25**	Str	*Second child*	It looks like railroad trains.	1:45
26	Teacher gives "but" signal again and tries to return to "step" metaphor: conflict of metaphors.	**26**	Reacts/Res/ Sol/Sol	*Teacher*	Like railroad trains. But that's how we can tell they're like steps, doesn't it? Because . . . is this the shortest or the tallest of all of them?	
		27	Sol	*Second child*	This one?	
		28	Responds/Sol	*Teacher*	This one, the very first one. What is that—is it short or tall?	
		29	Responds	*Second child*	Short.	
30	Child 1 makes an attempt to get in the guessing game.	**30**	Sol	*First child*	Guess what that is. [15 sec]	2 min.
31	Teacher answers immediately and counters with a question.	**31**	Responds/Sol	*Teacher*	Short. And this one is what? Is it . . . ?	
32	Child 1 now tries again to get back to his original observations about the thicknesses: "skinnier."	**32**	Responds	*First child*	Skinnier.	
33 to 42	Teacher begins a whole series of questions inflected in such a way that anyone would know the answers are "yes." (In fact, we have played this part of the tape to people who did not know the topic, and they all answered "yes" right on cue, just as the children do.)	**33**	Sol	*Teacher*	Is it taller than this one?	
		34	Responds	*Second child*	Yes.	
		35	Sol	*Teacher*	And is this one taller than this one?	2:15
		36	Respond	*Both*	Yes.	
		37	Sol	*Teacher*	And this one is taller than that one?	
		38	Respond	*Both*	Yes.	
		39	Sol	*Teacher*	And is this last one a little taller than that one?	

Commentary		Moves	Actor		Time elapsed
	40	Respond	*Both*	Yes.	
	41	Sol	*Teacher*	So, how did I put them? [15 sec]	
	42	Responds	*Second child*	It goes up, up, up.	
43 Note that Child 1 tries again with "biggest," and the teacher acts as though Child 1 had said "tallest" on cue.	**43**	Reacts/Sol	*Teacher*	That's right; from the shortest to the—	
		Respond	*First child*	Biggest.	
	44	Responds/ Reacts	*Teacher*	Tallest, right—biggest.	
	45	Str	*Second child*	I wish we could see our faces, what we were doing. [15 sec]	
	46	Responds	*Teacher*	Well, some day they'll have television tape recorders, and then you'll be able to see yourself, too.	2:30
	47	Responds	*First child*	I know why . . . and yeah, well . . . you can see yourself when we talk.	
	48	Sol	*Teacher*	All right, now, if I took this one, where would I put it in these steps?	
	49	Reacts	*First child*	Um, bum.	
	50	Responds	*Second child*	Hey, that's little. [15 sec]	2:45
	51	Reacts/Sol	*Teacher*	That's little, so where would it go?	
	52	Respond	*Both*	Here, here, here.	
	53	Reacts	*Teacher*	Right, it would go right there.	
54 While it is difficult to detect without listening to the tape recording, there is frequent competition between the teacher and the children for the "speak space" —e.g., 4, 5, 16, 41, 54, 59, 60, 61. This kind of competition is very frequent when wait times are short.	**54**	Responds	*First child*	And this one would go there.	
	55	Reacts/Str	*Teacher*	Would it? Take a look.	
	56	Responds	*First child*	No, it would go over . . .	
	57	Str	*Teacher*	Find the place where it would go.	

Commentary		Moves	Actor		Time elapsed
	58	Responds	First child	Let me see. [15 sec] Not there. I found it.	3 min.
	59	Reacts/Str/Sol	Teacher	Very good. Gail, I want you to try one. Where would this one go in here? (Sound effects.) [15 sec]	3:15
	60	Responds	First child	I know, I know where it is.	
	61	Sol	Teacher	Tell me, how are you finding out where they would go?	
	62	Responds	First child	Because they's . . . one's bigger than the other.	
	63	Responds	Second child	It keeps getting bigger and bigger and bigger. [15 sec]	
64 Teacher responds with four solicitations and a structuring move—all with no interval for children to respond.	64	Sol/Sol/Sol/ Str/Sol	Teacher	So what do you have to do to the two sticks to show? How do you tell where it should go? What is Gail doing right now? Do that again. What is Gail doing right now?	3:30

Does a student ranked at the bottom of the class recognize when he is being rewarded for a correct response and when simply for effort? If he does not, the effect of the reward would be to reinforce an incorrect response.

In one in-service experiment, each of fifty teachers taught science to two first-grade children whom they had not previously known. The teachers knew the children had been grouped in combinations of two high-verbal children, or two low-verbal children, or one high- and one low-verbal child but were not told which combination they had. At the end of the lesson, each teacher tried to decide which combination she had. To the delight and dismay of everyone in the experiment, the teachers usually misjudged the combination. Most often they classified low-verbal youngsters as high-verbal. The interaction of children with materials along with the protracted silences of the teachers apparently "turned on" children who usually "tuned out."

RESULTS

When the fifty teachers returned to their classrooms and experimented with increased wait times, they reported

Transcript 8-2

	Moves	Actor		Time
1 Observation 1	Resp	*James*	Well, I put this nail on and I pulled it up, and it was like a force against it. (Observation.) [3 sec]	
2 Observation 2	Resp	*Dotty*	I put a compass and it began to vibrate. (Observation.) [7 sec]	15 sec
3 Observation 3 [inference 1 (magnet)]	Resp	*James*	The compass went down. (Observation.) [2 sec] The magnet was pulling the needle down. (Inference 1.) [6 sec.]	30
4 Observation 4	Resp	*Paul*	I used the tape (magnetic) and when I put it ober it, it came down. (Observation.)	
5 Inference 2 (Paper clip)	Resp	*Alice*	It could be a paper clip. (Inference 2.)	
	Resp	*Whole class*	No! [3 sec]	
7 Observation 5 used to argue for inference 2	Resp	*Jill*	I found the little nail sticks to paper clips. (Jill uses her own observation to argue for Alice's idea and shows a nail and clip.)	
	Resp	*Class*	Well, you magnetized it.	
	Resp	*Teacher*	Jill thinks it might be a paper clip too.	45
10 Argument based on evidence	React/Resp	*Paul*	Impossible. When you put a magnet on these, it won't stay on there unless it is on in a special way; a paper clip can't make the magnet move. (Argument based on evidence.) [6 sec]	
11 Argument based on evidence	Resp	*George*	Freddy said he had a compass and it went around. It wouldn't do this with paper clips. (Argument based on another child's evidence.)	1 min
12 Change of mind based on evidence	React	*Jill*	The compass experiment convinces me. (Changes her mind *on the basis of evidence.*)	1:15
13 Evaluates evidence: direct versus indirect	Resp	*James*	This is direct observation. That one with the paper clip is indirect. (Evaluates pieces of evidence.) [7 sec]	
14 Inference 3 (Nail)	Resp	*Jill*	But I don't think it could be a big nail in the box, because it wouldn't fit. (Limits the inference.)	1:30

that children who did not ordinarily contribute began to take a more active part in doing and talking about science.

The teachers' own questioning behavior also varies with wait time. As wait time increases, teachers begin to show much more variability in the kinds of questions they ask. Students receive more opportunity to respond to

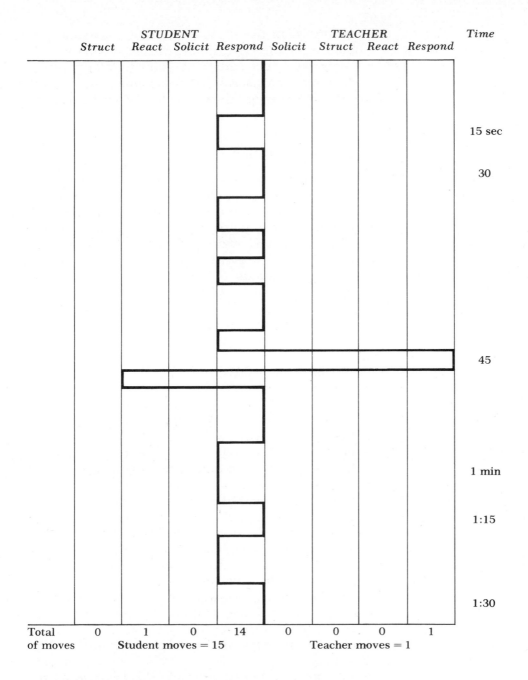

	STUDENT				TEACHER			Time
Struct	*React*	*Solicit*	*Respond*	*Solicit*	*Struct*	*React*	*Respond*	

								15 sec
								30
								45
								1 min
								1:15
								1:30

Total	0	1	0	14	0	0	0	1
of moves		Student moves = 15				Teacher moves = 1		

thought rather than straight memory questions. When the pacing is fast, teachers often ask and answer their own questions. ("What color was it? It was green, wasn't it?") For some reason when teachers gain control of wait time, questioning becomes less barragelike and more flexible in form. Questions asked by the teacher begin to reflect a genuine interest in the ideas of students. Slowing down the whole interchange rate among the players in the classroom seems to produce satisfying gains for all concerned. See, for example, Transcript 8-2, in which the students try to infer the contents of a box based on observations they made.

Effect on students (See Figure 8-5.)

1 *The length of students' responses increased.* Under a fast schedule, responses tend to consist of short phrases and rarely exhibit explanation of any complexity. Data from the chart plots suggest that the second wait time, when it is prolonged, contributes measurably to the appearance of longer statements.

2 *The number of unsolicited but appropriate responses by students increases.* This outcome is more responsive to the second than the first wait time, but is influenced by both.

3 *Failures to respond decreased.* "I don't know" or no responses were often as high as 30 percent in normal classrooms, i.e., in classrooms where the mean wait time fell at 1 second or less. This outcome is more susceptible to manipulation by the first wait time, the pause that the teacher allows before calling on another student or repeating the question. (It also happens to be responsive to the reward incidence.)

4 *Confidence, as reflected in fewer inflected responses, increased.* Under a fast schedule, responses tend to be phrased as though the child were saying, "Is that what you want?" In the middle of a prolonged, fast sequence you ask a child his name, and it will not be unusual to have him respond with a question mark in his tone. This confidence indicator, inflected responding, is also susceptible to the reward variable. As reward increases, so does the incidence of inflected responses.

5 *The incidence of speculative thinking increased.* This is influenced by both classes of wait times. We do not have a satisfactory test of how the reward schedule influences this outcome variable as yet.

6 *Teacher-centered show-and-tell decreased and child-child comparing increased.* Under a fast

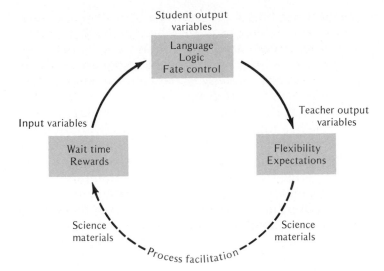

Student output
variables

Input variables

Teacher output
variables

Science
materials

Science
materials

Process facilitation

FIGURE 8-5
Postulated relationships among variables.

schedule and a high reward or sanctioning schedule, children "stack up" waiting to tell the teacher. There is very little indication that they listen to each other. (This observation will be discussed later in connection with a simulation experiment and additional research still to be done.)

7 *More evidence followed by or preceded by inference statements occurred.* Under a fast schedule, the incidence of qualified inferences is extremely low. When the second wait time is lengthened, this outcome variable changes in a desired direction.

8 *The number of questions asked by children increased, and the number of experiments they proposed increased.* Students do not ask questions very often. When they do, the questions are usually for clarification of procedures and are rarely ever directed at other students. This outcome variable seems to be susceptible to both classes of wait times.

9 *Contributions by "slow" students increased.* Under the fast schedule, most responses came from a particular faction of the class. When wait times were increased, the sources of response increased. The same held true for students in micro-teaching settings. Interestingly, this outcome gradually influenced teachers' expectations. Although we have not had time to investigate it in any detail yet, this fact seems to be both surprising

Inquisition

60

55

50

45

40

35

30

25

20

15

10

5

0 sec

and rewarding to the teachers. It would be of some interest to determine whether the reward pattern to this group gradually changes toward a less ambiguous form as the rate of responding goes up.

10 *Disciplinary moves decreased.* In some classrooms which shift from a fast schedule to a slow schedule, the number of disciplinary moves which a teacher makes, e.g., calling people to attention, stopping unsocial behavior, etc., tends to decrease. This variable has not really been studied in relation to changed wait times. Children maintained on a rapid inquisitorial pattern show signs of restlessness and inattentiveness sooner than do children on lower "bombing" schedules.

Effects on teachers

Once wait time is changed and behavior is stabilized for a period, certain characteristics of "teacher-input" variables change. They are regarded here as outcome variables because they are influenced by the wait time factor.

1 *Teachers' responses exhibit greater flexibility, as indicated by the occurrence of fewer discourse errors.* Under a rapid schedule, the probability that a detectable discontinuity in the discourse occurs increases. Conversation does not build into structural propositions. Instead the sequence of discourse resembles a smorgasbord line in which everyone goes along commenting on what he passes or picks up, but no one pays any attention to or gives any indication that he has heard the comments of others.

The flexibility index is computed in much the same way that the index of responsiveness for a computer-assisted instruction program is calculated. If the machine asks a question and the student responds with something that is not in storage, the machine either goes on to the next question as though nothing happened, or it cycles back and repeats—sometimes with progressive cuing. In either case a "discontinuity" is scored against the discourse. Frequently the teacher on a fast schedule achieves a less-favorable index than does a moderately good computer program. At least the computer program has the advantage of leaving the response time up to the students. The flexibility score improves with increases in wait times.

2 *The number and kind of questions by the teacher change.* The total number of questions decreases per 15-minute interval because student responses become longer, and the incidence of unsolicited but appropriate responses increases. The number of questions that call for reflection and that ask for clarification of meaning increases. Teachers at almost any grade level tend to ask questions that require little of the student except simple recall.

3 *Teachers' expectations for the performance of certain children seem to change.* In microteaching situations, we grouped children whom teachers did not know into pairs consisting of two children rated by their school as high verbal or two rated as low verbal, or we paired one high with one low verbal. We informed the teachers that they had one of these combinations and the task was to do some science and employ a longer wait time; then they were to judge with which kind of combination of children they were working. At the end of 20 minutes they made their judgments. They tended to make the following kinds of errors:

a They rated a high and low combination as two highs.

b They tended to rate two highs correctly most of the time but occasionally rated them as a high and a low.

c Two high verbals were occasionally (about 15 percent of the time) evaluated as a high and a low.

It should be pointed out, however, that we have not had an opportunity to discover whether the effect on expectations is general or how long it persists. Neither do we know how it may change the real performance of the students rated at the bottom of the class, given that the pattern of responding could be sustained.

VERBAL PATTERNS THAT CUT INTO WAIT TIME

In their eagerness to prompt responses from children, teachers often develop verbal signals that create addi-

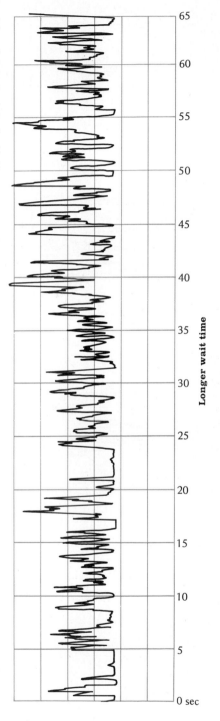

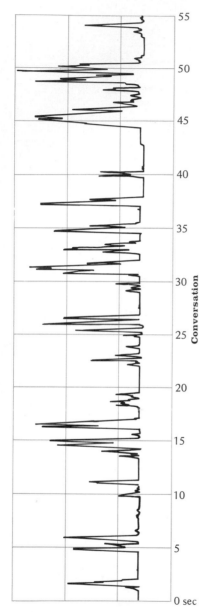

tional mental hazards for the children. These responses tend to cut down or intrude into the wait time.

"Think!"

Sometimes teachers command children to "think!" when they cannot answer a question. In our observations, confronted with materials and a problem, certain children stopped trying to find a solution after a few tries, and just sat. In response to my question, "What are you doing?" one child replied, "I am putting on my thinking cap." Nothing more happened until I asked, "And what does your thinking cap tell you to do?" "I don't know. She [referring to the teacher] just tells you to put on your thinking cap whenever you don't know the answer, and you keep guessing until you get it or she asks someone else."

This child had disengaged from the problem early, and he needed specific suggestions in order to be able to re-initiate activity with the system being investigated. Vague commands like "Think" or "Put on your thinking cap," while they often reflect the exasperation of an overworked adult, may be self-defeating, since they contain no specific suggestions for starting the process or for getting it going again once the sequence breaks down. When followed by a specific suggestion, by a reminder of some forgotten piece of information, or by an invitation to ask questions, commands to "think" may help a few impulsive responders to improve their answers. If the command is accompanied by *time* to think, responses may be more thoughtful.

Mimicry

If we examine teachers' verbal patterns, we find that a great many teachers have developed a habit of repeating the last word or phrase that the child spoke, so that we get a dialogue of the sort illustrated in Transcript 8-3. Note that the pattern of repetition is so extensive in this little bit of dialogue that at some point the children begin to turn the tables. When they say a phrase and the teacher repeats it, they in turn repeat the teacher's phrase. There is some humor on their part in this, but it could eventually, of course, lead to management problems that might prove to be severe. In essence, children are saying, "Please talk to me and stop mimicking."

After almost every observation or inference in Transcript 8-2, the teacher repeated the response of the child. Exactly what function mimicry serves is not immediately obvious. It must have some adaptive value for teachers; otherwise the pattern would not be as widespread as it is. (Note its incidence in Transcript 8-1 as well.) It may constitute an attempt on the teacher's part to be certain that everybody in the class hears a communication from a child. Or it may simply be a habituated response that has the function of minimizing the amount of wait time the teacher must endure. Most probably it serves the function of maintaining the centrality of the teacher in the communication net. In short, it is not at all unlikely that the pattern of mimicry existing in so many conversations of teachers with children serves the function of maintaining stronger control over the classroom. When wait time increases and the flow of conversation in toward the teacher tends to decrease, there is less opportunity to mimic.

Many teachers report that they experience a brief period of uncertainty about who is in command in the classroom while passing through that transition state from relatively short to relatively longer wait times, and sometimes find themselves doing more mimicking than usual.

Under a high mimicry pattern it is not surprising that children tend to answer in short sentences or in short phrases and to answer to some extent with a questioning tone in their voices. They learn quickly that if they can somehow trip off the correct word in a phrase it may not matter a great deal if they understand the context or if they understand exactly what the word means, since it will produce a new response in the teacher and remove the child from the inquisitorial hook.

If improvement of communication skills on the part of youngsters and an improvement in the quality of their responses or the cognitive complexity of their responses seem like reasonable instructional goals, then it is to our advantage to examine the extent to which we mimic, and to question whether the practice of mimicry influences the quality of classroom discourse.

Mimicry may be a variable with which to experiment. With a small group of children, try to use a very high value of the variable, namely, to mimic everything, and note how they respond. Then try reducing mimicry to zero or near zero to find out if their response is in any way different. Compare Transcripts 8-2 and 8-3.

Observing changes in a thermal system, Transcript 8-3.

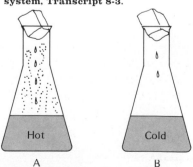

Transcript 8-3

Analysis of a transcript to illustrate high incidence of mimicry and rewarding. Experiment: Observing changes in a thermal system, fifth grade.

						STUDENT				Wait	TEACHER				
Item	Repeat	Reward		Dialogue	Time	Str	Rea	Sol	Rsp	time	Sol	Str	Rea	Rsp	
1			C1	Ice is melting.				1			1		1		Rsp
2	1		T	The ice is melting. What do we mean by melting?							1		1		Rea/Sol
3			C1,C2	Getting smaller				1							Rsp
4	1	1	T	Getting smaller, very good.									2		Rea/Rea
5			C2	Shrinking				1							Rsp
6	1		T	Shrinking									1		Rea
7			C2	The ice is reducing.				1							Rsp
8	2	1	T	The ice is reducing, that's a good word, reducing.									3		Rea/Rea/Rea
9			C1	And water is dripping and the ice. (Inaudible.)	15 sec			1		1+					Rsp
10			C2	Oh, I know what happens. Well, when the ice is dripping it causes water vapor.				1							Rsp
11	2	2	T	Water vapor, good, that's very, very good. Water vapor. what else? You both are looking at the hot bottle, the one with the warm water in it. What about . . . (interrupted.)	30 sec / 30 sec						2	1	3		Rea/Rea/Rea/Sol/Str/Sol
12			C1,C2	Hot air, hot air, hot air.				1							Rsp
13	1		T	Hot air. Why is there hot air?							1		1		Rea/Sol
14			C1	Because there is no space for the new clean air to get in.				1							Rsp
15			C2	No room for oxygen.				1							Rsp
16	1	1	T	For oxygen, that's right, You see the hot air here. (Points to A.) What about here? (Points to B.)							1	1	2		Rea/Rea/Str/Sol
17			C2	You don't see any	45 sec			1							Rsp

TOTALS

9	5			45 sec of transcript; average wait time = 0.4 sec		0	0	0	10	1 sec	5	2	13	0	

Student moves = 10 Teacher moves = 20 Total moves = 30

STUDENT | | | | TEACHER
Struct | React | Solicit | Respond | Solicit | Struct | React | Respond

"Yes . . . but"

Although the pattern of mimicry rarely appears when adults speak to each other, "yes . . . but" and ". . . though" constructions do appear frequently, especially if their views diverge. If during a discussion meant to explore ideas or exchange information we get a feeling of "no progress," the probability is high that "yes . . . but" and "though" signals are sprinkled liberally through the discourse of one or both speakers. They signal an impending rejection or negation of an idea. The probability is high that the user does not really receive and explore the new ideas. Instead, he immediately counters with his own ideas.

Swimming upstream against a conversational flow full of "yes . . . but's" and "though's" is like a salmon migration—only the hardiest survive the first few barriers. If we examine children's transcripts to see what comments provoke "yes . . . but," we find that the most likely culprit (about 78 percent) is a speculative statement, a low-order inference, or the use by the child of an analogy or metaphor. Furthermore, if a child in the first through the third grades tries to make a teacher understand what he understands about an experiment, he is likely to stop trying after encountering "yes . . . but" two times. A few hearty individuals may last through more attempts, but in cases where we have transcripts extending over two science sessions in a row, such children do not often appear again in the discourse.

Preliminary data on "yes . . . but" and "though" constructions imply if teachers use those forms less, the likelihood increases that children will exhibit a higher level of thinking more of the time. Or, to put it another way, if learning to intuit answers and making testable inferences about phenomena are acceptable goals, then the reduction of the negative forms "yes . . . but" and "though" may improve everyone's chance of reaching those goals.

These two phrases of negation put the actors in the system into a game stance in which the ideas that develop are not nearly so important as who wins. "Yes . . . but" and "though" are verbal decoys. On the surface they seem to indicate that an adversary has been heard and his argument attended to, but transcripts almost never show a teacher with a consistent negation pattern of this kind using a child's idea as a basis of thoughtful conversation.

Alternative forms of producing fruitful argument

that may eventually lead to a better selection of variables or determination of relationships among them by children might be phrases spoken by the teacher such as:

"*If* that is so, *then* why . . . ?"

"I don't understand what you mean. Try telling me again."

"What evidence are you using?" Or simply, "What is your evidence?"

"I am not sure I can agree with that, because . . ."

These modes model the logical form, "If . . . then . . ." and help children explore the logical consequences of their speculations. Eventually these modes will begin to appear in the children's own discourse as wait time by the teacher increases and they hear more "If . . . then . . ." arguments.

VERBAL DEVICES THAT PRODUCE COMPLIANCE

Some phrases that teachers use might be called *rhetorical*. However, the effect that they have on the class interaction pattern belies the soft meaning of *rhetorical*. Certain phrases place two speakers in a relationship to each other that requires one of the speakers to agree with what has just been said. If he does not agree, the only way in which he can express another point of view is to come into conflict.

In a classroom situation where there is, after all, a hierarchical status relation (namely, an authority figure—the teacher—and junior figures—the students) it is relatively unlikely that a difference in view will be verbalized in the student group. Actually, rhetorical phrases are not intended by the teacher to cut off conversation. They do, however, have the effect of winning compliance with the view that the teacher is expressing at the moment. In science we are interested in the quality of the response rather than the source.

"Isn't it?"

The teacher makes some sort of statement and concludes with ". . . isn't it?" The children usually confirm the statement. To disagree with it is too costly. In fact, in the transcripts we find few times when the teacher uses the "isn't it?" phrase that children will disagree. We have even tried having some teachers make patently incorrect inferences or observations about laboratory material to find out what children do when confronted with a conflict between the authority of the teacher as expressed in the phrase "... isn't it?" and the authority of the observations. Children who are not specifically trained to rely on their observations as a basis for their statements will tend to agree anyway. Sometimes they just nod their heads, sometimes they say "Yes," and sometimes they just say nothing. So the "... isn't it?" construction needs to be used with considerable care. (For more on this topic, see Chapter 17 on evaluation.)

"Don't you think that . . .?"

Another phrase which makes it just as difficult for the other speaker to voice a contrary opinion is the phrase "Don't you think that . . . ?" You may know immediately that you don't think *that* at all, but the phrase implies that all the speaker expects from you is a "Yes." If, however, the speaker says "I think that . . ." instead of "Don't you think that . . . ," the respondent is far more likely to tell the listener his own views. The flow of conversation is greatly facilitated when the phrase "Don't you think that . . . ?" is replaced by "I think that . . . . What do you think?"

"Why did you . . . ?"

The phrase "Why did you . . . ?" will be discussed when we deal with techniques of question asking in the next chapter, but it also has the properties of a habituated phrase. The effect of this "Why did you . . . ?" phrase on many children is to put them on the defensive. In the home environment as well as in the school environment, children who have done something that adults don't expect or especially approve of will often be asked, "Why did you do that?" Many experiences with that "Why did you . . . ?" phrase have made children gun shy on the "why" construction.

According to the evidence from analysis of 200 + hours of transcripts, the probability that children in the first to third grades will answer a "why" question is only about 36 percent. If the same information is solicited in a

"How come . . . ?" format, the probability of a response jumps to 72 percent.

Another provoking version of the "why" construction that is used with good intent but unfortunate consequences involves the phrase "Why did I . . . ?" If you will recall, in Transcript 8-1, item 9, the teacher set up some dowels and said to the children, *"Why did I do that?"* There is no earthly way children could know *"Why"* she did *"that"* or why anyone does anything. The phrases "why did I" and "why did you" include personal pronouns, and are essentially a question about someone's motives. No one can really know about such things. Sometimes teachers ask the question meaning it to be an open-ended or "thought" question that children are supposed to interpret as "Why did that happen that way?" Unfortunately, young children interpret language literally, as Transcript 8-1 indicates.

Our experience, then, is that children tend very often not to answer questions that begin with "why." This may be partly because the questions are essentially unanswerable anyway and partly because the children associate "why" constructions with the requirement that they justify their behavior. (See Chapter 11 on conversation versus interrogation for a more extended discussion of "why" questions, and also Chapter 18 on philosophy of science.)

"Right?"

In addition to the phrases ". . . isn't it?" and "Don't you think that . . . ?" we noted another habituated behavior whose effect, judged from transcripts, is to win compliance. The teacher makes an assertion and concludes with the remark "Right?" Children inevitably nod or say "Yes" following a question "Right?" "Right?" has an inflectional equivalent in Socratic dialogues where the teacher makes an assertion in the form of a question which, because of its form and tone, may only be answered in one way, usually "yes" or "no." We saw this particular pattern illustrated in Transcript 8-1. The teacher conveys selected information by making a series of assertions intoned as questions. The combination of tone and semantics cues the listener to say "yes" or "no" so obviously that he need never understand a thing about the content to know how to answer satisfactorily.

By bunching together a succession of these phrases,

teachers can produce in groups of children small facsimiles of the Greek chorus. Soon all the children are nodding or answering in unison.

As Transcript 8-1 indicates, we cannot be certain that at the end of such a sequence children will arrive at the answer they were intended to make from the beginning. Witness what happened near the conclusion of such a sequence in Transcript 8-1.

Teacher:	*And is this last one a little taller than that one?*
Both children:	*Yes*
Teacher:	*So how did I put them?*
Second child:	*It goes up, up, up.*
Teacher:	*That's right, from the shortest to the—*
Second child:	*Biggest.*
Teacher:	*Tallest, right—biggest.*

Note that in spite of everything, the children still cling to "biggest." There may be some times when it is just more honest and expeditious to tell children what we want them to pay attention to than to play a game that can only be frustrating to all participants. Telling may still fail to convey a particular message, but it must produce at least as much learning as the "pseudodiscovery" format illustrated in the transcripts, and considerably less tension for both parties.

TECHNIQUES OF STIMULATING DISCOURSE

Entering a group

The problem is to enter a group without asking a question. Some techniques that seem to function well as stimulators of discourse are discussed next.

Join the group with no comment at all. This is another version of wait time. Become an observer of the phenomena the children are examining and talking about. Speak when you are able to make an observation or some other statement about the system.

Join the group at its eye level. Pull up a chair or stoop down, but get down to the head level at which the children are working. The videotapes show children turning away from phenomena to speak to a teacher who is standing.

This disengagement is avoided by joining the group at the common head level.

If it is necessary to ask a question, try to avoid asking one that begins, "Why did you. . . ." Analysis of tape recordings shows that the probability of getting a response to a question in this form is considerably less (approximately 30 percent) than if the same information was requested in some other question format.

Lose eye contact. At first children try to mediate their arguments through the teacher. The flow of discourse directly from one child to another increases when the teacher loses eye contact with the speakers.

Group process facilitation

Make most comments, especially in the early stages of helping children to work collaboratively, on processes you observe going on between them. This function of facilitating processes need not be served exclusively by the teacher: the children can learn to do it for their own work groups.

One of the process-facilitation techniques has a close analogue with skills being taught in the science program. It contains two or three statements, depending on conditions. The speaker says:

"I observe x."	*Where x is any statement that he can make about the group, e.g., "I observe that someone interrupted Gregory every time he spoke."*
"I infer y."	*Where y is an inference based on the observation x, e.g., "I infer that you are not interested in what he has to say."*
"I feel z."	*Where z is a statement about how the observation-inference feels to you, e.g., "I feel bad about that."*

Training in group process facilitation seems to produce an environment that encourages productive discourse.

In response to the changed dynamics in classrooms where teachers are working under schedules of low rewards and extended wait times, role relations change. Certain kinds of decisions that formerly belonged exclusively to the teacher now shift gradually to the children. Students now face the problem of making the resources in their groups available—i.e., getting all the ideas out and evaluated. More organizational problems and stresses of interdependence develop. The presence of scientific phenomena that provoke controversy creates a situation which is nearly ideal for teaching children how to maximize group productivity. The data of H. Wiethake suggest that even when children trained in process facilitation move to other classrooms, the effect of the training is still detectable. Some social-psychological variables that influence the quality of work in elementary science are discussed in Chapter 14.

We are in search of factors which create conditions in which children find it useful and interesting to develop language and logic, as well as confidence that they can shape both physical and social systems. Can they come to believe that they do in fact have some control of their own fates?

SUMMARY

1 There is probably a relationship between the quality of inquiry in elementary science and two variables controlled by the teacher, wait time and rewards. Wait times tend to be very short unless a conscious effort is made to increase them.

   a The amount of time teachers wait for students to begin a reply to questions averages between 1 and 2 seconds.

   b The amount of time teachers wait after a student makes a statement tends to average 1 second.

2 When average wait times are increased to 3 seconds or longer, certain student variables change in a direction that makes for better inquiry.

   a The average length of students' responses increases.

   b Students initiate more responses.

   c More students succeed in answering questions more of the time.

   d More alternative explanations are offered.

   e Students make more and better connections between evidence and inference.

3 Certain variables controlled by the teacher change

when longer average wait times have been established.

   a Teachers are more flexible in their responses to students.

   b Teachers' questions show more variability.

   c Teachers' expectations regarding the performance of students rated as relatively weak improves.

4 Certain habituated verbal signals tend to cut down wait time.

   a The command "Think!"

   b Mimicry in which teachers repeat what students say.

   c "Yes . . . but . . ." and ". . . though" constructions that signal rejection of an idea.

   d Phrases that produce compliance: ". . . isn't it?" and "Don't you think that . . . ?"

5 There are ways to join a group of students working on an experiment such that there will be minimal interference with their flow of thought.

   a Observe but make no comment until you can make an observation; i.e., avoid a question.

   b Lose eye contact with individuals.

   c Try the sequence of comments: "I observe . . ."; "I infer . . ."; "I feel . . ."

6 There is a possible relationship between the input variables of wait time and reward and outcome variables having to do with language, logic, and fate control. These variables will be discussed in succeeding chapters.

7 As students spend more time doing science in small, task-oriented clusters, they need to acquire some communication skills. New science programs work on an intrinsic motivation model.

8 A very high rate of overt verbal rewards and punishments (positive and negative sanctions) may teach the student to distrust his own judgment. Students will be more afraid to venture new ideas in an atmosphere that is heavily judgmental.

ACTIVITY 8-1

OBJECTIVE

To recognize structuring, soliciting, reacting, and responding moves

What to do:

Read the transcripts in this chapter. For each one, construct a table like the one shown here. Enter the totals for each kind of move in the table.

	Teacher	*Student*	
Structuring	————	————	
Soliciting	————	————	
Reacting	————	————	
Responding	————	————	*Transcript #* ————
Total	————		

ACTIVITY 8-2

O BJECTIVE

To identify feelings that develop during instruction

What to do:

To get some sense of what it feels like to be involved in a fast-paced exchange, try role playing the parts in the transcripts. Get someone to speak the teacher's lines, and you speak the students' lines. Try varying the pace.

ACTIVITY 8-3

OBJECTIVE

To study the influence of wait time

What to do:

1 Teach a science lesson to two or more students. Tape-record the lesson. Choose the lesson from any of the new science programs or prepare one of your own.

  a Transcribe the tape recording, at least 15 minutes of it. It takes time to transcribe a tape, but the process will focus your attention on how much interaction there is in 15 minutes.

  b Listen to the tape and mark on the transcript where there are wait times. What is the total wait time? Find this by adding together all the pauses.

  c Classify the statements in the transcript according to whether they are structuring, soliciting, reacting, or responding. Examine the distribution of these moves among the two players: the teacher and the students.

	Teacher	*Students*
Structuring		
Soliciting		
Reacting		
Responding		

  d Calculate the average length of students' responses.

2 Design your own investigation into the influence of wait time. Select those outcome variables of most interest to you.

ACTIVITY 8-4

OBJECTIVE

To recognize pauses on a servo-chart plot.

What to do:

1 Compare chart plots. Find the total wait time for each plot. (The needle tracks horizontally when there are pauses.)
2 (Optional.) Calculate the percent of wait time for each chart by dividing the total time shown on the chart into the total of pauses.

$$\text{Percent of wait time} = \frac{\text{Sum of pauses}}{\text{Total time consumed}} \times 100$$

REFERENCE

Mary Budd Rowe: "Science, Silence, and Sanctions," *Science and Children,* vol. 6, no. 6, March 1969.

CHAPTER 9

"How we live is like in a box. You go home. It's a box. They're always at you for something. School, well, that's just another box. You keep hoping you could find a nicer place, but if you do, some guys are already there and they don't want you cuttin' in. So what's a guy to do, man?"

—GHETTO SIXTH-GRADER AFTER OBSERVING MEALWORMS

SCIENCE AND SOUL: SOME MUSINGS ON FATE CONTROL

OBJECTIVES

On completion of this chapter and its associated activities, you should be able to do the following:

1 Identify those teaching techniques that are likely to encourage the development of a sense of fate control on the part of students.

2 State the probable relationship between early instruction in science and the development of a sense of fate control.

3 Identify student behaviors that probably indicate a developing sense of fate control.

INTRODUCTION

One of the attributes that marks science is the focus on "what might be" rather than on "what is." Perhaps the biggest contribution science makes to Western societies, borne out by the way Western peoples have absorbed the philosophy, is its emphasis upon intervening in one's own future. When we can move in our imagining from *what is* to *what might be* and can engineer the route from a present reality to a new reality, we are acting *as though* we believe our fates are mostly under our own direction.

This chapter is about the relationship of early training in science to the development of a belief that one can, in some measure, determine his own destiny. In a world which is becoming more complex, the maintenance of that belief and the development of the analytical skills which will make it possible to cope with complexity become a vital part of general education. For children in any culture who grow up in environments marked by passivity, governed by superstitions, bound by fear, emptied of dreams, or ruled entirely by forces outside themselves, science has something special to say. If we wait until these children can read or if we depend on the home to develop a belief that what they do and how they do it matters, we may pass the time when we might accomplish this end.

Science, properly taught and energetically pursued, may provide innumerable opportunities for learning new cause-and-effect relationships, that is, *conceptions of causality.* I invite you to join me in an investigation which is only just beginning, and to which teachers can make a substantial contribution. Consider now the relation between early science instruction and the development of a belief that we can in fact intervene in our own destinies.

A part of what underlies the development of a sense that one can control one's own fate has to do with language (see Chapter 12). Another part has to do with conceptions of causality, and another has to do with what kind of reinforcements our environments make available to us, their source, and their distribution (see Chapter 10). Still another aspect has to do with the richness of our imaginings and our freedom to try some of them out.

CRAPS VERSUS BOWLING

According to their various histories, individuals differ in how they relate events to one another. Our ideas of cause are intimately tied to our notions of what part luck or chance plays in the events that we experience. When we believe that outcomes have little to do with our actions and a great deal to do with chance, or forces outside ourselves, we need take little responsibility for our actions, since there is little advantage to be gained: fate will determine the future, and we simply gamble on a set of unknowns.

Take a concrete example as a metaphor for conveying the relation between our conceptions of *cause, chance,* and *fate* control. Suppose we put dice in a cup and shake and roll the dice to try to produce a particular combination of numbers that will win us some money. Call the game *craps,* if you like. In this game, skill or our ability to intervene to make one outcome more likely than another is very low (given, of course, that the dice are unbiased). Once we shake and roll, that is it. Practice will do little to improve the outcomes. On the other hand, bowling is an example of a game where figuring out the right variables and acting on the ball accordingly can increase the probability of achieving some preferred outcomes. In some sense, we can affect the future (the outcome) in bowling, but we are left to the mercy of a capricious world in throwing dice. Even though the ball, like the dice, must leave the hand before we can know an outcome, the ball carries with it a kind of message; it carries constraints on its freedom that we put there.

The business of building some sense of fate control is like moving a person from dice playing to bowling, from games of fate to games of fate control, from a low expectation that he can affect an outcome to a relatively high expectation that what he does will matter. To the externally controlled people (the would-be craps players) the kind of planning that marks a technologically based society makes no sense. Their early experience, devoid of the ingredients out of which fate control could be compounded, makes participation in the shaping of their own destinies less and less possible.

Science and prediction go together. The more I know about a system, the more likely I am to be able to act on it in definite ways and expect certain results. *Prediction*

rests on a belief that events are not totally capricious, that what I do to the system makes a difference in how the parts act. I can, in some way, act to control the fate of the system. Probably the building of this belief represents the single greatest contribution science can make to the education of any "disadvantaged" child.

To all young children the world is whimsical. They do not see much connection among the events of today and virtually none at all between the events of today and those of tomorrow. Magic and the gods control their world (gods include any powerful people in children's lives, such as parents, teachers, and other adults). If children fail to emerge from this stage, as happens to some, they grow up prey to superstitions, unable to act in their own behalf to improve their conditions of life. For such children, grown into adults, there is no point in planning, because they believe that all power to control is vested in others or in nature. That means that an individual cannot be responsible for what happens to himself. Planning is irrelevant, since whatever happens is just a matter of luck. There is no point in trying, because although something may turn out well this time, it is just as likely to turn out badly the next. Luck plays an enormous and erratic role in the lives of such people. For them, time as a dimension collapses to "now." Enjoy what there is *now*, because any minute luck may change what is happening; or, conversely, endure what is happening now because it may change in some way, depending on what the powerful people do or on the whims of fate. Since things can get better or worse at any moment, the only thing to do is to take what you can get when you can get it. Live for the moment. Never focus your attention on anything very long, because you do not know where threat will come from next. Accept the box, because you cannot change it.

The children who acquire conceptions of the world based on chance or luck—that is, the craps players of the world—tend to maintain one of two social postures. They may be passive, perfectly welded to the conditions around them; or continually in conflict, threatening and being threatened by others, for that is what it takes to survive in the box. Trust and collaboration, as well as sustained effort toward any goal, are irrelevant to the craps players because the chance model of the world assumes virtually no connection between events.

When youngsters who believe that control rests almost entirely outside themselves do occasionally protest, they are in trouble. Unaccustomed to reasoning forward in time, to examining evidence and making predictions so that they might choose the best means for intervention on their own behalf, they react to frustration with brief, intense outbursts of violence rather than with any extended strategy for change. The course of their lives is marked by such outbursts of violence between protracted periods of indifference to the flow of events around them. On the other hand, the bowlers—adults who learned as children that they could by their own actions intervene in their own fates—puzzle about the passivity and social disorganization of the disadvantaged.

Unfortuantely the natural institutional response of the schools, and very often of the teachers in them, to the social disorganization, the indifference to learning, and the short attention of children operating with a craps model of the world is to deny them access to science. One hears comments like these: "They cannot even get the basics. How do you expect them to do any science?" "If we try to teach them science, they get too excited and we can't get them settled down. Anyway, they think science is magic. They don't get the principles."

These comments represent a common point of view among teachers in general but are especially strongly held by teachers of disadvantaged and handicapped children. In a sample of responses to questionnaires given to teachers who took part in various science programs where children were expected to work with materials, the comments above appeared on more than 40 percent of the replies. Rural groups in Colorado as well as inner-city teachers in New York City expressed the same view.

To the externally controlled people, the kind of planning and prognostication that marks a technological society makes no sense. Their early experiences, devoid of the ingredients from which fate control could be compounded, make their participation less and less possible in a technological world (Figure 9-1).

Developing a belief that one can act to control his own destiny requires certain kinds of support from teachers while children are doing science. If teachers bomb youngsters with questions rather than engaging in conversations with them, and if they distribute rewards (praise and blame) in the indiscriminate manner that the data suggest they do, it seems inevitable that all but a few

FIGURE 9-1
No matter what the cultural and environmental context is, the student must learn to cope with it. Each context presents its own problems. Try to identify characteristics of each situation. (Courtesy of Paul Kirouac.)

of the most hardy will learn that powerful others do control their outcomes and that dealing with the world is more like playing dice than like bowling.

The rate and duration of questioning often are faintly reminiscent of the inquisition, and the politics of the reward system are inordinately complex. On innumerable occasions children are confronted with some soul-searing choices. They have intriguing science materials in front of them and a command to learn something from them. They hardly start before the teacher begins asking questions, talking, demanding attention. They try to contend with both the demands of the teacher and the attraction of the materials. In some classes children learn that safety lies in making a choice to give up investigating the materials in favor of closely monitoring the teacher. In other classrooms, where children need to make no such choices, they can and do try out ideas, talk about them, and gradually learn to get their reinforcements from things that happen between them and the materials. It is important to the development of fate control that children have sufficient time to work with materials. Humans rarely do one-trial learning, so they need plenty of opportunity to repeat events until they have extracted meaning from them and have discovered that they are replicable (i.e., that the same thing can be made to happen again).

LANGUAGE AND CONCEPTS OF GHETTO AND SUBURBAN CHILDREN

Part of the utility of constantly studying handicapped, disadvantaged, and suburban children side by side, so to speak, comes from the contrasts that help to focus attention. Something happens in one group, and that starts us looking for it in the other. Sometimes it makes us pay attention to phenomena we would otherwise miss or ignore: the high incidence of fantasy and storytelling with objects that marks the talk of so many inner-city children; the tremendous anxiety of suburban children about bodily functions. Here are some examples.

The place was a first-grade classroom in Harlem. Four small boys leaned over a little aquarium watching the guppies and snails. One pointed to a guppy. "Hey, look. I think it's shit."

"The snail is doing it, too."

I went over to look at the tank. The boys became

quiet, as they often do when a teacher or visitor approaches. One boy pointed to the brown object trailing behind a fish. "What is that?" he asked.

"What is your idea?" I countered.

He hesitated. "Shit?"

I nodded. "Looks like it."

The boys went back to examining the tank. There was no sound. Suddenly a boy who had not spoken looked up, "Do they piss, too?" I told them that it was harder to see, but probably fish did. Silence. Then one small boy shivered a little. "You mean they swim around in all that stuff?" He looked up for a moment and said, "It's sort of like the garbage strike, isn't it?" At that time the New York City garbage strike was in its fifth day. First-graders do not often reason analogically, but these children did.

Three days later and 10 miles away, in classroom in an upper-middle-class suburban school, first-graders looked at the organisms in the aquarium supplied for the "Organisms" unit of SCIS.[1] There was a lot of giggling and obvious embarrassment. The children were making essentially the same observations as the city youngsters did, but they somehow thought that what they observed would not be acceptable to talk about in school. When I approached one group, a boy pointed to two guppies. "What is that brown stuff?"

"What do you think it is?" I asked.

"Well, it could be eggs, but—." He stopped.

"But what?"

"Well, it's the wrong color." He paused again. "I think it's his bowel movement," he whispered. This announcement produced much giggling and obvious embarrassment.

Both groups eventually learned terms like *feces* and *urine*. But whereas the terms simply became acceptable substitutes for the more graphic language of the city children, the suburban children seemed to find substantial relief that there were words they could use with less embarrassment.

The story points up some kinds of learning and communication problems faced by each group. Pregnancy, birth, death, waste, and violence are part of the daily experience of many inner-city children. They have words for telling about "how it is." If teachers let young children *start by using their available language,* the children

---

[1]Science Curriculum Improvement Study.

learn alternatives by *using new words in appropriate contexts* rather than by definition. At this early stage the transition to a "new" language learned in the context of concrete events goes fairly smoothly. That is the beauty of some science programs—they provide specific settings (materials) and situations where children can experiment with the difficult business of *converting experience to language.* When children have trouble getting an idea across, they can resort to showing what they mean with the objects they are using. *So there is always a way for them to communicate* once they start working with the science materials—if anybody will listen. As the research reported in the chapter on wait time suggests, finding someone to listen may be one of the biggest problems students face.

Consider for a moment the inner-city children's counterparts in suburbia. In the area of life science, especially, these children also need help—but for different reasons. Sometimes they have all the words, the correct labels, but the emotional tie-ups over the words, and the phenomena they apply to, tend to keep the children isolated from adults. They hide behind polite forms or lapse into silence to cover their feelings. Caught between curiosity and taboo, it takes time for them to learn that it is safe to talk about phenomena like death, pregnancy, and evacuation. When they do, the flood of questions and observation is enormous. *The teacher has to be prepared to listen.* But these children too have trouble finding listeners. Aside from the fact that listening may be one of the most humane things a teacher can do, it is a major way for the teacher to get data that will help in deciding how to proceed.

Children attend to the same phenomena in an aquarium whether they come from the inner city or from suburbia, but sometimes they treat the phenomena differently.

When guppies and snails die in city classrooms, there may be some arguments about sharing animals that are left; but on the whole, death and disappearance (especially disappearance) do not surprise ghetto youngsters. If some of the guppies disappeared overnight (as they often do) the ghetto children did not ask, "What happened?" or "Where did they go?" nearly as often as the suburban children did. The difference in response to such phenomena probably has several origins. Often people come, stay awhile, and disappear with little explanation to the ghetto child. Turnover among teachers is high. Objects get taken. The familiar does not provoke inquiry. It is a chance world, and one simply accepts what exists now. On the other hand, if an animal dies and it remains in the aquarium, some children will develop elaborate but untestable explanations about what happened. One small boy looked at a dead guppy floating in a smelly aquarium. "Probably he had bad companions, and they poisoned him. That happens." He said his uncle had died the day before because of bad companions who poisoned his tea. (His uncle died, but of an overdose of narcotics.) Here the child's explanation consisted of a metaphor.

Suburban children confronted with the missing guppies ask all kinds of questions that boil down to "What happened?" The disappearance provokes theorizing followed by simple experiments to find out. *For the suburban child, things do not just disappear without a reason.* In suburbia, dead guppies stimulate a thousand questions and speculations: How did it happen? What will happen to the eggs (after a pregnant guppy turned over)? Maybe there wasn't enough food. Maybe the snail did it. Maybe it can only be pregnant once, etc. Suburban children particularly want to talk about death. They seem to be as matter-of-fact about it as the ghetto youngsters but curious and concerned over their parents' responses.

One small girl said, "My grandfather died, and my mother keeps crying. Why does she do that? Crying won't change anything. I wish she would stop."

Suburban and ghetto children do not think about causation in the same way. Only a part of the difference has to do with language per se. The rest probably has to do with the cultural context of their lives. Young ghetto children and many Southern black children, as well as poor whites, think that all that happens to them, good or bad, happy or sad, is a matter of fate. If an outcome was good, say on a test, or they received a bit of praise from the teacher, they say they were lucky. If an outcome was bad, they were unlucky. "That's how it is," they say, and they shrug—or, depending on circumstances, they erupt in a sudden burst of violence and then settle down again to the inevitable. Unlike suburban children, they rarely try to figure out and test ideas about events such as missing guppies, largely because the events are accepted at face value. For these children, events have no past, only a present.

That a sense of fate control is evolving may very well be indicated by the quality of speculations about previous and antecedent conditions surrounding some event e.g., when students start asking, "How come?" The children who speculated about what happened to the baby guppies and *what might be done* to prevent a recurrence were already exhibiting behaviors that indicate some progress along the fate-control dimension. For them, events have causes. If they do not want the baby guppies to disappear, then their speculations about what happened will govern their decisions about what to do to prevent another disappearance. They, in contrast to the other children, believe they *can* change the fate of the system by what they do to the system. The potential to do that lies between them and the properties of the system—that is, in how they interact with the system. Change the properties or the variables, and you change the outcome. Children low on the fate-control continuum can only divide what is left of the guppies and leave it to chance that the next round of babies will not disappear. Thus their fortunes, measured in guppies that grow up, diminish to nothing—not a very happy prospect.

Probably one of the most exciting and at the same time most puzzling contributions new science programs make to the education of disadvantaged children is the general stimulus they provide for children to talk. But the talk is not always what we would expect. The objects frequently start children telling about themselves and their lives—and we do not really know how to deal with such communications.

Consider, for example, what happened when I took some mealworms into a Harlem fourth grade classified as mentally retarded but educable. Before the start of the science lesson, I watched a painful language arts session with them. They sat back, sullen, silent, and staring straight ahead. It was as though the teacher was not there.

It was just before Thanksgiving. One little boy had not spoken since school opened in September. I put a handful of the worms into each of fifteen shoe boxes and gave every boy a box. I sat down next to the silent boy, who stared in front of him with his arms folded. Gradually his curiosity got the better of him, and he looked into the box. We sat silently watching together for a few minutes as a brown mealworm and a white one approached each other. Suddenly he spoke. "Look, look, they are going to fight. Whenever brown and white meet they fight."

I held my breath and kept still. The worms passed each other. Some of the worms started up the side of the box. A brown one moved straight up and a white one crawled up toward it at an angle. The boy spoke again. "Look, the white worm will catch the brown worm and pull it down." That happened.

The worms kept going up the sides to the top of the box, and just as they would get to the edge, he would flip them gently back. Finally I could not contain my own feelings and spoke: "Don't you want to see if they can get all the way out?"

He turned and looked at me for the first time. "No, because when you are in prison, you don't get out, ever."

Just then a neighboring boy stuck his pencil in at one of the worms and received a whack on the arm. "I don't want my worms hurt." The boy turned to me again. "I don't like to hurt things. I don't like to fight. Do you like to fight?"

I told him the truth, "No, I'm mostly too scared."

"I don't like to fight," he said. "Some people think we should get out on the street and fight, but I don't like to. I'd rather go to the park and look in the cracks."

Then he began to talk more. He knew it all—how the insects changed from fall to winter and what happened in spring—and he knew it in amazing detail. Soon he began talking about the cockroaches in his apartment. He knew them, too—where they hid and had their young, what they ate, and when they would come and go.

Eventually the regular teacher took over the class and began the authorized ritual so familiar in some classrooms, "What did we learn?" The boy looked up, startled. He shrugged, crossed his arms, and slumped in his seat—gone again.

Out of what is for them the greatest reality—the events of their daily lives—children build private stories about how the world functions in relation to them. When that world is harsh, unpredictable, controlled arbitrarily by powerful others, when adults take little time to converse with children and interpret events for them, things happen to the way children reason.

Consider the operational test for his hypothesis that a second-grader gave me. I left two chickens in an inner-city classroom for a week. After a week the children began telling me what they had observed. Jose pointed to one of the chickens "This one is the mother, and this one is the father."

Chickens being what they are, I was surprised by the observation and asked him, "How did you decide that?"

"I'll show you," he said. "Whenever you put your finger in by this one, she pecks it, but she just pecks it soft. That one is the mother." His face took on a kind of gentle expression and he continued, "She never tries to hurt." He held my finger near the chicken so that I could feel what he meant. Then he moved my hand toward the other chicken, and he frowned. "This one is the father. See, it hurts when he pecks you. He always tries to hurt you. This one is the father." The second chicken did peck harder, and it did hurt. For the evidence Jose had, the inference fit. (The "acceptable" explanation for the rather astute observation that one chicken consistently pecked harder than the other probably has to do with the fact that a pecking order develops between two chickens in the same enclosure.)

DEVELOPING THE SENSE OF FATE CONTROL

It is important to the development of fate control that children have sufficient *time* to work with materials. As has been mentioned, human beings rarely do one-trial learning, so they need plenty of opportunity to repeat events until they have extracted meaning from them. By adjusting the systems, they learn to change the outcomes in predictable directions. (That is one purpose served by controls in an experiment. Controls help keep some variables from fluctuating, so that we can study the effect of changing other variables.)

Time to investigate means that the would-be investigator can get a better idea of how well his mental model explains the relationship between what he did to the system and what happened as a consequence. Doing something and getting a consequent event comes more and more under the control of the child as he gets enough practice with simple physical systems to build up some concepts of how they probably work and what he can do to change the way they work.

Mapping experience into language

Children need a great deal of opportunity to try to put their experiences and thoughts into communicable language. That process of mapping experience into communicable language takes time. Data in succeeding chapters will show how slowly the language and thought-mapping process goes on for a child as compared with an adult. Robbed of opportunities to struggle with communicating whole thoughts by the rapid-fire demands of their teachers, children can become increasingly inarticulate. In spite of the bridging function which the science materials and scientific phenomena may serve between children and teachers, the gulf widens when the adult, confronting his own anxieties about management, fails to listen to the cries from the box.

Using evidence

Learning to build arguments on the basis of evidence probably has a great deal to do with progress in developing fate control. Interesting physical and biological systems give children opportunity to see how evidence and inference can function to alter what they come to believe about a system and what they can do with the system as a result of how they do their imagining. To get some idea of how well some second-graders in the Science Curriculum Improvement Study were learning to trust their own ability to explore a novel system, to extract information from it, and to argue in favor of their view against a "powerful adult," I presented a whirly bird to ten SCIS children, one at a time. Ten controls from another school in the same part of the ghetto also worked individually with the whirly bird, a useless but interesting contraption that has many variables to be controlled in it. The task was to find out how putting rivets in the arms changed the *number* of turns or the *amount of time* the arms turned when the contraption was wound up. In this particular version of our investigation, we were interested in what kinds of things the children do to the apparatus, what observations and inferences they make, and what they do when the teacher (the experimenter) gives them an argument. It happened that many of the children in the control group could do little more than wind the machine up and let it run. They could not make connections between the number of rivets and the number of times the arms revolved. There was not much to argue with. In the experimental group, however, eight of the children did seem to develop strategies for finding relations. Every time they made an inference, they heard a contradictory statement from the teacher, "No, I do not think it works that way." If the children had internalized the belief that they could make systems behave in predictable ways and that evidence stood higher on the list of values than fiat, they would reply by arguing or by repeating the events and showing the results. Eight children did just that. Two others found relationships but backed down in the face of an argument, so we can imagine them as still in conflict between the authority of a powerful other who decides by fiat and the authority that stems from argument based on evidence.[2]

Understanding the concept of cause

Our conceptions of cause govern how we search the environment. When young children are pressed to furnish explanations *before they have sufficient experience* or even interest in imagining what exists that they cannot see, you hear conversations like the following (six-year-olds in a suburban classroom examining rocks):

> *First child:*   *I have a rock that sparkles, and brown goes through it.*
>
> *Second child:*   *I have a rock that has other rocks in it.*
>
> *Third child:*   *I have a rock that looks like a piece of meat. (Note the simile.)*
>
> *First child:*   *This looks like rock candy, but it isn't because rock candy has strings and it comes in a roll.*
>
> *Teacher:*   *Where do rocks come from?*
>
> *Child:*   *God made the rocks, and He made the whole world!*

So much for science. Some powerful person made the world, and there is no need to bother one's head about that. Consider how a fourth-grader responded to the request of the teacher to explain what made coupled pendulums behave the way they do. The girl shrugged, "I don't know. They just do, that's all."

Constructing explanations

Part of what goes into the development of fate control must lie in the kinds of explanations we eventually learn to construct. That, in turn, implies that we would do well to present children with phenomena they can have a reasonably good chance of coming to understand and that we avoid asking them questions like the one about rocks where there is no possible sequence of moves they can make to uncover events that lead to a particular outcome.

[2]Note that this approach has implications for evaluation in science and will be reconsidered in Part 3.

While the coupled-pendulum problem, drawn to its ultimate explanation, is also very complex, nevertheless, the children can go as far as attempting to build a model that would act in the same way (assuming that the nature of the coupling was hidden initially). They can find out what kinds of relationships between objects would produce essentially equivalent results. They can, in short, act on the environment in such a way as to make a new system behave like an old one. They can, that is, if anyone will let them.

Middle-class students have their problems, too. Sometimes they transfer language appropriate in one context to another context. For example, one group exposed photographic paper to sunlight. All the children were excited, but note how a suburban first-grader described what happened.

> Child: *It turns purple when it's distracted by the sunlight.*
> Teacher: *What do you mean—distracted?*
> Child: *You know, when the sunlight annoyed it.*

A kind of propositional thinking occurs in the suburbs when first-grade children try to decide what is in a mystery box by doing simple experiments on the box. The mystery container is just a closed shoe box with a magnet and some nails taped to the inside walls. The black box models the idea that there is a limit to the analysis or direct observation which a scientist can do. He constructs ideas of how a system probably works and essentially says, "If it is built like this, then it ought to act this way." As long as the mental model and the physical system conform, he assumes that he has correctly determined the structure.

> James: *Well, I put this nail on and I pulled it up and it was like a force against it.* [Observation.]
> Dotty: *I put a compass, and it began to vibrate.* [Observation.]
> James: *The compass went down.* [Observation.] *The magnet was pulling the needle down.* [Inference 1.]
> Paul: *I used the tape [magnetic] and when I put it over it, it came down.* [Observation.]
> Alice: *It could be a paper clip.* [Inference 2.]
> Whole class: *No!*

Jill:	*I found the little nail sticks to paper clips. [Jill argues for Alice's idea and shows a nail and clip.]*
Class:	*Well, you magnetized it.*
Teacher:	*Jill thinks it might be a paper clip, too.*
Paul:	*Impossible. When you put a magnet on these, it won't stay on there unless it is on in a special way; a paper clip can't make the magnet move. [Argument based on evidence.]*
George:	*Freddy said he had a compass, and it went around. It wouldn't do this with paper clips. [Argument based on another child's evidence.]*
Jill:	*The compass experiment convinces me. [Changes her mind on the basis of evidence.]*
James:	*This is direct observation. That one with the paper clip is indirect.*
Jill:	*But I don't think it could be a big nail in the box because it wouldn't fit.*

Examples of such sustained arguments on the basis of multiple sources of evidence rarely occur in ghetto classrooms until the middle of the second year of a science program marked by many opportunities to explore and *discuss* ideas. (See Chapter 8 for discussion of wait time as a variable that appears to be related to the incidence of conversations like the above.)

When children have enough experience with a variety of objects and the teacher models types of arguments based on evidence, the children begin to follow suit. We still do not know to what extent science programs that give every child access to materials help to develop propositional thinking. It is worth finding out, especially when so many youngsters who normally are not highly verbal seem to become so with scientific phenomena.

Once a person believes that some set of events is patterned—i.e., contains some relationships that are not random—he operates differently in relation to the events and even extracts different information from a situation. If the pattern is so invariable and repetitious that he soon learns to expect no change, he stops attending altogether. If it contains some regularity and some unpredictable elements, and he feels he can reduce the uncertainty by what he does to the system, he learns something about the relationships that exist in the system and his attention will tend to be maintained. If, on the other hand, he believes that how the system behaves is totally a matter of chance or under the control of someone else, he stops trying to discover a pattern in it or transfers his attention to the "someone else." In other words, where he thinks the reinforcements will be coming from seems to determine how he will act and what he will learn in any particular situation.

FATE CONTROL AND TASK PERSISTENCE

The effect that a dice-playing conception of the world can have on task persistence may be inferred from an experiment performed in 1962 by Holden and Rotter[3] using an ESP (extrasensory perception) task and money. Three groups of adult subjects each received two dollars in nickels and were told they could bet a nickel on each trial as to whether or not they would be able to name the card correctly. They could keep going until they ran out of money, or stop at any time and keep the change. One group of subjects were told that the outcome was totally a matter of chance. Another group was told that skill was involved. A third group received no information; this was called the *ambiguous* condition. The frequency of reinforcement was maintained as a constant across all three groups: that is, no matter what guess the subject made, half the time he was told he was correct. The group who had been told skill was involved stopped soonest. Apparently this group would have reason to think the reinforcement pattern should improve, and when it did not they withdrew. Almost twice as many trials were required to convince the other two groups to withdraw. Here we may imagine that if one does not know anything about the state of nature (in this case, whether ESP is a real or imagined thing), it will take more moves before one becomes convinced that there is in fact no relation between the phenomena (here, between what one guesses and what card turns up).

[3]K. B. Holden and J. B. Rotter, "A Nonverbal Measure of Extinction in Skill and Chance Situations," *Journal of Experimental Psychology*, vol. 63, pp. 519–520, 1962

In another experiment Phares[4] told one group of volunteers that they could avoid an electric shock by pressing the correct button and that they could learn by inference which was the correct button. This instruction has the consequence of making the player believe that there is a pattern and that he can discover it. Another group were told that they could press any of the buttons and it would be a matter of chance whether they would experience a shock. Both groups had to learn some nonsense syllables. Although the number and pattern of shocks actually delivered to both groups was the same, the group which had been instructed that they had some control of the situation exhibited better recognition of the syllables. This kind of experiment may seem irrelevant at first glance, but it has implications for science instruction. Subjects who feel they have control of the situation are more likely to exhibit perceptual behavior or other adaptive behavior that will allow them to cope with new situations than subjects who feel that chance or forces outside themselves determine whether or not their behavior will be successful. When a person perceives a task as controlled by the experimenter, the teacher, chance, or some other indefinable conditions, he relies less on his past experience and on reason. He actually learns less. In such cases we would expect random guessing and other random behaviors to increase, since the outcomes are perceived to be controlled by forces outside the individual. The outcomes in Phares' experiment resemble in certain respects the relationships of teachers to children in some classrooms.

HOW THE CONCEPT OF INTERNAL AND EXTERNAL CONTROL AFFECTS LEARNING

Although most of his work describes experiments with adults, the work of Julian Rotter[5] at the University of Connecticut on internal versus external control of reinforcement is closely related to the notion of fate control

[4] E. J. Phares, "Perceptual Threshold Decrements as a Function of Skill and Chance Expectancies," *Journal of Psychology*, vol. 53, pp. 399–407, 1962.

[5] Julian B. Rotter, "Generalized Expectancies for Internal Versus External Control of Reinforcement," *Psychological Monographs: General and Applied*, vol. 80, no. 1, Whole no. 609, 1966, pp. 1–28.

as we have discussed it so far. Rotter maintains that the effect of a reinforcement on some consequent behavior of an individual depends on whether he perceives a causal relationship between his own behavior and the occurrence of the reward. When a person persistently attributes the occurrence of rewards to forces outside of himself, he is said to have a belief in *external control*. If, on the other hand, he perceives an event as contingent on his own behavior or characteristics, Rotter describes him as believing in *internal control*. Rotter believes that this variable has much to do with how different individuals learn in various situations. Individuals differ in the degree to which, in any given situation, they are likely to attribute desirable or undesirable outcomes to their own actions. Rotter developed tests of internal-external controls that would indicate how individuals differed on this variable and how groups differ.

Rotter also makes the point, as a result of his studies, that psychological learning theory has little to do with how one goes about learning in real-life situations. Most real-life situations are perceived to be at least partly controlled by the skill of the individual, whereas in most concept-learning studies, for example, the experimenter controls the tasks and the schedules of reinforcement. He suggests that "experimenter control" may be equivalent to "chance control" in that the subject cannot effectively act on his own behalf to change the outcomes or the pattern of events. Here, again, we can infer a relationship between how, and to what extent, the teacher controls ideas and rewards and how adroitly children engage in things scientific. Children can come to believe that outcomes are subject to their own skill and the ingenuity with which they conceptualize the factors or variables at work in a situation. Alternatively, they can learn that all rewards and punishments come from a capricious adult who decides what should be praised and what should be blamed.

In general, performance on the internal-external control test (I-E) shows negligible correlations with intelligence but may have a great deal to do with acquisition of information. It seems that people tending to rate on the internal side of the scale make more attempts to get information that they could use to better their lives or to control the environment. The I-E scale seems to measure a psychological equivalent of the sociological concept of alienation, or a sense of powerlessness to change conditions. Seeman[6] used a modified I-E test and found a significant correlation between internality and the amount of incidental information reformatory inmates had acquired about how the reformatory was run, what was required to win parole, etc. "Internals" tended to know more, even though they did not exhibit appreciably different scores on measures of intelligence. Seeman and Evans[7] also found similar relationships between the amount of information matched pairs of tuberculosis patients had about their own condition, the degree to which they questioned doctors and nurses, and their degree of satisfaction with the amount of information they were getting. Internally controlled individuals were more active information getters. *So there may indeed be a relationship, apart from intelligence, that exists between fate control and information-seeking behavior.* I am suggesting that science appropriately taught may contribute to improving the sense of fate control and that this improvement, in turn, will increase the amount of voluntary learning and investigating that people will engage in.

Of course, we might anticipate that being at least in partial control of one's fate can produce some anxiety and a potential for excessive self-blame when things go wrong. It does seem to be the case that suicides are more prevalent among middle- and upper-class groups, which Rotter shows are generally more likely to exhibit somewhat higher scores on the internal-control side of the ledger. On the other hand, homicides are more prevalent among groups who are more generally dominated by an external-control model of the universe. Clearly, performance at either extreme of the I-E scale might have pathological consequences.

According to the Coleman report,[8] Negro children tend to perform as externals on the Rotter I-E scale. (Coleman called the I-E a measure of fate control.) He found that Negro youngsters who rated on the internal side of the scale also performed better in class. He commented that it was also interesting to note that high

[6]M. Seeman, "Alienation and Social Learning in a Reformatory," *American Journal of Sociology,* vol. 69, pp. 270–284, 1963.

[7]M. Seeman and J. W. Evans, "Alienation and Learning in a Hospital Setting," *American Sociological Review,* vol. 27, pp. 772–783, 1962.

[8]James S. Coleman, "Equality of Educational Opportunity," USOE Publication OE-38001, 1966.

schools in which children were predominantly on the E side of the scale had fewer laboratory facilities. Coleman felt that each child faces a two-stage developmental problem: first, he must learn that he can, within rather broad limits, act effectively upon his surroundings; second, he must evaluate his own capability for mastering the environment.

If highly external people have limited experience with situations which could be affected by their own actions, then it is not unreasonable to suppose that by providing children with numerous small physical and biological systems that provoke curiosity and by reasoning together with them, they might gradually develop an internal-control model. If, in addition, we can provide these materials in settings *where parents who do not ordinarily engage in joint mental ventures with their children might also investigate the systems,* the probability that children and parents might exchange ideas could be increased. Crandall and Katkovsky[9] related the interaction between parents and children to each child's sense of responsibility for his own actions. In two studies they found that supportive, positive relationships with children are more likely to foster beliefs in self-achievement and that interactions between father and child seem to influence the child's internal-external control more strongly than do those between mother and child.

In another experiment Julian and Katz[10] found that in a competitive game where the subject was given the option of relying on his opponent's expertise to earn points at no cost to himself, internals preferred to rely on their own skill even when reliance on the opponent might have yielded more points. This differential preference for relying on oneself occurred not only under skill-determined conditions but also on tasks where outcomes seemed to be controlled by luck.

Whether or not a child must make a prediction in advance of doing an experiment probably determines what he will eventually learn about the system under study. *The need to predict outcomes is a motivational component of internal-external control orientations.*

[9]Virginia C. Crandall and Walter Katkovsky, "Parental Antecedents of One Motivational Determinant of Intellectual Achievement Behavior," ERIC number: ED 020 223, 1967.

[10]James W. Julian and Stuart B. Katz, "Internal Versus External Control and the Value of Reinforcement," *Journal of Personality and Social Psychology,* vol. 8 (1, Pt. 1), pp. 89–94, 1968.

Forcing a prediction may serve to focus attention selectively on some features of the system and encourage the student to gain some control of it. If the prediction is confirmed, the experience is generally reinforcing. If the prediction is not confirmed, then new search behaviors may be initiated, *provided one has the right to be wrong.*

Beliefs and complex attitudes such as the one under discussion—fate control—are dependent on outcome variables. They arise from behaviors that precede them. It is more customary to suppose that attitudes cause the behaviors with which they are associated—i.e., that attitudes are an independent variable and the behaviors are the dependent or outcome variables. But as this discussion on fate control may have demonstrated, beliefs are under the partial control of the behaviors that led to their formation.

If we can accept the indications that some people operate in the world with beliefs that put most of the control outside of themselves, and others operate under the notion that more of the control of outcomes lies in their own hands, then we may ask what kinds of experiences a person must have to develop some belief in his own ability to control fate. Better still, we should ask what conception of how the world operates will help him *act as if* he can affect his own destiny. What conception will help him take responsibility for his own acts?

Whether he plays as if the game were dice or as if the game were bowling, he is free to dream—but only the bowler may one day realize his dream. It is ironical that what kind of a player a child becomes must, in some sense, depend on the people around him, including you, as his teacher. In a way you do control his fate. How you talk with him matters. How you let him explore matters. How you determine his rewards matters. Whether you are willing to let him meander occasionally and find his own way matters. What skills you teach him matter. And whether or not you have high hopes for him matters.

SUMMARY

1 Regardless of what science program you teach, it would seem to require at least the following properties if it is to make a contribution to the development of a sense of fate control:

a Materials must be put into the hands of every child—and perhaps be made available to their parents.

b The teacher must:

(1) Do a great deal of *listening* and *watching* (see Chapters 8 and 11)

(2) Keep rewards to a minimum during problem-solving sessions (see Chapter 10)

(3) Give children plenty of time to investigate and talk about their investigations

(4) Build language in context rather than by definition (see Chapters 7 and 12)

(5) Encourage students to ask questions

(6) Model arguments based on evidence

(7) Engage in conversation rather than inquisition

(8) Expect success

2 Fate control is a variable which is related to how much sense a person has that what he does matters—that is, that he is capable of influencing the outcomes of events.

3 Problem-solving behaviors seem to differ according to how people rate on fate-control measures. Those who score relatively higher on such measures tend to perform better.

4 Concepts of causality and probability or chance are probably related to the development of a sense of fate control. Science deals with concepts of causality and change.

a Prediction is a procedure that allows us to plan in relation to the future. It rests on the belief that events are not entirely capricious.

b Prediction based on analysis of past and present events is the basis of prediction. It suggests the most probable outcomes.

c Given a prediction, an individual can decide whether to intervene to change outcomes. Thus he gains some degree of control over the system.

5 Students' questions are one indication of a developing sense of fate control. Content and frequency of questions suggest what conception of causality the students have. Frequency indicates the vigor of their information-gathering efforts.

6 Those science investigations which provoke some conceptual conflict which the student can successfully reduce are rewarding. A sense of fate control is more likely to develop when rewards are perceived by the student to come about as a direct result of his behavior. (Chapter 10 shows that many teachers have a whimsical reward system that would tend to suppress the development of a sense of fate control.)

You can help choose the student's game: Will it be craps or bowling, fate or fate control?

ACTIVITY 9-1

OBJECTIVE

1 To identify rewards.
2 To relate reward frequency to the number and kinds of moves made by students and teachers.

What to do:

1 Classify the moves in Transcripts 9-1 and 9-2. Organize the data in a table.
2 Construct a histogram that shows how the moves are distributed between the speakers, where Rsp = responding; Rea = reacting; Str = structuring; and Sol = soliciting.
3 Count the number of rewards in each transcript.

		Frequency	Percent of player's moves
Teacher	Rsp		
	Rea		
	Str		
	Sol		
Student	Rsp		
	Rea		
	Str		
	Sol		

ACTIVITY 9-2

Design a study to investigate the influence of overt verbal rewards on inquiry. Choose your own outcome variables.

ACTIVITY 9-3

What teaching techniques are likely to help encourage the development of a sense of fate control?

ACTIVITY 9-4

Design an experiment to study the relation of science instruction to fate control. What behaviors would you take to be indicators of fate control?

ACTIVITY 9-5

State a relationship between prediction and fate control.

REFERENCE

For more detail on the Colorado population of teachers see:

M. B. Rowe and P. Hurd: "The Use of Inservice Programs to Diagnose Sources of Resistance to Innovation," *Journal of Research in Science Teaching*, vol. 4, no. 1, pp. 3–15, 1966.

CHAPTER 10

"Mostly what I learned is it's bad to make mistakes. If you try to talk over your ideas with someone else, she says you're cheating. Then she tells you to ask her questions if you don't understand something, but when you do she just bawls you out and says you weren't listening." —FOURTH-GRADE GIRL

"Sometimes she says it's good when you know it isn't. She's just trying to make you feel better—but I don't feel so good." —SIXTH-GRADER

"I'm always guessing what she wants. If I don't guess right, she looks so disappointed. I wish I didn't have to worry about it." —SIXTH-GRADER

SCIENCE AND SANCTIONS

OBJECTIVES

On completion of this chapter and its associated activities you should be able to do the following:

1 State a probable relation between reward rates and self-confidence in an investigation.

2 Design a simple classroom experiment to study the influence of reward frequency on inquiry-related behavior of students doing science.

INTRODUCTION

To "grow" a scientific thought system takes time and a great deal of shared experience, free of the notion of cheating. It is in talking about what we have done and observed, and in arguing about what we make of our experiences that ideas multiply, become refined, and finally produce new questions and new experiments.

To make a classroom safe for inquiry, students need to be able to work under conditions in which teachers *rarely* make either praising or blaming statements. As discussions later in the chapter will show, teachers do a great deal of overt verbal rewarding of students. As much as 25 percent of the talk of some teachers falls into the category of evaluative talk. These evaluative reactions to what students say and do—e.g., "Good," "Fine," "OK," "You are doing well"—actually seem to interfere with the development of sustained inquiry by students. While high-reward schedules of one kind or another may help students to acquire certain basic skills or to memorize some segment of information, such schedules appear to block sustained, productive search in which students try to find more than one way to think about something. It is in preserving for ourselves *the right to be wrong* that we gain the courage to try new ideas, to explore more than one alternative, to evaluate our own work. It is very difficult for students working in a highly evaluative atmosphere, one marked by a great deal of overt verbal rewards, to explore freely. The disposition is to do what is most likely to produce reward. Rewards function to distract attention from the system under investigation. The drive to move on to the next step comes from something external to the system being explored.

Science is one area where children can appraise their own work through sharing, comparing, and tearing apart, when appropriate, the results of their experiments. Nature, not the teacher, can be the final arbiter.

Science is essentially a social enterprise. It thrives on intellectual conflict. In fact, someone once described scientists as people with a quarrelsome interest in the doings of their neighbors. Reward comes for the scientist when he generates a new idea that proves fruitful or he conjures up a beautiful experiment, the results of which will help the scientific community to choose between two competing theories.

New ideas do not come without cost. Many experimental paths, probably about eight in ten, do not lead to an expected event. Some lead to a totally unexpected outcome which then shifts the whole direction of a research effort. More lead nowhere. In addition, ideas that once seemed "right" are replaced. The point is that scientists who are trying to grow their own thought systems reserve to themselves the *right to be wrong*—many times. Why should we not do the same? All this is not to say that scientists do not suffer some severe disappointments, but rather to suggest that if they can take risks, if they find it profitable to tolerate the uncertainty of not knowing for sure what the end result will be before they start an experiment, then why should we not, at least occasionally, give ourselves and children similar leeway in teaching and learning as we and they struggle to make some sort of sense out of our experiences?

The focus of this chapter is on the influence of overt verbal praising and blaming on the investigatory behavior of children. Almost all modern science programs put emphasis on developing in students a disposition to engage in productive inquiry. Part of productive inquiry requires that students interpret their experiences as they move through an investigation and, on the basis of the interpretation, make decisions about what next steps are reasonable. What part do patterns of reward and censure play in the decision-making processes of students doing science? We shall be examining data with one question in mind—what patterns of reward and censure are most likely to encourage children to maintain themselves in a constant state of readiness to encounter new and more complex scientific ideas? Joy, adventure, uncertainty, frustration, and excitement are all part of the experience of inquiry. What conditions of reward and censure are likely to enhance this kind of mental and emotional adventuring? The content of this chapter is controversial and incomplete in many respects because we do not know enough yet. It is definitely an invitation to further inquiry.

How do overt verbal rewards affect the development of sustained investigatory behavior? In this chapter we will look at samples of dialogue between teacher and students and among students to see what kinds of evaluative talk occur and under what circumstances. We will compare behaviors, language, and some of the logic exhibited by children who are taught science under a high positive-reward schedule with those of children taught under a markedly reduced reward pattern.

PATTERNS OF VERBAL SANCTIONS BY THE TEACHER

The average rate of delivering verbal sanctions (positive and negative) is apparently fairly regular for most teachers, regardless of what is going on, and differs somewhat between teachers. In extreme cases it may reach 25 percent of the total talk by the teacher.

In science the positive or negative evaluation of outcomes lies basically in the system of materials and what consequences come from the way one thinks about what happens. In the classroom, on the contrary, a great proportion of the judgments as to the worth of an idea seems to come from the teacher. One-trial learning more nearly characterizes classroom verbal dialogue as well as test patterns. This prevailing pattern runs counter to the pattern that makes science so dynamic. Scientists progress in part because they make frequent use of negative instances; some alternatives simply prove less fruitful than others. Some ideas which prove useful at one point may even turn out later to be clearly mistaken. How much opportunity is there for children to learn that negative instances contribute information which may help to refine a research strategy? Scientists compare their outcomes and argue energetically over interpretations. In a modern elementary science program, the students are meant to engage in similar discussions. Through this process they originate more ideas, correct misinterpretations, and develop confidence in their own capacities to search out explanations.

If our goal is to teach people to learn science in such a way that they will reorganize their conceptions as science changes, we probably have to give them practice at doing just that. To learn science, children have to make mistakes, just as scientists do. They have to try out ideas and decide *on the basis of evidence rather than fiat* which ones to keep and which to let go (Figure 10-1).

It takes a great deal of trust to pursue a modern science program (Figure 10-2). Children have to learn to trust their own ability to get evidence and make something of it. Teachers, for their part, have to learn to trust

FIGURE 10-1
Students evaluate ideas on the basis of evidence. (Courtesy of Paul Kirouac.)

FIGURE 10-2
Modern science programs tend to be based on the belief that scientific phenomena are intrinsically interesting.

children enough to let them attempt something which they themselves probably never experienced. After all, how often did *our* teachers and professors make it safe for us to make mistakes or to explore novel byways?

In an analysis of thirty-six transcripts of talk in first-grade science lessons, teachers seemed to exhibit different patterns of reward with students rated by them as "bright" and those rated as relatively "slow." The basis for rewarding the poor student was often more ambiguous than that for rewarding the better student. That is, the rewards were as likely to follow incorrect responses as correct responses. In addition, children rated slower by the teacher received more admonishments to "think" when they failed to answer, but had less time to do so. (We shall consider later other unhelpful pieces of advice in Chapter 15, on management and control.) Teachers in this sample actually gave more rewards to poorer students. Presumably, they rewarded effort, but the question is whether the students could distinguish between feedback meant to tell them the response was correct and feedback meant to convey appreciation of effort. It is of some interest to know if children learn to distinguish between the various bases of reward. It may also be pertinent to ask what the children who do not receive reward but hear it given to someone else are likely to learn. Can children distinguish between rewards given for trying and rewards given to signal acceptable responses? We might hazard the rather inflammatory proposition that short wait times plus a *consistently* high pattern of overt verbal rewards can turn the most imaginative science curriculum into chaos and drive all but the most hardy inquirer into hiding. Are children on high, often indiscriminate, reward schedules likely to check their ideas by resorting to experimenting on physical systems, or are they more likely to continue to rely almost totally on the word of the adult?

EFFECTS OF THE REWARD SCHEDULE

Modern science programs for the elementary school seek to develop self-confidence in children by allowing them to work out their ideas in experiments. Children find out how good their ideas are by living with the results. When predictions no longer work or when new information makes a point of view untenable, then they are free, at least in principle, to change their views. The point is that *the authority for change comes from the results of their experiments rather than from the teacher.*

We might speculate that a high pattern of rewards from the teacher would increase the likelihood that information would flow almost exclusively from the teacher. This would mean that in the classroom we might expect to see a good deal of "show and tell" behavior during a science lesson, with children waiting impatiently to show the teacher in order to garner rewards. We might also expect the number of disciplinary moves to be higher under the high reward schedule as children grow impatient waiting for their chance to display what they have accomplished. On the other hand, if the teacher removes herself as the primary source of reward by simply reducing overt verbal rewards, we might reasonably expect the pattern of communication to become more chainlike or circular. We might expect the children to depend less on the teacher and to do more comparing of results among themselves, given that this was not regarded as cheating.

These things do, in fact, appear to happen when the teacher's average rate of overt verbal rewards is reduced. Children demand less of the teacher's time and make more use of each other as a resource. They do more comparing and arguing about results. They are more prone to use evidence as an arbiter of arguments rather than the teacher. (One notes, for example, that incidence of eye-checking with the teacher tends to be higher under a high reward schedule than under a low reward schedule.)

To contrast the effects of a high reward schedule on the discourse of students with those of a low reward schedule, consider two lessons on thermal equilibrium. One is conducted under a relatively high schedule of overt verbal rewards, the other on a minimum reward schedule. Versions of this experiment appear in a number of elementary science texts and in the curriculums of two major cities (Transcripts 10-1 and 10-2).

Each of two milk bottles has a piece of ice lodged in the neck. One bottle is about one-third full of hot water, and the other is filled to the same level with cold water. The children try to account for differences in appearance that develop. The walls of one bottle fog up, while the walls of the other bottle remain clear. In 1 minute of con-

Transcript 10-1

Experiment on thermal equilibrium

1	*Teacher*	OK. Now I want you each to take one of these ice cubes. Each put your ice cube in the neck of the bottle, each in one bottle. Let's see what happens. (Pause.) Good. OK. Let's watch and see what is going to happen to the ice cubes. Do you think they are going to go through?
2	*First child*	The ice is slipping.
3	*Teacher*	Good. Slipping. How do you know?
4	*Second child*	Melting.
5	*Teacher*	Melting. Good. Which one?
6	*First child*	It's smoking. See, it's smoking. (The walls of one of the bottles fog up.)
7	*Teacher*	That's right. That is not really smoke, but it looks like it.
8	*First child*	Smoke. It's from the hot water. It comes from the steam.
9	*Teacher*	All right. And what is happening to the other bottle?
10	*Second child*	The ice is melting, but not as fast. It's not in hot water.
11	*Teacher*	Right. What kind of water was in this?
12	*First child*	Cold.
13	*Teacher*	Right.

Transcript 10-2

1	*Child*	You can see right through this bottle. Here (pointing to another bottle) it's all steamed up.
2	*Child*	It's like when your mother is steaming up some hot water to make Jell-o; then the windows steam up. Or maybe the hot water comes out of the cooking.
3	*Teacher*	Is there anyplace else?
4	*Child*	In the bathroom. Sometimes when you're running water to take a bath or something.
5	*Child*	Or you take a shower and the water comes down and makes steam.
6	*Teacher*	Right. You think it might be the same kind of thing?
7	*Child*	Yes, after someone in my family takes a shower, I look in the mirror, and there's a whole bunch of steam like this hot bottle.
8	*Teacher*	Do you think clouds could be formed like this?
9	*Child*	I don't see how. You would have to have hot water and where would you get it?
10	*Child*	The top there (points to bottle that is fogged up) is water in little droplets. Looks like there are all little, tiny hundreds and hundreds of drops all grouped together on the bottle.
11	*Child*	It looks like it's getting hotter and hotter down by the water. It is much hotter than it is up above the water. And down on this bottle (pointing to the bottle that has cold water) it is much colder where the water is than up above.
12	*Teacher*	Have you ever heard of a liquid turning to a gas?
13	*Child*	No. (Several answer together.)

versation recorded in Transcript 10-1, eight verbal rewards were given by the teacher; six of them followed statements by children. Verbal rewards include phrases like the following: "Good," "Fine," "OK," "All right," "Right," "You are doing well." Notice in particular that eight times in 1 minute the teacher in Transcript 1 repeats phrases which the children use. He rewards five of these phrases. Although it is somewhat debatable whether the teacher's repetition of children's observations constitutes a kind of reward, this is mentioned here to call attention to the phenomenon. It is common for teachers to repeat portions of what students say, as if giving tacit approval. The habit at least serves to maintain the star configuration for information flow. In transcript 10-2, however, reward is reduced to a minimum. Notice that explanations by students tend to be less fragmented. There is also evidence that students are paying attention to comments made by other students. Phrases like "I disagree with George . . . ," and "It didn't happen that way in ours . . . ," suggest that students in Transcript 10-2 hear each other. There is no evidence in Transcript 10-1 that such is the case.

Creative behavior in nonevaluative, time-free settings

The contribution that *sufficient time* and a *non-evaluative situation* can make to the innovative quality of children's thought finds support in a study of creative behavior of fourth-graders working under two different test conditions. O'Brien and Boersma gave fourth-graders the Unusual Uses (verbal) and Figure Completion (non-verbal) tests of creativity.[1] Half the children took the tests under the evaluative, time-controlled conditions that mark the usual school setting. The other half worked in a nonevaluative, group-play setting, and had as much time as they wished to complete the tasks. This latter group scored significantly higher on both measures of creativity. In addition, the correlation between creativity and intelligence was substantially lower. With emphasis on success minimized and with the pressure of time removed, children displayed significantly more creative behavior, even on measures that ordinarily correlated rather strongly with intelligence. The experimenters gave the children all the response time they needed and withheld praise. The children in their study began by giving common responses at a relatively high rate. Then the rate slowed down and the children began to produce more unusual answers. In the nonevaluative, time-free setting the children generated more cognitive associates and more unique associates. It should not be so surprising, then, to suggest that science instruction and learning might benefit from some reduction of reward and censure rates as well as from the more deliberate use of wait time as a manipulable variable.

Working in a setting free of evaluative stress and unrestricted as to time, Wallach and Kogan studied the

[1] K. G. O'Brien and F. J. Boersma, "Differential Relationships Between Creativity and Intelligence under Two Conditions of Testing," Session 2.5, AERA, Feb. 8, 1968.

creative behavior of fifth-grade children confronted with a variety of tasks and contents.[2] Most measures of creativity used by other investigators show a strong correlation with intelligence scores. The time-free, nonevaluative technique used by Wallach and Kogan, however, resulted in a new measure of creativity that is largely independent of intelligence. They found children in their sample who could be classified as both creative and intelligent, some who could be classified as creative but not particularly intelligent, some classifiable as intelligent but not creative, and some classifiable as neither creative nor intelligent. By the fifth grade, then, a creative factor whose main effect is independent of intelligence may be identified. While it remains to be seen what events lead to its development, it is unlikely to thrive in science settings where the pace is fast and the teacher is the exclusive source of approval, and not a very reliable source at that, since the pattern of reward is often indiscriminate. In short, we might hypothesize that innovative solutions to problems and the invention of alternative explanations are less likely to occur under a high-frequency reward schedule than under conditions that could be termed neutral.

Whereas a highly evaluative school setting in which time is constricted favors children of high intelligence, it does little to foster their creative development. The apparently dramatic shifts in overt patterns of responding in science that young children exhibited when teachers increased wait times and decreased sanctions may come about because these two variables, high wait times and low overt verbal rewards, especially favor the display and practice of creative behavior.

As science tasks or problems become more complex, the effect of rewards on the thinking process needs more careful examination. It is not altogether unreasonable to suppose that rewards administered while children are doing a problem may function like *noise*. They may interrupt logical thought processes.

Rewards and problem solving

Sometimes it is useful to simulate a process in order to understand how the process produces effects. Francis

---

[2]Michael A. Wallach and Nathan Kogan, *Modes of Thinking in Young Children,* Holt, Rinehart and Winston, Inc., New York, 1965, chap. 2.

X. Lawlor simulated three different reward regimens found in elementary science in order to study the influence of rewards on problem solving.[3] The most frequent regimen resembles a randomly administered flow of overt verbal rewards where it is difficult to decide just what is being praised. Incorrect responses are about as likely to be rewarded as are correct responses.[4] A second kind of pattern is also characterized by a high reward frequency, but the rewards are for the most part pertinent to students' statements. A third, relatively rare, pattern is characterized by no overt verbal rewarding; for convenience, we will refer to this pattern as a *neutral reward condition*. Lawlor focused on the influence of these three kinds of reward schedules on the problem-solving efficiency of 202 second-grade pupils who had been taking part in a modern elementary science program, the Science Curriculum Improvement Study(SCIS).

By observing the impact of reward patterns on the way children working alone did simple, meaningful sorting tasks like those suggested in levels of the SCIS, SAPA, and ESS curricula,[5] among others, Lawlor could record exactly how each individual child responded. Lawlor focused on problem-solving efficiency. He used the *People Blocks* kit (ESS) for one set of categorization tasks and a set of varied geometric shapes of his own design for another task. Students in one group received praise from the experimenter after each correct categorization. That is, they received pertinent rewards. Those in another group received praise on a fixed-time schedule which simulated the random condition common in many classrooms. It did not matter, in other words, how the children in this group categorized. They were praised at random—sometimes in the middle of what they were doing. This was the random-reward schedule. A third group worked in a nonevaluative setting with no verbal

[3]Francis X. Lawlor, "The Effects of Verbal Reward on the Behavior of Children in the Primary Grades at a Cognitive Task Typical of the New Elementary Science Curricula," unpublished doctoral dissertation, Teachers College Press, Columbia University, 1969.

 Also published as an article under the same title in the *Journal of Research in Science Teaching*, vol. 7, no. 4., pp. 327–340, 1970.
[4]Bellack et al. found similar random patterns in high school social studies classes. A. A., Bellack, H. M. Khebard, R. T. Hyman, and F. L. Smith, *The Language of the Classroom*, Teachers College Press, Columbia University, New York, 1963.
[5]SCIS: Science Curriculum Improvement Study (Rand McNally). SAPA: Science— A Process Approach (Xerox). ESS: Elementary Science Study (McGraw-Hill, Webster Division).

rewards delivered by the experimenter. This was the neutral or no-record condition.

If rewards functioned to divert attention away from the system, then children who received many randomly administered overt verbal rewards should solve the problems less efficiently than those on low reward schedules. Pertinent rewards might encourage pupils to focus on the teacher rather than on the system. However, efficiency should be somewhat better for the pertinent reward condition than for the random reward condition. Children who received no rewards, Lawlor predicted, should solve the problems most efficiently.

The efficiency indicator that Lawlor chose, the E-ratio, was the number of acceptable sorts divided by the total number of sorts.

$$E = \frac{\text{Number of acceptable sorts}}{\text{Total number of sorts}} \times 100 \text{ percent}$$

So, for example, if a student made fourteen groupings, seven of which were correct, his efficiency would be $\frac{7}{14} \times 100 = 50$ percent.

Unacceptable sortings were those in which children failed to base their groupings on properties of the materials. The children in the no-reward and pertinent-reward conditions had higher E-ratios than did those in the random-reward condition. Both boys and girls do well under the no-reward condition, but girls do better than boys in the pertinent-reward condition; this seems to indicate that girls are more attentive to verbal cues from the teacher and that they know how to use them to guide behavior. Boys performed better under the *neutral* condition.

If the number of unacceptable sortings is taken as an indicator of randomness in behavior, then it is of special interest that Lawlor found the random-reward schedule to produce more random behavior. Teachers may be doing a great deal of rewarding simply out of habit.

The two tasks Lawlor used varied slightly in their stimulus complexity. The *People Blocks* kit required finer discriminations and offered more sorting alternatives than did the geometric shapes of different colors. Nevertheless, neither task was especially difficult, and it is surprising, therefore, that the children were at all sensitive to the different reward conditions. Performance on the people-blocks task proved to be somewhat more influenced by the various reward conditions.

This leads one to speculate that as the task or problem becomes more complex, a high reward rate, either pertinent or random, will be even more likely to interfere with efficient problem solving and perhaps may even block it altogether.

The whole subject of the relation of overt verbal rewards to inquiry processes needs much more investigation. Lawlor's simulation involved one student at a time, but in fact students more often work in groups. That means some of them collect rewards and others hear rewards given. Another investigator, L. Sechrest, has suggested that the effects of a reward on the unrewarded members of a group may be greater than the effect upon the person meant to receive it.[6]

At this point in the state of knowledge about the influence of rewards on inquiry behavior, it appears to be a safe rule to suggest that overt verbal rewards be reduced to a minimum. This is not to imply, however, that teachers should not show normal pleasure in the things students do and say. Instead, the work to date indicates that teachers should be cautious in giving praise. Situations that are not evaluative are psychologically safe for innovative responding. (Some Skinnerians would approve this advice on the basis that an intermittent reward schedule will be more likely to elicit the desired search behaviors during inquiry.)

Rewards and skill learning

You will note that most of what has been discussed in relation to rewards or to sanctioning in general was confined largely to the formulation and solving of problems. We made only passing reference to the use of rewards to teach children specific skills and particular pieces of information. We have not talked in any detail about reinforcement schedules designed to teach specific content. Instead we have focused attention on the relation of rewards to information seeking and decision making in the context of particular problems or situations.

The distinction between rewards used to encourage learning of skills and the influence of reward on problem solving must be maintained for the moment. Most science programs that depend on laboratory learning as a part

[6]L. Sechrest, "Implicit Reinforcement of Response," *Journal of Educational Psychology,* vol. 54, 1963.

of instruction operate on an intrinsic-motivation model. They assume that some physical or biological stimulus will provoke curiosity because of its novelty or because it produces conceptual conflict. Students will seek to satisfy their curiosity or reduce the mental conflict by operating on the system. The cues that guide students through a problem are meant to come from their inter- actions with the system. Praise and blame may divert attention from the system. What is pertinent depends on what they know or think at each stage in an investigation. There are ways teachers can assist students, but in general, high reward patterns probably will hinder more than they will help the development of confidence on the part of students in their ability to conduct investiga- tions. Under a low reward schedule, students will be more likely to ask for assistance and to be able to specify what kind of help they need. Under a high reward sched- ule, students will tend to be less adventuresome in their thinking. At least these are predictions worth testing.

Rewards and affective responses

Learning goes on through the use and modification of mental models we have about the world. But the feel- ings we have control our willingness to explore. *Fright- ened people do not venture as freely as do confident people.* Studies by Edward Zigler suggest that our affec- tive systems may be more responsive to instruction than our cognitive systems.[7] For this reason, as well as for reasons of what we wish to accomplish with respect to the views of science that children acquire, the study of the effect of overt verbal rewards and sanctions re- quires more detailed investigation, especially by class- room teachers.

If, for convenience, we separate what in practice are never separated, namely, the cognitive and affective components in any learning situation, then we may imag- ine situations in which much is learned and little is liked. We may also conceive of situations where little is learned but the experience is pleasurable. We can imagine situa- tions where much is learned, and the excitement that accompanies the learning maintains some momentum that transfers to other situations. What is learned may

[7]Edward Zigler, *An Overview of Research in Learning, Motivation, and Percep- tion,* Yale University Press, New Haven, Conn., 1962. (ERIC code: ED 020 799, PS 001 011.)

have consequences for the cognitive system, but how it is learned may determine what happens to the affective system. High rates of overt verbal rewards and sanctions in a modern elementary science program may function in ways not anticipated.

We do not know enough yet about the subtle blending of our feelings with the way we think. How that mix comes about in science certainly eludes us. But one thing seems evident—science materials do provoke excitement and pleasure, and if children are given a chance, they will do and say all kinds of content-relevant things. The potential for operating on an intrinsic-motivation model exists in science. But we really have not investigated how to exploit opportunities to drive children's thinking toward the construction of more and more interesting and sophisticated explanations or to have them feel the excitement many scientists feel as they engage in that kind of discourse.

A divergent view: the Bereiter-Engelmann program

At least one major program of instruction that includes science relies heavily on strong cues and rewards from the teacher. To teach content, the teacher follows a script exactly as written. Originally developed to teach reading, the program was expanded to include mathematics and science content. S. Engelmann and C. Bereiter maintain that no thinking goes on unless students acquire substantial amounts of content. Thus they prepare a script which the teacher follows and in which room for divergent responses by students is cut to a minimum. Successful performance nets tokens for students, who then use the tokens to buy time to do things they want to do. For example, as part of the attempt to teach the distinction between "more" and "less," the teacher displays two balls of clay that are equal in size and asks:

> Is one of these balls bigger than the other?
> (Wait)
>
> Do these balls have the same amount of clay?
> (Wait)
>
> Listen and see if you can figure this out. I want to make one ball bigger than the other ball. . . . What do I want to do?
> (Wait)

But I am not going to do anything to this ball! Who can tell me how I am going to make this ball bigger? (Wait)

The teacher follows a script for an entire lesson, issuing rewards and giving cues at a high rate. It should be noted, however, that this use of structure and reward is designed simply to transfer information from the teacher, who has it, to the students, who do not. The pace is deliberately fast. Divergent responses cannot easily be accommodated. The objective is really to .teach basic discrimination skills and language. It remains to be seen how well students on a sustained regimen of this sort will be able to engage in investigations of the kind called for in many of the other modern elementary science programs.

Rewards and fate control

Recall the discussions of fate control in Chapter 9. There, the distinction was made between people who believed that the world was governed only by chance, the craps model, and those who believed there was some order in it, the bowling model. We might guess that the random-

FIGURE 10-3
A sense of fate control may be nurtured in an atmosphere which is relatively free of sanctions, contains sufficient wait times, and allows people to inquire together.

reward schedule would foster the craps model. Pertinent-reward and no-reward conditions might favor development of the bowling model. (Figure 10-3.)

Praise of persons versus praise of tasks

There may be some value in distinguishing praise of a task well performed from praise of a person. The first contains specific feedback and may encourage a particular class of behaviors, but the second may act more like buckshot—when it hits you, you tingle all over, but you are not sure just what part is hit. Diffuse praise contains nonspecific feedback and may produce some anxiety.

The distinction between praise of a task, e.g., "Good, you solved that problem in a new way," and of a person, e.g., "You would make a good scientist," may be small in the mind of the teacher but appears to present different consequences for students who receive the praise. Specific praise of a task might encourage a particular class of behaviors, such as seeking novel solutions. Praise of a person, on the contrary, leaves the student in doubt about exactly what he did that merited praise and what behaviors he should continue to exhibit. For these reasons, if praise is directed at the *task* rather than at the *person,* students are more likely to respond with continued action in the task, e.g., selection of another task: if, on the other hand, the teacher directs the reward to the *person* (e.g., "You're a good student" or "You would make a good scientist"), the probability that the activity will continue declines for a period.

Sometimes a teacher notices something a child does and praises him, only to learn that he was not the first to make the discovery but got it from someone else. Some bad feelings may then develop among the children over the adult's natural expression of pleasure. That is another reason why reducing overt verbal rewards often improves the working conditions in the classroom. The visibility of science activity makes knowledge general, whether you want it that way or not.

In listening to children talk and joke with each other after these two kinds of rewards have been administered, we may have identified one source of the difference between their effects. We have found it not at all uncommon that when a teacher addresses praise to a child rather than to an act, the child takes a considerable amount of teasing from his peers when the teacher departs from the scene. If, on the other hand, the task is reasonably praised or no evaluative comment is made about it, the probability that the child will be teased is low, and the chance that he will be asked about what he did by his peers increases.

It may be important, then, to investigate further the relation of the *phrasing* of statements of praise or blame to the development of inquiry skills in science. Zigler and Williams;[8] Terrell, Durkink, and Wiesley;[9] and Rosenhan[10] report differences between social classes in response to these two forms of reward. My observations and manipulation of these variables during science lessons failed to expose a difference.

Perhaps we should deemphasize the success-failure aspect of interactions in the classroom and emphasize instead evaluation by students themselves of outcomes in terms of what they find out about a physical or biological system. We have said that one way to encourage this is to produce problems structured in such a way that they contain an element or even several elements of surprise or uncertainty. In the course of the dialogue in the classroom, the teacher listens carefully to what children say in order to pick up issues that are essentially conjectural, points of view that would suggest different procedures, or inferences which students make concerning the same data but which do not seem compatible. Properly adjudicated, these serve as fuel to drive the conversation on and push inquiry to more advanced levels. For scientists, logical argument and empirical testing followed by more argument is a process that contains its own self-corrective properties while at the same time propelling scientists toward new discoveries. Why should that process not serve the same ends for students, at least sometimes, in the science classroom? If there must be praise, be judicious about it. If, one day, it comes from students themselves, so much the better.

Students will find praise of tasks more useful than praise of persons, since the feedback implicit in praise of tasks is more specific.

[8]E. Zigler and J. Williams, "The Effectiveness of Two Classes of Verbal Reinforcers on the Performance of Middle and Lower Class Children," *Journal of Personality*, vol. 30, pp. 157–163, 1962.

[9]G. Terrell, K. Durkink, and M. Wiesley, "Social Class and the Nature of the Incentive in Discrimination Learning," *Journal of Abnormal and Social Psychology*, vol. 59, pp. 270–272, 1959.

[10]D. L. Rosenhan, "Effects of Social Class and Race on Responsiveness to Approval and Disapproval," *Journal of Personality and Social Psychology*, vol. 4, pp. 253–259, September, 1966.

SUMMARY

1 Three patterns of overt verbal rewards appear in elementary science classrooms:

   a Random, in which it is difficult to identify exactly what behavior is being rewarded.

   b Pertinent, in which only correct responses are rewarded.

   c Neutral, in which almost no overt verbal rewards are given.

2 It is hypothesized that a nonevaluative pattern, the neutral condition, may be most suitable for large portions of inquiry-based elementary science programs. Classroom observations of children subject to a high reward schedule while doing science experiments indicate that the incidence of errors, the necessity of repeating steps, and the frequency of checking with the teacher are significantly higher than when children operate under a lower reward schedule.

3 Most teachers would find some improvement in the self-confidence of students if positive and negative sanctions were greatly restricted.

   a Use rewards to get acceptable social behavior, e.g., "You did a good job on cleaning up."

   b Use rewards in drill, "Right, this ball is bigger."

   c Avoid rewards during the course of an investigation.

4 When patterns of overt verbal rewards are high, students will show low self-confidence, as indicated by:

   a Answering many questions with an inflection that seems to say, "Is that what *you* want?"

   b Doing more eye checking with the teacher, even when materials are in front of them.

When patterns of rewards are low, these effects tend to diminish or disappear.

5 When the pattern of overt verbal rewards is high, students' responses tend to occur in short phrases, with little or no amplification, and their explanations tend to be terse and incomplete. When the frequency of rewards is reduced, students' explanations tend to become longer, and they more often state alternative explanations.

6 When the pattern of overt verbal rewards is high, children will be less likely to compare results with each other and to use each other as resources for ideas and information. This is indicated by:

a More waving of hands and "oohs" and "ahs," as they compete for the teacher's attention.

b Less evidence of listening to each other's ideas and building on these ideas.

As a result, the teacher's management problems increase. When the frequency of rewards is reduced, there is less dependence on the teacher and more manifest interest in the findings of other students.

7 When the frequency of overt verbal rewards is high, children will be less likely to value doing science for its own sake; evidence of how they value science may be found in what they choose to do in their leisure time.

ACTIVITY 10-1

OBJECTIVE

To find some behavioral indicators for the fate-control variable

In this chapter a concept called *fate control* is discussed. The problem is to find some way of converting fate control into a variable that can be investigated.

What to do:

1 Think of some science problem to be investigated. Imagine how two students, one who is relatively high on fate control and one who is relatively low on fate control, would face the problem. List the ways in which you would expect them to differ. (List some indicators you would use to infer the presence of a fate-control variable.)
2 List the factors in instruction that probably contribute to development of a reasonable level of fate control.

ACTIVITY 10-2

OBJECTIVE

To identify some behavioral indicators of fate control

What to do:

1 Read Transcript 11-2 in Chapter 11.
2 In statements 9 to 13 there is conflict between the authority of evidence from the system and authority of the teacher.

a Which of the boys probably would stand higher on a fate-control measure? State the evidence.
b Which of the boys probably would stand lower on a fate-control measure? State the evidence.

CHAPTER 11

"It is the right of the teacher to ask, and the duty of the student to answer."   —KIKUYU BOY IN KENYA

"If the teacher asks me and I do not know, my friends also will not answer. They will tell me after, perhaps, but they will not make me look foolish."   —HOPI BOY IN ARIZONA

"If she asks me and I know the answer, then I like to answer. If I don't know, then I keep hoping she will miss me. But I may raise my hand anyway, because sometimes she calls on you if it looks like you don't know."   —FIFTH-GRADE BOY

INQUISITION VERSUS INQUIRY

OBJECTIVES

On completion of this chapter and the activities associated with it, you should be able to do the following:

1 Demonstrate an acceptable variety of question types during a teaching session.

2 Demonstrate an acceptable rate of asking questions. (Normally rates are too high.)

3 Plan a series of lessons to teach students how to ask questions.

4 Identify four kinds of moves that teachers and students can make: soliciting, responding, reacting, and structuring.

5 Distinguish between inquisition and inquiry.

6 State a relation between conceptual conflict and inquiry.

7 Distinguish between directed and diffuse statements and questions.

INTRODUCTION

Traditionally, the relation of teacher to student has been as the Kikuyu boy described it—the teacher asks, and the student answers.

Aschner calls teachers professional question askers.[1] They may ask 2,000 questions or more a week. In modern elementary science programs, where students are supposed to be getting practice at inquiry, a study of 300 tape recordings indicated that students actually ask very few questions. In tape-script analyses of lessons on "Grandma's Button Box," Science Curriculum Improvement Study (SCIS) done with first-graders, "Measurement of Angles," Science, A Process Approach (Measurement 17, SAPA) done with fourth- and fifth-graders, and "Thermal Equilibrium" (an experiment that appears in some form in many texts and in at least two "big city" curriculum guides) carried out with second-, third-, and fourth-graders, the number of questions asked by teachers ranged from a low of fourteen to a high of seventy-two for an average 10-minute segment of discussion. The number of questions asked by students ranged from a low of zero to a high of six for the same period. Most of the questions asked by teachers called for facts or data. Only one question in seventeen required students to do any complex thinking. These questions tended to be very incompletely answered. Students had too little time to think, and teachers took too little time to hear them try to reason their responses. The questions asked by students served mainly to clarify procedures or to request that part of the directions be repeated.

In the context of modern elementary science programs, it is appropriate to ask two questions:

1 Why rush? Is it necessary to ask so many questions in such a short time?
2 What can we do to help students become better question askers?

It takes time to study natural phenomena, to construct explanations, and to evaluate those explanations by examining data. Mankind did not achieve its present state of knowledge overnight, and neither will children.

[1]M. J. Aschner, "Asking Questions to Trigger Thinking," *NEA Journal,* vol. 50, pp. 44–46, 1961.

If many students observe and think about some experiment at the same time, you can be very certain that when you hear what they observe and think, the total pool of observations and possible explanations will exceed your wildest imaginings. If students learn to listen to each other, they may compound even more explanations and find themselves in frequent disagreement. To settle their differences, they must frequently reconsider the evidence. In this way they open themselves to huge amounts of information which they must constantly evaluate or to which they must react. Gradually they learn to model the type of contentious discourse that gives science so much vigor. But if all this is to happen, teachers and children must give each other *time to think. There is a distinction between inquiry and inquisition. Inquiry is something teachers and students may do together. Inquisition is something teachers do to students.* Modern elementary science programs depend more on developing productive techniques of inquiry than on indoctrination. Thus there is less need for inquisition. Be mindful of the anguished complaint of one fourth-grader: "Everything is rush, rush, rush. They don't like you to think about anything even though that's what they're always shouting at you—think! All you're supposed to do is give answers, answers."

THE GAME MODEL OF THE CLASSROOM

For the moment imagine the classroom as a system consisting of two players—a teacher and a set of students. The set of students is considered to be one player in a game where the other player, the teacher, controls the rewards and the pacing. Imagine that each player can make four kinds of moves:

1 Soliciting—asking questions
2 Responding—replying to questions or to statements from the other player
3 Reacting—evaluating statements made by the other player, expressing feelings
4 Structuring—making suggestions about how to proceed, starting a new line of reasoning, etc.

Traditionally, the teacher monopolizes three of the moves—soliciting, structuring, and reacting. The students hold a corner on the fourth kind of move, responding. (It is not uncommon, however, for teachers to answer their own questions.)

Under the two-player model of the classroom, productive inquiry is more likely to occur when both players have equal access to all four kinds of moves. Teachers need to learn how to ask good questions—and so do students.

Questions do not necessarily serve the same purpose for both players. Students are supposed to be inquiring about physical and biological systems. Teachers, on the other hand, have both the students and the laboratory phenomena as foci for inquiry.

IMPROVING THE QUALITY OF STUDENTS' INQUIRY

Suppose we neglect for the moment what children do when the teacher asks them questions and ask, instead: What are their ways of knowing, or what are their ways of getting information? In the context of science they seem to have three sources: the physical system or biological system, each other, and the teacher or some authority such as a book. It appears that their mode of getting information from the teacher is to listen. They do not generally interrogate the teacher. From their peers they get information by initiating a conversation or, possibly, by listening to what they say when the teacher asks questions. From the physical or biological system, they get information by observing and acting on the system to change it in some fashion. These interactions with the physical system amount to questions that the student asks of nature.

Students need to be taught how to ask questions of themselves so that they can improve the quality of their own inquiry. Analysis of tape scripts made while children "do" science in small groups in which the teacher is not present suggests that while students may often be puzzled, they rarely address questions directly, even to each other. Instead they make statements. Their questions are often hidden away in the statements and suggestions. Consider, for example, the sample of discourse taken from a transcript made in a Cumberland Mountain school where children from eight to sixteen years of age were in the same class. They were working with batteries and

Transcript 11-1

		Dialogue	Analysis
			(The children were trying to hook up lightbulbs and motors.)
1	*12-year-old*	Golly, look at that.	Gee-whiz stage.
2	*His partner*	What did you do?	
3	*12-year-old*	I just put this here and this here and the thing went on.	
4	*8-year-old*	Hey, look what I got. I got them both working. Let's see if you can hook yours into mine and we can get them all going. (Suggestion is accepted, and all three begin combining their systems.)	Start of investigation—a structuring suggestion is made.
5	*Partner*	Not that way, you dope. It won't work that way. You have to put them one after the other.	A difference of opinion develops. Conflict of procedures.
6	*8-year-old*	No, you don't. Look, if you do it this way, you can turn out one light and the others will stay on. (Shows them—after a brief struggle for command of a wire.)	
7	*12-year-old*	What would happen if we got more wire and bulbs and stuff? Let's see if she has more. (Goes off to ask for additional materials.)	Concrete inference diffuses.
		At this point the boy and teacher arrive with more materials. The teacher stands a while watching and finally says:	
8	*Teacher*	I think you can get that many bulbs to light and use fewer wires. I think you have three wires in there you don't need.	Attempt to produce cognitive conflict.
		The teacher then left the group, and the following remarks ensued:	
9	*8-year-old*	If we take out this wire, there won't be any way to get the juice from the battery to the motor.	Concrete inference—direct elimination.
10	*Partner*	Who cares? I just want to put this stuff in and see if it works.	Concrete inference—diffuse addition.
11	*12-year-old*	Well, if we could save some wires, we could get more things hooked up. I think we could take out this wire (pointing). Anyhow, maybe she's (the teacher) just putting us on.	Concrete inference—directed elimination.
12	*Partner*	Well, she wouldn't say it if she didn't know she was right, would she?	Challenge of source that produced conflict.
13	*12-year-old*	Well I want to see if she's right. (He begins switching wires around, and an argument develops over what they are trying to do.)	Immediate goal in doubt.

bulbs, an activity that appears in virtually all science programs at some point or another (Transcript 11-1).

When several children act on a physical system at the same time, they may all be wanting to ask a different question or perform a different operation, and that can make for some hot social interaction. If the intervention of the teacher from time to time with questions and observations can keep the members focused on the same investigation, there may be differences of opinion, but the conflict will tend to be useful. It will revolve around variables in the system. If, on the other hand, the questions have the effect of splitting the goals of the group, then the content of the problem may be lost in useless social conflict. The problem that the teacher faces in moving from group to group is discovering where each group is in its deliberations.

Recall that we said a physical or biological system acquires a history. That simply means that it changes over time. The time that is relevant may be very short (even fractions of a second, as in the case of an explosion) or very long (as in the case of germinating plants or gestating animals). But most of the systems children study do change or are acted on within the span of a few minutes, or at least within the usual class period. As the teacher moves about the classroom from system to system, the problem of discovering through what stages each group of children and the phenomena have moved becomes more difficult. As the groups begin to vary in their progress according to what happens in each system and according to what the members try to do, the teacher has to sample the activity of each group more and more efficiently. The children sample (or take data from) the physical system, but the system of interest to the teacher is more complex. It consists of all the various student systems and the nature of the encounters the various groups have with the phenomena. There has to be a way to find out how students interpret their experiences. Eventually the instructor must find a way to teach the children to help him or her understand "where they are at," as one boy put it. Usually the means to that end get in the way of its achievement. Under pressure of time, numbers and variety of activities, and differing durations of interest, teachers often develop a pattern of inquisition that is self-defeating.

There are ways to learn from observation and listening. Sometimes all that is necessary is to watch and listen for a while in order to establish the context. It is also possible to train groups to report what has happened thus far. That procedure encourages students to give their individual versions of the *sequence* of events and the kind of evidence they think relevant. The process of reporting benefits the group as much as the teacher, since it invariably happens that if the teacher checks to see whether everyone agrees with what one child reports, at least one child will not agree or will report something the others missed. The function that this kind of "telling" serves for the teacher is clear. It furnishes the information that helps him decide whether to (1) listen and leave, (2) encourage discussion among members as a way of exposing more data or increasing the sophistication of the ideas developing in the group, or (3) help the group to clarify its most immediate objective. The function reporting serves for the group is to help it arrive at some consensus regarding its procedures, observations, and inferences. Students can be taught to give two kinds of information at this stage: (1) what was observed; (2) the *sequence* in which events happened. Until they get considerable practice, students frequently garble the sequence.

IMPROVING THE QUALITY OF QUESTIONING BY THE TEACHER

The peculiar relation which getting information, making inferences, and hypothesizing as processes hold to each kind of content area in the curriculum probably needs special examination. It may be more necessary in other subjects than in science to rely on secondary sources of information and to argue by justification or by invoking authorities. In science the physical phenomena can be made directly available to everyone. For the same reason, there may be less need for teachers to ask so many questions when they teach science than when they teach other subjects. Although tape recordings made of elementary science classrooms indicate that without training on wait time the rate of question asking tends to be high, teachers may simply be transferring to science habits acquired in teaching other subjects. Questions by the teacher seem to be used for three purposes: (1) *evaluation,* in which the teacher tries to find out what the student already knows or remembers; (2) *control,* in which the teacher carries on a kind of inquisition whose implicit function seems to be to reduce the need for overt disciplinary moves; and (3) *instruction,* in which the teacher uses questions to point children to resources, to point out discrepancies, and in other ways to produce some level of cognitive conflict.

The kindly inquisitor: the Socratic method

Socrates, that most famous of teachers, conducted his instruction largely by questioning. His technique placed the learner first in a state of conflict. When a student expressed an opinion, Socrates would get him to expand the idea, to expose the extent of the idea. Then Socrates would "unsettle" the view either by exhibiting some data that threw doubt on the notion or by pointing out some inconsistency within the statements made by the student. His style of interrogation led students to make the responses that he intended they should make. "Is it not true that . . . ," he would begin, and the student would usually answer with "yes" or "no," depending on the cues. Thus it was the style of Socrates to invite confirmation of his own logic after having once made the student vulnerable by producing doubt at an early stage in the student's argument.

If we examine the kinds of questions that Socrates asked and the sort of responses he expected from the student in the discourse shown in Transcript 11-2, we note that his treatment of the Greek slave is remarkably consistent. Socrates states a fact in the form of a question that simply invites the boy to agree. Occasionally the boy has to count and to make an inference: ". . . and I want to know whether you still say that a double square comes from a double line?" The prevailing mode for the boy's responses is "yes," "true," "certainly," or "no."

Note, however, that in the discourse Socrates really had two pupils—Meno, who in a way was learning to be a teacher, and the slave, who served as the pupil. The task of the slave was to solve a mathematical problem; the task of Meno was to infer from the behavior of the boy that knowledge may be produced by inquiry ". . . about that which he does not know." Notice, that Meno, too, gradually begins to answer as the boy did: "The fact, Socrates, is undeniable." "Yes." "Obviously." "I feel, somehow, that I like what you are saying." And finally Socrates agrees that he too likes what he has said but lets Meno in on the

Transcript 11-2

1   *Soc.*   Tell me, boy, do you know that a figure like this is a square? **Sol/**

2   *Boy.*   I do. **Resp/**

3   *Soc.*   And you know that a square figure has these four lines equal? **Sol/**

4   *Boy.*   Certainly. **Resp/**

5   *Soc.*   And these lines which I have drawn through the middle of the square are also equal? **Sol/**

6   *Boy.*   Yes. **Resp/**

7   *Soc.*   A square may be on any size? **Sol/**

8   *Boy.*   Certainly. **Resp/**

9   *Soc.*   And if one side of the figure be of two feet, and the other side be of two feet, how much will the whole be? **Sol/Sol/** Let me explain: if in one direction the space was of two feet, and in the other direction of one foot, the whole would be of two feet taken once?

10   *Boy.*   Yes. **Resp/**

11   *Soc.*   But since this side is also of two feet, there are twice two feet? **Sol/**

12   *Boy.*   There are. **Resp/**

13   *Soc.*   Then the square is of twice two feet? **Sol/**

14   *Boy.*   Yes. **Resp/**

15   *Soc.*   And how many are twice two feet? count and tell me. **Sol/Str**

16   *Boy.*   Four Socrates. **Resp/**

17   *Soc.*   And might there not be another square twice as large as this, and having like this the lines equal? **Sol/**

18   *Boy.*   Yes. **Resp/**

19   *Soc.*   And of how many feet will that be? **Sol/**

20   *Boy.*   Of eight feet. **Resp/**

21   *Soc.*   And now try and tell me the length of the line which forms the side of the double square: this is two feet—what will that be? **Sol/**

22   *Boy.*   Clearly, Socrates, it will be double. **Resp/**

23   *Soc.*   Do you observe, Meno, that I am not teaching the boy anything, but only asking him questions; and now he fancies that he knows how long a line is necessary in order to produce a figure of eight square feet; does he not?

24   *Men.*   Yes.

25   *Soc.*   And does he really know?

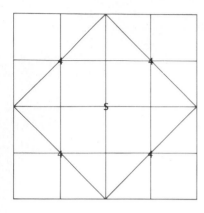

26   *Men.*   Certainly not.

27   *Soc.*   He only guesses that because the square is double, the line is double.

28   *Men.*   True.

29   *Soc.*   Observe him while he recalls the steps in regular order. (*To the boy.*) Tell me, boy, do you assert that a double space comes from a double line? /**Sol**/ Remember that I am not speaking of an oblong, but of a figure equal every way, and twice the size of this—that is to say of eight feet; and I want to know whether you still say that a double square comes from a double line?

30   *Boy.*   Yes. **Resp/**

31   *Soc.*   But does not this line become doubled if we add another such line here? **Sol/**

32   *Boy.*   Certainly. **Resp/**

33   *Soc.*   And four such lines will make a space containing eight feet? **Sol/**

34   *Boy.*   Yes. **Resp/**

35   *Soc.*   Let us describe such a figure: Would you not say that this is the figure of eight feet? **Sol/**

36   *Boy.*   Yes. **Resp/**

37   *Soc.*   And are there not these four divisions in the figure, each of which is equal to the figure of four feet? **Sol/**

38   *Boy.*   True. **Resp/**

39   *Soc.*   And is not that four times four? **Sol/**

40   *Boy.*   Certainly. **Resp/**

41   *Soc.*   And four times is not double? **Sol/**

42   *Boy.*   No, indeed. **Resp/**

43   *Soc.*   But how much? **Sol/**

44   *Boy.*   Four times as much. **Resp/**

45   *Soc.*   Therefore the double line, boy, has given a space, not twice, but four times as much. **Resp/**

46   *Boy.*   True. **Resp/**

47   *Soc.*   Four times four are sixteen— are they not? **Sol/**

48   *Boy.*   Yes. **Resp/**

49   *Soc.*   What line would give you a space of eight feet, as this gives one of sixteen feet;—do you see? **Sol/**

50   *Boy.*   Yes. **Resp/**

51   *Soc.*   And the space of four feet is made from this half line? **Sol/**

52   *Boy.*   Yes. **Resp/**

53   *Soc.*   Good; and is not a space of eight feet twice the size of this, and half the size of the other?

54 *Boy.* Certainly. **Resp/**

55 *Soc.* Such a space, then, will be made out of a line greater than this one, and less than that one?

56 *Boy.* Yes; I think so. **Resp/**

57 *Soc.* Very good; I like to hear you say what you think. And now tell me, is not this a line of two feet and that of four? **Sol/**

58 *Boy.* Yes. **Resp/**

59 *Soc.* Then the line which forms the side of eight feet ought to be more than this line of two feet, and less than the other of four feet? **Sol/**

60 *Boy.* It ought. **Resp/**

61 *Soc.* Try and see if you can tell me how much it will be. **Sol/**

62 *Boy.* Three feet. **Resp/**

63 *Soc.* Then if we add a half to this line of two, that will be the line of three. Here are two and there is one; and on the other side, here are two also and there is one: and that makes the figure of which you speak? **Sol/**

64 *Boy.* Yes. **Resp/**

65 *Soc.* But if there are three feet this way and three feet that way, the whole space will be three times three feet? **Sol/**

66 *Boy.* That is evident. **Resp/**

67 *Soc.* And how much are three times three feet? **Sol/**

68 *Boy.* Nine. **Resp/**

69 *Soc.* And how much is the double of four? **Sol/**

70 *Boy.* Eight. **Resp/**

71 *Soc.* Then the figure of eight is not made out of a line of three? **Sol/**

72 *Boy.* No. **Resp.**

73 *Soc.* But from what line?—tell me exactly; and if you would rather not reckon, try and show me the line. **Sol/**

74 *Boy.* Indeed, Socrates, I do not know. **Resp/**

75 *Soc.* Do you see, Meno, what advances he has made in his power of recollection? He did not know at first, and he does not know now, what is the side of a figure of eight feet: but then he thought that he knew, and answered confidently as if he knew, and had no difficulty; now he has a difficulty, and neither knows nor fancies that he knows.

fact that he, Socrates, had been doing a kind of experiment.

> . . . *Some things I have said of which I am not altogether confident. But that we shall be better and braver and less helpless if we think that we ought to enquire, than we*

would have been if we indulged in the idle fancy that there was no knowing and no use in seeking to know what we do not know; . . . that is a theme upon which I am ready to fight, in word and deed, to the utmost of my power.

In the same spirit let us investigate the subject of questioning and inquiry in science instruction and learning. Let us start with Socrates. Suppose, for example, we construct a picture of the kind of dialogue in which Socrates engaged. It might look approximately like Figure 11-1, which shows statements 1–17 from the dialogue categorized by type.

Because of the form in which Socrates casts his questions, the slave and Meno need only make short replies. Mostly their task is to confirm what Socrates has said: "Yes," "It is true," "Certainly," etc. By means of this technique, which relies on strong cues, Socrates changed the state of doubt in the slave. He remarks to Meno concerning the slave:

He did not know at first, and he does not know now, what is the side of a figure of eight feet; but then he thought that he knew, and answered confidently as if he knew, and had no difficulty; now he has a difficulty, and neither knows nor fancies that he knows.

FIGURE 11-1
The first seventeen items of Socrates' instruction, drawn on the two-player grid. Complete the analysis.

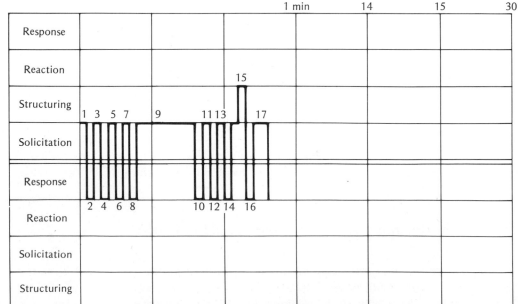

Socrates knew the part that conceptual conflict could play in prompting inquiry. There is no inquiry without doubt. To produce conceptual conflict, he played the part of inquisitor. The flow of logic was under his control. While this method may occasionally be useful, there are other models that probably are more suited to modern science programs.

Relation of wait time to the pattern of the teacher's questions

If wait times preceding and following a question are increased from the present average of 1 or 2 seconds to averages that exceed 3 seconds, certain characteristics of the verbal behavior of children begin to change.

1 The length and number of students' responses increase.
2 "I don't know" and failures to answer decrease.
3 The incidence of speculative thinking increases.
4 More evidence—followed by or preceded by inference—is expressed.
5 The number of questions asked by children increases, and the number of experiments they propose increases.
6 Contributions from "slow" students increase.

When children begin to respond differently, the questioning patterns of teachers tend to undergo additional changes. (See Figure 11-2a and b.)

1 Teachers ask more varied questions. While the number of questions that call for strict reporting of facts, or cognitive memory questions, declines somewhat, the number of questions that call for more complex kinds of thinking increases.
2 The contingent responding of teachers changes. They exhibit more flexibility in the range of responses accepted and used to progress or maintain an argument.

Possibly (although this is sheer speculation) as children exhibit more of what they think, there is more about which the adult becomes genuinely interested and curious. Students are given more opportunity to respond to questions that encourage thought rather than just strict recall. When the pacing is very fast, teachers work much harder. They often ask and answer their own ques-

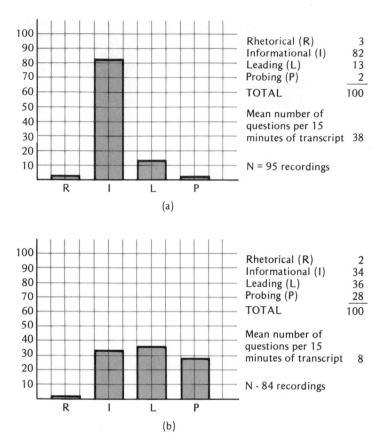

FIGURE 11-2
a **Typical distribution of types of questions before wait-time training.** *b* **Typical change in distribution of types of questions once average wait times of 3 seconds or more have been achieved.**

tions. ("What color was it? It was green, wasn't it?" "What made the bulb light? Wasn't it the switch?") When teachers gain control of wait time, questioning becomes less barragelike and more flexible in form, even if the teacher has not had specific training in question-asking techniques. Of course, the total number of questions asked by teachers in an average 10-minute interval tends to be lower as wait time increases. While it is not entirely clear why there is a change in the pattern of questioning by the teacher when wait times are extended, we might hazard a guess that this change comes about in response to the shift in the kind of thinking the children are exhibiting. Just as in any normal conversation each speaker is responsive to what the other speaker says, so the teacher who has increased wait times is exposed to more variability in what the children say.

As wait time increases, flexibility or responsiveness on the part of the teacher increases. There are fewer strictly repetitive cycles and discontinuities in the logic of the conversation. Consider, for example, the discussion recorded in Transcript 8-2 (page 256). Note how the children build on each other's observations and propositions and how relatively little talking the teacher needs to do. This is an example of a joint inquiry rather than an inquisition by the teacher.

Effect of increased wait time on discussion by students

Children on a longer wait-time schedule usually become more fussy about what evidence leads to or supports a particular inference. The various views in a group serve to produce some self-correcting kinds of situations. For example, one class of second-grade children whose teacher experimented with wait times over a period of several weeks visited an aquarium that had, among other organisms, a shark in a large tank with other fish. The conversation went as follows:

Teacher: *Tell me what you observe.*

[*Pause of 3 seconds.*]

First student: *The shark is hiding near the bottom waiting to catch a fish.* [*Note the implicit inference. At first glance it appears the child made an observation, but "hiding" in order "to catch a fish" is an inference.*] **(Inference.)**

[*Pause of 15 seconds. The teacher says nothing, and the children continue to look at the tank.*]

Second student: *I don't think that is right. Look how fast the shark can swim. It can swim faster than the fish. It does not need to hide. It can catch up with any fish, it wants.* **(Refutation, using evidence.)**

[*Pause of about 7 seconds. The teacher is still silent.*]

First student: *I don't know. My dad says policemen wait to catch speeders that way, and their cars can go faster. They hide because they want to catch you by surprise.* **(Metaphor.)**

[*The teacher continues to be silent. She said later she was at a loss to know what to do about the last response. Note, however, that the children took the problem out of her hands as they continued their dialogue.*]

Third student: *Probably the shark just catches fish when it is hungry. Otherwise it would be swimming all over just tearing them up. If we looked long enough, we could see him eat.* **(Evidence – inference.**]

Questioning and groups at work

In general, the following advice seems warranted.

1 Ask fewer questions. Make each question yield as much information as possible.
2 When possible, find a conversational mode.
3 Teach students how to ask questions.
4 Give time for thought.
5 In a modern science program, children need to learn to trust their capacity to extract information from materials, to build arguments on the basis of evidence, and to *value* doing that. To help that process along, the teacher can do two things:
   a Pause after asking a question. Wait at least 3 seconds.
   b After a student answers a question, pause again. Wait at least 3 seconds. Gradually the whole form of discourse in the classroom will tend to change. As a result, the pattern of questions by the teacher will change.
6 Use more questions calculated to produce conceptual conflict.

   Many of the units in modern science programs excite children, start them investigating, and stimulate them to pursue ideas in many directions. Commonly the first encounter with a new stimulus sends the students into a "gee whiz" stage. They may then begin to do things to the system to discover how it works. But they may exhaust their reservoir of interest and ideas very soon. Unfortunately, that initial burst of motivation is rarely sponstaneously rekindled in such a manner as to prompt them to ask more sophisticated questions, acquire more complex skills, or design more refined experiments. Instead, there is a great deal of lateral branching out from the problem in search of more novelty; the level of cognitive complexity stays about the same. Thus children, left un-prompted, will usually tend to hop from system to system rather like grasshoppers, sampling the fare casually and moving on to a new leaf. Appropri-ately stated questions, challenges, and compari-sons made by the teacher can reenergize their brains and feelings with respect to a particular system.

7 When groups report, train them to give two kinds of information before they state their inferences and explanations:

a What was observed.

b In what *sequence* events happened.

When students are prompted to report their obser-vations and to tell about their speculations or in-ferences, they may discover that they do not agree among themselves on what sequence of events happened. Thus they often argue on the erroneous assumption that each member of the group "saw" the system in the same way. A part of their training in how to inquire involves teaching them to check what was observed and in what sequence events happened. If students mix up the sequence of events, then it is unlikely that they will be able to infer relationships between variables. Finding relationships between variables depends on know-ing in what order or sequence one did things and what events happened as a result.

INQUIRY TRAINING FOR CHILDREN

For five years, beginning in 1957, J. Richard Suchman, then a psychologist at the University of Illinois, studied the inquiry behaviors of elementary school children with a view to developing procedures for teaching them skills that would facilitate inquiry.[2] Suchman found that child-ren exposed to a puzzling physical system (e.g., a siphon where water runs "uphill") asked remarkably few ques-tions in view of the amount of information needed to ex-plain the operation of the system. The questions they did

[2]J. Richard Suchman, *The Elementary School Training Program,* a project of the Illinois Studies in Inquiry Training, National Defense Education Act of 1958, grant no. 7-11-038, 1962. This effort has since been extended to a full-scale science program marketed by Science Research Associates.

ask generally seemed unrelated to each other. This observation by Suchman may bear on the earlier remarks about wait time. Children who previously have been subjected to a rapid rate of questioning and given little time to frame responses, and who may also be subject to a whimsical reward schedule, probably do not learn to listen to each other in recitation settings. Survival demands that they reply to the teacher's next question and less often requires that they amplify or extend something another student has said. (Certainly they do not get into the habit of asking questions.) Questions asked by students showed little indication of a systematic search strategy. Since the questions asked by students seemed unrelated to each other, a group of students were rarely able to pursue an idea to the point where they could analyze the relationships among the components in the system being studied. Suchman remarked, "It was clear that the children lacked a functional understanding of the essence of experimental design and the rules of logical inference."[3]

Suchman devised a plan to teach inquiry skills. First he filmed some phenomena that he suspected would be sufficiently surprising or contrary in outcome to what students might expect to capture attention. In one film, for example, water runs uphill (in a siphon). The students observe the event, and then the teacher says, "What made that happen that way?" All talk is tape-recorded for later use by the students when they try to improve their questioning skills.

Students were permitted to ask questions which could be answered by "Yes," "No," or "That is partly right and partly wrong." The teacher supplied only these answers. The object was to teach children how to ask directed rather than diffuse questions, how to organize information to support inferences, and how to analyze a situation to uncover relationships among the variables.

The purpose of inquiry training "is to impose on the child's intuitive approach to searching a systematic and logical scheme, to make discovery the result of planning more than luck."[4]

Categorizing students' questions and statements

The system for categorizing questions and statements suggested in the chart on page 349 is adapted from Such-

[3]Suchman, p. 16.
[4]*Ibid.*, p. 20.

Category system for studying inquiry
Procedure statements:

Verbal statements in declarative or question form that describe, clarify, or verify directions or procedures, or that verify previous observations.

    1 Diffuse: Garbled or vague procedures or directions.

    2 Directed: Directions or procedures precisely stated.

Evidence statements:

Identifies properties of objects or systems. States conditions of a system at specified points in time. Describes events. Describes evidence of interaction.

    1 Diffuse: Vague or metaphoric descriptions.

    2 Directed: Evidence precisely stated. If a metaphor is used, the relations between it and the system are stated in terms of properties.

Analytical statements:

Separates objects, systems, and events into components. States necessary, sufficient, or both conditions for an event to occur. States the sequence in which events occur. Compares the same system at different stages or compares two systems on corresponding components. States assumptions.

    1 Diffuse: Vague or metaphoric descriptions.

    2 Directed: Components, conditions, and sequences precisely given.

Empirical inference:

Describes or predicts what would happen as a result of certain manipulations of the system.

    1 Elimination—describes or predicts what would happen if x were removed or its value lowered (where x is an object, condition, or a variable). "If we didn't soak it in water, it wouldn't get dark."

    2 Addition—describes or predicts what would happen if x were added or its value increased (where x is an object, condition, or a variable). "If we left it in light longer, it would get darker."

    3 Substitution—describes or predicts what would happen if some object, condition, or a variable were replaced by another x (where x is an object, condition, or a variable). "If we just used ordinary paper instead of blueprint paper, it wouldn't turn dark."

        a Diffuse: relationship between the independent and dependent events is vaguely specified. "If we left it in light it might change."

        b Directed: relationship between the independent and dependent events is precisely specified. (See examples 1, 2, 3.)

Implication statements:

Explains relationships in the system. Justifies empirical inferences. States probable functional relationships between events or variables. Puts together ideas in new ways to produce a new discovery or new questions. Synthesizes an explanation.

    1 Diffuse: Nature of a relationship is vaguely stated (e.g., "I think it has something to do with rain").

    2 Directed: Nature of a relationship or an implication is precisely stated (e.g., "If the water vapor condenses, it would show up as drops and we would see rain").

man's work. It rests on the assumption that learning will proceed to higher levels of complexity if the inquirer gradually becomes conscious of what kinds of mental and empirical operations are likely to produce answers to the questions: *What happened? When? Under what circumstances? How do you account for it? Can you make it happen again?* The search itself can be exciting, and the successful pursuit of an explanation that satisfies is in itself rewarding.

Students are great brain pickers. Given a problem, they will often fish in the teacher's head for the answer. When you hear the phrase, "Does it have anything to do with . . . ?" then the student's thinking is diffuse. For example, if a student observes water running uphill, and asks, "Does it have anything to do with air?" he has made a diffuse inference. Past experience has taught him that his teacher will respond to this cue by assuming he has supplied an explanation. A relationship between uphill movement and air is not stated. On the other hand, if the student asked, "If there were no air in the tube, would the water still run uphill?" he would be asking a *direct-inference* (elimination) question. The relationship between the moving water, as one variable, and the absence of air is directly stated. He has predicted that water will run uphill if air is removed from the tube.

Students in the training group should learn to use the information gained from each question to guide them in deciding what to ask next. *Part of the training includes teaching students to listen to each other.*

Normally, approximately 15 minutes of inquiry may be allowed. Then there is a pause while the group caucuses in order to pool all possible explanations. Out of the caucus comes a new flood of questions meant to help them converge on an explanation.

At some point, usually on the next day, the teacher plays back portions of the tape. Students try to distinguish directed questions from diffuse questions. They work to improve their skill at asking directed questions or at making directed statements.

As they listen to tapes, students frequently recognize when members of the group are repeating questions. Feedback from the tapes helps them to focus on what they can learn from questions asked by others. After a number of such training sessions, the sequence of questions should begin to be less random.

Verification statements.   In the early part of an inquiry session, students should ask questions that allow them to *verify* the *contents* of the system (e.g., "Is that water in the tube?") and the *correct sequence of procedures,* (e.g., "Did you blow into the tube before you put the clamp on it?").

Evidence statements.   These include questions or statements concerning the condition of the system at various points in time as well as statements of evidence of interaction in a system.

> *Diffuse:*   *"It looks like beer."*
> *Directed:*   *"It turns yellow and foamy when we blow in it."*
> *Directed:*   *"When you push down on the switch, the motor goes on."*

Analytical statements.   Such statements identify the variables, state the necessary or sufficient conditions for an event to occur, identify the assumptions, and compare two systems.

> *Diffuse:*   *"Does the pressure have something to do with the moving water?"*
> *Directed:*   *"The air pressure outside the tube (siphon) is greater than the air pressure inside the tube. Will the water in the tube start to move?"*

Empirical inferences.   Students may perform mental experiments and try to guess at answers (Figure 11-3). They do this by imagining what would be the result of certain manipulations on the system such as *eliminating* some part (e.g., if we took out this wire, would the bulb still light?), *adding* something to the system (e.g., if we made this wire four times as long, would the bulb still be as bright?), or *substituting* (e.g., if we put Nichrome wire in here in place of the copper wire, will the bulb still light up?).

> *Diffuse:*   *"Let's see what would happen if we added more wires."*
> *Directed:*   *"If we added more wires, then these bulbs should be brighter."*

Implication statements.   Implication statements are statements, and questions, in which students seek to

FIGURE 11-3
An experiment is a way of asking questions of nature.

explain relationships among variables. They may use a model, such as the idea of a circuit to explain the interactions in an electrical system.

> *Diffuse:* "*Does water vapor have something to do with the rain?*"
>
> *Directed:* "*If the water vapor condensed, then we would see drops.*"
>
> *Directed:* "*The reason the motor turns on when you close the switch is that there is a circuit.*"

Turn back to Transcript 11-1 to see how some of the statements might be categorized.

Steps toward productive inquiry

To help students learn to inquire more productively, do the following:

1 Demonstrate a phenomenon that provokes curiosity either because it is novel or because it acts in a way which seems contrary to expectations.

2 Tape-record questions and statements students

make as they try to explain or account for the event.

3 Play back the tape recordings. Help students to do the following:

   a Distinguish between diffuse and directed statements

   b Identify points where two or more people asked the same question

   c Restate questions or statements

How frequently should you engage in this kind of training? Teaching students to ask questions is not meant to constitute the whole science program. The training can be either spaced over time or concentrated into a few weeks. There is some advantage to spacing, since the students will then be exposed to frequent reminders concerning the kind of questions they ought to be asking and the kinds of thought in which they ought to be engaging.

The one difficulty that inquiry training poses for the teacher concerns the depth to which he or she understands the relationships in the system about which the students are to inquire. The teacher should choose phenomena he understands well or phenomena which someone, who knows what variables are involved, can help him learn enough about to answer questions. The explicit goal is to focus on the process of productive questioning.

INQUIRY TRAINING FOR THE TEACHER

You can teach yourself to ask questions which provoke students to do some fairly sophisticated reasoning. There are six categories of questions which you might ask. (This is only one of many possible ways to categorize questions.)

   1 *Problem identification.* Questions or statements designed to encourage students to identify a problem. For example, you might present some data that contain some inconsistencies to determine whether students identify the inconsistencies or can state possible reasons for them. For example, several students might perform the "same" experiment but get different results.

   2 *Information; facts; observations; data.* Questions or statements intended to prompt students to give information previously learned, state observations made on a system, or present data collected during an experiment. The response could be presented in oral, written, pictorial, or graphical form. The content of responses in this category is generally noncontroversial.

3 *Procedures; skills; design.* Questions or statements that encourage students to demonstrate or describe the sequence of procedures they used to demonstrate the techniques or skills they used (e.g., focusing a microscope), to identify the input and output variables, and to state which variables were controlled.

4 *Inference; empirical relations.* Questions or statements intended to prompt students to use evidence as a basis for stating relationships between variables. [E.g., when the length of the string on a pendulum is increased, the time the pendulum takes to make a complete cycle increases. The length of the pendulum (the input variable) is related to the period of the pendulum (the output variable).]

5 *Interpretation; explanation.* Questions and statements that prompt students to put together a sequence of at least two ideas, in order to explain how a system works or to compare two systems. (E.g., if the pressure on the liquid inside the tube drops and the pressure on the liquid outside the tube stays about the same, then the liquid will rise in the tube. The high-pressure area pushes it into the low-pressure area.)

6 *Application.* Questions and statements that encourage students to interpret new experiences using concepts they already have; questions or statements that ask students to give additional examples; questions and statements in which students attempt to evaluate how appropriate an idea is to a given situation. (For example, once the concept of a simple circuit is developed, then students should be able to apply it in a variety of situations to find out why something like a motor or a light is not interacting.)

Ordinarily the highest proportion of questions fall into categories 2 and 3. Students need practice in identifying problems—converting problems into direct statements which clearly identify the variables to be investigated. Students also need practice in connecting inferences and explanations with evidence.

Through questions, the teacher tries to help students approach each new investigation in a somewhat analytical fashion. Hunkin reported that students in sixth-grade social studies gained more knowledge when their text materials required them to do more analysis and evaluation of content than relatively simple recall and comparison.[5] Presumably the same thing would happen in science. Questions which encourage analysis and evaluation of results or serve to produce conflict, by pointing up differences in data or reasoning, probably prompt students to mentally process information over and over again—but in different orders. Thus they not only uncover more relationships but actually rehearse the information and so increase the probability that more of it will be retained.

Certainly it seems reasonable to suppose that the particular kinds of activities which new science programs ask teachers to undertake with their students at different points might also determine, to some extent, how rich the opportunity for asking cognitively complex questions can be. Donald Flory, for example, chastizes the writers of the Science Curriculum Improvement Study in one of their own publications for the high (if inadvertent) emphasis that the early versions of the lessons place on demonstration and drill. Flory analyzed tape recordings and then described how the lessons differed in their potential for producing divergent inquiry.[6] In spite of the fact that students had materials that could prompt inquiry, the writers rarely suggested ways to exploit the opportunities.

As long ago as 1912, in a study of questioning behavior by teachers, Romiet Stevens decried the high rate of questioning by teachers and the low level of thought demanded. She reported that most of the questions in classrooms she observed required simple recall and only rarely required students to compound explanations. This pattern does nothing more, she speculated, than train memory and encourage superficial judgments. Certainly

[5]Francis P. Hunkins, "The Influence of Analysis and Evaluation Questions on Achievement in Sixth Grade Social Studies," paper presented at the meeting of the American Educational Research Association, New York, February 1967. (Mimeographed.)

[6]Donald L. Flory, "Dynamics of Classroom Behavior: An Informal Study," *What Is Curriculum Evaluation? Six Answers*, Science Curriculum Improvement Study, University of California Press, Berkeley, 1968, pp. 27–37.

it does nothing, she claimed, to help boys and girls become self-reliant, independent workers who enjoy mental activities.[7] Forty-eight years later, William Floyd, studying elementary classrooms in a different part of the country confirmed Stevens's observations. In his sample, 42 percent of teachers' questions assessed memory and 23 percent called for statements of facts or information. He made the point that *questions seemed to be used more for evaluation than for instruction;*[8] i.e., they check up on what a student knows rather than on how he thinks about what he knows.

Alan Kondo did a more quantitave analysis of teachers' questioning behavior in the Science Curriculum Improvement Study (SCIS) unit "Material Objects," but he arrived at a similar conclusion. The content of lessons he studied differed in their effect on the variability of question-asking patterns. Some lessons seemed to drive the questioning behavior of teachers more strongly toward routine and cognitive memory questioning than toward evaluative and divergent questioning. Kondo reasoned that the three types of lessons that make up SCIS units probably differ in the extent to which they encourage more variable questioning patterns. The "Material Objects" unit is organized into sequences of *exploratory, invention,* and *discovery* lessons. The exploratory lessons generally give some preliminary experience with new phenomena for which the teacher will later provide a verbal label during the invention lesson which follows the unit. A discovery lesson follows an invention lesson and is intended to give the students an opportunity to broaden the concept by exposing them to a range of phenomena which represent more examples of the concept. Discovery lessons provide more opportunities to apply the new concept in different contexts. (In psychological terms, the discovery lesson has the effect of producing stimulus generalization.) Kondo reasoned that since the psychological intent of each of the three kinds of lessons was different and since questions ostensibly mirror the kind of learning that is meant to take place, he should expect to identify distinctive patterns of questioning for each of the three kinds of lessons. Invention lessons would be more

---

[7]Romiet Stevens, *The Question as a Measure of Efficiency in Instruction,* Contribution to Education, no. 48, Teachers College Press, Columbia University, New York, 1921.

[8]William D. Floyd, "An Analysis of the Oral Questioning Activity in Selected Colorado Classrooms," unpublished Ed. D. dissertation, Colorado State College, Greeley, 1960.

FIGURE 11-4
Teachers can sometimes learn to model inquiry behavior by actually engaging in investigation of a system which is novel to them.

likely to produce memory and convergent questions, as teachers try to relate the exploratory activities to the new term to be learned. Discovery lessons ought to encourage divergent questions, since this is the stage in which students try to apply the new concept to new situations.

Kondo analyzed tape recordings of six lessons, two each of discovery, invention, and exploration. For each of the four teachers who took part in his study, he had two examples of each species of lesson—that is, a total of six lessons for each of the four teachers. (That may not sound like much, but it represents about eight hours of recordings and many more hours than that in transcribing.) He found the differences in complexity of questioning to be greater between teachers than between lessons. To put it another way, each teacher appears to develop a pattern of questioning and maintain the pattern with small variations as she shifts from one content to another. The patterns appear to be relatively stable: a teacher who uses a high proportion of cognitive memory questions and a relatively low proportion of convergent and divergent questions will tend to maintain that pattern with a particular class. But a teacher who uses a more varied mix of questions will tend to maintain a more complex pattern,[9] regardless of whether she is teaching an exploration, invention, or discovery lesson. In short, teachers tend to develop characteristic patterns of questioning.

There are other kinds of questions asked by teachers which normally receive little attention but which have a great deal to do with improving the general atmosphere for inquiry.

1 Questions that prompt the student to make additions to her answer; e.g., "Tell me more. It's not clear what you mean by that."

2 Questions or statements that prompt more discussion and encourage students to listen to each other; e.g., "George, do you agree with Mary?"

Teachers can learn to vary their question-asking pattern. It will begin to exhibit more variability naturally as the pace slows down. With categories of questions in mind, teachers can make sure that they give students opportunities to try to respond to more questions which require analysis, inference, and explanation. They can help students learn to substitute direct for diffuse statements. They can be on the alert for expert brain pickers.

As more students become self-starting and self-maintaining investigators, teachers move out of the role of trainer into that of consultant. Students ask questions. Teachers try to help them find better ways of knowing.

SUMMARY

1 Teachers who are insensitive to wait time tend to ask a very large number of questions at a very rapid pace. There is, as a result,

a Insufficient time for students to think

b Insufficient time for teachers to evaluate responses properly

2 Investigations show that teachers, for the most part, ask questions which call for stating facts or reporting observations. Students may not be get-

[9]Alan K. Kondo, *The Study of the Questioning Behavior of Teachers in the Science Curriculum Improvement Study Teaching the Unit on Material Objects,* unpublished Ed.D. dissertation, Teachers College Press, Columbia University, New York, 1968.

ting enough practice at responding to questions which call for analysis and interpretation.

3 Students rarely ask questions. A part of inquiry training consists of teaching students to ask questions.

4 Concern for the quality of thought is only part of the educational package. Emotional atmosphere has a great deal to do with learning. A distinction must be made between inquisition and inquiry. Inquisition probably develops an unfavorable emotional atmosphere.

5 Soliciting, responding, reacting, and structuring are four kinds of moves which teachers and students can make.

    a In inquisition, teachers do virtually all the soliciting, structuring, and reacting while students confine their moves to responding.

    b In inquiry, students participate more broadly— that is, they solicit, structure, and react as well as respond.

6 The focus of inquiry for students is the biological or physical system. The focus of inquiry for teachers is the system consisting of the student plus the phenomena he is investigating.

7 Both teachers and students need to learn how to ask questions about their respective systems.

8 Conceptual conflict can prompt inquiry provided the teacher makes it safe. Well-chosen questions can produce conceptual conflict.

9 In groups which have become accustomed to wait times, teachers' questions tend to be more varied than in groups which operate under short wait times. Teachers seem to become genuinely interested in students' ideas.

10 Some teachers apparently employ a high rate of questioning to help maintain control of the class. There is some evidence that this procedure is self-defeating. Students apparently tire more quickly.

11 Discussions among students have the following advantages:

    a They reduce the number of questions that have to be asked.

    b The variety of views discussed and evaluated

tends to make students more fussy about what evidence supports an inference.

c They produce inadvertent rehearsals of concepts and relationships.

12 To help improve students' inquiry behaviors:

a Ask fewer questions in a given period.

b Give more time for thought.

c Teach students to ask questions.

ACTIVITY 11-1

OBJECTIVE

To identify four types of questions asked by the teacher

There are many systems for classifying questions by the teacher. The four categories used in Figure 11-2 are based on the system developed by T. W. Parsons.

Rhetorical: All questions which are asked in such rapid succession that there is no opportunity for students to respond. All questions for which the teacher either supplies an answer or does not expect an answer.

Informational: Questions which ascertain whether students have assembled information. All questions which call for naming, identifying, and describing information.

Leading: Questions which clue students either to answers or to processes that could be used to find answers. Usually these questions supply students with some information and ask them to infer a relationship.

Probing: Open-ended questions which prompt search for additional data or relationships or which encourage explanation are counted as probing questions. Questions which call for application of concepts or principles.

Others: Questions which do not fall into the above categories. Usually these are concerned with classroom management.

What to do:

1 Transcript 8-1
   a Read Transcript 8-1 and code the teacher's questions according to Parson's system for analysis.
   b Design a data table to present the findings.

c Construct a bar graph to show the frequency of each type of question.

2 Transcripts 8-2, 9-2, and 12-1: Analyze these transcripts in the same manner.

ACTIVITY 11-2

OBJECTIVE

To identify categories of students' responses

What to do:

1 Read Transcript 12-1. Code the statements there according to the system shown in Figure 11-1. Organize your findings into a data table. Recode in Suchman's system.

2 Examine Transcripts 8-1, 8-2, 8-3, 9-2, and the passages of conversation given in this chapter. Try to identify statements by students that could be coded according to the system adapted from Suchman's investigations. Organize a data table to show the results.

3 Suggest reasons for the differences in results. (Hint: Can you connect either the teacher's questioning pattern or wait time to the outcomes?)

ACTIVITY 11-3

OBJECTIVE

To demonstrate a variety of types of questions

What to do:

Teach a lesson in which you demonstrate a variety of types of questions. Categorize the questions. Construct a bar graph to show the distribution of different types of questions. (See Figure 11-2.)

ACTIVITY 11-4

OBJECTIVE

To produce a plan for teaching students to ask questions.

You might accomplish this in a number of ways, including modeling the behavior (see Figure 11-5).

REFERENCE

Parsons, Theodore W.: *Guide and Self-analysis System for Professional Development Education Series: Teaching for Inquiry*, Schedule A. Questioning Strategies, 1971. (Available from GSA, 2140 Shattuck Avenue, Berkeley, California.) This manual presents a simple way to examine your own questioning techniques. (The data presented in Figure 11-2a and b are based on the GSA category system.)

CHAPTER 12

"*Pumpkin seeds fell off the leaf. The plant is getting too big for the shell.*"

—FIRST-GRADER

Teacher: *How did the algae get inside the intestines?*

Student: *If that daphnia was in one of the jars, maybe it was green water and then the daphnia could eat it all like we wanted to do it. And I don't—I do think it's that green we saw when we looked through those round things; I think it's the green dot, because it was near the whiskers in back of it.*

Student: *I don't agree with Laura, because she said it was the tail but I don't think it is the tail.*

Teacher: *Well, what do you think it is?*

Student: *I think it's the bones.*

—FIRST-GRADE CLASS DISCUSSING
DAPHNIA IN AN AQUARIUM (SCIS)

LANGUAGE IN USE

OBJECTIVES

On completion of this chapter and its associated activities you should be able to do the following:

1 Recognize the two parts of a scientific concept: the relationship and the operation.

2 State at least three instructional procedures for improving students' competence at problem solving.

3 State a probable relationship between language development and exposure to science phenomena.

4 Design an investigation to study the process of problem solving.

5 Recognize that to be effective, communication must be a two-way process.

INTRODUCTION

Modern elementary science programs provide a rich milieu in which to develop language and thought. Confronted with phenomena and given some freedom to investigate, children work hard at converting their experiences into language. Just as a person might draw a map to show someone how to get from one place to another, so children construct a language map that expresses the relationships they discover and the ways in which they interpret events. Their experiences compel them to conversation.

Children probably get more active practice at mapping experience into language in a laboratory setting than in language arts or mathematics classes. During one observed science session, students worked in small groups with materials from the unit "Material Objects" of the Science Curriculum Improvement Study (SCIS). Analysis of tape recordings made of the discussion which followed the laboratory work showed more than twice as much content-relevant speech by students during the science period as during the language arts period. Students want to talk about scientific phenomena. Teachers can take advantage of the motivation afforded by scientific materials to foster development of language and thought.

A map is a kind of abstract representation of where things and places are in relation to each other. It leaves out many details, but it preserves key relationships that make it possible for a person to plan a journey, to choose desirable routes, and to estimate the time of arrival at each location. Similarly, language maps leave out many details, focusing instead on relationships among ideas. Language enables students to manipulate variables mentally and to anticipate possible outcomes of experiments. They can pick out routes to explore which are most likely to produce desirable results. Concepts, principles, and generalizations are the markers on a conceptual map. These markers become connected into a complex network of mental highways over which the student travels during problem solving. Such networks are unlikely to develop in instructional programs which fail to give students direct access to phenomena, time to investigate, and opportunity to discuss their work.

To better understand the relation between language and thought, we need first to investigate how students use concepts to guide their search for answers to questions.

Most concepts in science, if they are completely stated, contain two parts—a part that describes a relationship of some kind and a part that tells what one must do in order to produce evidence of the relationship. Recall Chapter 2 on measurement, which points out that to say, for example, that an object is 10 centimeters long implies a knowledge of how long a centimeter is and how to perform the measurement operation—by duplicating the centimeter unit ten times. All that information is hidden within the concise statement, "The object is 10 centimeters long." With more complex concepts, one has to be even more careful to be on the lookout for the hidden part of the concept. In the study to be described next, some concepts concerning magnetism are shown to have both explicit and implicit content. Failure to pay sufficient attention to the implicit content seems to have the effect of putting roadblocks on the conceptual map.[1]

USE OF CONCEPTS—THE NEGLECTED INGREDIENT

All the current emphasis on inquiry brings the problem of using concepts to the forefront. After all, what good are concepts if students do not know how to employ them in some systematic manner? Teaching students how to make *better use of concepts they already know* probably represents the major task to be accomplished in inquiry training.

We worry too much about what scientific concepts children learn and not enough about *how children employ the concepts they already know*. In solving problems, students must *select* and *order* varied types of information or data. Presumably they accomplish these two tasks using concepts that they know. But how? In what way do they or should they *use concepts that they already know* to select and order data? As teachers and former students ourselves, we can remember how often we knew the necessary concepts but could not solve a problem. To be able to state a set of concepts is one thing; to be able to use the set effectively is another.

Unfortunately, we usually leave the teaching and learning of how to use concepts to chance. In evaluation

[1] Mary Budd Rowe, "Influence of Context-learning on Solution of Task-oriented Science Problems," *Journal of Research in Science Teaching*, vol. 3, no. 1, pp. 12–18, 1965.

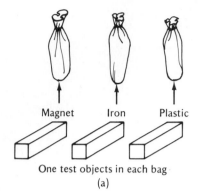

Magnet Iron Plastic

One test objects in each bag

(a)

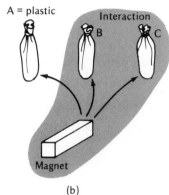

A = plastic

Interaction

B

C

Magnet

(b)

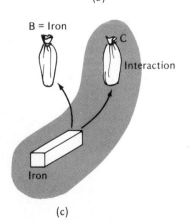

B = Iron

C

Interaction

Iron

(c)

FIGURE 12-1

a **The problem is to find out which bag contains which object.** *b* **If the magnet test object produces evidence of interaction, then by deduction (elimination) one can infer which bag contains the plastic.** *c* **If the iron test object produces evidence of interaction, then the concealed object must be a magnet.**

we do not usually attempt to keep tabs on the child's methods of using concepts. Instead we are prone to look at the end product of his thought—that is, whether the answer is right or wrong—without paying much attention to the *process* by which he arrived at a result.

AN INVESTIGATION INTO CONCEPTS: MAGNETS

The concepts used in this investigation are commonly taught in the primary grades and may be stated as follows:

1 There are things called *magnets* which can be identified by the way they act when they are brought near each other or near iron.

2 Two magnets sometimes attract each other, depending on how they are arranged.

3 Two magnets sometimes repel each other.

4 Magnets attract iron if they are brought near iron.

5 Magnets do not attract some objects that are brought near them.

6 The force of attraction between two magnets is greater than the attraction between a magnet and a piece of iron.

Before presenting the problem to be solved, each of sixty first-grade boys taking part in a study had four magnets of different shapes, a piece of iron, and a heavy piece of plastic placed in front of him. All the children had previous experience with magnets. The purpose of this preliminary activity was to establish what concepts they could *state* and *demonstrate*. As the boys worked with the materials, they were encouraged to talk about what they were finding. Statements of the following kind were typical:

"Look, it magnets together." (Concept 2.)
"This one and this push apart." (Concept 3.)
"When you put it this way, it sticks; but this way it like pushes apart." (Concepts 2 and 3.)
"If you put the iron and the magnet together, it doesn't stick so hard." (Concepts 4 and 6.)
"It won't pick this plastic up." (Concept 5.)

After a child both demonstrated and verbalized the concepts in some form, the magnets were removed and replaced by three closed leather bags, each of which contained an oblong object (Figure 12-1). All three bags looked alike; and the shape of the objects in all the bags was the same, as was the weight of each bag. Each boy received the following information: "Here are three bags. One holds a magnet, one holds a piece of iron, and one holds a heavy piece of plastic. Which bag has the magnet, which bag has the iron, and which bag has the plastic? Try to find out without opening the bags."

There was no way to tell from the appearance of the bags or by fingering them which bag contained which object. Once a boy had made his decision, the first set of three bags was removed and an identical second set replaced it for trial two. The same problem was presented. There were three such trials.

Four boys performed operations that permitted them to correctly identify all three bags on each trial. Fifteen boys made incorrect decisions on the first two trials. They persisted in trying to make decisions on the basis of how the bags and objects felt. These boys finally resorted to guessing on the first two trials.

After two trials, if the student had made no correct decisions, the investigator provided one cue by holding up an object and saying, "Suppose I met you around school one day, and I told you that I found this piece of metal. I thought it was a magnet, but I was not sure. Could you help me find out whether it was a magnet or not?"

No matter what response the subject made to this, the investigator simply replied: "I see . . . . Well, here are the three bags again. One of them has a magnet in it, one has a piece of metal that is not a magnet, and one has something in it that has nothing to do with magnetism. Which one has the magnet, which has the metal, and which has the plastic? The cue was designed to remind the student that in order to make a discovery about magnetism, he would have to perform an *operation* of some kind. One cannot detect the presence of a magnetic field unless he moves into the field some object with which the magnet will interact.

A concept in science has two parts—one of which is not explicitly stated but is taken for granted. There is the statement of a relationship. (E. g., "Magnets attract certain metals.") *Implied* in the statement is an *operation.* (Here, to detect a magnetic interaction, move a piece of metal or move the magnet.) In teaching scientific concepts one has to be careful that students learn both the explicit part and the implicit part. They must learn what the relationship is, and they must also learn what operation to perform (i.e., what to do) to produce evidence of the relationship.

Ten of the fifteen boys who received the cue just before the third trial adopted a successful strategy on the third trials. The other five apparently remained unaffected. These five simply repeated what they had done on the earlier trials; they were not focused on the operations that would produce evidence. The cue prompted the students to *think of operations that related to the concepts*. One may hold a concept, but if it is to be useful to him in practical circumstances, he must also know what kind of *evidence* would support it and how to get that evidence. Twenty-one boys achieved a partial solution. They succeeded in correctly identifying one of the bags but were unable to distinguish between the objects in the remaining two bags.

What distinguished the successful, the partially successful, and the unsuccessful groups from each other?

The twenty-one children who were successful in solving the problem differed from those who were unsuccessful in the way they *used* the six concepts on magnetism. The most successful employed *two or more concepts in sequence*. They used either two different concepts or the same concept twice, applied in a slightly different way. A number of boys, for example, began by touching a magnet to each bag (see Figure 12-1*b*). Two bags would be attracted by this procedure, the bag containing a piece of metal (concept 4) and the bag containing a magnet (concept 2). At this point the students had to deduce that the bag which was not attracted must contain the plastic (concept 5). Of the two bags with which there had been detectable interaction, one contained metal and the other a magnet. The problem was to find a way to decide which was which. The partially successful group got this far but seemed unable to find a strategy for distinguishing the iron from the magnet. Instead they resorted to poking and lifting the bags as the unsuccessful children had done.

The successful problem solvers employed a variety of strategies. A few correctly distinguished between the magnet and the metal by recognizing that they had to pull harder to separate the magnet from one of the bags than from the other. They reasoned that the pull between two magnets would be "stronger than the magnet with metal" (concept 6). (The sequence of concepts that they employed was 2, 4, and 6.)

A few boys chose a different and more powerful strategy. They also employed the concept that magnets can repel each other ("push away" property, concept 3). They put one end of the test magnet to each bag, and then they reversed the magnet and repeated the procedure. The bag containing the metal would be attracted no matter which end of the magnet was used (concept 4). But the bag containing the magnet would be attracted and then repelled depending on which end of the test magnet it was exposed to (concept 2 followed by concept 3). Thus they could make the bag containing the magnet *move away* from the test magnet.

Sometimes a boy started with a piece of metal as a test device rather than a magnet. The metal will be attracted to the bag holding the magnet, leaving two bags to be distinguished, those containing metal and plastic. He would then switch to using a magnet to pick out the bag containing the metal. Throughout the procedure he employed only one concept, "magnets attract metal" (concept 4), but he used two different test objects, a piece of metal and a magnet.

Successful problem solvers, then, used two or more concepts to govern a sequence of information-gathering activities. Presumably the successful problem solvers knew both the implicit and explicit part of the concepts they used. They knew the relationship and recognized the necessity of performing an operation in order to produce evidence.

Some sequences provide more checks against the possibility of errors than do others. For example, the partially successful problem solvers employed only one of the concepts and employed it only once. They could identify only one bag correctly. The advantage to be gained from sequencing—i.e., using one concept after another—was lost.

When a subject uses two or more *different* concepts to guide the sequence of gathering data, he gets more information than he needs; the extra information serves to confirm his other findings. Subjects who had efficient, error-free patterns, for example, used both the property of attraction and the property of repulsion. Subjects who used two or more different concepts built a kind of network of concepts to trap the data. In this way they added surplus information to the information-processing system and so decreased the chance of making a mistake.

One rule to use in teaching successful inquiry strategies or problem-solving techniques might be, *"Refer to the concepts on the mental list and use them to shop*

for different items of information." Recheck the list of concepts and make certain that more than one concept is being used. Deliberate resequencing of concepts can provide the surplus information or redundancy necessary to make a decision or find an answer with the least chance of error.

USING CONCEPTS IN INQUIRY TRAINING

Inquiry training addresses itself primarily to the business of using concepts and only incidentally to learning concepts, although an end product of any inquiry process may be the production of a new idea or concept—or a new invention. To make students more effective inquirers, it may be helpful if they are taught to do the following:

1 Make the implicit as well as the explicit part of the concept visible. That is, students should learn the relationship stated in the concept and what they have to do to produce evidence of the relationship.

2 Make a mental list of the concepts that may be applicable to a problem.

3 Select more than one concept from the list. "Use the list to shop for information." Unsuccessful inquirers apparently failed to shop from the list at all. Partially successful inquirers usually employed only one concept from the list. Successful problem solvers sequenced two or more concepts to gather the necessary evidence.

4 *Order* the information gathered, so as to be able to make inferences from it.

Of course, one must be cautious about overgeneralizing from a study of so few children. More studies like it could easily be done; and if the information gained from such studies was then pooled, a substantial contribution could be made to our knowledge of the processes that are probably involved in learning to be an effective inquirer. The goal to be attained in the magnet problem was clearly stated and apparently well understood by the children. The routes to attainment, however, were open and under the control of the children. Feedback was not mediated by another person; instead, the children had to interpret the data and use them to make a next decision. Certain activities, by their design, lend themselves well to the study of concept use. If a group of practitioners got together, found additional activities, and performed similar investigations, perhaps with the help of practice or intern teachers, they might collect their data and publish the results in a magazine like *Science and Children*, which is put out by the National Science Teachers Association for elementary teachers. *Science and Children* often contains articles by and for classroom teachers.[2] If teachers begin to act as investigators, the whole quality of instruction may gradually improve because more of our decisions will be based on knowledge of the process of inquiry rather than on ignorance of how students arrive at solutions.

CONTEXT—A CRUCIAL FACTOR

The magnet problem illustrates how important it is for teachers to observe and discuss process with students. The teacher needs to know the context out of which each student speaks. To illustrate how important it is for the teacher to discover the context from which a student is speaking, consider the following quotation taken from a tape recording: A first-grader speaks: "Pumpkin seeds fell off the leaf. The plant is getting too big for the shell."

Do you understand what he said? Surely you recognize all the words he used; where, then, does the difficulty in understanding lie? It cannot be in the words alone. Possibly it is the way he put the observations together. What do plants and shells have to do with each other; and what kind of shell, "seed shell" or eggshell, is he talking about? And after all, pumpkin seeds do not ordinarily fall off leaves. What you are missing is the *context* out of which the sentences came. To get some grasp of the context, you need to experience the system about which the child is talking. Perhaps if you could see it, you would know what he meant. Look at Figure 12-2. Now you know what he meant when he said, "The plant is getting too big for the shell." You see the *system,* but how does that explain his comment, "Pumpkin seeds fell off the leaf"?

To grasp the sentence about pumpkin seeds, you need some *history* of what happened between the child and the system over some period of time. Eight days earlier everyone in the class had planted pumpkin seeds. Some days

FIGURE 12-2
The seed coat adhered to the first leaf of the pumpkin plant.

[2]Write to the editor, *Science and Children,* a publication of the National Science Teachers Association, 1201 16th Street, N.W., Washington, D. C., 20036.

after that, this child observed, "The seeds came out of the ground stuck to the leaves." *Now* he says, "Pumpkin seeds fell off the leaf." The communication becomes intelligible when we know the context.

Shared experiences ensure a common referent for language in use. Conversation flows easily when teachers and students jointly accumulate experience with physical and biological systems.

When people confront a novel phenomenon, they often try to tell what it means to them or how they think the system works by using analogies, metaphors, or both. The boy with the pumpkin seeds, for example, referred to the seed coat as a shell. Whether one person's communication ends up being essentially private or whether it does convey meaning to another person depends upon whether the hearer shares the analogy or metaphor. Since we know that different people will attend to different aspects of a system, and will use words whose referents may be ambiguous to express what they are thinking, we should not be surprised that the listener also screens what he hears. The words must pass through noisy mental circuits. In spite of ambiguity in the referents and in spite of the way in which the hearer, on account of his expectations, bends their meaning to make a fit between what he hears and what he thinks, messages do get through.

How easily changing contexts slip into and out of small words! Take the almighty "it" for example. See what *it* does to an explanation. If the meaning of a statement depends so strongly on context in the simple examples already described, think what happens when we move from description of phenomena to explanation of phenomena. Explanation requires the speaker to infer relationships among events. Often those events happen at different points in time, as in the case of the pumpkin seeds, and to different parts of the system. In a simple experiment on thermal equilibrium, children and their teacher observe the events in Figure 12-3 and try to explain them. In 85 seconds of Transcript 12-1, nineteen of the ubiquitous little "its" passed between children and teacher. Even with gesturing and the immediate availability of the system, the speakers and the listeners confuse their meanings as the little pronoun slips along from one referent to another.

One young classroom teacher who heard the tape recording of this conversation insisted that the children and teachers really knew to what each *it* referred. To

FIGURE 12-3
Bottle A contains hot water. Bottle B contains cold water. A piece of ice sits in the neck of each bottle. (See Transcript 12.1.)

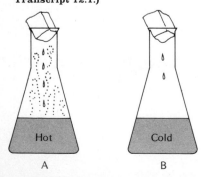

Transcript 12-1   **The Almighty "It"**

Teacher	Saul said, "It's [1] getting foggy." Would you describe that bottle as being fogged up?
First child	Well, I'd explain it [2] as a lot of wet air, moist air.
Second child	Wouldn't it [3] still be foggy?
Teacher	What do you mean when you say foggy?
First child	Well, it's [4] not so clear.
Second child	It [5] means that you can't see it [6] so clear.
Teacher	What's on the side of the bottle? Do you know?
First child	Moist air.
Teacher	Good, Peter, you say moist air. Can you describe anthing more? Can you explain what else it [7] might mean?
Second child	Well, um, cold water.
First child	No.
Teacher	Is this cold water in this bottle?
First child	No—hot and cold water combined together, fogging it [8] up a little.
Teacher	Good. What's the cold that's making it [9] fog up, then? You have hot water in there but what's . . . ?
First child	Hot would make this thing, and then the cold would just combine with it [10]—making it [11]—instead of going around.
Second child	Hot would . . . Hot would . . . Hot would do something different. When it's [12] real hot, the water's real hot, it [13] gets kind of foggy-like . . . .
First child	Yeah, but wait. Yeah, but it [14] steams. No it [15] stays there, but . . .
Teacher	Just a minute. Let Saul finish first.
Second child	But the cold water is different. The cold water doesn't have steam like the hot water—so that means . . . so that it [16] won't get foggy-like inside.
Teacher	Uh-huh. Good. Now, what were you going to say, Peter?
First child	Well, I was saying—as usual, the hot water makes steam, so it [17] would be cold . . . just—the coldness—just pressing it [18] against the glass, making it [19] moist air.

prove her contention, she taught the same lesson, tape-recorded the conversation, and got essentially the same result. Then the class listened to the tape and tried to decide what each *it* meant. The teacher found that it took the class nearly an hour to unscramble all their misunderstandings over what they thought each *it* meant. (Incidentally, the teacher who tried the experiment in taping exemplified what it means to inquire in science. She disagreed with the view that children did not follow the subtle shifts in meaning, so she did a simple experiment to get some data. The data did not conform to her expectations, but she became convinced that the discussion by the children after the experiment would make their communication more precise and increase their knowledge of phenomena. The quality of discourse may gradually be improved by occasionally playing back to a class portions of discussions. Analysis of the talk will make students more conscious of language, logic, and listening as factors in effective communication.)

In the conversation on thermal equilibrium, each speaker's intention governed what words he used; each listener's expectations governed what interpretation he put on what he heard. As Figure 12-4 illustrates, to convey *meaning* from one person to another requires that the would-be communicators not only share the same words but agree on the referents to which the words apply. The expectations each has also act to change the meaning of a communication. Somehow these differences must be recognized and rationalized in order for meaning to be transmitted.

The phenomena of science provide a place for children and teachers to start to work on communication. Together they develop a series of small histories of shared experience with physical and biological phenomena. They invent variables according to their needs, and gradually they come to share the same referents. At points of conflict they return, as scientists do, to the physical system. They do all that, however, only if it is part of the teacher's plan and if the teacher does not exempt himself from the requirement of listening and determining how effective his own words and referents are. The teacher may model effective communication behavior for the students.

In order to understand how an adult and a child may come to talk together about a system, we need to keep in mind that each of them acquires a history in relation to the system, and that the system itself usually has a history, especially if it is a dynamic rather than a static system. The child and the teacher usually do not share exactly the same experience with the system being studied, since the teacher must also interact with other children

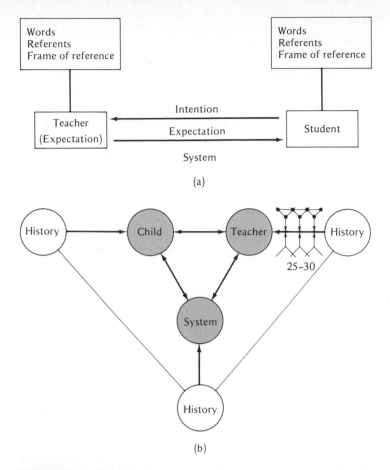

(a)

(b)

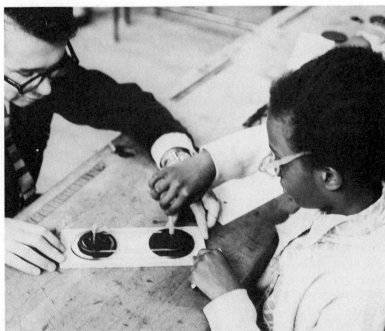

FIGURE 12-4
a **The problem of "tuning in"—how to communicate with each other.** *b* **Tuning in is a double problem—finding out what has happened in each child's system and finding out what will be helpful to him.** *c* **Finding out what the student has learned about the system.**

and the phenomena they are studying. Their problem, if they wish to speak together, is to find a way to give and get enough of the history of what has happened to form a basis for conversation and further inquiry. To picture the problem each child faces when he wants to speak about phenomena with the teacher, and the complementary problem the teacher faces, examine the interaction model in Figure 12-4*a* and *b*. The child may have a continuous history of observations and interactions with the system, interupted only by his peers or by the teacher. The teacher, on the other hand, moves about the classroom "sampling" a great many systems, each of which may be in a different condition. Each child must find some way to talk about his system that will allow the teacher to discover enough of the *context* to move the conversation along or to make appropriate suggestions regarding next steps.

When a teacher joins a child and interacts with him about a system which they can both observe, the child uses his language, at whatever its level of development, to convey the substance of his experience and thought to the teacher. The teacher watches and listens. If she asks diagnostic questions—questions that will genuinely help her to understand what experiences the child has had with the system and how the child thinks about those experiences—they may communicate. In short, both child and teacher must solve communication problems to make their encounter useful and fun (see Figure 12-4*c*). A group of students can be taught to report what they have been doing and finding out as a step in starting off a conversation. That saves the teacher from having to fish for information with a set of questions. Conversation is better than inquisition, since it puts the teacher in the role of consultant rather than inquisitor.

FAMILIARITY AND COMPREHENSION

Scientific phenomena, experiments, and games provide a unique opportunity for children to develop elaborative language patterns that are conducive to analytical thinking and problem solving. The continuity of experience which the teacher and children may achieve together, by virtue of the fact that the phenomena can be jointly observed and talked about, provides a rich soil for the cultivation of skills of cue elaboration.

Two children will differ in the rate of comprehension of specific content, depending on their familiarity (previous experience) with that material. *Familiarity* means that the children know what ideas usually go together and increases the probability that they will infer the meaning of new concepts or words from the *context* in which they occur.

Each of the language skills facilitates comprehension by decreasing the range of possibilities of what is likely to occur next. The listener builds up a progressive expectation of what will follow. (In fact, one form of humor is based on knowledge of such expectations: the association between the punch line and what preceded it is relatively improbable.) For the person who knows the probability characteristics of his language or of a particular discipline (e.g., what ideas occur together in what order), the "surprise value" of a communication will be relatively low. That is, the amount of news a communication contains or what has to be learned from it will be less than it will be for the person who has less knowledge of the sequential relations. In other words, the amount of real information that a person must extract from a given communication is a function of his knowledge of the language and of the *ideas* expressed in the communication.

NOVELTY AND LEARNING

At this juncture we may ask what science curriculum materials should be like if they are to help students develop the ability to elaborate their observations and thoughts in standard forms. The answer which logic suggests is that substantial portions of the content ought to be strange or novel to the children concerned—not familiar and close to their past experience, as so many educators suggest. It is possible to select material which is new but not too complex. Novel or unexpected events arouse interest, prompt inquiry, and furnish children with an opportunity to begin new patterns of verbalization uninhibited by past learning. If, in addition, children can take home pieces of equipment or science objects for a short time, in the same way that they borrow books, then they and the adults may be prompted to talk together in situations where both are genuinely interested and puzzled. For example, teachers in one of the SCIS project schools in an inner city gave first-graders an opportunity to borrow electric wires, small motors, and lights that they had experimented with in class. The average number of additional discoveries children made and experiences they could describe after one week was six. Some of the new experiences came about because older children or fathers became interested and talked with the children. At another time, the same children took home magnifiers with three different lenses mounted on them, to continue explorations started in school. Again the interest of other family members was captured. More school systems are experimenting with provocative "take-home" materials that will encourage two-way communication. There is an attribute of normal instruction that probably impedes growth of analytical thinking and verbal patterns. If you watch what young children do with objects like magnifiers, magnets, and electrical circuits that are left around, you will find they play for a while and then leave the objects. If the children are let alone, they eventually return to the objects, sometimes doing the same or similar operations over and over. They may return on several occasions to the objects, quite unpredictably. This fact often annoys teachers who have moved on to a new topic or who think that this is a child's device to avoid more routine but necessary work. But another interpretation of this behavior is that thinking patterns develop through frequent short encounters with objects and phenomena, and that the process of elaboration is going on during these times of exploration. The meaning of such internally prompted experiences increases for children as they develop more connections between the experiences and their own thought systems. These repeated encounters help children consolidate and stabilize their learning. It is by this means that they develop connections among ideas in their conceptual maps.

The argument, then, is for curriculum formats with more individual variation (e.g., opportunities to return to some contents and experiences when the *learner* decides) and social productivity (e.g., by bridging the gap between school and home with high-interest science materials). Probably the preschool, kindergarten, and first grade represent the most effective stages for using science to mediate language mismatches between home and school, but there is no necessary reason why it cannot serve this function for older children as well.

SCIENCE AND LANGUAGE DEVELOPMENT

Science may be employed to help children learn analytical language patterns. We need to be aware of the fact that certain logical operations in science require that children have a fair command of syntax. Think for a moment how much information we store in the final phonemes of many words—e.g., tense, number, and comparisons (*-er, -est*). Children who speak certain dialects tend to omit or de-emphasize the final phonemes that are such important clues about what kind of mental or physical operation is called for. Such children will talk freely when confronted with phenomena, but they use an inferior syntax that must eventually be corrected. In the context of shared experience with science materials, it is relatively easy to identify and work naturally on these problems. The concrete experiences afforded by the presence of the materials allow teacher and students to build new language maps.

Recall the very simple but fundamental example of mislabeling described in Chapter 1. Many first-graders confused two words, *soft* and *smooth*. The kind of operation one performs to distinguish a soft object differs from the operation for distinguishing a smooth object. To establish smoothness, one moves the fingers horizontally across a surface. To establish softness, one squeezes the object—i.e., moves the fingers up and down at right angles to the surface. As soon as students learned the distinction between the two operations, the confusion in their use of the two terms disappeared.

For students with language problems—use science

The communication gap produced by different histories of experience, and by variations in the semantic and syntactic structure of languages used by individuals, is especially marked between teachers and the children of minority groups. Educators rarely use the most obvious resource available to them for bridging this gap—early and regular exposure to a sequence of experiences in science. The manipulation of science materials, either in ways invented by the children or in ways specified by their teachers, creates opportunities for teachers and students to interact in the context of *shared experiences*. It provides an opportunity for teachers and children to invent and use language with little risk that they will misunderstand each other. The physical system is right there in front of them, and they can repeat an event as often as necessary to achieve some degree of consensus about the language mappings being used. The shared experience allows teachers to model language patterns, and it provides an opportunity for children to construct their own versions out of those models.

In practice, the terms we use to describe experiences are less restrictive in their application than their dictionary meanings might suggest. What is more, the meaning of sentences does not lie in the sum of their component words as much as it does in how the words are related— i.e., in the structure of language. It makes sense to teach young children new terms in the *context of experience*. In this way they come to recognize how variable the circumstances are to which the terms could apply. But mostly they begin to experience all the kinds of relationships that can exist between ideas. Obviously science instruction for young children cannot go on effectively with respect to growth of language unless two conditions are met: (1) *all children should have plenty of opportunity to use and hear language in conjunction with direct exploration of phenomena,* and (2) *formal definitions should be avoided in favor of using words and phrases in context.* If students are forced to learn formal definitions of terms before they have a sufficient pool of experiences to which the terms apply, the probability that they will be able to use the ideas implicit in the terms in new situations becomes very small. Teaching definitions out of context produces limited transfer of learning. On the other hand, learning language, including the specialized language of science, proceeds quite easily when the terms are constantly heard while the students are immersed in the appropriate contexts. While children can do a great deal of thinking, even with very limited language, they can do more thinking of a higher order if they have more language facility.

Labeling and language

Try a simple experiment. Arrange the twelve objects in Figure 12-5 in groups, on the basis of their common properties (or better yet, ask children of different ages to sort the objects). Label each class of objects according to their shared properties and keep track of which objects belong in each class. Now form new categories based on some

FIGURE 12-5

a The description of this assortment of objects depends on the basis for categorization. *b* One grouping is according to the variable of corners: 3 corners, 4 corners, no corners. Try another grouping.

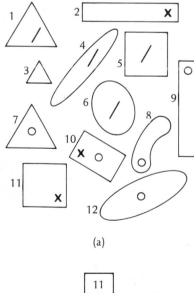

(a)

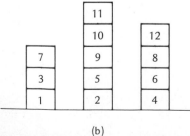

(b)

new set of properties, and reclassify the objects. See how many different kinds of groupings are possible. Note that the objects now cluster in groups in different combinations. As the basis of categorization changes, so do the labels and, in fact, so does the system of objects. The relationship in which the objects stand to each other changes every time you select a new variable as the basis of classification. There is something in what the philosopher says—when you change the variables, you automatically change the relationships among the parts. To understand a communication, you must find out what variables are governing the relationships.

To illustrate how flexible the labels we use to describe the properties of objects are, and to show how subtly the referents change, examine the three objects pictured in Figure 12-6. Label the objects according to the property of size: *big, bigger, biggest.* Now relabel the objects on the basis of size as *small, smaller, smallest.* Note what happens by simply shifting the context. The same object, say object A, first has the label *biggest* and then the label *small.* Now, nothing changed in the objects themselves— neither their absolute size nor their physical arrangement with respect to one another. What is more, the labels match the way many people "feel" they perceive the objects. Object C seems small and object A seems big in comparison to it, and the labels do not change that fact. Row 1 of labels (*biggest, bigger, big*) really has to be read from right to left to make the words and the objects seem to match. Row 2 of labels (*small, smaller, smallest*) can be read comfortably from left to right, except that it is difficult to call object A *small* while you can still see objects B and C, and after you have just finished calling it *biggest.*

Of course, what shifts here ever so subtly is the implicit referent. Any object can be called *big:* the object can be its own referent. But to call some object *bigger* implies that at least two objects must exist in fact or in principle—the object you are labeling and the one you are comparing it to, the referent. To use the label *biggest* implies three or more objects, the one being labeled and two or more referents.

Labeling, then, is a function of context, the way in which the objects seem to be related to each other. The teacher must become an astute observer of context. The labels attached to an object can change according to the relationships or functions which the object serves.

FIGURE 12-6

The same object may at one time be labeled "smallest" and at another time labeled "big." Context determines which label is appropriate.

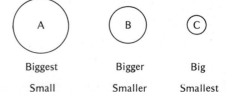

A	B	C
Biggest	Bigger	Big
Small	Smaller	Smallest

(Recall the example in Chapter 1 where an object could be called a *table,* a *barrier,* or a *platform,* depending on its use.)

This simple experiment in perception and labeling illustrates something of the complexities faced by all of us when we try to map experience into language. The shifts in referents as well as the location of the observer with respect to the system create communication hazards. The kind of shift in context that allowed the same object to be labeled *biggest* at one instant and *small* at another is analogous to the use of symbols in science and mathematics. How many times, for example, have you sat as a student in a science or mathematics class and watched in confusion while a professor used the same symbol to mean one thing at one time and something entirely different at another time, or used different symbols to represent the same thing? Unless you knew the context well enough to shift with the speaker, his meanings escaped you. Naturally, in such a situation one's confusions accumulate, with the result that while the course progresses, one's understanding grinds slowly to a halt.

It makes no sense to teach by definition when the pool of experience is so limited. (In fact, we may suppose with some accuracy that the reason so many teachers dislike science results from the fact that they were taught science by definition. The novice learns, in a restricted fashion, concepts that are in fact rich in meanings. But only one event fits in a category so learned; the concept, then, has little generative capacity.) Definitions are formalizations and restrictions placed on words *after* we have had varied encounters with them. Sometimes we deliberately restrict the meaning of a word or invent an entirely new sound to label a concept which is new to us or which has to fit together in a particular way with other ideas. But restrictions placed too early on the contents of categories may block the kind of free-associational thinking that probably constitutes a necessary, if not sufficient, condition for creative thought and productive problem solving in science.

It is clear from these few examples that the business of categorization or the formation of concepts is an active, flexible process. The words we use should be connected with our conceptualization processes instead of with unvarying, static dictionary meanings. In practice we employ words with great ingenuity and stretch their meanings according to our needs or the dictates of the flow of our experience. Sometimes we store the same concept under different labels; at other times we use the same labels to refer to different concepts.

The language we develop maps our thinking processes and experiences only approximately. The variety of kinds of experiences and feelings we, as individuals, tuck away in the "same" words—i.e., words that sound the same—is enormous. Communication in and of itself constitutes a remarkably difficult interaction, particularly when there is no immediate or past shared experience between speakers. We achieve some consensus about meaning when we come from the same or a similar community of experience. If we come together with different experiential histories and if, in addition, the semantic and syntactic properties of our languages differ, then the communication gap becomes enormous. Two physicists, for example, may be able to talk together and achieve reasonable comprehension of what they heard with relative ease. But a physicist and a psychologist would have more trouble communicating. Their principal difficulty does not lie exclusively in the jargons of their fields, but in the fact that they do not share relevant experiences that can serve as referents for what is being said. Thus, they can talk past each other—a capacity we all share to some degree.

A few remarks on reading

In one sense, reading is just another kind of communication process. But its difficulty is great in comparison with spoken language, for the reader cannot interact with the communicator to clear up misunderstandings. Students can be taught to diagnose their learning problems when they read science material. They can learn to ask themselves questions about the material:

What *variables* are mentioned?

What examples of the variables or ideas are given?

What words do not make sense in terms of my present understanding?

Students often feel discouraged when they do not understand some written material. They should be made to understand the following points:

1 The author frequently is not clear or gives too few examples. (One book for slow learners in biology was actually made by cutting out almost all the examples. This had the effect of making the content even more difficult to learn than that of the original version, since there was even less redundancy. Omitting most of the examples meant that the rate at which new ideas were introduced per page was excessive.) Teachers and students should look for more examples.

2 It is good to seek help when one does not understand. A book represents a one-way communication system; two-way communication systems are more effective. Students should be encouraged to seek help from other students as well as from the teacher.

Videotapes clearly indicate that some teachers become upset if students help each other. There are several probable reasons for this unfortunate response: teachers often associate collaboration between students with cheating; they do not want to share even a small part of their role as teacher or helper; or they fear some students will become too dependent on others.

Books, like teachers, are a resource. Students can learn to use them as another source for acquiring information. Just as students who want information from another human being must ask questions, so students who seek information from printed materials must learn to ask questions. When students have had a substantial amount of laboratory experience with the content of what they are reading, the language and thought in the book will be grasped more quickly. If students go to books because they really want information about something, the motivation to read through even fairly complex subject matter will be high. With a few analytical skills, they often can get some help from books.

POOR LANGUAGE DEVELOPMENT AND LEARNING

There is a danger in supposing that poor language development necessarily implies poor mental development. While there is a relation between language and thought, children with relatively meager vocabularies have been shown to be capable of normal cognitive activity. McGlathery found that lower-class students performed as well as middle-class students on science tasks that allowed them to demonstrate results—that is, tasks where the score depended on making the proper decision and not on verbal evidence. But when evidence of competence in science required verbalization, the middle-class group made better scores.[3]

The kind of verbal models to which students have access makes a great deal of difference. Some teachers refuse to use the language of science in context. After analysis of a tape recording made during science periods in third- and fourth-grade classrooms, Altman reported that inner-city teachers conducting a modern science program exposed students to fewer verbal cognitive interactions than did suburban teachers.[4]

In the course of physical maturation, the basic capacity for language develops. Although children exhibit signs of cognitive functioning long before they use language, they will not actually synthesize language if they do not get the raw materials from adult speech. The latent capacity for speech may be built during the first two years of life, but if (as in the case of deaf children) a person has no access to the sound of language, then the materialization of a language structure may be delayed or fail to develop at all.

Educators particularly should keep in mind that cognitive processes, while they may be expressed in language and subject to the effects of language, also go on independently of language. Mentally deficient children may display greater language development at the time of starting school than do deaf children, but the sophistication of their play does not exceed that of the deaf. For example, deaf children set up trains, figure out switch combinations, and build complex forms with construction sets.[5] These behaviors are indicators of well-developed cognitive operations.

When children come to school with language and thought that do not match the demands imposed by the new situation, each environmental encounter is that much more complex, and may easily exceed their mediational skills. For example, when a group of kindergarten youngsters in a Portland ghetto received a small bag of

[3]G. E. McGlathery, "An Assessment of Science Achievement of Five and Six-year Old Students of Contrasting Socio-economic Backgrounds," ERIC Report ED 026371, 1968.
[4]Altman, I. M, "Teacher-Student Interaction in Inner-City and Advantaged Classes Using the Science Curriculum Improvement Study," unpublished Ed.D. dissertation, University of California, Los Angeles, 1970.
[5]Eric H. Lenneberg, *Biological Foundations of Language,* John Wiley and Sons, Inc., New York, 1967.

objects for sorting, several of them burst into tears. One little girl hid the bag under her dress, and a little boy immediately stuffed three of the objects into his pocket. No words came from the children during the first period. For the most part, they just sat holding and fingering the objects or guarding them from the view of others. Their teacher wisely let the children keep the bags in their desks. From time to time in the next few days, the children would take some of the objects out. They began to compare and talk about them, first with friends. On the fourth day, the teacher started the lesson on sorting that she had originally intended to teach. The children began the difficult business of trying to convey what they discovered about the objects. Had the teacher tried to launch the lesson on the first day, she and the students might well have been too discouraged to ever try again. Their teacher would have reported that the language and concepts were too difficult for the students.

Young children with language handicaps do solve problems. Children with relatively small vocabularies and a restricted grammar can sometimes solve rather complex science problems as long as they can work with concrete objects rather than with abstractions. Such children of necessity make the words in their repertoire do more for them.

Language synthesis is far from a passive process in which children simply mimic patterns passed on to them by adults. Children actively build language out of the sounds that adults furnish them. Unlike parrots, however, they experiment with *patterns of sound* rather than exact word-by-word productions. It is at this point that a close interaction between children and adults becomes vital to the development of patterned language structures. The sounds of words uttered by children at twelve to eighteen months of age are crude replicas of the adult words. The adults have to make the translation to recognizable words. Human beings have a remarkable capacity for interpreting speech distorted in pitch, or loudness, or inflection, even against a great deal of background noise. They can do this partly because of the nature of speech itself, which is a highly redundant process. To a person who knows the patterns of a language, it is often possible to hear only relatively few parts of a message in order to be able to figure out its total content. It is the *patterns* that children try to acquire, rather than each separate constituent. *No amount of drilling on separate words will ever teach children the structure of language, since the meaning of a sentence is never equivalent to the sum of its referent words.* Meaning and comprehension depend heavily on syntax. That is why new scientific terms need first to be learned in context—with many examples.

Keep in mind that the power of language lies mainly in its patterns and structural relations and in the *flexibility of its categorization processes.* Language learning is not solely a paired-associate phenomenon in which one word represents one object. Our brains could not store that much information, to say nothing of being able to operate with it. Nevertheless, some adults persist in teaching language, including scientific terms, to children as though they were parrots. In science instruction it makes little sense to teach young children formal definitions for terms before they have had considerable concrete experience with the referents of the terms and before they have heard the terms used in context many times.

Unfortunately, we do not know very much yet about how children transform their experience of objects and phenomena into language. In the early stages of education, we would do well to allow children to experiment liberally with labeling their concepts and constructing their language out of science experiences which we share with them to some extent. We can appreciate the problem of the preschool child who said to this teacher in puzzled dismay, "I have a stomach ache in my head." For the time being, he had to make old words do for a new experience.

If teachers became oriented toward inquiry about the teaching-learning process, they might at least try to model the language of science for children, remembering that *new patterns are learned by repeated exposures to the sounds, coupled with a variety of experiences.* One outcome seems certain: children may acquire the language patterns of science if they are exposed to them—they never will if teachers or parents deny them the ingredients.

SUMMARY

1 Language development will probably progress more rapidly when language is learned in the context of direct experience. Science provides opportunity for students and teachers to build language maps based on shared experience.

2 Concepts in science contain two parts:

  a A statement of a relationship (e.g., "opposite poles attract each other")

  b A statement of an operation necessary to produce evidence of the relationship (e.g., "when two magnets are brought together . . .")

Sometimes insufficient attention is paid to the *operation*.

3 In solving a problem it is helpful to do the following:

  a Make a mental list of the concepts that may be applicable.

  b Shop for information, using two or more concepts from the list.

  c Order the evidence so as to be able to make inferences or draw conclusions.

4 Successful communication between teachers and students depends in part on how familiar each is with the context. Students need to learn how to convey details of the context to the teacher.

5 *It* is a word whose use needs to be carefully monitored. Find out to what each *it* refers, or there may be unnecessary confusion about meaning.

6 The effectiveness of communication can gradually be improved by occasionally playing back and analyzing tape recordings made of discussions. These encourage students to focus on:

  a Language in use

  b Reasoning

  c Listening behavior

7 Novel rather than familiar experiences probably provide a better opportunity to work on the development of new language patterns.

8 Students need time to repeat, retrace, and "retalk" about phenomena. In this way they build connections between ideas and so gradually construct a conceptual map.

9 Early, extensive experience with scientific phenomena may be an especially powerful means for developing language capabilities among students classified as disadvantaged.

10 In spite of poor language development, students may exhibit good reasoning. Teachers sometimes make the mistake of equating poor language development with poor mental development.

ACTIVITY 12-1

OBJECTIVES

1 To identify observations, inferences, and operations

2 To note the effect of *sequence* of observations on the inferences students make

Background:

Transcript 12-2 was furnished by Henry Wiethake, a fourth-grade teacher who had been experimenting with wait time. He was teaching Science: A Process Approach (SAPA). This is a portion of a discussion which followed a laboratory activity that focused on controlling variables. Students studied the influence of light and immersion in water on blueprint paper. Note that once Mr. Wiethake had started the conversation, the students took over.

What to do:

Read Transcript 12-2 through carefully.

1 What evidence is there that the students are listening to each other?

2 List or circle all the *observations* made by students.

3 List or mark all the statements which tell what someone *did*—i.e., what operations or procedures were performed actually or hypothetically. (An example of a hypothetical experiment is item 23, in which the student predicts a result of an imagined experiment.)

4 List all the *inferences* or attempts at explanation.

Transcript 12-2 **(Third grade)**

1	*Teacher*	Yesterday we did some work with the blueprint paper and light. What results can you see by looking at the various groups, papers, and whatever happened?
2	*Child*	Amy, you don't want to do it now?
3	*Child*	The, ah, longer we let the, ah, light hit it, the darker it

got. We had different times; most-used time was 10, 5, 3. If it was 3 minutes that it was kept under . . . (Tape messed up) It was 5 minutes that came in between.

4 *Child* Well, um, one of the things that you'll . . . one of the, um, the three strips of paper—um, the results don't seem to go along with what you said, David, because the 10 and the 3 are the same, and the 5 is a little darker.

5 *Child* I disagree with you, because, um, what David said was—well, when you keep it under longer, it gets darker. I support, agree with, Davey, and I don't agree with you at all.

6 *Child* Well, ah, in, ah, some cases some people didn't exactly know what to do, so they could've made a mistake and maybe put the whole slip in the, in the, ah, light, in the pockets we put them in, and therefore could not really tell that much.

7 *Child* Well, I think at one point, ah, there's a time where it gets the darkest, between 10 and 5, and then it seems to get lighter, because when things are there it does look a little lighter than the 5. So one point—I'm just guessing—but one point in between that probably would be the darkest point there, and then it gets lighter.

8 *Child* I don't think it was supposed to get darker as it was exposed to light, because we did it, and when we exposed it to light the color came off, but when you put it in water and you let it dry it got darker.

9 *Child* Well, most of them look the same, from here, not really all of them, but most of them, they all look pretty dark.

10 *Child* I think it was because the, um, light too—if you have a dull, um, light it wouldn't show up too much, and if you have it like a real bright light it will react more—like, it'll get a shade that will be darker.

11 *Child* Well, I think the more time you have it under the light, the darker the part that isn't under the light gets.

12 *Child* I disagree with you, because, uh, it's the, um, side that is in the light gets darkest.

13 *Child* I agree with Kathy, because how could anything happen to the part that like just isn't in the light? What happens to the part which is in the light?

14 *Child* I disagree with Kenneth because he said that the part that was hidden from the light got darker, the part that was in the light got darker . . . not hidden from the light.

15 *Child* Well, I don't think the water really affected the color that much, I think it was just the light that did it, 'cause when we took it out you could see the difference already without putting it in the water.

16 *Child* Did it get any darker when you put it in the water?

17 *Child* Well . . .

18 *Child* Well, not really.

19 *Child*   Well, um, what . . . what Kathy said, um. It really is true. It just gets a little feel of the water when you put it in the water. It gets a little clearer.

20 *Child*   The thing that happened with ours was when we tested ours and we took it out, it didn't look like anything happened to it, and then when we put it in the dark and put a paper towel over it and left it overnight it got much darker the next day. Like today, when we looked at it.

21 *Child*   Well, um, some people walked around with the strips while they were getting ready to experiment. And when they put it in the light they could have already been a little darker.

22 *Child*   Well, I . . . I agree with _____, because when we did our experiment and everything . . . um, when we tested it, ours turned out like, um, white on the other side of it. And, um, then when we left it overnight it turned dark.

23 *Child*   Well, I disagree with John, he said, like, before the experiment if we walked around with it, it wouldn't make any difference if we didn't dip it into water. Say we got paper and we brought it up from the art room into Mr. Wiethake's room, does it get darker?

24 *Child*   Yes, but I disagree with Sal because that's a different kind of paper, Sal. And it might have an effect because we were keeping it in a book, and it was dark there, and as you were walking around, the light could have affected it, and it's not the same kind of paper as the normal paper we get out of our notebook. So I agree with John.

ACTIVITY 12-2

OBJECTIVE

To observe how labels change when the context changes

When you change the basis for categorizing objects, you change their relationships to each other. The relationships we observe "out there" in the world around us depend upon where we focus attention. That prompts some philosophers to muse that there are no fixed relationships "out there." We invent them. We require, however, that the relationships bear some kind of correspondence with what we observe.

What to do:

1 Reexamine Figure 12-5. Find at least two other bases for categorizing the objects. Assign labels to the categories.
2 Construct histograms to describe each sorting. Do the shapes of the histograms remain constant?

ACTIVITY 12-3

OBJECTIVE

To observe individual differences in the way students go about solving a problem

Task:

To design and conduct an investigation into the process of problem solving

What to do:

1 Select a relatively simple problem from any current science series or plan one of your own.
2 Give the task to a pair of students. If possible, tape-record their conversation. Keep a record of the *observations, inferences,* and *operations* they perform.
3 Give the same task to a second pair of students. Again make a record of observations, inferences, and operations.
4 Compare the performances of the two pairs of students. In what ways were they similar and in what ways different?

CHAPTER 13

There always is a noise when it is dark!
It is the noise of silence, and the noise
Of blindness!

The noise of silence, and the noise of blindness
Do frighten me!
They hold me stark and rigid as a tree!

—JAMES STEPHENS, FROM "IN THE NIGHT"

DOING SCIENCE WITH HANDICAPPED STUDENTS

OBJECTIVES

On completing this chapter and its associated activities, you should be able to do the following:

1 Adapt some science activities for use by blind students and deaf students.

2 Analyze the content of a scientific experiment to determine what variables are important as regards adaptation.

3 Decide what evidence would normally be associated with the variables defined in item 2.

4 Identify the possible modalities that could be used in collecting evidence. Combinations of touch and sound can often substitute for vision.

5 Adapt the apparatus as necessary.

6 Devise a technique for having handicapped students record data.

INTRODUCTION

Time is the variable which, more than any other, distinguishes the learning behavior of blind children from that of their sighted peers, of deaf learners from that of those who can hear, and of some emotionally disturbed and mildly retarded students from that of normal children. Blind children have no lead time, no opportunity to size up an event before they are in the midst of it. Deaf children usually get less experience at abstracting information and gathering it into convenient bundles for mental manipulation; their response time, consequently, may be too great for the situation. Emotionally disturbed youngsters often cannot suppress competing responses or ignore one stimulus to pay attention to another; as a result, their lead time—time in which to anticipate the course of some event and adjust accordingly—shrinks. Mentally retarded children often cannot integrate events, assign meaning to them, and pick out an appropriate response. For all these children, prediction over a short interval of time may be difficult, but the reasons for this difficulty are different and depend on the kind of handicap.

How science may serve children who must operate under some handicap is the topic of this chapter. Relatively little systematic investigation of how young children with different kinds of handicaps may be reached, or how they may be helped to interact with their environments through participation in science activities, seems to have found its way into the literature.

A number of ingenious instruments exist for assisting blind children to collect data, especially in England, but these were developed mainly for older students. Some adaptations that can be made with simple materials will be discussed here. An argument will be made to support the suggestion that some socially handicapped children might be better taught if they were regarded at first as functionally deaf, with science instruction adjusted as for deaf children. Emotionally disturbed youngsters able to remain in school seem to have a special affinity for science. Mildly retarded children have difficulty abstracting and integrating information, but they may accomplish a good deal, given sufficient time to work with physical systems.

The contents of this chapter really amount to another open invitation to inquire. Development of science activities and instruments suitable for use by young children with different kinds of handicaps has received little attention. The possibility that early science instruction might actually facilitate the acquisition of compensating behaviors and help children to gain some sense of control over their environment seems not to have occurred to many people.

MISSING MODALITIES

Different modalities take in information at distinctive rates. Eyes, for example, can display a whole spatial array for their owner at one time. When either the owner or the objects in the array start moving in relation to each other, the eyes keep track of that information. By contrast, information that comes in over auditory tracts apparently must be strung out in time and sequenced by the listener, and the patterns in it discovered, before it becomes intelligible.

The wide range and depth of distance over which eyes may pick up information permit people to "see ahead in time." Before an event reaches its conclusion, or even before it takes place, people who can see may anticipate it and adjust their responses accordingly. They can follow the trajectory of a thrown ball and move to meet it. They can observe changes in a physical system, select variables, and choose appropriate times to make measurements. When necessary they can take evasive action to avoid calamity. In a sense, vision permits the sighted to influence the future over a short span of time because information brought to them by the eyes allows them to plan alternative outcomes. Because vision permits interaction at a distance, it provides a little lead time in which to adjust response before an event happens.

Blind children ordinarily do not have that kind of lead time. To experience events they usually must arrive in the midst of them. They may use sound and proprioceptive cues; but since these serve over a much shorter distance and range than vision, the lead-time variable must necessarily be shorter. The visual cues, which tell an inquirer into a physical or biological system what to look for and when to collect data, must be supplanted for blind children with other devices.

Almost anyone venturing into a new environment or confronted with a new problem will experience some anxiety. Since blind children have so little information before arriving on the scene, in comparison with sighted children, they require more time to collect the comparable cues. The spatial arrangements of parts, their contiguity, and their motions in relation to each other give important information about interactions in systems. Often sighted children may take in this kind of data at a glance. Blind children must acquire comparable data through touch, sound, the use of special sensors, or instruments. Since that information must usually be collected in smaller chunks per unit of time because the modalities that must be employed have not the simultaneity available under the visual mode, that touch of anxiety which accompanies new experiences at first may take a little longer to disappear.

Deaf children, on the other hand, miss little of the visual information which might be pertinent to a science investigation. Provided their language development has moved along fairly normally, they can proceed in science as would normal children. However, it is more often the case that deaf children rarely get sufficient early practice at representing experience in some kind of language context. The task of abstracting information from the environment and then accumulating it into language bundles which may be logically manipulated depends on the availability of language models or appropriate communication substitutes for sound. Deaf children sometimes pass the peak period for language learning before formal instruction becomes available to them. Even then, schools for training of such youngsters frequently spend an exorbitant amount of time teaching language per se rather than language in the context of some concrete events. As a result, deaf children are often denied even the chance that normal youngsters get of trying to map experience into language through science.

Once I watched two young teachers try to do some science with a group of deaf nine-year-olds. They did what teachers with normal youngsters often do when they feel that the children are not getting the principle: they talked faster and faster, and louder and louder. The children smiled up at them, hardly replying to any questions and absently fingering the materials. The voice of a teacher may draw the attention of children who can hear away from their materials, but these children were impervious to the intrusions. Finally the teachers resorted to tapping the children on the shoulder or lifting their faces up, pointing at their own mouths. The children were effectively drawn away from the materials, just as sometimes happens with normal children. But their attempts to respond gradually dwindled to nothing.

When the class was over, the two young instructors shook their heads. "You see," one said, "it is too hard for them. They are nine years old, and we only used activities from the first-grade program. They still couldn't get it." We sat down then to look at the video-tape recording of their sessions. The tape showed increasing interference, or "helping," from the teachers. Not only did the words come faster, a fact that would not have mattered, since the children were protected by their deafness, but the teachers' hands appeared increasingly in the systems the children were trying to learn about, moving the parts and gradually stealing the action from the children. It was a perfectly natural impulse; frustration makes most of us step up our pace and tricks us into taking on more of the functions that belong to others. In teaching, the impulse must be fought against.

Whereas blind children may suffer from a kind of "time binding" at the point in inquiry where the physical or biological systems to be investigated must be observed, deaf children may become bound in the present at the point of converting experience into abstractions. Since the collections of experience into abstractions frees children from the perceptual binding imposed on them by the appearance of things and the necessity of manipulating factors concretely rather than mentally, deaf children especially need to engage in science activities where they can observe the history of systems. Deaf children require at least as much time to explore the system as normal children faced with a comparable problem. Indeed, they probably need more time, because without ready access to conversation, argument, comparing, and sharing activities—all of which help to evolve and refine their logic and language—they will not develop a sense of a negotiable future. Blind children, for their part, usually come to use verbal information very efficiently. They usually can hold in memory longer chains of directions and verbal information than can sighted children.

DOING SCIENCE WITH BLIND CHILDREN

Exploring spatial relations

Probably the first major conception which blind children must acquire has to do with dimensionality. Space and

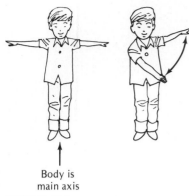

Body is
main axis

FIGURE 13-1
How blind children may use them-selves as a frame of reference to break space up into sections.

FIGURE 13-2
Using the body as a frame of refer-ence, a blind child can perceive the shape and dimensions of an object by moving his hands in from some starting point, as is shown in Figure 13-1.

(a)   (b)

time, which may be taken for granted by the sighted and which must eventually be dimensionalized for them, must also be dimensionalized for the blind. A possible sequence of activities that would help to develop a strategy for exploring spatial relations in a system might progress through the following steps:

1 Use of the body.   Use the whole body as a frame of reference. Take some large objects, such as boxes of different dimensions and shapes, and have children "scan" them with their hands and arms as shown in Figure 13-1. This procedure will teach them to explore space and objects by dividing space into approximately rectangular coordinates. Contrary to what would usually be the procedure in working with blind children, begin with large objects, not small objects where the children's bodies may serve as the center of the coordinate system (see Figure 13-2).

2 Serial ordering.   Begin work on the concept of serial ordering, again using large objects such as the boxes mentioned in item 1. With the main part of the body as a guide, the children try to order boxes according to length, then width, and then height, by sensing how far out or close in their arms are to their bodies as they feel each object. Whereas a sighted child learning to order serially can keep the visual display constantly in front of him for comparison, the blind child must retain in memory the muscular cues which told him how far apart his hands and arms were for each object. That is the information he must use if he is to order objects serially, whether along a linear dimension or along a weight dimension.

3 Surfaces.   Once a system for determining the approximate dimensions of objects is established, then the shape of their surfaces may be explored in more detail, by the simple process of first getting the dimensions and then by sliding the hands over surfaces, looking for edges, corners, and cues that suggest the changing of position from one of the coordinate directions to another. A curved object, for example, may first be explored "as if" it were rectangular to establish its approximate size. Then the hands may be slid around it, with the shape of the hands and their position, especially at the wrists, being used to give information about the direction of change of a surface. See Figure 13-2 for an illustration of one such procedure. A physical concept of area can emerge from such activities.

4 Measurements.   In these early stages of instruction—
the primary years—*measurement* is more important to
blind children than to sighted children. The reason for doing measurement at all in science is so that the magnitude
of change in a system may be noted. Sighted children
often can see changes, and their magnitude is a matter of
minor interest. The change is so obvious that there is no
point in measuring it. Not so for blind children. Often the
only way blind children can know that any interaction has
occurred in a system is by noting the changes in the value
of certain of its variables through measurement. The
magnitude of changes in many cases may be too small to
be detected by the use of body cues.

    Length. Cuisinare rods make good basic units of
length, although dowels cut into convenient lengths will
do well as long as they are rectangular instead of round
(to prevent rolling). (See Figure 13-3.) Making such units
so that the smaller values will be even multiples of the
larger values will help students to acquire a sense of a
hierarchy of values in which larger units subsume smaller
units. Measurement of an object in smaller units of length
will yield a higher number than measurement of the same
object in a larger unit. The larger the basic unit, the
smaller will be the number necessary to express the measure. That principle holds whether the unit of measure
happens to be length, weight, or temperature.
    Sighted children who measure the same object and
come up with markedly different results can usually see
that others are using measurement devices of different
unit size. They use that information to clarify any communication problems. Such a process of clarification not
only teaches them that disagreements may be reasonable
in terms of the operations performed but also makes argument legitimate. Science thrives on argument. Blind
children need to learn the same attitudes, but the way in
which they collect the information will put more pressure
on communication by words and force more reliance on
tables of data.
    Consider, for example, how a comparison of results
obtained by two children who do not see might be accomplished. Give each child a long flat stick, such as a meter
stick or yardstick, but unmarked; a large sheet of wrapping paper, three feet or more in length and about 30
inches wide; and some pieces of masking tape or other
sticky markers fastened to a piece of wax paper. To measure something, the children use their fingers to line up

FIGURE 13-3

Rulers for blind children. *a* **Measuring stick with raised strips, which
can be made of adhesive tape.** *b* **Measuring stick with holes and side
notches.**

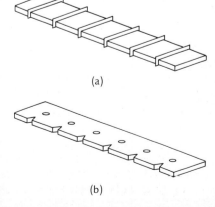

(a)

(b)

one end of the stick with the edge of the object to be measured. Then they slide a hand along to arrive at the other end of the object. By taking hold of the stick at this point and pasting a piece of sticky tape on it—or sliding a rubber band along it, so that the edge roughly corresponds to the position of the finger marking the point on the rod that corresponds to the length of the object—they make a first record of their results. By following a similar procedure, they can simply transfer the information to the brown wrapping paper: place one end of the rod on the left side of the paper, and put another piece of sticky tape or masking tape on the paper at a point that corresponds to the location of the tape or rubber band on the measuring stick.

A convenient, quick way to compare the length of an object at two points in time or the lengths of two objects at the same point in time is to use the back of the hand and the forearm or a stick. Put two rubber bands around the arm or stick. Lay the stick along the object to be measured, and slide the rubber band along until it corresponds to the length of the object. When the second object is similarly measured, the child can compare the location of the two rubber bands by sliding his free hand along the surface of the stick or his arm until it comes to the first band. When the second rubber band lies beyond the first, then the object is longer by an amount equal to the distance between the bands or markers.

Weight. Blind children may build and calibrate their own weighing devices. They may proceed in either of two ways or may perhaps eventually follow both methods. First, they need some standard units of weight. As was mentioned in Chapter 2, you might give them large washers of different sizes.

Hang an object of unknown weight on a spring by dropping it into a cup attached to one end of the spring (see Figure 13-4). At the point where the rubber band and the paper clips or hook that hold the cup meet, make a mark on a stick. This can be done with masking tape, but a second rubber band that may be slid up and down the stick is more convenient. With this location on the stick marked as a reference point, remove the object of unknown weight and replace it with the unit weight measures. Keep adding weights until the reference point (the rubber band) is reached. Equal weights will stretch the spring about an equal distance; thus the weight of the unknown and the weight of the collection of unit measures

FIGURE 13-4
Weighing devices.

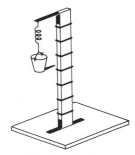

(a) Spring balance

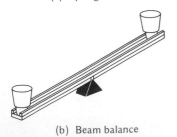

(b) Beam balance

will be equal when the rubber band arrives at the original mark.

An alternative procedure or one which might follow next in the sequence would be to calibrate the stick by marking off points on it that correspond to the distance the spring or rubber band stretches when increasing numbers of washers are added to the cup. The stretch of a spring is linearly related to the stretching force. That linear relationship between distance stretched and the magnitude of the force permits the weighing device to be calibrated in a more simple fashion. Mark the zero point with a line or notch in the stick. Mark the greatest stretch permitted by the spring on the stick, using the standard weights (the washers) to find this point. Then divide the distance between the two reference points into equal intervals that correspond roughly to addition of two of these intervals. Holes can be drilled on the back surface of the stick to correspond to the numbers represented by the notches. The arrangement and number of holes would follow the normal representation of numbers in braille, but the reference point would always be at the location of the notch on the front surface or one edge of the stick.

A *beam balance* for comparing equivalent masses of material may also be constructed for use by blind children, with only one major change in design from those described in the chapter on measurement (see Figure 13-4*b*). As is illustrated in Figure 13-4*b*, a stick, which is about as broad as the widest mass likely to be used, has two rails glued to it and is grooved along the side. The fulcrum is set low, so that when the system tilts the beam will touch the desk, cuing the children by sound as well as by touch when the system is not in balance. Plastic cups may be fastened to corks that fit snugly between the rails. Objects to be compared can be dropped into the cups. The system is balanced by adding and removing weights, or by sliding the cups to different positions inside the rail. Objects that are small enough can be placed inside the rails without a cup, and the reference washers can be stacked to balance them.

Temperature. To measure temperature, we must resort to commercially prepared systems and forego the luxury of allowing children to make their own instruments.

Time. With only a small distorting effect on the system, blind children can use pendula to measure time, as is suggested for children who can see. Time is marked by comparing two events which run simultaneously. If a sufficiently heavy mass is used for the pendulum bob, the system will retain enough momentum to run for some time, in spite of the small damping effect which the children's fingers will have as they count its oscillations. They can count swings by bracketing the pendulum string with their fingers, near the top, and noting when the string returns to the referent finger.

A metronome adjusted for different frequencies may also be used, of course. This is especially useful when a group of students work on an experiment in which they simultaneously collect data for comparison. As with pendula, an inverse relation holds between size of units and number used to express the time measurement: longer pendula require fewer swings than shorter pendula to measure the duration of an event. This is a relationship which students can discover for themselves.

Blind children should participate in the assembly of the apparatus they will use. It is by this means, i.e., having knowledge of the sequence of steps in the assembly and the spatial positioning of parts, that their concept of contiguity of parts will be developed. Constant checking of the approximate dimensionality of the system, using the method shown in Figure 13-1, will help to maintain spatial orientation.

ADAPTING SCIENCE LESSONS FOR USE BY BLIND CHILDREN

Blind children have one advantage at least over sighted children. Whereas children who see and hear may be forced by their teachers to learn almost exclusively from demonstrations—an unfortunate but common practice— blind children really must encounter the systems directly to grasp the concepts in them. The major caution to be observed by those who teach science to the blind, especially teachers who are sighted, has to do with talking and helping too much. That impulse needs to be kept in check, as it must also be by teachers of normal children.

To adapt any lesson for use by children who have little or no sight requires a careful analysis of the content to determine what variables probably are central to the purposes of the activity. (See Chapter 16 on task analysis.) Next, decide what evidence would normally be associated with those variables and consider how it might be collected. Having done that, decide what sense modalities a normal child might use to gather the data. Study the situation carefully to see whether comparable information could be obtained by some combination of sense modalities other than sight. Combinations of touch and sound, properly sequenced, can often make up for what would ordinarily be accomplished by vision.

Histograms and graphing

Recall that most of the information in a histogram lies in its shape. Once blind children can compare one length with another, they can begin to represent events in histograms, much as sighted children do. If the histograms are made of heavy-weight paper or of light-weight cardboard, the children, by touching, can easily monitor the shape of the display, exposing to themselves the relative lengths of columns as they move their fingers along the edge of the histogram.

When data in a histogram are to be represented somewhat more abstractly—that is, when units on the histogram correspond to some set number of unit measures actually made on the system—there is also a simple procedure to be followed. Give the children a collection of cardboard squares, which will serve as units on the histogram. Each square can be made to represent as many units of measures made in the physical system as the children wish. In the beginning, one unit of length might be represented by one square, or one unit of weight by one square, or one unit of temperature by one square. What the variable is does not matter. Later, for reasons of economy of space, two units of measure may be represented by one square, then three or four units, etc. If the units are pasted onto a piece of paper (again, heavy wrapping paper is useful here), not only will the children be able to read the histogram from its shape, but, if they need to check data for any set of measures, they will simply need to count the squares in each column. The line made by fitting the squares together can be felt with the fingers.

In putting together a histogram, the basic manual problem that must be solved if the histogram is to contain useful information in its shape is setting up all the columns so that their bases fall on the same line. There are two ways to accomplish this. If the children use large wrapping paper, then they can paste on the first column any way they choose. The columns that succeed it would then fit against each other. The children would only have to get the first square or counter of the next column in place beside the corresponding square of the first column. By running their fingers along the edges of the two squares they can achieve an alignment. An alternative procedure would begin by pasting a long thin strip of cardboard or heavy paper onto the wrapping paper, to act as a base line. Then, each new column would be set up by abutting it against the base line. Underneath each column, holes labeling the column would be punched in the paper.

Bivariate graphs—graphs that describe how two variables seem to be related—may be built by using pegboards on which lines that are sufficiently raised to be detected by touch are drawn along the board so that they pass through the centers of the holes (see Figure 13-5). The edges of the board can serve as the frame of reference, or, alternatively, strings may be strung along the board to represent the vertical and horizontal axes of the graph. Plastic pegs such as those often used in pegboard displays may be inserted in the holes to fasten the strings in place and to serve as "points" on the graph. Normally the intervals along each axis can be marked with a peg; one peg is inserted in every other hole, as shown in Figure 13-5. Children use the graph boards, which are easy to assemble and cheap to make, by finding the positions on the two axes that correspond to the values they want to represent and then sliding their fingers along the appropriate lines until they arrive at the intersection. When they locate the hole at that intersection, they stick a peg in the hole to mark the location. Depending on the distribution of all the points, they may then get some concept of the shape of the distribution by taking a piece of string, wrapping it

FIGURE 13-5
Stages in the construction of a bivariate graph for use by blind children.

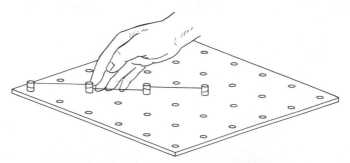

around the peg at the extreme left, then moving it along to the next point, wrapping it around that one, etc., until the point farthest to the right is reached. Then, by running their fingers over the string, the children may apprehend the shape of the curve. This running of the fingers along the string should be done by using the four fingers of one hand simultaneously, as shown in Figure 13-5.

Deciding when to collect data

Now that we have some means of collecting data by interacting with a physical or biological system, the next problem is to find some way of determining when to collect data. Since blind children are not cued by visual changes in a system, they must make other decisions about collecting information. Probably one of the best strategies for them to use depends upon a sampling process. They decide at what time intervals they will make their measurements. A system may change suddenly or gradually, or it may arrive at some state of equilibrium. But the values of the relevant variables will change as the system interactions begin, reach some kind of maximum, and decline or cease. Some of those interactions may be over with so quickly that their measurement is not practical; others will be subject to measurement. By working in small groups and apportioning the data-collecting jobs among the members, the children can usually collect the information they need to discover how the system operates.

If there are moving parts in the system, it may not be practical for them to explore the system with their fingers once it is in action. When this is the case, a flexible probe, which may be inserted in the system, will often help them find out what is going on. Plastic straws make fairly good flexible probes. A partially unfolded paper clip will also function as a good probe. If the upper portion of the clip is left still folded, not only do the children have something bigger to hold on to, but the information picked up by the probe, the vibrations, will be transmitted to the thumb along a larger surface and so will be more easily detectable. The children will need to practice until they become accustomed to holding the probe lightly between thumb and forefinger. If they grasp the probe too strongly, they will not be able to detect small differences in the vibrations that result from the interaction of the probe with objects it touches.

Organizing data

Just as children with sight eventually face situations where they must find convenient forms for organizing and storing data, so must children without sight. They can organize data into simple tables, just as sighted children do, by setting up areas in which data of different kinds are collected. But the way in which they form the tables will necessarily be slightly more cumbersome. Two methods will be briefly described. One employs a small wooden or plastic frame on which wires are fastened, as shown in Figure 13.6, to form a simple grid. The frame is loosely taped to paper, preferably large sheets of wrapping paper, as described earlier. Whatever data are being collected or sorted then are dropped into the compartments. On the paper surrounding the frame, the student punches out his label or code, which tells what each column and row represent. In this way he can construct either univariate or bivariate tables.

An alternative technique starts out with the frame taped to the paper, which is placed over a soft matting such as foam rubber or even cardboard. With a stylus or a fine ball-point pen, the paper can be scored to mark off the lines that form the table. The paper can then be flipped over and data kept inside the boxes formed by the scoring. If the boxes of the table are made sufficiently large, then the squares of cardboard described earlier can represent data from the different categories. Alternatively, the children can simply punch holes in the squares, making one hole for each point that belongs in a particular square.

Blind children can learn science. Science lends itself especially well to the mastery of space and time relationships, one of the major classes of relationships which blind children must master. In addition, physical systems studied directly can lend physical substance to mathematical concepts, as is illustrated by the inverse relation between the magnitude of a measurement unit and the number used to express the value of the variable. It would,

FIGURE 13-6
Frame for keeping track of data. Counters may be dropped into each square.

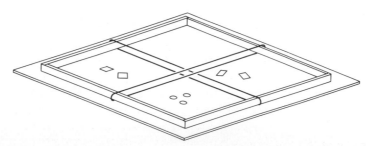

I think, be a pity to deny blind children access to the very discipline in which the primary goal is the exploration and explanation of physical phenomena. It is through science that men roll back the darkness and drive away their fears.

DOING SCIENCE WITH DEAF CHILDREN

Deaf children escape one feature of instruction that often afflicts those who hear—the bombardment of questions from their teachers that characterizes so many classrooms. (See Chapters 8, 10, and 11, which discuss wait time, reward patterns, and question-asking behaviors of teachers.) Nevertheless, their lack of hearing makes communication difficult. Their problem comes mainly at two points: talking over what happens in an experiment and getting directions. Deaf children must rely heavily on visual cues. It was suggested that blind children be encouraged to assemble all apparatus they use, or all that is practical for them to assemble; the same is true for deaf children. To establish some continuity between what one does to a system and the changes a system goes through during an experiment or activity, it is well for the children to experience the birth of the system.

If we adopt the position that thinking and speech originate independently but come after a time to interact in such a way that each influences the other, then what deaf children require for stimulation of thought is early and frequent exposure to physical and biological systems whose histories they can observe and change. Language in use is not simply a labeling process; it is more like a mapping process in which the words and the logical connectives work together to display the thought. It would be foolish, in my view, to withhold instruction in science simply because the problem of communication between one human being and another was not entirely solved. Let the physical and biological systems that they can experience together speak to them. Out of that experience they can build a communication system which contains some potential for mutual understanding. Deaf children need to learn language in some very compelling contexts. A similar argument may be put forward regarding youngsters who come to school from homes in which language and logic associated with anything except the most rudimentary kind of directives do not exist. Begin by treating such children as though they were functionally deaf. The semantic forms and the vocabulary usually employed in

Area = 4 square inches

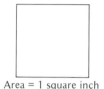

Area = 1 square inch

Area = 4 square inches

Area = 1 square inch

FIGURE 13-7

How many small squares, each 1 square inch in area, would be equivalent to the area of the big square? How many small circles, each 1 square inch in area, would be equivalent to the area of the big circle?

school may mean little to them in the beginning. But language may develop rapidly in the context of science activities where all the data are out in the open, available to every child. Deprivation of language experience, whether through real or functional deafness, may be remedied to some degree, at least, by frequent and somewhat prolonged exposure to directed experiments designed to focus attention on patterns of interaction in physical and biological systems.

Early successes in reasoning about what they observe and how systems respond to manipulation can help deaf children gradually pass to more elaborate forms of thinking. As they progress, they must become free of the need to solve problems at a concrete level by direct manipulation, just as normal children must. More complex problems often require more symbolic representation, and in fact many physical problems resist solution by directly concrete means. Transformed to a more abstracted form, such problems may be quickly solved.

For example, if a child or adult operating at a concrete level in respect to area has displayed before him a rectangle 4 square inches in area and a rectangle 1 square inch in area, he will usually solve the question of how many small squares would give the same area as the big square by cutting out small squares and fitting them into the big square. But if he is then shown two circles, one enclosing 4 square inches of area and the other 1 square inch of area, and asked how many of the small circles would be necessary to give the same area as the big circle contains, he will not find a solution. That problem is not amenable to a concrete solution, except approximately. To solve it, the child must move away from the perceptual bind imposed by the shapes, to the concept of area per se. He has to ignore shape and focus only on area. Then he may reason that if the large circle consists of 4 square inches (or 4 area units) and the small circle contains 1 square inch, he will need four such small circles to get an area equivalent to that of the big circle. (See Figure 13-7.)

With physical systems it is relatively easy to teach a logical concept like equivalence. All the activities designed to teach measurement, for example, contribute to the notion of equivalence as well as to the idea of conservation of quantity. Exposure to whole sequences of change in many kinds of systems should encourage the development of transformational thought and the evolution of language chains to represent thought and facilitate it. At least, as children encounter such systems, they expose clearly to the teacher by what they do, as much as by what they try to say, how they are thinking. Thus the diagnostic potential of science activities probably should not be ignored, especially by people interested in the full development of individual potential. Under that model, one does not think of norms and other kinds of product measures. Instead, one watches the process by which a child proceeds through a problem and intervenes accordingly. (See the discussion in Chapters 16 and 17 on evaluation for further discussion of these points.)

DOING SCIENCE WITH MENTALLY RETARDED OR EMOTIONALLY DISTURBED CHILDREN

There is no necessary connection between emotional disturbance and retardation in children. Nor is there just one kind of "emotional disturbance." All that this section is intended to do is to acquaint you with some interesting but puzzling observations made by some teachers who have tried to do science activities in classes for disturbed and retarded children. The two kinds of groups present a common problem in that attention spans seem to be notoriously short, although the reasons which might be put forward to explain the fact probably would differ. Almost without exception, however, teachers who try to do some science with either kind of group report that attention to science tasks persists much longer than attention to other tasks and that the children are more prone to return voluntarily to science tasks than to tasks from any other subject of study. I have observed that phenomenon myself on many occasions but am at a loss to explain it. But there is no point in trying to find an explanation for phenomena that are not sufficiently well documented yet. My guess about what may account for the persistence comes from watching both groups work with science materials. They often make the system go through the same interactions many times; it is as though they carry on a kind of silent dialogue with it. Perhaps this is one of the times when they can structure their own thoughts, for most of the rest of the day seems to be devoted to the necessary business of trying to respond to conventional modes imposed on them—a predetermined structure must be learned which may be a necessary part of the socialization process.

Perhaps too, bearing in mind the discussion of how the reticular formation operates (Chapter 7), we might hazard a guess that the moving parts of physical systems

—the interactions between parts which can be seen and felt—fire up the reticular formation, which then maintains the cortex in an alert condition for a time.

While early science instruction may be desirable for normal children, it seems almost imperative for the development of language and logic in handicapped children. To begin will not be easy, but that matters little: it is in the nature of beginnings that they are difficult. It is time to begin. . . .

SUMMARY

1 Time is a variable with special importance for handicapped students.
   a Blind students have no lead time.
   b Deaf students need more response time (picking up auditory information is slower than picking up lip or visual information).
   c Emotionally disturbed students need time to control competing responses.
   d Mentally retarded or slow students need more time for integrating events.
2 Different modalities take in information at different rates.
   a Vision allows one to see a set of events as they happen. On the basis of this information one can anticipate the direction in which objects will move.
   b Auditory information (sounds such as speech) has to be strung out in time. It takes longer to describe an event than to see it.
3 Measurement is an important process in science. Early emphasis on measurement is probably more important for blind than sighted students, since it permits them to detect the extent of change in a system. Sighted children often have less motivation to measure, because the changes in a system are often so obvious to them visually.
4 The potential for language development in the deaf probably could be enhanced through early exposure to science. Through such exposure, a community of shared experience can develop. When there are communication problems concerning "what happened," the students can resort to the physical or biological system to show what they did and what resulted. Thus the language

grows in the context of verifiable experience.

5 Much of what is done in modern elementary science programs can be adapted for use by blind and deaf students, for whom early science instruction may be even more important than for nonhandicapped students. To adapt materials do the following:

a Identify the variables.

b Identify the kinds of evidence that could be associated with those variables.

c Identify all the modalities or combinations of modalities which could be used to supply evidence which is equivalent to what would normally be collected.

d Adapt the apparatus where necessary.

e Devise a technique for recording data.

ACTIVITY 13-1

Invent ways of measuring liquid volume that blind students might use. (Hints: try devices that float; try plastic syringes.)

ACTIVITY 13-2

In Chapter 16, on task analysis, procedures for several science lessons are described. Examine these to determine how they might be adapted for use by blind students.

ACTIVITY 13-3

Design a light-weight metallic or plastic probe that a blind student might use for exploring systems. Describe its characteristics.

REFERENCE

The Science Curriculum Improvement Study (SCIS), a project located in the Lawrence Hall of Science at the University of California, Berkeley, is being adapted for use by blind students. Write to Dr. Herbert Thier at the Lawrence Hall of Science for more information.

CHAPTER 14

"I want that classroom quiet. If a parent walks in and hears a racket, he's going to think I'm not doing my job. I don't care if they move around some, but they'd just better not be running around."

—PRINCIPAL, DISCUSSING DISCIPLINE

"I've got three parents coming to help me teach science each week. At first I was afraid it would mean trouble—criticizing, and like having extra kids in the room. But now I can't see how I ever got along without them. They help with materials and they listen to the children. That's what we need, and they do—someone to listen."

—TEACHER OF THIRD GRADE, AFTER THREE
MONTHS OF USING PARENTS TO HELP

MANAGEMENT AND CONTROL—SOME SOCIAL-PSYCHOLOGICAL FACTORS

OBJECTIVES

On completion of this chapter and its associated activities, you should be able to do the following:

1 State four rules for forming and maintaining productive work groups in science.

2 Identify behaviors which distinguish healthy groups from sick groups.

3 State a relationship between expectations and performance.

4 Recognize functions which when performed help a group identify and progress toward its goals.

5 Devise skill-practice games to help students become more adept at working in groups.

INTRODUCTION

Children ordinarily are sorted into classroom "lots" for instruction. Administrative decisions based on beliefs about what mixtures of intelligence, reading skills, maturity, and race make for the best learning groups determine the classroom group to which a child will belong. Whatever the attributes of the mixture, the teacher must find some way to organize the classroom in order to promote the best possible outcomes for as many individuals as possible. No two "lots" of children are identical in all respects. A set of prescriptions simply will not suffice for all conditions or situations that science instruction can present. Instead, teachers need a framework for making decisions.

While it is common to attempt to apply findings from studies on the psychology of learning to improve instruction, there seems to be little interest in relevant research in the area of social psychology. Because so much of teaching is carried on in groups, however, principles of social psychology are applicable to teaching situations— especially in science instruction, where so much depends upon productive discussion of ideas. We will discuss a few ideas from social psychology that have special relevance to the teaching of science.

Pressure from a peer group has been shown to be extremely relevant to decision making, even in objective situations.[1] One study showed that adults could privately estimate accurately the length of a line compared with a standard; but when others were present who deliberately gave erroneous answers, about one-third of the adults changed their answers to conform to the group. If adults are subject to such pressures, how much more must children be influenced by them? Modern elementary science programs provide concrete reality for students to work with and discuss. The problem is to develop group skills that encourage independence of judgment while, at the same time, the group members cooperate in finding solutions to problems.

Organized groups, those in which there are rich interactions governed by some rules, are superior to unorganized groups in their ability to operate under stress and in ambiguous situations. There are phases during problem

[1]S. E. Asch, *Social Psychology,* Prentice Hall, Inc., Englewood Cliffs, New Jersey, 1952.

solving in science when the situation is ambiguous, the outcomes uncertain, and the level of frustration high. By applying the skills developed by the social psychologist, a group can be moved toward a goal without jeopardizing the independence of its members. Such skills can be taught to students.

Modern science programs rely more heavily on the authority of evidence than on the authority of status. It is important to recognize which factor—evidence or status— is influencing your students. In science, students check their impressions by experiments. If this alternative were not available, as is the case in most areas other than science, the opinions of the group would be more readily swayed by nonobjective views. Organized groups learn to rely on evidence for making decisions in science; and the skills introduced in this chapter should help them do so. Modern science programs make discussion a key factor.

Is there any evidence that the students are prepared for this field trip?

Experimenting with small groups to see how variables like participation, cooperation, task persistence, and efficiency are influenced in elementary science can be very rewarding. It is better to identify variables and try to use the knowledge of them to improve outcomes than to move blindly through the morass they can create when we act as though they did not exist. The nice thing about maintaining an inquiry-oriented stance toward teaching is that we can divest ourselves a little of the need to be right all the time. In science one pokes about, hopefully in a somewhat systematic fashion.

In this chapter we focus on group variables. Of course, many times our experiments may fail. The scientist guards his right to be "wrong." He expects to "mess about" at times. He knows that as a result of an experiment, he may find that a lovely hypothesis must be thrown out. Teachers who experiment with instruction behave in about the same fashion as scientists. When they start experimenting with teaching in order to uncover new variables or gain better control of the learning process, it is natural to experience some anxiety at first. Just as the scientist does not accept a "one-trial" answer, teachers often need to repeat teaching experiments, adjusting variables to see what happens. By persisting in this investigatory attitude toward classes, we feel much less upset when something does not "work." Instead, we start thinking about what can be done the next time to help students achieve a better result.

SOME BASIC PROPOSITIONS

Consider the following propositions:

1 Science is a social enterprise in which arguments over interpretations of data drive researchers to more advanced levels of investigation. Modern elementary science programs depend on such differences among students to provoke discussion and new investigations.

2 Some groups function in such a way that they encourage maximum development of each member's resources. The members can learn from each other (see Figure 14-1). The variety of ideas and experiences in the group makes the work rewarding to everyone. We shall call these groups "healthy."

3 Some groups function in such a way that they inhibit the development of individual resources. No one listens to anyone else. The variety of ideas and experiences in the group is small. There is little impetus to search for the use resources that others have. We shall call these groups "sick."

4 Individuals have unique histories which must be brought to bear on the problem-solving efforts of the group. Each individual is a potential resource for the group.

5 Soon after a group forms, members develop expectations about the ways in which individuals in the group will function. These expectations influence the performance of each individual in the group. When expectations are low, performance tends to be poor. When expectations are high, performance tends to be correspondingly high.

In science, children usually work in groups. Even if it were financially possible to provide every child with all the science equipment and directions necessary for him to pursue his learning individually all the time, we would not necessarily choose to do so. (This point is treated in Chapter 7, which discusses two functions of argument in learning science.) In any case, that is not a prospect which most of us are likely to face for some time. Economic realities being what they are, elementary schools rarely provide all the objects needed for science at a ratio of one per child. Consequently, most of the time children work in groups when they are doing science. How do we

FIGURE 14-1
Teachers face the problem of forming productive work groups.

distinguish effectively functioning groups from poorly functioning groups? The first management task that confronts you is to find ways to *compose* productive work groups. The second management task is to *maintain* productive work groups once they have been formed.

Collaboration may involve use of the same equipment, or it may mean that a different operation is performed by each member of the group. . . .

COMPOSING PRODUCTIVE WORK GROUPS

Effects of groups

Recall the discussions of physical and biological systems, where it was frequently pointed out that when a system forms through interaction, it acquires its own unique set of properties. The system becomes a new "thing." None of the components has the same list of properties as the new entity. This is also the case when a collection of people with different histories form a work group. The group is a new system which quickly acquires its own set of characteristic properties. These properties, in turn, influence the behavior of the members. For years, experienced teachers have moderated the behavior of individual students by changing their work groups or the seating arrangements in a room. Disruptive children assigned to different groups developed desirable behavior patterns often enough to encourage teachers to use the technique as one way of solving discipline problems.

A group that stays together for a considerable period of time acquires a social structure marked by fairly predictable patterns of interaction, stable expectations about the performance of its various members, ways of treating conflict, and devices for managing deviant members. Depending on how it operates, that structure can help or hinder the development of each child's ability to do science. It can control the extent to which the child is free to explore, to try out new ideas, to find himself in error, and to learn from experience. In some science groups, students develop specialties. Instead of rotating tasks among members, one member records all the data, another cleans up, and another assembles apparatus. Each student in such a group engages in a limited range of activities. In other groups, such specialized tasks are rotated among the members. The members of a group develop expectations about the kind of contribution each person is likely to make toward solution of problems. When expectations about a member are generally negative—for example, "You always goof"—then the quality of that child's performance often deteriorates and the range of activities in which he participates shrinks. At this point, the teacher needs to evaluate what is happening in the group. It is important for the teacher to monitor groups carefully in order to know when a change in group composition would create more variety for all the members or when it would be beneficial to talk with a group to find out how it is operating.

It is appropriate, then, in the context of modern elementary science programs, to pay some attention to small-group variables that may influence students' performance in and attitudes toward science. Managing the social system of the classroom so that it helps, rather than inhibits, learning involves the application of theory and research from social psychology. Science materials make the ways in which students work together visible—and audible. Teachers can observe interactions of students with each other as well as with the materials they have in hand. Since the behaviors are so visible, it is also perhaps easier in science than other subjects to teach students to recognize when a work group is functioning poorly and to teach the skills necessary for effective collaboration. Students must come to believe that, through effective use of their individual resources, the product which they can produce jointly will usually be better than any they would produce individually.

Expectations and groups

Expectations are beliefs that we each have about how people will behave under various circumstances. Each year, teachers begin school with a new group of children and a set of descriptions handed on by their former teachers of what to expect from them. The children, in turn, may have advance descriptions of their new teachers. At first, this information substitutes for firsthand experience and provides the adults and children with a basis for deciding how to behave toward each other. Furthermore, after a few short weeks of interaction, both teachers and children usually confirm their expectations. The previous data serve to bias them. They bias each person in such a way that he will tend to ignore data about people if the data fail to fit his expectations. Thus, for example, if a student who has been doing poor work suddenly performs well, a teacher may suspect cheating or may think the good performance is a fluke. Studies have shown, for example, that teachers who have been given positive information about a student will tend to grade his essays more favorably than if they have been led to have poor expectations for his performance. Students, too, live according to their expectations. They may develop persistent beliefs about the abilities of their classmates. These be-

... Collaboration may also mean planning, experimenting, and observing together; and it may mean working individually and sharing results.

liefs will govern the kinds of things they do and say. When things go wrong during an experiment, for example, they sometimes blame a student with low status whether or not he actually was responsible.

New expectations are also developed, and these too serve to govern the kind and quality of interactions that follow. The basis for forming new expectations may be direct experience, or it may be characteristics of the person, such as race, reputation, and status. In any event, *expectations condition behavior*. Teachers make decisions and act on their expectations about what a particular group of children can do. These expectations are expressed through institutional decisions such as grades and promotion as well as other kinds of cues such as praise and blame. The expectation patterns that knit children and teachers into systems may function as an intellectual and emotional coffin from which neither can emerge. On the other hand, positive patterns of expectations can motivate a whole group to attain great heights.

When no one expects much of anyone else, or expects only trouble, then the quality of life in the classroom tends to deteriorate. When expectations are generally high, the quality of life improves. Because elementary science programs provide new and tangible things for students to work with and talk about, they provide a unique opportunity to do something about improving expectations.

Unless you guard against it, expectations developed in each classroom between children and adults tend to stabilize early and to be very resistant to change. Part of their stability lies in the fact that neither teachers nor children bother very often to check the validity of the data which govern those expectations. Often the members of a system assume limits where none necessarily exist. Children with a reasonable idea for an experiment have been heard to say of their teacher, "Oh, she wouldn't let us do that." Teachers for their part have been heard to remark about their children, "They couldn't do science; they can't even read," or to say of their principal, "He wouldn't let us do science this way; it is too noisy." Principals sometimes have described their teachers as "afraid to teach science because they don't know enough." As a result, both adults and children live in an unnecessarily restrictive environment, operating on expectations which they rarely seek to modify and of which many are false.

Once a pattern of expectations forms, it is difficult to change it. Teachers come to associate a certain level of performance with a student, assuming that his behavior is predictable and that not much can be expected to change it. This is unfortunate, since the quality of performance of an individual is very much influenced by the particulars of a task, the combination of people in the group, and the expectations others hold about what he will do and say. (See Chapter 9.)

How predictable is a child's behavior as he moves from situation to situation? In one study, seven-year-olds were independently rated on variables such as ability to follow the rules of the game, endurance and concentration, and reaction toward frustration. The children worked on construction of models and on problem-solving tasks. For each change in task, different peers worked with the child who was being studied. That is, both the tasks and the membership of the work groups changed. If individual characteristics are highly important in predicting behavior, we should expect the different judges to agree on their rating of each child's performance, and the ratings should not change much from situation to situation or as a result of changing the composition of the group. If, on the other hand, situational variables (e.g., the type of task and the people with whom one works) are a powerful influence on performance, then the judges will disagree on their ratings of each child, and the relationship between their ratings will tend to be random. That would be the case if a child's behavior does change in response to particular situations.[2]

It turns out that situational variables are of great importance. The investigators found no systematic correlation among the judges' ratings of an individual's behavior when both the task and the composition of the group changed. A person does not behave in the same way all the time. Often we attach labels to children and proceed to categorize them as relatively fast or slow learners, leaders or followers, disruptive or cooperative, persistent or easily discouraged, good or bad at following rules, and so on—and then we act according to those labels. We base our expectations on the labels we have attached, and we begin to modify our interaction with each child as though he were indeed a fixed or unchanging variable. The study suggests that any normal child probably would be evaluated differently under different circumstances. Persistent labels cannot be applied so easily, for real performance

[2]See Magnusson, Heffler, and Nyman reference at the end of the chapter, page 449.

changes as a function of the type of task, the setting, and the combination of students who work together. Modern science programs in which teachers permit investigation allow some students to exhibit ways of thinking and working which their teachers had not thought possible. I have heard many teachers say of a particular student who said or did unusual things during a science lesson, "I didn't know he could think that way." Sometimes they add reluctantly, "Maybe he has a special aptitude for science." We give up our old expectations in favor of new ones grudgingly; and, unfortunately, we rarely have to subject our expectations to the searching analysis that sometimes forces scientists to let go of their fondest notions.

Expectations are relative. They are largely determined by situations. A child moved from one group to another and from one task to another is likely to change his behavior pattern. The group, in its turn, accommodates its pattern of interaction in order to absorb the new member. When the behavior of children shifts, it can in turn reinforce or inhibit teachers, depending on how they value the new interactions. One thing is certain—teachers and students are bound together in a system, and no one in it can change much without producing consequences in some other parts of the system.

The behavior of an individual varies greatly, depending largely on two factors:

1 The characteristics of the particular group with which he is working
2 The kind of task the group is working with and the conditions under which the setting requires him to operate

Knowledge of personality characteristics, self-concepts, or mental ability within rather broad limits does not help us predict what a particular child will do on a particular unit in science, provided that he has some degree of freedom to investigate actual physical or biological phenomena.

Events or people may have taught us to have any one of a thousand positive or destructive beliefs about ourselves and our relationship to the world. But even knowing what the self-concept of a particular individual is, and how he probably came to form it, we cannot predict how he will behave in any given situation. *We cannot say why children or adults with similar histories and self-con-*

cepts behave so differently in the face of crises.[3] Similarly, given the unusual stimuli that science problems present to students, we can expect some unusual performances from students who might otherwise not be recognized. Our focus must be on performance—what we observe students saying and doing when they have sufficient opportunity to work with materials and to talk freely about how they interpret their experiences.

Observers who have no previous knowledge of the intelligence or creativity of the children in a classroom cannot tell from watching them perform how tests had classified them. Wallach and Kogan[4] sent trained observers into some fifth-grade classrooms to find out how children could be classified according to the following categories: high creative, high intelligent; low creative, low intelligent; low creative, high intelligent; and high creative, low intelligent. Did the children have manifestly different ways of behaving? The observers, who were not told how the children were rated on the tests, found virtually no behavioral patterns that distinctly distinguished boys classified as high creative from those classified as low creative. They did find, however, that creative girls behaved in some distinctive ways. These girls generally tended to be slightly disruptive. The girls classified as high creative, relatively low intelligent, exhibited particular deficiencies in coping with the achievement and social pressures of the school situation. These girls, except for occasional outbursts, were largely withdrawn in group-work situations and hesitant in academic-work situations. The girls classified as high intelligent, low creative, on the other hand, functioned rather well in the classroom. Kogan and Wallach were tempted to speculate that conformity brings more recognition than creative behavior does. New science programs value unusual but adaptive responses. If group pressures repress such responses, then much of the value of the new programs will be lost.

Since variation in tasks and in composition of groups produces marked variation in the behavior of individual children, it is well to have open expectations about what particular children can do. While it is natural and mentally economical to categorize individuals we work with

---

[3]See the Coles reference at the end of this chapter.
[4]Michael A. Wallach and Nathan Kogan, *Modes of Thinking in Young Children,* Holt, Rinehart and Winston, Inc., New York, 1966.

and to act according to those categories, we run the risk of helping to lock children into mental coffins from which there will be few resurrections. As further proof that such judgments derive from and are constrained by the structure of the particular groups and tasks in which we see individuals working, consider the results of an experiment conducted by Piers et al.[5] They found virtually no agreement between teachers asked to rate the same children on creativity, despite the fact that they supplied a very precise description of what they meant by creativity.

Modern science programs prompt a wide range of responses from children. The adult in the classroom cannot easily appreciate variety in outcomes if the variety seems to create management problems. According to the ideas the adult has developed about what kinds of outcomes to expect, he, as well as the students, has to decide how to evaluate unanticipated outcomes. The research on expectations should caution him to be sure that his judgments are based on the merits of the evidence offered by individuals and groups rather than on expectations about the way those individuals and groups usually perform. In science one can always resort to the evidence to settle differences, or at least to understand how inferences were formed.

Expectations, sanctions, and wait time as related factors

Expectations influence teachers' behavior in subtle but identifiable ways. In one experiment, twelve second-grade teachers each identified the five best and the five poorest students in their classes on whatever basis they chose—that is, they could use any criteria they wished to select the students. No one had trouble picking the strongest or the weakest children. Three science sessions and three arithmetic sessions were observed and tape-recorded to answer the following questions:

1 Do teachers ask the top and bottom groups, on the average, the same number of questions?
2 Do teachers address to both groups questions of equal difficulty or questions that require the same kinds of logical operations?
3 After teachers ask a question, do they give, on the

[5]E. V. Piers, J. M. Daniels, and J. F. Quackenbush, "The Identification of Creativity in Adolescents," *Journal of Educational Psychology,* vol. 51, pp. 346–351, 1960.

average, the same amount of time for slow and strong students to answer?

4 Are different patterns of praise given to each group?

To start with the last of these questions, the pattern of praise differed. The students classified as weak got more praise, but the reason for the praise was often ambiguous. As to the third question, teachers waited *significantly less* time in both science and mathematics for "slow" students to reply; that is, they allowed "bright" children more time to think. Can we hazard the guess that the shorter wait time and different pattern of praise reflect the expectation that poorer students will not know answers but need encouragement to try? We might surmise, further, that the more ambiguous pattern of reward delivered to the bottom group reflects the teacher's uncertainty about what to do with the children in this group in order to get them to act more like the children in the top group. As to question 1, teachers asked brighter children slightly more questions, but not significantly more. However, turning to question 2, the level of difficulty of the questions addressed to the two groups differed. Students rated as slow received more cognitive memory questions (e.g., "This is a *what*?") and low-level inference questions. The few divergent questions asked went to the top groups almost exclusively. (Question-asking behavior and questioning techniques are discussed in more detail in Chapter 11.)

It appears, then, that children rated as relatively less apt were given less time to think and fewer opportunities to practice higher-level cognitive operations, and lived under uncertain reward conditions. Thus, the low expectation for their performance is continually confirmed and reinforced by their teachers' patterns of interaction.

On receiving these data, the twelve teachers were shocked at first. They listened to sections of tape recordings to verify the findings, as they should. Then they justified the faith that underlies this book—that inquiry *is* the job of the classroom teacher. They began to experiment with wait time, increasing the average wait time for the students rated as weak to five seconds or more. Incidentally, it is of interest to note that teachers who find their expectations changing about particular children rarely alter their views suddenly. They usually begin by expressing surprise and pleasure at what a student starts doing. After a while they may report that the child "seems to have an aptitude for science" but will complain that he does not want to do anything else.

The research on expectations and on the behavior of groups suggests that the following classroom practices might be helpful in science.

1 Group membership should be changed under certain conditions.

    a When members show persistent task specialization (e.g., some always assemble apparatus, others always clean up) it is well to make a change.

    b When a predominantly dominant, aggressive, and talkative combination prevents participation by all members, a change is called for. A group can usually handle one or two such members, but not more.

        (1) Put the silent people together. Usually their level of participation increases if this is done.

        (2) Put several talkers together. This generally produces more balanced participation. Give them skill-practice exercises such as those described later in the chapter.

    c As a rule, it is better to change group membership between tasks rather than during tasks.

2 Provide variety in the kinds of investigations on which students work during the year. This will give students with special interests an opportunity to make valued contributions. Some units of work, by their organization and content, appeal strongly to certain students and less so to others. Thus a teacher has to be prepared to find that individual students will vary widely in productivity as they move from unit to unit or project to project. As a whole, however, if groups are well composed, they will produce at a high level of competence and with general enjoyment. Variety in talent and experience in a group is more likely to result in innovative work. A high level of interest among some members often stimulates interest in lagging members.

3 Hold feedback sessions on how groups worked. Occasionally, hold discussions in which groups

FIGURE 14-2
Children imitate one another. Under what circumstances should this be encouraged? (Photograph by Sally Cahur.)

talk over their answers to questions about their own operation. The following are examples of questions that can be discussed:

a Were the views of all members considered, or did some people feel it was safer to keep their suggestions and opinions to themselves?

b If group members had it to do over, what would they do the same way, and what would they do differently? What slowed the group down? What helped to move it on to its goal?

4 Examine from time to time the kinds of cues being used to form or confirm expectations concerning the performance of individuals. Are all students being given opportunities to participate, to be heard, and to be helped?

5 Give training exercises in skills, to teach members of groups how to improve their operation. (These exercises will be discussed later in the chapter).

6 Teach students to listen to each other (see Figure 14-2). Give them plenty of time for responding. Students as well as teachers can experiment with wait time.

MANAGING GROUPS

Control versus overcontrol

New science programs can really put a teacher in a bind. The writers of such programs frequently exhort teachers not to "overcontrol." But principals and supervisors, for their part, frequently want teachers to maintain tight control. The behaviors children exhibit in science sometimes have no precedent. If something is genuinely a problem for children, they often will go through a phase similar to one that scientists experience; that is, they do not know where to start, and they often do some things that look pretty foolish or have no meaning. There is no simple way to decide when behavior has degenerated from the purposeful to the random or even chaotic. What is more, all groups do not reach this "frustration" stage simultaneously. It is difficult to endure this phase of a problem. What cues should teachers use in deciding when to provide help, when to postpone an activity to a later time, and when to drop an activity altogether?

Noise

When excitement runs high, noise usually accompanies it. Things can get loud. That happens when new science materials appear in classrooms, especially for the first time (see Figure 14-3). Some teachers find it impossible to "do" the science lesson planned for the day. In some schools where children have had little chance to work with materials, teachers reported that children in the primary grades clutched the objects to them, just holding them. No amount of reassurance that the materials would be there the next day could persuade the children either to start on the lesson or to part with the objects. On such days, it is impossible to conduct a lesson. The children need time to calm down. The novelty of the objects will wear off if the children can keep them close by for a while, When this kind of thing happens, however, some teachers become upset: it looks to them like a management problem. The curriculum guide says to hand out the materials and do a certain lesson; but the children cannot seem to handle the situation. When this happens, relax. Take time. Do the lesson later or on another day.

Similarly, the amount of novelty that a group of children can tolerate at one time varies. In some classes,

FIGURE 14-3
Large-group discussions following a laboratory experience can be vigorous. What does discussion accomplish?

when there are many different materials in use simultaneously, children run from one group to another and from one kind of object to another—and no substantial work gets done by any group, at least at first. This is the kind of management problem that will gradually disappear as students become accustomed to doing science and as they learn how to work collaboratively—but expect it in the beginning.

There is no doubt that science materials provoke excitement, generate talk, and in general raise the level of noise in a classroom. That can make communication increasingly difficult. It may be no simple task for a teacher to win back the children's attention in order to give directions, terminate the lesson, or comment or convey information. I have seen teachers blink lights, ring bells, blow whistles, scream, and use hand signals to restore order. Some signal system on which the class can agree may need to be devised.

In principle, it seems a nice idea to give some of the children science lessons to start on while others work in reading groups and others do mathematics; but in practice it often turns out that the noise developed by the children doing science interferes with the work of other groups and draws away the attention of children who are supposed to be doing something else. In addition, the constant need for help in interpreting directions that young children and nonreaders require does not leave the teacher free to continue work with other groups. Noise creates some management problems for students as well as teachers. Teachers and principals say they can distinguish noise which is associated with productive work situations from noise which indicates that the system is moving toward chaos. It is of some interest to know whether students can be taught to make similar distinctions and to react appropriately. Noise is contagious. The problem is to keep it somewhat contained. Students need to learn why it is not practical for all of them to talk at once.

Getting the lesson turned off

When it is time to end a lesson that students are enjoying and when the work has not been completed, the announcement may be greeted with a groan or a protest. That does not make the teacher feel any better; in fact, it makes some teachers so angry that they become more reluctant to teach science. The teacher and students face a problem. Students are usually not yet as future oriented as their teachers. They do not feel the same necessity as their teachers do to get on to other subjects. I have heard teachers complain that children get so excited that it is hard to settle them down after a science lesson. Many teachers in self-contained classrooms wait until afternoon for science. They say this suits the more restless state that students are likely to be in toward the end of a day.

These are all natural reactions on the part of the teacher as well as the students. Occasionally it is useful for students and teachers to talk over their reactions. The decisions may still need to be the same (school schedules usually are made for the convenience of the institution), but simple acknowledgment of the feelings can lead to better relations.

Imitation

In the area of science, as elsewhere, children learn a great deal by imitation of others (see Figure 14-2). Sometimes they do not know what to do; and rather than ask, they will simply learn by watching others work with the materials. That is really rather astute of them. Science tends to be a visible kind of enterprise. Any kind of learning that moves in a desirable direction might ordinarily be valued by an outsider observing a system, but in highly competitive classrooms, getting help from someone else is considered cheating; in such classrooms, the watching and copying of behavior are surreptitious. What is worse, if under these circumstances a child being watched notices it, he will complain to the teacher. In such classrooms, I have observed children write down observations on a sheet of paper, which they pull in very close to them and cover carefully. Conversation with others, the free sharing of ideas and excitement on which modern science programs depend, is suppressed. Ideas are guarded until they can be used to please the teacher. Bickering over materials and procedures is common in such rooms. This whole approach is contrary to the philosophy implicit in most modern elementary science programs. Modern programs usually emphasize open discussion, sharing of ideas, and the development by students of skill in asking questions of each other as well as of nature and the teacher. Thus, the reward pattern as well as the teacher's attitude toward open discussion governs, to some extent, the quality of interactions between students and between teacher and students.

Sharing

Science presents some other problems of group management. Students, particularly those of primary age, find it especially difficult to learn to share. Even when all the children have some science materials, problems of sharing still crop up if the materials are not identical. For example, in the SCIS unit "Material Objects," pairs of first-grade children receive a bag containing an assortment of objects which they are to categorize according to properties. There are enough objects for each child to have several, but that makes little difference. Whether I have observed this lesson in an upper-middle-class first grade or in a school where there are many disadvantaged students, the same sequence of events occurs. An argument begins over control of the bag, who will open the bag, and how the objects will be distributed between the two. Each child watches carefully to see what the other gets and checks to see what others near him have. If the collection is not the same, a loud complaint may ensue. And the teacher has to arbitrate.

Sometimes an experiment calls for the assembly of equipment by a pair of children. It is very common to find one member of the pair with all the material gathered close to him and the other member just sitting, totally disengaged from the whole process. If the disengaged child complains to his partner, the chances that he will get a piece of the action are about fifty-fifty. If he complains to the teacher, he may get some action—but part of it will be saved for the schoolyard. I have found it useful to hold occasional discussions after experiments to help students identify and talk about their problems in collaboration.

Sometimes a lesson calls for distributing to students a large number of objects or pieces of equipment. Many teachers find that so much material makes it difficult for children to focus attention or to share materials. Very sensibly, some teachers have the children begin work with one or two pieces at a time. This helps students focus attention. The difficulty comes when teachers interpret the guide or manual so literally that failing to follow it exactly produces a sense of failure. Occasionally they remove these naturally unpleasant, if ill-founded, feelings by dropping science from the school day. Teachers must really survive the first year of a modern elementary science program. In the second year they usually have accumulated enough experience to begin to make judgments with less anxiety. The classroom group, not the manual, dictates the pacing.

Discovery games

Older children sometimes make a disconcerting response to discovery or inquiry-training lessons, which they occasionally regard as a special form of hide-and-seek. They will play the game for a while; but eventually they become tired or frustrated, and then they try to wheedle "the real answer" from the teacher. They are accustomed to playing guessing games where just one winning hand exists and the teacher holds it. They may, for example, work very industriously to produce an explanation for some phenomenon that they observe. If the teacher just leaves the explanation at whatever level the students achieved, with however much or little detail it contains, the students become upset and insist upon knowing "if that is it, or is there more?" This kind of tension really has some uses. It is not at all uncommon for such children to go home to ask questions of other adults. Sometimes they do an experiment at home, or look up something in a book, and appear triumphantly in class with "the answer."

On the other hand, when teachers eventually give all the explanations, some children stop their activity early and, on being interviewed, say that there really is no point in making more than a token effort because the teacher always summarizes the lesson; then they learn what it is they are supposed to have gotten all along. Students for whom a good mark is everything, or for whom being correct is all-important, simply cannot tolerate uncertainty. All these responses present a management problem for the members of the system, children and teacher alike. In one school near an important university, the children made only the most cautious responses to a variety of science materials that most children elsewhere found very stimulating. Finally, one boy revealed what was disturbing the class. Although it was only the fifth grade, the children wanted to know whether they were going to get a mark for science. If so, they did not want "any of this discovery stuff, because you can't be sure what mark you will get." In the same school first-graders commented after a science lesson that it was fun, but they did not choose to do any more science because, as one boy put it, "My parents did not send me to school to play." What students think others expect partly determines how free they will feel to inquire.

Discipline

Part of what constitutes expertise in teaching is having good control of the class: knowing how to maintain discipline.

Teachers hardly ever talk directly about discipline, but almost everybody thinks about it. Since maintaining good discipline—whatever that is for each individual or school—stands so high on the list of what it means to be a "good" teacher, teachers invest a great deal of emotion as well as energy in bringing about a livable classroom environment. If I as a teacher perceive that a new science program threatens my management or control of the classroom, I am likely to junk the program quickly. I may give a thousand and one reasons why I should not teach science, but rarely ever say directly that I cannot cope with the bedlam that sometimes results. To say that would be to admit that I cannot maintain the quality of control I think the principal and other teachers expect of me. What is more, I may not be psychologically free to ask for help. The degree to which we fear how our peers and superiors will judge us determines how much freedom we really have to experiment. Discipline is a highly charged area for teachers and principals.

A study of 115 male and 175 female elementary teachers illustrates the anxieties that a new laboratory-oriented science program can produce.[6] While the teachers agreed that children may learn a great deal by doing science themselves, they gave many reasons for not teaching science:

> *"Some children get too excited, and they can't settle down when it is time to do something else."*
> *"Keeping everyone busy is a problem."*
> *"Some think science is magic."*
> *"Some might get bored."*
> *"Administrators do not like noise or children moving around."*
> *"There is not enough time."*
> *"The class is too big."*
> *"Some finish before others."*

Excitement is perceived to create management problems by some teachers. The level of noise goes up, and the children's spontaneous demands to see and to show what happened disrupts the usual order. The fact that some students complete their work before others also presents problems in science. According to some teachers, it is not easy to arrange for such students to continue to the next lessons, since the logistical problems of supplying equipment, materials, and directions are more difficult to manage in science than in other subjects.

TEACHERS' AND PRINCIPALS' EXPECTATIONS

People in any role form, or have formed for them, a conception of what it means to perform that role. Teachers regard themselves as experts in the act of teaching. *They*

---

[6]See the Rowe and Hurd reference on page 449.

will reject new practices, even when those practices are consonant with their beliefs, if they think that their standing as experts may suffer.

New science programs can create trouble for teachers when the way of teaching the program requires fundamental changes in the organization and conduct of instruction. Not many people will forsake a sure, safe, economical pattern of behavior for one whose costs or consequences are still uncertain.

If it appears to a teacher that the goals or objectives of a new science program are acceptable in principle but that implementation may impair the quality of the teaching as viewed by herself or the principal, no experimentation will be tried. Teachers, after all, are no more exempt from pressure to conform to expectations than are other mortals.

While the thirty-eight administrators in the study mentioned above acknowledged that discipline was important, they appeared to feel that teachers just did not know how to teach science. "Teachers are afraid because they don't know enough content." The teachers, in their turn, felt that the way they had learned science in college bore little resemblance to the kind of thinking they would now have to do.[7] Clearly, arguments teachers give against teaching science are more diverse than the simple complaint that they do not know enough science. Fears concerning expectations about what constitutes good discipline also threaten the life of budding elementary science programs. From time to time during the implementation of a new science program, it may be well for teachers and administrators to talk over their expectations, beliefs, and prejudices concerning what constitutes a well-governed science classroom. New science programs which emphasize inquiry may call for new conceptions. Certainly such new programs demand more sophistication in group-process skills than do programs conducted in more conventional ways.

TEACHING GROUPS TO FUNCTION EFFECTIVELY

When a difference of opinion develops in a small group about what to do or what is happening, the argument, left

---

[7] See the Rowe and Hurd reference on page 449.

to go its course, will sometimes degenerate into a sequence of "It is. It isn't. It is. It isn't." Suddenly, the group or the teacher has a squabble to settle. For a group to work well together in science, the members need to be able to do the following things:

1. A group must recognize areas of agreement and disagreement.

This means that the group can state the facts and inferences which members agree on; the group can state the facts and inferences which the members disagree on. In science, where it is usually possible to repeat an experiment, there is a way to check the facts.

2. A group must recognize when to build on ideas rather than to add ideas.

In the early stages of a problem, it is useful to get out and keep track of a wide range of ideas. In the later stages it is more productive, as a rule, to focus on a few ideas that are likely to prove useful and to build on those.

3. A group must get information and ideas from all members, not just the talkative few.

When all the human resources are available to the group, then the quality of the final product is likely to be better than if the product is just the expression of one or two members.

4. A group must listen.

Group members need to recognize that when everyone talks at once, progress is slow since ideas are missed, procedures become mixed up, and data get lost. A group needs to agree on how it will control its own communications.

5. A group must recognize and understand three kinds of discussions.

The members must learn when it is best to move from one type of discussion to another. The three types are (*a*) review of facts (*b*) inferences of relationships, and (*c*) solution of problems.

a. Reviewing facts. This serves the purpose of letting the members and the teacher find out what everybody knows about the situation. The group members pool their observations concerning data and procedures. There are correct and incorrect responses in this stage. Facts must be correct. This is the first step in locating areas of agreement and disagreement. This phase should force students to consider all the facts. If there are serious disagreements at this level, the wise decision may be to repeat an experiment. This kind of discussion can go on in a large group, such as the whole class, or it can be conducted in small groups.

b. Inferring relationships. In this category of discussion, students try to interpret facts, state relationships, and evaluate ideas. It is best done in small, face-to-face groups. Reactions to ideas come from other students instead of the teacher. This kind of discussion simulates those in the world of work outside the school. During inferring discussions, the group needs richness in ideas. Students must learn to do the following:

1 Get ideas from all members; share ideas. No student in science can excuse himself on the grounds that he has had no experience, since all members engage in the experiments.
2 Avoid ridiculing members with different ideas. The objective at this stage is to form a pool of ideas and to build an atmosphere of respect for all possibilities.

c. Solving problems. In this phase there is a clear goal to be attained by the group. Students select from the pool of ideas those which can be integrated and built upon in order to form a product. For example, the problem might be to find a way to measure the volume of an irregular solid such as a ring or a rock. The goal is clear, but the students are free to invent their own solutions and to decide what steps will lead to it. In this kind of discussion, students synthesize and practice applying concepts to novel situations. The members of the group need to do the following:

1 Listen to ideas and try to build on them instead of adding new ones. Each member needs to avoid becoming so preoccupied with his own ideas that he cannot focus on the contributions of others.

2 Determine what organization and procedures group members should follow. They must usually arrive at a consensus about what steps are involved and in what sequence the work should be done.

3 Develop skill at asking questions of each other to clarify ideas as well as to get information.

There are no clear rights and wrongs associated with inferring and problem-solving discussion. Instead these rest on opinion backed up by evidence. Some alternatives will seem more probable than others. Some products of the problem-solving phase will be more elegant or more functional than others. Instead of deciding that some responses are right or wrong, what must be decided in inferring and problem-solving situations is which relationships and products are most probably based on the evidence or most valuable for particular purposes. Sometimes these two kinds of discussions make it difficult for the teacher to win back the central position in the discussion, since they are largely conducted by the students themselves with the teacher available as a consultant.

TEACHING GROUPS TO WORK TOWARD A GOAL

Certain functions need to be performed by a group if it is to make progress toward a goal. In research done by a Harvard psychologist, Robert Bales,[8] four kinds of processes seemed to be involved in moving a group toward its goals. When any of the four are missing, then progress is slow or stops altogether.

1 *Initiation.* There must be a mechanism for organizing the group, starting discussion, raising questions, and introducing new ideas.

2 *Clarification.* There must be a way of getting all the information out for consideration and for getting vague terms more precisely defined. Failure to agree on operational definitions can produce unnecessary confusion.

3 *Summarization.* There must be a mechanism whereby a group takes stock: that is, decides where it stands and what it has achieved, and identifies

[8] R. F. Bales, *Interaction Process Analysis,* Addison-Wesley, Cambridge, Mass., 1950.

areas of agreement and disagreement. This is not simply a matter of generating ideas. Members meet to force themselves to put ideas together into solutions to problems.

4 *Evaluation.* There must be a mechanism for appraising alternative suggestions, for remedying faults in the procedures, and for keeping members posted on how they are doing.

Often these functions are performed almost intuitively by different members of the group: some tend to be initiators, others are evaluators, etc.

Groups can be taught to deliberately engage in each kind of function when they seem to be having trouble moving toward a goal.

GAMES

There are some games which groups can be taught to play at the same time that they are learning science, in order to help the members identify and acquire some skill at carrying out necessary group functions. These games need not be played regularly. Once skills are developed, then they can be dropped.

1 *Repeating before continuing.* This game fulfills the objective of improving listening behavior. During discussions, each person who speaks must do the following:

   a Paraphrase what the person who spoke before him said

   b React to what has been said before or evaluate it

   c Add his own ideas

2 *Summarizing and clarifying.* Students "freeze" the action at five-minute intervals. They take turns summarizing and clarifying what has been done and said during the previous five minutes.

3 *Sharing information and ideas.* This game has the objective of teaching students how to use all the resources in the group and of making students aware of their responsibility to contribute. It often helps low participators to take part.

The teacher chooses a problem to be solved and prepares a list of clues, facts, and relationships. Each member of the class receives a slip of paper that gives just one of the clues, facts, or relationships. All sharing of information in the group must be done orally. No one may show his slip of paper to another. The class is to use all the information to arrive at a solution to the problem.

After the class has reached a solution that satisfies everyone, the following questions are discussed:

1 What problems did the group face in getting organized (initiation problems)?
2 How would they do it faster the next time?
3 What clues were ignored? What people slowed the group by withholding their information?

This game not only provides group-process training but also prompts students to think about the content of the clues in order to give them an opportunity to rehearse concepts.

RECOGNIZING "SICK" GROUPS

Among the more common problems of "sick" groups are apathy, confused decision making, and unproductive conflict.

Unproductive conflict is characterized by the following:

Ideas are attacked before they are even completely expressed.

Members take sides and fail to develop procedures for resolving conflicts. In science there is always a way to start again, since a group can redesign or reconduct an experiment.

Members attack each other personally rather than arguing the merits of ideas.

When things do not go as predicted, members make someone a scapegoat.

Members are impatient. Often they leave the group or begin to engage in loud, boisterous behavior.

Every suggestion is rejected.

The reasons for such behavior could be several:

Group members have not acquired skill at diagnosing and remedying their own difficulties. For example, they do not know how to listen, to identify areas of agreement, etc.

The task or problem seems impossible, or too ambiguous, or uninteresting.

Some members get very involved with one interpretation or one facet of the problem. They try to force the whole group to   adopt their view.

This kind of conflict, however, can contribute to good problem solving if the group skills described earlier are brought into play.

Apathy may occur when the problem seems trivial, or far too difficult, or when a few members run the whole show to the exclusion of others. Students will show their boredom by yawning, by physically withdrawing to another part of the room, by reading or doodling, by trying to get things over with too quickly, by moving restlessly, by teasing, by trying to get the group interested in something else, or by delaying the start of work. Apathy may occur if the group does not know how to initiate, clarify, summarize, or evaluate ideas. Training exercises in these skills can help sick groups develop productive ways of working.

SUMMARY

1 It is common for students to work in groups when they are doing science. There are skills which they can learn in order to improve the progress of a group toward solution of problems.

   a Learn to listen to each other.

   b Learn when to add ideas and when to build on ideas already stated.

   c Learn to identify areas of agreement before focusing on differences.

   d Learn to get ideas from all members of the group. (Conversely, all members should learn how and when to contribute information to the group.)

2 There are three kinds of discussions in which a group may engage.

   a Reviewing facts.

   b Inferring relations.

   c Solving problems.

   It is sometimes useful for a group to deliberately shift from one kind of discussion to another.

3 There are four task-related functions which need to be performed in a group.

    a Initiation of ideas, procedures, and questions.

    b Clarification.

    c Summarization.

    d Evaluation.

4 A group is like a newly formed system. It acquires properties of its own. These properties can influence the quality of work exhibited by its individual members. Changes in standards, organization, type of task, and expectations influence the quality of each individual's contribution.

5 In a healthy group, independence of judgment and action are maximized when cooperation and collaboration are optional. In a sick group, there is a great deal of dependent behavior; members are easily influenced to give up their views even when data support them. Poor organization and group skills make optimal cooperation impossible.

6 Patterns of expectation sometimes put restraints on an individual because the people around him, governed by their expectations, control the kind of interactions that he can have with them. Science provides frequent opportunities to reappraise and alter, where appropriate, the pattern of expectations.

7 To form work groups for science, keep the following ideas in mind:

    a A mix of as many different backgrounds as possible usually results in more innovative solutions.

    b Form some groups of children who are poor participators or nonaggressive. Eventually these students will take initiative.

    c Form some groups of children whose level of participation is high. Usually a distribution of participation will result.

    d Break up groups which show too much task specialization over a period of time.

    e In face-to-face groups, members tend to talk most to those opposite them. If you seat two overtalkative members side to side, they will be less likely to monopolize the discussion.

    f The responses of a disruptive member may sometimes be improved by a change of both group membership and task.

8 Groups need feedback sessions from time to time to improve the way they are functioning.

9 Arguments which are productive should be distinguished from those which are not. Nonproductive arguments block the group's progress toward a goal. Members usually take sides, fail to compromise, or fail to search for areas of agreement or points where differences arise. Productive arguments may be marked by tension, but members invoke group processes (e.g., see items 1, 2, and 3) to make progress toward the goal.

ACTIVITY 14-1

State some rules you would follow for forming and maintaining productive work groups in science.

ACTIVITY 14-2

How would you distinguish an effectively operating group from one that is operating poorly? What criteria would you use?

ACTIVITY 14-3

What is the probable set of relationships between the teacher's expectations and the performance of students?

ACTIVITY 14-4

Plan a short science lesson in which some students must work together. At the conclusion of the lesson, conduct a feedback session in which the group examines its own operation. State the kinds of questions that should be discussed during the feedback.

ACTIVITY 14-5

Listen to tape recordings of students discussing a laboratory experience.

1 Count the interruptions.
2 Identify instances where a student uses an idea introduced by another student. (This is an indicator of listening.)
3 Design a lesson in which students listen to and talk over recordings of their own discussions. What objectives could be achieved?

ACTIVITY 14-6

With a group of students, try the following games discussed in this chapter for developing active listening:

1 The repeating game.
2 The stop-action game.
3 The information-sharing game.

ACTIVITY 14-7

Design an experiment in which you try to study the influence of training in the three listening games on students' performance.

1 Choose the output variables you consider most important.
2 Devise a way to measure these output variables.
3 Tell how you would decide whether the training was effective.

REFERENCES

For those interested in practical applications of group-process research to the classroom, the following references will prove useful:

Coles, Robert: *Children of Crisis*, Dell Publishing Co., New York, 1964.

Crutchfield, R. S.: "Conformity and Character," *American Psychologist*, vol. 10, pp. 191–198, 1955.

Forces in Learning, Selected Reading Series Three, National Training Laboratory, Washington, D.C., 1961.

Fox, R., M. B. Luszki, and R. A. Schmuck: *Diagnosing Classroom Learning Environments,* Science Research Associates, Inc., Chicago, Ill., 1965.

Group Development, Selected Readings Series One, National Training Laboratory, Washington, D.C., 1961.

Magnusson, D., B. Heffler, and B. Nyman: "The Generality of Behavioral Data II: Replication of an Experiment on Generalization from Observations on One Occasion," *Multivariate Behavioral Research,* vol. 3, no. 4, pp. 415–421, October, 1968.

Piers, E. V., J. M. Daniels, and J. F. Quackenbush: "The Identification of Creativity in Adolescents," *Journal of Educational Psychology,* vol. 51, pp. 346–351, 1960.

Rowe, Mary Budd, and Paul De Hart Hurd: "The Use of In-service Programs to Diagnose Sources of Resistance to Innovation," *Journal of Research in Science Teaching,* vol. 4, pp. 3–15, 1966.

Schmuck, R. A., and P. A. Schmuck: *Group Processes in the Classroom,* Wm. C. Brown Company Publishers, Dubuque, Iowa, 1971.

Wallach, Michael A., and Nathan Kogan: *Modes of Thinking in Young Children,* Holt, Rinehart and Winston, Inc., New York, 1966.

CHAPTER 15

"Keys, keys, keys—my kingdom for the keys. Mrs. N. is absent; the principal is away. I can't get into the science closet."

—DISTRAUGHT TEACHER

"If we leave anything on the floor, like some of the experiments, he complains to the principal."

"In our school Mr. R really helps me. He cut up blocks for us for the force experiment and he put in hooks for the pulleys. I think he'd like to help with the teaching."

—TEACHERS SHARING VIEWS OF THE MAINTENANCE MEN

"If I use some of the stuff from the kit, she wants it back right away. How can I set up an interest center that way?"

—TEACHER ILLUSTRATING A SHARING PROBLEM

MANAGEMENT AND CONTROL—LOGISTICAL FACTORS

OBJECTIVES

On completion of this chapter and its associated activities, you should be able to do the following:

1 Devise a plan for identifying and solving the logistical problems associated with any science program that you have to teach.

2 Devise an inventory-control plan for a particular science program.

3 Devise a plan for identifying science resources outside the school—people and places.

INTRODUCTION

Most modern science programs require that children work directly with apparatus and materials. That means the teacher has logistical problems to solve having to do with procuring and distributing materials, collecting and cleaning apparatus, replacing and repairing consumed or broken items, and devising schemes for students to share items that are in short supply.

Most modern programs prompt students to engage in investigations and to talk about their work. Frequently, children get excited, with the result that the noise level rises. Inquiry-oriented science programs present teachers with some unique problems of noise as well as of logistics.

Management problems in elementary science fall into three classes: logistical, verbal, and social-psychological. Verbal factors have already been discussed (Chapters 8 to 11). Logistical factors will be discussed in this chapter. Some social-psychological aspects of group management were discussed in Chapter 14.

LOGISTICAL PROBLEMS

Before class starts

To do science there must be equipment and materials (see Figure 15-1). Some of the necessary realia may come from the environment—things that students and teachers find or make or buy locally. Some of the equipment and materials may be shipped to the school, in which case the supplies will usually come in one of two forms: organized into kits or not organized into kits. Once materials and equipment are on hand, the problem is to decide how to arrange them so that busy teachers will find it practical to do science.

Some system that makes the preparation time as small as possible needs to be devised. One plan that seems to have worked successfully for whole schools as well as for individual teachers involves boxing materials by lessons.

Shoe boxes or other containers, such as a small plastic dishpans, make suitable containers for storage. Each container holds the materials for one lesson. An inventory-control card resembling a library card accompanies each container; it lists all the materials that are supposed to be present. Consumable items—those which are likely to

FIGURE 15-1
Science involves many kinds of materials.

be used up during a lesson (such as chemicals)—are itemized on a different part of the card from the non-consumables. At the end of a lesson, the inventory is quickly checked and those items that need to be replaced are marked on the card. Older students or teacher aides can often take care of the inventory process. Sometimes parent groups can be trained to help with this part of the science program.

Where groups of teachers are sharing materials, some plan for replacing lost or consumed items immediately is necessary. There is nothing more maddening than to start a lesson only to find broken, missing, or inadequate supplies. When someone fails to manage materials which others must also use, two things happen: bad feelings develop, reducing the chances of cooperation on future projects, and the science program gradually comes to a halt as boxes and kits become depleted.

Even in schools which use a packaged program— that is, a program in which the materials come in kits— teachers sooner or later find it practical to use the box-by-lesson plan. The principal objection to the box-by-lesson plan has to do with equipment that is used repeatedly, such as magnifiers, measuring devises, and hot plates. Actually, the number of such items is less than one might suppose. Such items can be stored separately in labeled and numbered containers. The inventory card for the lesson has a note on it which directs the teacher to pick up the extra materials.

Boxing by lessons saves rummaging around in the kits and makes it easier to identify lost or consumed items. In addition, when teachers must share kits, more classes can be supplied by a few kits, since classes move at different rates. Before the school year is very far along, teachers at the same grade level are usually doing different lessons in the sequence.

In class

Distribution and collection of material. Let us assume that a teacher arrives in class with boxes of materials and equipment for a science session in which all the children are to be involved. The next practical problem to be confronted has to do with the *distribution* of the paraphernalia. Certain management problems can arise when there is no plan for getting equipment to the students expeditiously.

Some of the major management problems laboratory science presents for elementary teachers arise when the distribution and collection of materials takes too long. I have observed classes in which a poorly managed distribution plan meant that some students waited 15 minutes for materials. Things happen which create management problems if students must wait too long. First, *they become restless.* This is indicated by starting to tease, throwing objects around (if they have been told to wait to begin until everyone has the equipment), pushing and shoving. The noise level increases beyond reason. (But note that what is "reasonable noise" to one person may be intolerable to another.) Second, *the teacher's directions get mixed up.* Either the students do not hear what they are to do or they have to wait so long for materials that they forget what they were to do. In either case they must ask to have directions repeated. Third, *part of the novelty of the experiment is lost because the members of the class who are waiting for materials see the outcome achieved by those who first have the materials.* The teacher will know this is happening if he observes that the last part of the class assembles materials or performs the experiment more quickly, or that more of the last group just watch what goes on in other groups.

At the end of a lesson, *collection* of materials must occur in some ordered fashion; otherwise, materials are put back in such a jumble that they are not easily available for reuse. This makes the time required for distribution when materials are next needed even longer. Presumably, the materials for one lesson or unit need to be used during several class sessions, so getting them back in clean and ordered condition must be part of the management plan. When this phase is managed successfully, redistribution of materials for the next science session will go more rapidly than if the contents of the storage box are left in a jumble.

Distribution time, the time to get materials into the hands of all students who are to have them, should not usually exceed five minutes. In observing a science class, including one you teach yourself, determine how long the distribution and collection phases last. If more than five minutes are required, then ask whether there are ways to speed the procedures. Here are some suggestions.

Try a monitor system. Do not mix up the social pressure to give everyone a chance to do something with the need to solve distribution and collection problems. If a few children become familiar with the materials, they usually will see to their management (see Figure 15-2).

Try discussing this problem with the class. I have found that if I discuss distribution and collection problems with a class as young as second-graders, the children will suggest and carry out efficient procedures. For example, I had given second-graders working on a lesson on symmetry some 300 objects in fifteen different categories and was wondering how to get the objects back quickly in some condition other than a heap. I decided to ask the children what we should do. They said we should send fifteen people around with bags, each collecting a differ-

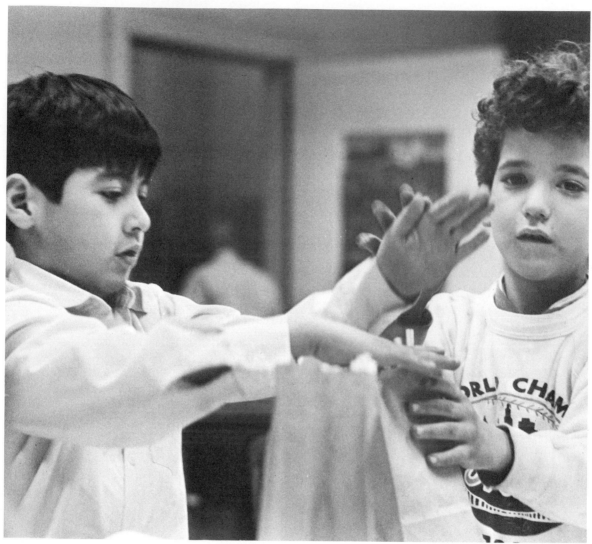

FIGURE 15-2
**Students can help with distribution
and collection of materials.**

ent category of objects. The rest would put the desks back where they belonged. For 2 minutes the place looked and sounded like a madhouse. At the end of that time, order was restored.

At the beginning of that same lesson, I had divided twenty-five students into five groups, given each group three trays and a box of assorted objects, and appointed a chairman to distribute the materials. That last move was a mistake. The one group that ignored the suggestion solved its distribution problems almost twice as fast as the other groups. (If distribution takes less than five minutes, forget this factor and think about something else, provided the collection process is orderly.)

Quality of equipment. Properly functioning equipment and materials distinguish modern science programs from older, more traditional "book" programs that require little material, usually only for demonstration.

However, quality control in the manufacture of items is not what it used to be. Pegs have a way of not fitting into holes, and balances often do not balance where they ought to. Materials sometimes are not as durable as they are supposed to be.

1 Before a lesson either you, an aide, or a student should note how parts of equipment fit together and function.

   a If parts fit satisfactorily, there is nothing to worry about.

   b If they do not fit satisfactorily, describe the problem along with any suggestions you have and give your comments to a supervisor or principal so that something can be done about the problem before the materials are to be used again. At least, do not lose the notes (e.g., "The hole through the ruler which is supposed to serve as a beam balance is not in the center, so the beam does not stay horizontal").
   Principal or Science Supervisor: Inventory control cards with the objects in question printed on them form the basis for a low-cost inventory-control plan. Teachers just check consumed items and broken or defective items and leave them in the school office to be picked up by the person responsible for servicing the program.

2 Notice whether the equipment is durable.

   a If it is satisfactory, there is no problem.

   b If it is unsatisfactory, specify the problem (e.g., "the alligator clips break off the copper wire").
   Observation: What items broke or fell apart during the session? How many?

3 Are materials present in sufficient amounts for the organizational scheme employed in a particular classroom?

a Is the equipment just for demonstration purposes?

b How many students have to share materials? *Observation:* How many children are there to a piece of equipment? How is the classroom organized to minimize this number? Be sure to talk these problems over with other teachers. You may solve a problem or learn about how someone else solved a problem. In that way everybody saves some time and a little grief.

4 How much of the material is the teacher supposed to gather? Be particularly careful of this item if you are using "complete" kits. A salesman's notion of what *complete* means often does not match the realities encountered in the classroom. Some "complete" kits come without the consumable items.

a Keep some record of the time it took to prepare a particular lesson so that you will know what to expect the next time, so that you can let other teachers benefit from your experience, or so that you can benefit from the experiences of other teachers.

(1) If you do not check up on what materials you need to do a lesson, you may find yourself lacking items when the time comes to do the lesson.
Observation: How long did preparation of this lesson take? What materials had to be substituted?

(2) In case the school's supply of petty cash evaporates, and you find yourself furnishing materials from home or purchasing small items, keep a careful record of costs. At least you can deduct them from income tax. The cost of aluminum foil, matches, and plastic bags has a way of mounting up as the year goes by.
Observation: What kind of materials and how much has the teacher supplied for this lesson?

(3) If the experiments call for items you do not have, are there equivalent substitutes that you or the children can construct (e.g., a drop of clear glue or water in a bobby-pin loop for a magnifier, or small beam balances made out of plastic straws and a straight pin)?

Observation: Who in the school or district takes responsibility for remedying problems like these? Do teachers feel there are regular routes to make their difficulties known, and that something useful happens when they report problems?

Observation: Is there any evidence that teachers talk over problems with each other or take the initiative in suggesting solutions for logistical problems?

GIVING DIRECTIONS

Since so many of the materials in a modern science program are novel, it is vital to give brief, easily understood directions if children are to use them successfully. Teachers often complain that children either do not or cannot follow directions. The evidence that they cite is reasonable. For example, children ask questions which indicate that they do not know what to do; or teachers receive unsatisfactory answers when they ask children questions to determine whether they can tell what they are supposed to do. Teachers often place the responsibility for the failure to follow directions in science on children, saying, "They fail to listen." (Note: this is an inference.) "They become too excited with all the materials." (Note: This is an inference.) "They cannot remember more than one step at a time." (Note: This is an inference.)

The distribution of materials may interfere with giving and receiving directions. The management problem with respect to distributing materials and giving directions for their use needs to be solved. Normally, directions should precede the distribution of materials. Both the teacher who gives instruction and the students who receive directions face certain problems that must be solved if they are to communicate effectively.

Problems of the giver of instructions or directions

1 Uncertainty concerning exactly what he wants done. Indications:

   a Changes in directions while they are being given.

b Use of elaborate phrases with a great deal of repetition.
2 Inclusion of too many factors at one time in instructions. Indications:
  a Mixing up of the sequence that students are to follow.
  b Failure to stop to allow for clarification and suggestions.
  c Expression by children of confusion or uncertainty about what they are to do, often by turning and whispering or talking to each other.
3 Failure to provide enough opportunity for questions. Indications:
  a Reprimanding children for not listening when they ask questions about procedures.
  b Failure to permit questions at intervals when a sequence of instruction is long or complicated.
4 Vague instructions. Indications:
  a Different interpretations by the children of what they are to do.
  b Confusion among the children about how to assemble equipment, if that is called for.
5 Expectation that children will not understand. Indications:
  a Reduction of the vocabulary level and complexity of sentences to an unnecessarily low level.
  b Refusal to use new terms in the context of children's experience. This latter way of behaving can block development of language competency in science.

Problems of listeners

Students, too, contribute to the management problem.

1 Careless listening habits. Indications:
  a Ceasing to listen before directions are completed.
  b Starting to talk or work as soon as the first step in a sequence is clear, and so failing to hear the whole set of directions.
  c Being so afraid of not understanding that they spend effort covering the fear or act as though they understand when they do not. (See solution 3, below.)

d Talking while directions are being given.

2 Failure to understand the words used. (I have observed, for example, that Spanish-speaking children in an English-speaking classroom watch what others do when they get equipment and quickly imitate them, sometimes with a few words of advice from bilingual friends. There is a considerable flow of nonverbal information in a classroom.)

3 Failure to ask questions when they do not understand.

4 Loss of interest in the work. Indications:
   a Breaking equipment.
   b Doing some other work. (See solution 5, below.)

What to do about giving directions

1 Give directions before distributing materials. Provide written directions for students who can read. Frequently, such written directions serve to encourage reluctant readers to try to read.

2 Give directions in short steps. Give time at each stage for students to clarify what they are to do. Make it psychologically safe for students to ask questions. Sometimes the next set of directions comes before they have finished thinking about the previous step.

3 Demonstrate the procedure or provide an assembled piece of apparatus when part of the directions calls for students to construct an item for use in an investigation.

4 Give no more direction than necessary to get a job done. Save extra talk for later.

5 Be as precise as possible when giving directions.

6 Ask occasional questions to check on how carefully students are listening.

7 Give training in listening skills. This may involve short exercises such as the following:
   a Providing simple pieces of apparatus to be assembled according to oral directions.
   b Giving a short burst of directions and then asking to have them repeated.
   c Having students work in pairs with one member of the pair giving directions. This provides practice in giving and receiving directions.

EXTRA RESOURCES—PEOPLE AND PLACES

Within the community there are frequently people and places that can play a part in the science program. Some of these resources may prove useful for the whole class; others may help the development of individual students who have special interests or are working on special projects. Just as an inventory of equipment and materials is vital to the success of a science program, an inventory of people and places can be an invaluable aid for teachers interested in finding opportunities for enriching their programs. The problem is to locate, develop, and catalogue these external resources.

Finding people and places

Frequently parents work in scientific, technological, or health-care professions. In addition, some parents have hobbies such as radio and electronics, bird watching, and conservation programs. Often people in science-related professions or those who have science-related hobbies can help supplement the instructional program by arranging field trips or programs connected with their specialties or, in the case of hobbyists, by working with individual students interested in the same topics.

To find these people, as well as others with resources that might contribute to some part of the educational program, one or more of the following procedures can be followed.

Interviewing parents. Almost every teacher sees at least one parent of each child for a conference before Christmas. During these conferences, during parent-association meetings, or both, teachers can collect the basic information. During such an interview there is information to give as well as to receive. Many parents do not realize that they can really help. They think that the children would not be interested, or they feel that they would not know how to go about making their skills available. The teacher needs to assure them that many people have such feelings at first, but that a little practice usually shows both the parent and the teacher what works well and what does not. Assure the parent that the teachers, and probably some class members, will help plan the program or field trip as well as the follow-up activities.

While the interview may go on in an informal setting, definite information of the kind shown on the sample resource-planning sheet shown on page 464 should be obtained. Sometimes a parent, once needs have been identified, can suggest other people and places in the community that would be of interest. Enter this information on the interview sheet. Particularly, find out whether the parent would help introduce you to the people who need to be interviewed.

Survey by the students. As a combination science-social studies activity, students in the upper grades can plan and conduct a survey of human resources—parents and other people—for the whole class. This procedure gives students practice at collecting and organizing social data, since they must design a survey form for interviewing parents and recording information. As a result of the interviews, the students investigate many kinds of work and hobbies they might otherwise not know about.

Letter to parents. A letter describing the need for resources, accompanied by a survey form, can be sent to all parents. While this method usually does not yield results as good as those just described, it does yield some results and may be a good way to start on identifying resources.

Cataloguing information

Once the information has been gathered, it needs to be catalogued. It is to be hoped that the identification of resources will be carried out as a project of the school rather than of individual teachers. When data are in hand from all grade levels, in addition to extra resources identified during interviews, a plan must be developed for organizing the information so that it is helpful. The librarian, if there is one, can usually suggest possibilities.

As a part of the cataloguing system, data should be kept on each resource as it is used. The following information, at least, should be added to the file on each person or place:

1 Date used.
2 Grade level.
3 Teacher.

Resource planning sheet

Name of parent _____   *Name of interviewer* _____
Address   _____   *Date of interview*   _____

Potential resource description:

Additional resources suggested during interview:

4 Details of arrangements—logistics, phone numbers, names, etc.
5 What preparation was necessary?
  a Of the class.
  b Of the person or place.
6 What problems arose, if any?
7 What did you expect to get from the use of this resource?
8 How well did it go?
9 Recommendations. What improvements should be made the next time? Should the resource be dropped?

This information will let a teacher using the resource file find out who has used a resource and with what success. Certain resources sometimes are overexploited. Students have been known to make the same field trip or hear the same speaker four or five times in the course of an elementary school career. Records of the kind described can help prevent that kind of repetition.

Feedback sheets that give students an opportunity to express their reactions to a visitor or visit can prove valuable in appraising a resource. Often students can make helpful suggestions for improving the way a resource is used in the future. When possible, students should be involved in planning how a resource will be used. Their participation in planning will help make the

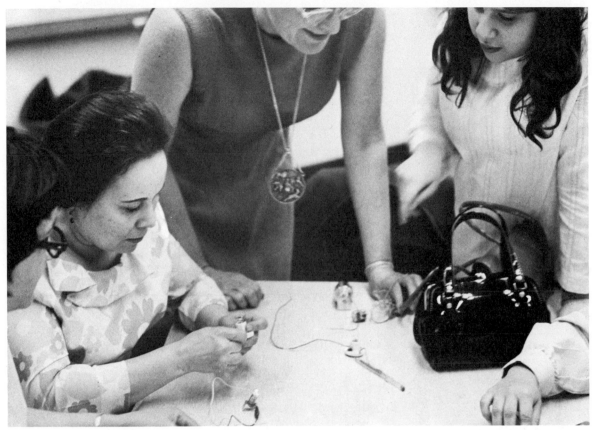

FIGURE 15-3
Sometimes a good basis for discussions between parents and teachers comes from giving parents firsthand experience with materials.

program more relevant to them. Usually students can anticipate the kind of management problems that are likely to be encountered.

People with hobbies that might be of interest to only a few students can be encouraged to work with those students regularly. Sometimes provision for this kind of cooperative work effort between individuals from the community and children from the school requires some help from the teacher. Sometimes the adult as well as the student is hesitant or shy. Normally, if the adult starts right in with direct work that involves some construction or immediate firsthand experience with realia, any initial problems in communication will solve themselves. (See Figure 15-3.)

The library as a resource

Even though most modern science programs focus on inquiry, investigation, and direct experimentation with physical and biological phenomena, there is still a place for books and films. Not everything can or should be learned through direct experience. The process is too slow. Books can be an invaluable source of information and enjoyment for students. Frequently, students who do not like to read find books on scientific subjects attractive. What is more, science materials can be checked out from the library for independent work.

Schools vary in their arrangements for getting books into the hands of students. In some schools, classes make periodic visits to the library. In others the classroom teacher tells the librarian what topics are currently being taught and all the pertinent books are sent to the classroom for as long as necessary. When the topic changes, the books are replaced with a new set appropriate to the new topic.

Whatever the plan is, teachers must make their needs known to the librarian. The more the librarian knows about the purposes of a unit, the more likely he is to be able to give good service. Modern school librarians often know about book and film resources that teachers would find useful. Consider the librarian as a resource person.

The school maintenance engineer as a resource

There is usually one man in the school every teacher interested in doing science should get to know well—the maintenance man. He knows where all kinds of odds and ends are that would help solve some problems. Often, the maintenance man can fix something that requires a little mechanical know-how.

Occasionally, a room in which science is going on gets a little messy. That can disturb the maintenance crew when it goes about its clean-up routines. For example, suppose that one day school ends before the students have completed assembling some apparatus, and that there is no place to store the partly assembled materials except on the top of each desk. The clean-up crew would object, because when it comes into a room it stacks chairs on desk tops to make sweeping easier. The decision to leave apparatus out, then, will create problems for the maintenance people. If things like that happen very often and the head maintenance engineer is not on your side, then there will be complaints, which you will usually receive through the principal. It is important, therefore, to ally yourself with the maintenance engineer. He can be an invaluable member of the science team. Since so many maintenance people must operate on small budgets and must know how to do small repairs, they usually are full of ideas for solving the sort of logistical problems that students doing projects frequently encounter. For example, I have seen these men show students how to build animal cages, repair a leaking aquarium, and drill holes in wooden strips for beam balances. They frequently think of relatively inexpensive ways to do things. Since science budgets in the elementary school are often minuscule, having someone around who can suggest cheap substitutes for some materials can prove very useful. Keep the maintenance man on your side.

SUPPLIES AND EQUIPMENT

Keys

The matter of keys may seem trivial, but enormous logistical problems can be created by a poor plan for distributing keys. Often, supplies and equipment are stored in locked cabinets or closets. If only one person holds the keys and that person is absent, then the science program for everyone who needs things from those closets suffers. Furthermore, in many schools I have visited, the principal keeps the key to the science storage area. If he is in conference, out of his office, or away from the school, then the keys are not accessible. Some schools keep such keys in the main office. If someone neglects to return the key promptly, then the next person is delayed. Small discouragements of the kind produced by failing to establish convenient access to materials stored in locked closets can undermine a science program.

If all teachers have keys to closets which contain materials they are likely to use, then there must be a good inventory-control procedure established to ensure that certain materials are replaced. Some system for solving the problems of keys must be devised in every school where materials and equipment must be locked up. Some system for inventory control, also, must be established for materials and equipment to which various people can have access. Some teachers hoard materials and refuse to share with other teachers. This behavior is sometimes justified on the basis of past experience, but a satisfactory plan for inventory control and maintenance should make people more willing to share when necessary.

Begged, borrowed, or stolen materials

Science materials get stolen, or taken, or borrowed, depending on what term suits your view of the situation. Some materials "get gone." That is a fact. The disappearance of objects disturbs many teachers, especially when they have little reassurance that the school system will replace depleted or lost materials, or when the school holds them accountable. Science programs are especially afflicted with this problem if the lessons interest the children at all. In many classrooms, the materials disappear into pockets, desks, and lunch sacks. Mouths are favorite hiding places for small objects.

I became interested in this problem while directing a Trial Center for the SCIS (Science Curriculum Improvement Study). I was curious to know what children did with the objects and whether their science activity continued outside the classroom. In one of the schools of the Trial Center, where materials disappeared at a great rate, I suggested that teachers think of the objects like books. Books can go home with children, so why not science materials? Since the materials came from the Trial Center, the loss would not present problems to the teachers. The Trial Center would replace the losses. Every few days, I suggested, "Ask whether anybody has discovered new properties or interactions or anything puzzling." Gradually, objects began to appear back in the rooms where teachers tried this experiment. The children had a great deal to tell. At the end of the year, inventory in those rooms was about 80 percent complete, whereas in rooms that did not follow the practice, inventories ranged from 30 percent to 60 percent complete. Inventories approached 100 percent complete only in those rooms where the teacher taught no science.

SUMMARY

1 The success of a modern elementary science program depends in large part on how well problems having to do with procuring, distributing, maintaining, and replacing equipment and materials are solved.

2 It is usually best to organize materials by lessons. This is the "box-by-lesson" plan.

    a This plan minimizes the preparation time that the teacher must spend.

    b The plan also makes it possible for fewer materials to supply more classes.

    c The plan makes inventory control easier.

3 Inventory-control cards make procurement of replacements and maintenance of the program easier.

4 Distribution of materials in class should be done quickly in order to minimize discipline problems that can arise when students become impatient.

5 Directions for use of equipment and materials can be given orally or in writing. Both the teacher who gives directions and the students who must follow the directions face some communication problems. The teacher should do the following:

    a State exactly what is to be done, in the correct sequence.

    b State the directions in simple terms with a minimum of elaboration.

    c Give opportunity for students to ask questions. Do not wait until the end of a long string of directives to give this opportunity for checking.

    d Give directions before materials are distributed and provide a model, when pertinent, of what is to be assembled.

The students as receivers of directions must learn

    a To listen.

    b To ask questions when something is not clear.

    c To keep track of the *sequence* of directions.

6 There are resources outside the school that can be identified and used to enrich the science program. These resources fall into two categories: people and places. A catalogue of these should be made, maintained, and continually referred to.

7 The librarian can supply relevant books. Reading

is still an important way to get information in science.

8 The maintenance engineer at a school can often supply invaluable advice and mechanical know-how to the science program.

9 There should be a workable plan for making available keys to locked closets in which science materials are stored. Failure to establish a workable plan can mean failure for the science program.

ACTIVITY 15-1

For your own school or for one you visit:

1 Identify the logistical problems through interviews with teachers and through observation.
2 Suggest procedures for solving the problems.

ACTIVITY 15-2

Tell how you might organize in your classroom to manage the distribution, collection, and maintenance of science materials. How would students be involved?

ACTIVITY 15-3

Design an inventory-control card. Then select one experiment from any elementary science book and enter the items on the card.

WE SUFFER from a legacy of secrecy and selectivity when it comes to evaluation. Because resources are scarce, not everyone can have access to the riches of the world—or so the argument goes. Some people must be selected to attend the colleges; to be the scientists, lawyers, and teachers; to head big companies. The rest must take the leavings. Colleges and employers want to know which people will be most likely to function best for them. Institutional efficiency depends on making correct predictions about the most suitable people to work in each setting. Testing programs of elementary and secondary schools, for the most part, serve gatekeeping functions—that is, they facilitate institutional decision making. If individual teachers and students learn anything helpful from the testing, that is a purely fortuitous outcome.

Since more people must be kept from gaining access to a given set of resources than may be admitted to them, it would seem to follow that if individuals do learn anything from tests, that learning mostly has to do with their sense of self-worth. We might hypothesize that most programs of testing, while they serve institutional needs, may introduce such significant negative side effects for individuals that their use should be challenged. In any event, the gatekeeping mentality which marks institutional testing permeates the elementary school and influences expectations, aspirations, and probably real accomplishment.

We can look at tests as instruments inserted in a social system and ask, as we would for any physical measurement process, how appropriate the instrument is to the intent of the investigation. Recall that virtually all measurement in physical and biological systems requires that the measuring device be inserted in the system and that the system interact with it. It is hoped that the amount of energy diverted from the regular flow of events in the system will be small enough that the intrusion will not materially disturb the functioning of the system. We can ask of tests or other kinds of obtrusive measures, In what way do they disturb the functioning of the system, and how tolerable is that disturbance?

The gatekeeping philosophy which pervades most school testing means that children who could achieve a particular set of skills, and competence in particular areas, but only at a slow pace or in an atypical manner, or both, find themselves condemned year after year to bad grades, a fragmented education, and a lessened sense of self-worth. The system puts them in double jeopardy. Because of its pressure for everyone to perform at the same rate as everyone else, slower students rarely are able to finish anything and very fast students frequently do not extend themselves in interesting ways. Tests usually signal the end of one phase of instruction and the beginning of another. Teachers rarely decide with individual students when they shall take a test, nor do they usually make it clear what function a particular test is supposed to serve as far as the student is concerned. How well could you answer a student who asks of a test you give him, "What is in it for me?" or alternatively, "Why should I take it now?"

Testing, especially of the gatekeeping variety, is only part of evaluation. More to the point are other kinds of procedures that help the teacher and the student to diagnose teaching and learning problems. The research on context learning shows how varied the routes to solution of even relatively simple problems can be. Impelled by common knowledge but not necessarily governed by the same logic, children pursue learning in unique ways. To become interested in the kind of evaluation that focuses one's attention on the *processes* by which students arrive at answers or originate investigations of their own is to venture into relatively unexplored territory. If we make a decision in favor of instruction that is oriented toward inquiry rather than indoctrination, then how we choose to go about evaluation must reflect that decision. *Our philosophies govern what we do in evaluation.*

Suppose, for example, we had to choose between two alternative programs, of which one taught students what they should believe and the other taught them how they should decide what to believe. Of course, a satisfactory program will contain some mixture of both kinds of instruction. To evaluate the progress of students for the first type of alternative would be simple, compared with the problems posed by the second alternative. But it is that second alternative to which we have given and will give most attention in the chapters which follow.

In one way or another, all of Part 3 is about evaluation. But you must not think about evaluation in too conventional a manner, or the relevance of some of the topics will escape you. Evaluation involves more than just testing. Instead, think about it as an inquiry into the functioning of some hugely complex human systems.

A great deal of technical knowledge has accumulated about how to pick out the people most likely to succeed at the next level of schooling, given that it continues as it is, or those most probably suited to engage in a certain profession or to complete the work of a particular college. But, strangely enough, until recently very little psychological technology has been devoted to helping people learn to monitor and guide their own development. Instead, most of the technology tells the student and teacher, "You made it," or "You failed to make it." How much diagnostic information is there in that?

Until recently nobody paid for development of a technology devoted to describing and diagnosing modes of learning exhibited by individuals. Tests were something you did to people for the benefit of institutions. (Some student radicals say that tests are a technique to get people to inform on themselves. There is some merit in this argument, since the results do signal those who use them to decide who shall pass and who shall fail; who shall enter college and who shall be kept out.) The only supposed benefit to the individual was the information that his test profile resembled the profiles of people who succeeded in a particular profession or institution or, on the contrary, that it resembled the profiles of people who failed.

It is argued that the institution or business in question does the student a favor by telling him that his chances for success will be good or poor, according to the profile.

Of course the students who are under discussion in this book are not yet taking tests involving employment or higher education, but the whole mentality connected with this kind of testing pervades elementary as well as secondary education. Testing practices generally follow a "keeping out" rather than a "keeping in" philosophy. In the discussions of evaluation appearing in Part 3, a "keeping in" philosophy motivates the inquiry.

Before we can evaluate a science program we need *contemporary* answers to certain questions. Science, like any other human enterprise, is a captive of time, bounded by the properties of the culture in which it is embedded. Its modes and models of thought change in each era. We have to begin with the most current view we can gather, knowing that it will still fail us—although to a lesser extent than an outdated view would—because we cannot completely control the future. As we live in the world, we change it, but toward what ends? In what relation do we or should we stand to the physical world? The sorts of answers we supply for those questions determine what kinds of emphasis instruction must have.

Furthermore, we cannot determine any kinds of goals or say anything much about how to teach and work well and happily with children, or even with each other, until we decide upon the conception of human beings toward which we want to work. Science as one kind of human enterprise carries some implicit answers to those questions. The teacher as its purveyor contains part of the answer. The environment of children is mostly people and nature. Out of their interactions with these two, children one day become men and women. What shall they be like? Wordsworth said, "The child is father to the man." How then shall we treat these fathers of future men? What is our dream for them?

Of course, you cannot escape yourself when it comes to a consideration of evaluation. What are your priorities, and how are they expressed in the classroom? For many elementary teachers, science stands low on the list of priorities. Part of any decent evaluation process requires that you face up to how you feel about science. What reasons do you give for whatever priority, high or low, you set on it?

How do your own styles of learning and your own patterns of knowledge and beliefs influence what your students learn and how they learn it? After all, you yourself have some "fate control" with respect to the students. Can you teach science to children in such a way that its content is quickly and flexibly available as a resource for guiding their own learning, for decision making, for problem solving? Did you learn science that way? Do you like science? All those questions belong to the domain of evaluation, and your honest answers to them will tell you something about the probable quality of the instruction you will give. Would you suppose, that someone could watch you working with children for a while and infer what the answers to those questions might be? *You* definitely occupy a place in the evaluation process.

You could make up your own science program, or you could take advantage of any of a number of programs available commercially. No matter what program you finally elect to use, you need to answer three questions:

Which knowers are you to trust?
What kind of knowers do you want children to be?
How should the program be adapted for your own situation?

In view of the fact that scientists have had an enormous influence on the content of many elementary science programs developed in recent years, especially those initially funded by the United States government, we will do well to ask what kind of people scientists are. Are they trustworthy knowers? What conception of man do they have and want spread in the world? How are their views and beliefs expressed in curriculums? As data for thinking about these questions, we shall consider some of the results of investigations in which scientists were the subjects of inquiry.

Your students' parents may hold opinions about what science is and what your decisions (or lack of decisions) about science are doing to their children. Parents can become a valuable source of data about children as well as willing collaborators in the education of their children. In a way, the system of interest in instruction is not just a group of students; it is a group of students and their parents.

The people with the biggest stake in the whole business of education rarely find themselves directly consulted. But even very young children can speak quite lucidly about life in the classroom. They can act out how teachers function in relation to them, and they can tell what their teachers' expectations are for them. Their commentary can be a useful part of the evaluative process. Hardly anyone asks for their help, however, so after a time there is not much point in their trying to tell anyone. One second-grader spoke of his classroom teacher as follows:

She does all these things to us like gives us mealworms and stuff and tells you to find out about them. She doesn't do any of it herself. . . . But once we found some things in a pond and that was good because she got excited, sort of laughing. She was trying to find out what they were too. It wasn't just make-believe like she does sometimes.

Although we shall be closely involved with philosophy and goals in the process of evaluation, you will be no more exempt from searching for evidence, designing careful inquiries to collect pertinent data, and bringing statistical ideas to bear than you were in Part I, when the topic was physical systems rather than social systems. Compounding observations into variables and measuring the variables are part of coming to understand how things work. Knowing how things work, in turn, can help us to make better judgments and decisions. In teaching, we make judgments and decisions all the time, but we might as well get some conscious sense and beauty into it.

Men emerge from the grasp of nature in proportion as they come to understand phenomena, as they move to gain control of them, and as they learn to use what they know to build new dreams of what might be. When they can learn from their mistakes, their collective as well as individual intelligence expands. When they cannot learn from them, their dreams gradually shrink away to nothing and are never realized. Fearful, anxious people do not dream; they have nightmares. Think, then, what in the school, in curriculums, in play, in homework, in you and your way of being with children creates dreams and what, on the other hand, produces nightmares. Go at the inquiry critically. Demand of yourself that you find evidence, and then interpret it with care.

CHAPTER 16

"What's supposed to happen? They did all kinds of things. I think they had fun, but what did they get out of it?"

—THIRD-GRADE TEACHER

"We had the test before I was ready. I couldn't get the scale to work, so I didn't finish—and she didn't care. Just do it—how could I?"

—FOURTH-GRADER

"Some of the children get very excited, and they do lots of things; but I am always surprised at what they come up with —not what the book led me to think. I think they get better ideas, but what about the test? They have to cover the material, don't they?"

—FIFTH-GRADE TEACHER

"I've only been doing science for a little while. Don't I do it well?"

—FIRST-GRADER COMMENTING TO AN OBSERVER

TASK ANALYSIS:
ONE BASIS FOR DECISION

OBJECTIVES

On completion of this chapter and its associated activities, you should be able to do the following:

1 State some uses of task analysis.

2 Perform a task analysis of a unit.

3 Use a task analysis to identify the minimum set of observations and inferences that must be made in order to progress through a unit.

4 State a relationship between diagnostic evaluation and task analysis.

INTRODUCTION

Scientific knowledge is not something gained by introspection alone. In contrast to the humanities, where the main test of an idea is whether it makes you "feel right" and is accepted by others, in science ideas must be subjected to objective verification. In science one comes to realize that an idea is not necessarily valid just because it seems right or reasonable. The idea must be tested against the performance of nature and against the network of other ideas into which it is connected or which it refutes. Modern elementary science programs seek to develop a scientific approach to obtaining and using knowledge. To that end they involve students in a series of tasks designed to teach them how to search for solutions and how to evaluate the appropriateness of their solutions. Tasks are chosen that are meant to stimulate conceptual development. There is always a question, however, whether a curriculum is adequately designed to accomplish its purposes.

Any curriculum in science can be systematically analyzed to determine what it is most likely to teach. Clusters of activities occurring in lessons or units form the tasks out of which concepts, principles, inferences, and deductions are eventually supposed to emerge. There is always the possibility that the instructional intent of tasks will not be understood with the same meaning by the people who prepared them as by the people who are supposed to learn something from them—i.e., the students. Task analysis is a technique for examining a lesson or a curriculum in order to learn:

1 What procedures must be followed
2 What minimum set of observations will need to be made in order to permit the minimum set of inferences and deductions to be formed
3 What sequence of ideas, concepts, principles, or generalizations must be developed
4 What defects must be remedied
5 What evaluation activities would be desirable

Tasks, at least as they apply to the curriculum, are collections of activities that often come close together in time and share a common purpose to some degree. The term *tasks* is heuristic, applying as it does to some arbitrarily bounded set of activities. When the student completes a series of tasks, however, he is presumed to have made progress toward certain goals. A careful analysis will sometimes show that progress is blocked by one or two simple things—a missed observation, a mixup in procedures, an illogical inference. Task analysis makes these failures less likely.

In this chapter, one technique for task analysis will be presented. Rather detailed analyses of several lessons are given in order to illustrate how one goes about task analysis. The reader will need to take time to study the examples if he wishes to learn to apply the technique.

There are many uses to which task analysis can be put. For people interested in programmed instruction or evaluation, or both, the technique is essential, since it yields information concerning the minimum set of observations and inferences that must be made at any point. A school administrator or group of teachers might do well to organize a summer workshop to produce analyses of the science units making up the elementary program. Out of such a procedure could emerge variations in lessons which require less costly materials, remedies for deficiencies in lessons, tasks for assessment of learning, programmed instruction materials, and many other benefits. Task analysis has been put to use in the following ways:

1. *Revision of units.* The analyses will show which concepts need to be expanded and which can be dropped. It will show how many times and in what contexts certain ideas are rehearsed. It will indicate the extent to which the stated objectives correspond to the content of a unit.
2. *Preparation of units in different formats.* Task analysis will provide one means of adapting units so that learners with different patterns of aptitudes can learn more effectively.
3. *Preparation of programmed instruction.* Since it exposes the sequence of concepts and the minimum set of observations necessary to move through the sequence, task analysis is a logical first step on the way to converting an existing curriculum to units of programmed instruction.
4. *Evaluation.* Task analysis provides a basic tool for the construction of appropriate items to be used in assessment of learning. Test construction, which uses task analysis as a source for items, is more likely to provide diagnostic information useful to students as well as teachers, since the items

will correspond closely to the actual, rather than stated, objectives.

5 *Classroom diagnosis.* Since the task analysis shows the minimum set of inferences that must be made to progress through a unit, it provides a guide for the teacher in observing the work of children. When difficulties arise, the teacher can begin diagnosing by checking the information, observations, and inferences made by the children.

6 *Sequencing of units.* Task analysis will provide a basis for determining in what order units ought to occur. Thus for a district using a unit system, the analysis becomes a means of making decisions about which materials might be combined at each grade level. Since analyses of units show the ideas developed in them, it is possible to produce a display of scope and sequence for a total program. Then teachers can decide how appropriate the content is for their purposes.

7 *Identifying needs for new units.* Since the task analysis sometimes indicates "holes" in the development—i.e., missing elements—it can give curriculum developers information about the need for additional units.

8 *Preparation of catalogue.* The information produced in a task analysis can be used to compile unit abstracts that describe the program and objectives accurately. Thus it is useful for discussions with school boards, granting agencies, parent groups, and classroom visitors. When such descriptions are available for a number of programs, they facilitate comparisons between programs. For new teachers entering a system, such a catalogue provides information about objectives, flow of ideas, possible difficulties, etc.

9 *Training of teachers.* Similarities and differences between programs can be exposed by comparing analyses of them. It is conceivable that out of this comparison a course of training for teachers would emerge which would make it highly probable that they could function successfully in any one of a number of programs. The analysis would show what the minimum set of training experiences for a particular program ought to include. Thus, it would be useful as a basis for designing an in-service training program. Instead of being a mech-

anistic approach to curriculum construction, as some of its opponents suggest, task analysis forms an empirical base upon which to make much more humane instructional settings than we might otherwise.

When you "buy" a new curriculum, it is a little like buying the same size clothing for all your children. You have to plan on doing a little taking in or letting out to fit the situation. Teachers, like scientists, must have a certain flexibility in their approach to phenomena. Task analysis provides some guide to how to do the tailoring. No one can design a set of procedures and objectives which will fit each class so well that all teachers will get exactly comparable results. Each operating condition has some uniqueness about it that requires modification of recommended procedures. Teachers need to feel free to make changes. The curriculum designer imagines what range of experiences children might already have had and what kinds of reasoning they might be expected to do, given those experiences. That knowledge is necessary to him if he wishes to incorporate activities which are novel to learners or which could produce conceptual conflict. Recall the discussion in Chapter 7 in which both novelty and conceptual conflict were described as factors that motivate inquiry. People are not usually prompted to inquire about what is familiar unless it suddenly appears in some unusual context. With all the different environmental contexts in which children are immersed, the curriculum writer must depend on teachers to slant the activities so that they provoke speculation and investigation. It is at this point that the joining up of teachers with a curriculum makes all the difference. Curriculum designers can write activities calculated to produce conceptual conflict, but only teachers can control whether that happens. Designers have to imagine what children will be likely to infer or conclude from a series of investigations. Designers make guesses about what logical operations the children will probably perform, provided that teachers help.

Individual children tend to exhibit highly variable routes to the solution of problems. Logical threads in a curriculum can be mercilessly stretched and bent by children. Again, if teachers team up with writers to help adjust the activities and their interpretation, then the result for the children is likely to be somewhat better than it might be if a program is interpreted rigidly.

What would you do when he returns to the classroom? How do you think he would rate this activity? (Photograph courtesy of Phyllis Marcuccio.)

Unfettered by a network of established connections between concepts, preoperational children and children without a substantial fund of accumulated experience in reasoning frequently make a travesty of the rational linkages on which the curriculum writer depends to motivate inquiry. The teacher must determine, then, how to adjust the examples and tasks.

TWO VERSIONS: THE CURRICULUM ON PAPER AND THE CURRICULUM IN PRACTICE

If you based your whole conception of what doing research in science is like on published accounts of investigations, you would get a very distorted notion of how the men and women in the various disciplines actually function. You might gather that hypotheses, variables, procedures, instruments, etc., materialized easily and out of strictly logical necessity. Published accounts leave out the "messing about" phases of studies, in which one plan after another may be tried and discarded. The accounts rarely disclose how long it took to accomplish the published study. Final reports seldom include discussions of aspects such as persistent failures of machinery to perform according to expectations, or the number of experiments aborted by the presence of extraneous materials in the system or by human error. To be a professional scientist requires a high tolerance for frustration accompanied by a certain flexibility in regard to objectives, for an investigation that starts out with one purpose may well terminate by meeting objectives which were not part of the original intent but which emerged during the study.

In a somewhat similar vein, one could get a distorted notion of how objectives and plans associated with a curriculum are meant to function in particular classrooms. Just as with reports of scientific investigations, published curriculums exhibit some standard forms of presentation that make them appear cut and dried, or, as some teachers describe it, "mechanistic." In practice, however, equipment sometimes does not work, students do not draw the conclusion predicted, and it is often necessary to retrace steps. Sometimes the students emerge having learned something unanticipated but valuable. The curriculum in practice looks different from the curriculum on paper. Task analysis provides data the teacher can use to ensure that certain minimum objectives are met.

Even the curriculum writer goes through a messing-around stage. You could get the mistaken notion that curriculum writers always thought of the objectives they wanted to attain and then prepared lessons designed to achieve them. After observing and participating on a number of writing teams whose missions were to prepare new science programs, I can report that it rarely ever happens that way. On the contrary, the usual route in production of lessons runs in the opposite direction. Someone gets an idea for a series of lessons that might fit somewhere within a general framework and begins to write descriptions of the activities, frequently messing about with simple pieces of equipment until something works easily. It is in the *process of writing* that the specific objectives which such lessons or units might serve emerge. These objectives appear in the presentation near the beginning of a unit so that the would-be consumer can quickly determine what the activities might reasonably be expected to accomplish. Similarly, in a scientific publication, the objectives that evolved and became the focus of the study appear near the beginning of the report, so that the consumer will have a frame of reference for interpreting what follows.

A curriculum on paper and a curriculum in practice are two entities which have some kind of correspondence to each other, but sometimes that correspondence is rather remote. Task analysis, however, can help teachers to adapt the curriculum so that there will be closer agreement between the proposed purposes and the accomplished purposes.

QUESTIONS TASK ANALYSIS CAN ANSWER

Task analysis supplies information about concepts, procedures, observations, and logical operations pertinent to a set of tasks.

1 About concepts:
   a What concepts are introduced in each lesson?
   b What concepts are practiced in the lesson and in how many contexts? (Any lesson or unit may contain new concepts and may also employ concepts introduced in earlier lessons. There must be a reasonable balance between new and familiar ideas.)

c How concrete or abstract are the concepts?

d In what sequence do the concepts appear?

2 About operations or procedures:

a What operations, skills, and techniques are involved in each lesson?

b What operations are meant to rehearse or practice concepts?

c How are data stored? (In memory, in tables, in graphs, etc.)

3 About observations:

a What combination of observations constitutes the *minimum* necessary for children to discover the relationships or to learn the concepts?

b What information do students need in addition to that which can be gained by direct observation?

c What information comes from experiment and what must be obtained from books and other sources?

4 About logical operations (Here, observations provide the "stuff" on which the child's brain must operate logically):

a Given the minimum set of observations and given the network of ideas already existing, is it logically possible for children to make the correct deductions or inferences?

b How close is the tie between evidence and inferences? (Are conclusions based more on decree than on argument?)

This last kind of analysis often picks out a key observation; if this key observation is not made, the expected deductions and inferences may be prevented from occurring. Thus the teacher can be alerted to note whether students make the key observations. Discovery becomes more probable as linkages between the observations and the conceptual network increase; coherence becomes especially important for older children. Rationality is at a maximum in tasks where the necessary observations accumulate to form the basis for inferences. Children who are preoperational can function well enough at an empirical level to begin to assimilate the rudiments of what will later evolve into a network of established ideas. They develop meaning out of concrete experience.

At more advanced levels, both the beauty of discovery and the quality of thought depend on how well ideas fit into a system of mutually supporting propositions. Rationality at this level of functioning depends on possession of a fund of knowledge organized so that problems orginate and their "givens" are established from logical necessity —from what the network of ideas would lead one to expect. Understanding of many ideas depends upon having acquired some sophistication and having attained some minimum level of cognitive maturity. Certain ideas cannot be mastered on an intuitive basis, since they can be expressed only in abstract terms. Rationality in such cases is based not only on knowledge but on whether students have matured sufficiently and have been frequently exposed to situations that would encourage them to deal with problems abstractly as well as concretely. See, for example, Figure 13-7, showing two geometric problems which are apparently similar but which require different levels of solution.

FIRST STEPS IN DOING A TASK ANALYSIS

You will need felt pens in three colors and a worksheet like the one shown in Figure 16-1.

1 Read through a unit or portion of it.
   a Identify all statements that describe procedures which you or the children are to follow. Underline these statements in one color.
   b Identify all statements which describe observations to be made or evidence to be gathered. Underline these in a different color.
   c Identify all statements concerning concepts, principles, inferences, or deductions. Underline these in a third color.

   I often do this underlining routinely to a unit that I am planning to teach, since it quickly signals to me what kind of operations I am supposed to be carrying out, what observations the children should be making, and what concepts are supposed to emerge. This cursory kind of analysis has immediate utility for people teaching a unit for the first time.

2 On the task-analysis worksheet, do the following:
   a Enter the first procedure in the left column.
   b In the second column list the minimum observations or phenomena to which students must attend.

FIGURE 16-1
Task-analysis worksheet

1. Procedures	2. Observations, phenomena	3. Concepts, principles, inferences, deductions, etc.	4. Logical operations (optional)

Miscellaneous

---

    c Continue to the next procedure. List the observations.

    d When inferences, deductions, concepts, or principles are supposed to emerge, list them in the third column opposite the last set of observations.

When you have completed step 1, you will have done a task analysis. Step 2 constitutes the recording of it.

In setting up worksheets for analysis, leave space at the head and foot of each page for summaries and comments. Usually the space at the top of the page is reserved for recording cumulative information emerging from the analysis that relates to goals or general principles. A page of analysis might, for example, contain several subconcepts that result in the eventual formation of some major idea. Such major principles are generally entered at the top of the page as well as in column 3. In addition, a set of activities might also represent teaching that has some attitudinal outcome as its goal. If the import of activities seems to be affective (e.g., a point of view about scientists would be an affective outcome), that would also appear at the top of the page.

The space at the bottom of each page collects all miscellaneous comments and observations. The analysis might show, for example, the same idea being rehearsed in two or three different contexts; this fact would be noted in the space at the bottom. One trial is rarely enough. Inconsistencies between procedures or concepts in earlier and later parts of a unit would be exposed by analysis, and the fact of the inconsistencies would be entered in the bottom space, along with the locations of inconsistencies, as shown in the analysis. In one unit, for example, the writers said that children should learn to keep the equipment they use clean and in order, but later on the teacher was directed to collect and clean the equipment. This is a small example of an inconsistency between the principle to be taught (cleanliness and order) and the procedures suggested. Principles and procedures should be consistent; here, if there is to be consistency, the children should be responsible for cleaning up.

Once observations are entered at the bottom of the page, the teacher can decide whether changes, additions, or modifications should be made. Before analysis, teachers might not be aware that any modifications warrented consideration. After analysis, they may elect to ignore some or all of the observations; but if they do, at least this will be a conscious decision, based on knowledge.

EXAMPLES OF TASK ANALYSIS

To study the examples, do the following:

1 Read through the portion of the original curriculum that is given. Identify and mark procedures, observations/phenomena, inferences/deductions, and concepts.
2 Locate each on the worksheet, which shows how the unit was analyzed.

Example 1: "Spinning Tables"

One page from a unit called "Spinning Tables" illustrates a case where the writers do not tell what the minimum set of observations must be. (See Figure 16-2.) They do ask

14 | For these activities you will need the smooth table, colored chalk, and a damp cloth or eraser. If you draw more than once on the chalkboard, use a different colored chalk for each trial, so that you can make comparisons.

Take some time to play with the table. What things catch your attention? Spending time initially on investigation is something the children should do too. It will give them an opportunity to become familiar with the equipment, and it often leads to interesting activities. Experimenting with the equipment by yourself beforehand will help you understand your children's reactions when they begin to explore the possibilities of the tables.

Below is a top view of the table spinning clockwise. Can you predict what kind of pattern you will get if you use the chalk to draw a straight line across the table as it spins? You should be able to make a light stroke with the chalk so that the table won't slow down too much. (The dotted line in the diagram below represents the motion of your hand.) Draw on this diagram what you think the chalk line will look like after the table stops.

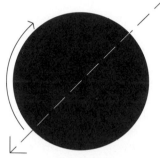

What would happen to the pattern if you drew your hand across the table more slowly, but kept the table spinning at the same rate? Record your prediction on the same diagram.

The first activity is always exciting in the classroom. Seldom does any student predict the pattern correctly. One girl was convinced, when she saw the result, that her hand must have moved according to the pattern on the table. An interesting class discussion followed on how she could keep the

motion of her hand straight. Eventually a couple of classmates decided to hold a yardstick horizontally about an inch above the table for her to use as a guide. Once the children were convinced that the hand's motion was straight, they tackled the problem of what caused the strange pattern.

What pattern will you get if the table is spinning more slowly? Draw your line across the table at the same speed as in the first activity.

Will spinning the table in the opposite direction give different results? Try it.

FIGURE 16-2

A section of the "Spinning Tables" unit. Published by the Elementary Science Study of Education Development Center, Inc., Newton, Massachusetts. Copyright © 1968 by Education Development Center, Inc.

that several variables be manipulated and their effects studied. The unit generally employs a special form of a lazy Susan, but any lazy Susan will work reasonably well. A piece of chalkboard or a piece of paper is fastened to the top of the lazy Susan, and the actual procedures of the unit begin as shown in Figure 16-2.

First, notice that in the format in which the lesson appeared, the procedures, questions, and observations to be made are all mixed in a kind of conversational form. To do the task analysis, you must read analytically in order to classify the various operations and concepts. One problem is to identify the input and output variables.

The second observation to make about the page con-

Children usually spend quite a bit of time trying différent speeds after these initial tries. Encourage them to predict what they think will happen in each new situation.

Predict what pattern you will get if you slowly draw from the center to the edge as the table spins. Will the pattern be different if you start at the edge and go to the center? What will happen if you spin the table in the opposite direction?

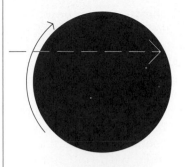

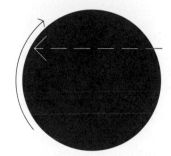

Will the patterns in the situations above be alike?

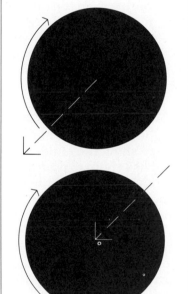

Spin your table slowly. Can you draw some kind of figure on the spinning table that will end up looking like the one below? (It's hard to do, so don't worry if it isn't perfect.)

15

Your first reaction will probably be to make a very quick stroke with your hand. This is one way of doing it. Try it again, only this time move your hand more slowly. In order to do this, you must move your hand in a circle *with* the spinning table while drawing the line.

cerns the variables. These are never explicitly talked about, and they are changed with each successive procedure. Reading units with this kind of format requires close attention to every sentence—otherwise, the structure concealed in the unit will not be uncovered. (From the teacher's point of view, the task analysis helps to bring into some kind of order what could well be merely a welter of unrelated information.) Table speed, hand speed, and direction of spin are all variables which are supposed to be manipulated at one time or another. One teacher might experiment with the unit just as it is, leaving it to chance that children will discover patterns and the ways in which they are altered. (A lower level of learning would require only that the children discover that there are patterns and that they are somehow different when some condition of the system is changed. A more advanced level of learning would occur when the children could associate input variables with specific pattern changes.)

Ultimately the unit aims to develop the concept that what you observe depends on your point of view—i.e., where you are in relation to other things. At the end of the lessons the writer tells you, "A motion as seen from the classroom's point of view is the same as the movement you make with your hand, and the same motion from the spinning table's point of view is the path left on the table." This unit must be very interesting to children, since they frequently spend long periods of time with it when the apparatus is left available for use. A complete analysis of the entire unit would show what content goals, and possibly what process goals, the unit serves (Figure 16-3).

Assessment.   To evaluate outcomes from just this one page of activities, in which several input variables are to be manipulated, you might choose to show the children a succession of different patterns and ask them to postulate the conditions under which those patterns were probably formed. (See Chapter 17 for examples.) They can always check their predictions by performing the experiments which they think produced each of the patterns. You would not only listen for the correctness of their predictions; you would be especially attentive to their reasoning. If the children recognize what variables are relevant and how they are related, then the message on that page of the unit has been realized. In Chapter 17, there are examples of evaluation items which might be suitable for the portion of the unit which has been analyzed.

Example 2: Interaction and systems

Units of the Science Curriculum Improvement Study (SCIS) exhibit a somewhat different format. The example chosen for analysis comes from an early version of a SCIS unit, commonly taught in the second grade, called "Interaction and Systems." The unit, which is meant to take up approximately half of one year's work in science, has seven parts, all of which demonstrate in one way or another concepts of interaction and systems. Changes in systems are generally interpreted as evidence of inter-

FIGURE 16-3
Task analysis of page 14 from the unit "Spinning Tables"*

Procedures	Observations, phenomena	Concepts, inferences
Use different colored chalk for each trial.	Make comparisons between trials.	
Play with the table.	Miscellaneous activities and observations.	Familiarity with the equipment.
Spin table clockwise and draw a straight line across the table as it turns (basic condition).		
1 Predict what the pattern will look like and draw it.	Any drawing is acceptable. First predictions are seldom correct.	
2 Perform the operation.	Curved pattern appears. Direction is clockwise.	The hand moved in a straight line, but the chalk pattern is curved.
Spin table at same speed, but move hand across it more slowly (variation 1: keep table speed as a constant, and slow hand).		If you change a factor like the speed of your hand, the curve changes. If you keep the table speed as a constant, then the faster you move your hand, the flatter the curve will get. The slower you move your hand, the deeper the curve gets.
1 Predict and record the prediction.		
2 Perform the operation.	The new curve is more pronounced. Its bend is deeper.	
If students think their hands are not moving in a straight line, have them invent ways to check.	Various procedures will be tried out to verify that the hand moved in a straight line.	The curved pattern is being produced by the spinning table.
Spin table more slowly to see what happens to the pattern (variation 2: slow table speed).†	The loops get bigger, and there are fewer of them.	Slowing the table down changes the pattern.
Spin the table counterclockwise.†	Curve starts out in opposite direction (counterclockwise).	The pattern changes in one way. When the direction of spin changes, so does the direction of looping.

*This unit was published in 1968 by the Elementary Science Study of the Education Development Center. It is now distributed by the Webster Division of McGraw-Hill.

†Note that the directions fail to say whether the hand should now be drawn across the table rapidly or slowly. Independent variables introduced to this point; i.e., the input variables are speed of the table and speed of the hand holding the chalk. In principle, four combinations of input variables are possible, each of which could produce a different pattern or output variable (dependent variable): (1) both fast; (2) both slow; (3) the table fast and the hand slow; (4) the table slow and the hand fast.

The writer may elect to leave it to chance that children will investigate the combinations, or he may choose to point it out to the teacher, who can then decide how to employ the information. At least the task analysis alerts the writer to a possible omission.

action. Dissolving is one kind of interaction, and part five of the SCIS unit, which deals with this concept, has the following three stated objectives:

1 To keep track of a system even though the objects in it change in appearance.

2 To interpret dissolving, color change, and heating as evidence of interaction.

3 To experiment and write reports individually.

The first lesson from part 5 "Making Copper Chloride Solution," deals with dissolving as an example of interaction. Consider what happens to the concept in this SCIS lesson.

Assessment and commentary.   At the end of lesson 1 of part 5, "Dissolving," the writers suggest that the process of dissolving copper chloride could be repeated inside a plastic bag, and the children should try to decide whether the system is the same or different. They should, according to the writers, say that the system is the same system since the parts which interact have not changed. That, it is claimed, would represent a response indicating progress toward acquisition of the idea of conservation.

Although it was not suggested by the writers, the trial of dissolving inside the plastic bag suggests that the second step of the experiment, evaporation, also be tried inside a plastic bag. If the first system was the same in all respects, why should not the same reasoning apply to the second system? By the simple rule given in the first example, this second system is identical because nothing was added or removed. It happens that such an arrangement could serve to remedy somewhat the incompleteness of the concept of evaporation as it now stands in the activity, since the only place the water could go would be into the bag. The children might observe some evidence of evaporation, some condensation of moisture on the bag, and a small amount of blue residue. Depending on how much liquid had to evaporate and depending on the starting condition of the air in the bag, some evidence of interaction would result. Children could conceivably infer that the more rapid and complete evaporation, which occurs when the system is not confined to a plastic bag, may be associated with more space for the water to move into.

Note also that the second item under optional activities, which suggests that children might redissolve and reevaporate their copper chloride crystals, probably should be required rather than considered optional. The activity would allow completion of a complete cycle: dissolve, evaporate, recover, redissolve, evaporate, recover. This makes the logic of the unit somewhat tighter, since

FIGURE 16-4
Task analysis of Lesson 1 in Part 5, "Dissolving," from the unit "Interaction and Systems"*

Procedures	Observations, phenomena	Concepts, inferences, etc.
Demonstrate how to get copper chloride into a tea bag and how to fold the bag over the edge of a tumbler.		
a Children imitate procedure.	Blue crystals.	
b Put enough water into each tumbler to just wet bag.		
c Look for *evidence of interaction*.	Solution turns bluish. Bag becomes empty. Schlieren (children often describe them as "kind of like ropes").	Copper chloride *dissolved.*† It might still be present, because the crystals were blue and so is the solution.
Prepare a report‡ which includes three categories.		
a System of interacting objects is specified.		
b Evidence of interaction is recorded.		
c Picture story of the whole process is included.		
Compare results.		Different children may have made different observations or have thought about the observations differently.
Try out ways to get copper chloride back again.		
Get back copper chloride in solid form by *evaporation*. Use a controlled experiment design.	When the water evaporates, a blue substance remains. It is powder-like.	Even though the blue substance looks different, it is *probably* copper chloride. (The residue substance is more powdery.)
a Copper chloride solution		
b Plain tap water	Some whitish residue.	
c Distilled water	No residue.	Evaporation is a way to get back materials dissolved in water.◀
Optional activities These provide some rehersals of the concepts in different contexts. Use the tea-bag technique to study the interactions of other common materials.	Depend on what substances are used. Some may not even dissolve at all.	
Add water to the residue crystals and let them dissolve again, then re-evaporate.	Solution turns blue as it did originally. After evaporation a blue residue is present again.	Even though the copper chloride residue looked different from the original pile of crystals, it interacted in the same way.

*Prepared by the Science Curriculum Improvement Study and Published by Rand McNally, 1970. Pages 73–76 are analyzed.

†The word *dissolve* is used in context and not directly defined. At this point it still is an incomplete concept in that the conservation notion which is relevant to it has not yet been introduced: i.e., the material dissolved must still be present, even though it is in a different form (transformed). Check to see how the concept *dissolve* grows as a result of the succeeding activities.

‡There is some question concerning what would be the minimum set of items which would make the report acceptable: i.e., no criteria are specified, and the function of the report is clear. Reports prompt our memories, and they serve to communicate findings. Check to see how the reports are used.

◀Check earlier parts of the program to see whether this is the first introduction of *evaporation* or whether it is simply an application of a concept already explored. Note, however, that the water "control" gives a chance to observe the disappearance of water without copper chloride in it. The idea that the water might nevertheless still be around somewhere—i.e., conserved—is not pursued. This should signal the writer and teachers to expand the concept of evaporation to include conservation of the water at some point in the sequence, otherwise children may think that evaporation violates the conservation rule. Note that the suggested assessment activities could well constitute an extension of the lesson to cover these difficulties.

it confirms that while the residue crystals look different, they still interact in the same manner. The task analysis makes this apparent (Figure 16-4).

Example 3: Science—A Process Approach

This is a program originally developed with government funds. The format of this unit differs from those examined so far, but not so much as one might expect in view of the fact that the program of Science—A Process Approach (SAPA) has a reputation for "high structure," whatever that means. As indicated by the analyses completed to this point, all units have some degree of structure even though that structure may be well masked. SAPA makes more of the structure explicit.

In the lessons analyzed as examples so far in this chapter, the commentary has suggested what concepts introduced in the unit or lesson must have come earlier in the program. The analysis suggests what the teacher must be certain the student already has learned if he is to be successful in doing the new unit. The SAPA plan tries to save teachers some of that trouble by presenting a series of simple flowcharts on the front of each unit, which show what processes were treated in each of the preceding units. For example, the lesson that will be analyzed comes from Part C, frequently taught at the second-grade program level. "Classifying 9" (meaning the ninth lesson in the series that emphasizes the process of classifying) is titled "Separating Materials from Mixtures." On the cover of the booklet appears a scheme or flowchart that tells the teacher which other lessons in the program contribute most directly to success in doing what "Classifying 9" requires. In addition, the cover of the booklet specifies the minimum set of behaviors that children might reasonably be expected to exhibit at the conclusion of the lesson. In effect, SAPA exposes a portion of the task analysis to its consumers and thereby risks building an image of some kind of repressive structure. But such an image is empirically no more justified than it would be for units of the other programs, which do not suffer from the reputation of being repressive, because they have not been so explicit about their expectations.

As the task analysis clearly shows, "Classifying 9" exhibits neither more nor less structure than the other units analyzed (Figure 16-5). The source of irritation probably comes, as the analysis indicates, when the writers invade the decision-making domain of the teacher. There occur throughout the lesson a number of suggestions that tell the teacher how to run her shop, and since the advice is not particularly astute and since styles of work in each classroom may differ, the advice can only detract from the value of the unit. Unfortunately, many SAPA lessons are loaded with pedagogical directions that teachers will do well to ignore. Indeed, they must ignore them if they want to exploit the program to its fullest.

Assessment or appraisal. With the same thoughtfulness that went into identifying preceding lessons on which this particular lesson, "Separating Materials from Mixtures," depends, the writers furnish a procedure for finding out what kinds of competence the children exhibit at the end of the activities. An exact appraisal procedure, along with directions for scoring, appears on the back cover of each pamphlet. In this case, for example, a child receives a new mixture consisting of materials he has not previously used and three separating devices: two troughs and one set of sieves (Figure 16-6).

First, the teacher who administers this procedure to an individual child tells him to separate the mixture into component parts by any means he wishes. For each component separated, the child gets a point. Then he must describe the process. (Communication is one of the processes emphasized in the SAPA program.) Next, the child orders the components according to size of particles. Finally, he orders them according to their weights or volumes. Directions for scoring are supplied.

ADDITIONAL COMMENTS ON TASK ANALYSIS

Task analysis is a singularly humane process, although some educators classify it among the operations they accuse of being "mechanistic." It deserves to be better considered. In teaching we often inadvertently punish children for not performing according to our expectations. Many factors may contribute to this situation; one explanation is suggested by information that emerges from task analysis. Either the children did not have adequate exposure to the ideas in a unit which should have been developed beforehand, or the unit did not contain sufficient examples, sequenced to encourage the kind of

FIGURE 16-5
Task analysis of "Classifying 9" in Part C of Science—A Process Approach, "Separating Materials from Mixtures"*

Procedures	Observations and phenomena	Concepts, inferences, etc.
Shake up a mixture of pebbles, coarse sand, fine dry clay in a jar *without* water.	Materials get scrambled.	
Question: How could you find out the weight or volume of each material present?		
1 Show a bag full of a mixture of three sizes of marbles.	There are three different sizes of marbles.†	
2 Separate the marbles into groups according to size and measure the *time* it takes to do it. Divide the material and work in five groups (variable 1: time).	Five separate times for sorting are recorded.	
3 As soon as a group finishes, dump marbles back into main container. Use time from start to finish of all groups as total time (variable 2: total time).	Total time of groups from start to completion of all sortings = _____.	
Question: Is there a way to shorten the sorting time?		
1 Show the class an open-bottom expanding trough, and have two children dump all the marbles in it.		Fewer people were able to sort more rapidly with the help of the trough.‡
2 Measure total sorting time.	Total sorting time is less. Fewer children worked on the task.	
Show the class a dry mix of gravel, coarse sand, and fine sand.§	Miscellaneous.	
Question: How can the components be separated?		
1 Show a graded screen trough in which the *mesh interval* is a variable (variable 3: mesh interval).		
2 Use the screens in the trough to separate the components of the mixture.	The mixture sorts into three piles each of which is mostly made up of one component but does not have contaminants.	Particles fall through holes that are bigger than they are.

Procedures	Observations and phenomena	Concepts, inferences, etc.
3 Measure the volume of each pile and compare it with the volume of the original mix.	The total volume is less than the sum of its component volumes.	Infer that the volume of the total is less because small particles get tucked in between big particles.

Note:
This activity could equally well lead to the notion that the law of conservation is being violated, unless the weights of the total mix and of the components are also obtained. The weight of the total will equal the weight of its components.

Then follow a series of rehearsals in which the variables type of mixture and size of screen mesh are altered.	Miscellaneous.	The smaller the mesh, the smaller the particles it will allow to pass through.
Children are encouraged to weigh as well as measure the volume.		Weight is conserved. Volume is not.

Note: In view of the note on conservation, this aspect of the activities might well be given as much emphasis as the measurement of volume, or even more.

---

*Published in 1967 by the Xerox Corporation.

†The directions say that the teacher is to *tell* children that *she* notices three different sizes. This is a good example of why pedagogical procedures should be kept out of a unit or categorized in the unit in a separate place. A teacher may choose to let children find out for themselves how many different sizes are present. Even here the teacher has options; she can ask how many different sizes they observe or provide even a lower degree of cuing by waiting to see whether they spontaneously notice the fact that there are different sizes. All such decisions are the prerogative of the teacher, not the writer.

‡Again, the directions invade the pedagogical domain. They say, "*Emphasize* that fewer people sorted more rapidly." Should that be something the teacher points out, or should it be an observation which emerges from the viewing of the results? How strongly do the phenomena cue the students?

§Showing the class a mix of something already prepared may not be so powerful as actually mixing the materials in full view so that they can observe how the system came into being.

Notice also that the directions do not call for determining the total volume of the mixture before starting to separate it. Thus, the teacher can arrive at the end of the activity only to find that the volume comparisons called for cannot be made. (Task analysis points out to the writer omissions that he ought to do something about. This kind of omission can make a teacher unhappy with an activity and—if it happens often—with a program.) The whole quantitative aspect is lost. Similarly, the writer fails to allow for weighing the total mix made before separating components, so even the conservation aspect of mixtures and components cannot be explored.

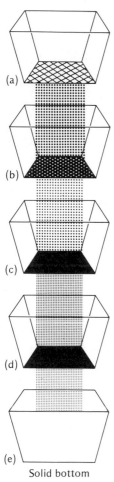

Solid bottom

FIGURE 16-6
Troughs and sieves for separating mixtures.

thought intended. It could also be that individual children failed to make certain pivotal observations. With the help of task analysis, such probable difficulties can be anticipated.

Task analysis also provides a procedure for diagnosis. Once a learning difficulty has arisen, teachers may use the analysis to find its possible sources. Diagnosis is the first step in the process of helping. When the helping process begins without sufficient diagnosis, its effectiveness is likely to be impaired. The teacher becomes like a doctor who gives the same prescription to everybody, regardless of what his malady is.

From the analyses given as examples in this chapter, you may see other ramifications of task analysis. For example, information emerging from task analyses would help to settle many conflicts that develop among advocates of different programs. Proponents of various programs naturally make claims for them; analysis will provide data on which to determine the validity of those claims. If a program develops an "image"—of being characterized by "high structure" or "low structure"—analysis will provide an empirical basis for determining what "structure" means in the context of the program, and what kind and degree of structure it actually possesses.

The use of task analysis to expose the network of implicit or explicit ideas in a unit is especially important for people who want to construct individualized learning packages. A common problem in any kind of programmed instruction concerns the unintentional loss of structure. Inferences which students must make depend on the acquisition of an ordered network of ideas, not on the simple accumulation of information. Frequently that network gets so fragmented in programmed instruction that essential meanings, which depend on the building of a context, are lost. Task analysis of individualized learning packages can provide protection against fragmentation.

Finally, task analysis is essential to some phases of evaluation. Its special utility is its more humane use of data—that is, it uses data in assessment for the benefit of individual learners. Out of the analysis, one can compound a set of tasks which students may administer to themselves or which teachers may help students try out in order to discover what a unit of instruction probably taught them.

The use of task analysis for improving the quality of

life in the classroom depends on trust. Program writers ought to furnish this kind of information and trust classroom teachers to use it wisely.

SUMMARY

1 Task analysis is a technique for evaluating a unit of instruction in order to determine the following things:
   a The minimum set of observations and inferences to be made
   b The sequence these should occur in
   c What defects must be remedied
   d What evaluation activities would be desirable

2 Task analysis is useful in the following kinds of activities:
   a Revision of units
   b Preparation of units in parallel formats
   c Programmed instruction
   d Evaluation
   e Classroom diagnosis
   f Sequencing of units
   g Identifying needs for new units
   h Preparation of catalogues
   i Design of in-service programs

3 Discovery becomes more probable as linkages between observations and the conceptual network increase.

4 In doing a task analysis of a unit, first read through the unit to identify and mark the following kinds of statements:
   a Procedures
   b Observations/evidence
   c Inferences/deductions

5 Some curriculum writers do not state the minimum sets of observations and inferences. They do not trust teachers with this information, fearing that teachers will turn the unit into a drill, which would defeat its purpose.

6 Knowing the minimum set of observations and inferences helps teachers to diagnose learning problems of students. By identifying those procedures, observations, inferences that were missed, teachers are in a better position to take remedial action.

7 Task analysis is a technique that yields information helpful in diagnosing learning problems in science.

8 A complete task analysis can probably be effectively done only by someone thoroughly familiar with the science content of a unit.

ACTIVITY 16-1

OBJECTIVE

To distinguish procedures, observations, and inferences in a lesson

What to do:

1 Set up a table like the one shown in Figure 16-1 and perform a task analysis. Enter the procedures in the left column and the observations in the middle column. Inferences, principles, and conclusions go in the third column. Omit column 4.
2 Identify the input variables.
3 Identify the output variables.

ACTIVITY 16-2

A unit called "Powders," which was part of the African Primary Science Program, is the basis for the activities that follow. A task analysis has been done to show what *procedures* must be followed, what *concepts* are involved, and what kind of *logic* must be employed by students.

The unit begins by having students note observations that can be made directly with the sensory apparatus of the body. From this information a concept begins to be built about each material. Salt, for example, is white, is shaped like boxes (the crystals are often described that way by children), and has a distinctive taste. Similarly, the other powders acquire a list of properties that constitute their empirical definition. Then the unit progresses to the use of substances which interact with the powders. Here the concepts are further expanded to include the list of ways in which certain liquids make each powder react. Gradually, the list of properties attached to each powder grows large enough so that when mixtures of the powders are formed, there are ways the components can be identified. The unit in this version never suggests, however, that there might be some benefit in having children make up their own combinations of powders and then attempt to identify what they contain. This last part of the operation would finally put the whole process under their control. They not only could identify or detect and infer combinations of powders; they could mix their own combinations and verify or test their ideas.

What to do:

1 Find some students and teach this unit. Tape-record if possible.
2 Keep a careful record of the students' observations. Check to see whether the minimum set necessary has been made.
3 At the conclusion of the unit, devise some activities which will assess the learning.
4 Tape-record samples of conversation among students. Analyze the tapes for
   a Content
   b Types of questions
   c Wait time
   d Rewards

OVERVIEW OF THE "POWDERS" UNIT

The unit teaches the following important concepts:

1 You can use the senses of your body (vision, touch, taste, and smell) to make observations about objects (powders in this case).
2 When you do not know what a substance is, you can find out by comparing its properties with properties of things that are known. (You should be cautious about tasting.)
   Note: This requires comparing and contrasting properties of powders to tell one from another.
3 Keeping records helps you remember your observations.
4 Some ways of arranging records are more useful than others.
5 You have to be careful not to contaminate (make "unclean") powders if you want to find out what the powders are.

Note:
One feature of the unit, which the task analysis uncovered, has to do with the concepts of mixtures and cleanliness. The idea of a mixture is never explicitly taught either by discussion or through the performance of a task. Powders 5 and 6, which are mixtures, are simply delivered to children. Since they have had four powders that are not mixtures, the question is raised by the task analysis as to whether it may be useful to introduce a brief lesson or demonstration to show children what a mixture means in the context of powders. This question is especially pertinent because the next point made in the lesson concerns the question of contamination of the powder samples by the children ("unclean powders," e.g., children may not brush all the old powder off their hands before experimenting with a new powder). Contamination or unclean powder in this sense is a concept based on the concept of mixture. A contaminant is just a mixture that has something in it you do not want, i.e., "unclean" substances in the powders unit are simply special cases of mixtures.

Materials:
Baking soda, starch, sugar, salt, water, iodine, and vinegar.

Summary of the key content observations upon which concepts and ideas to be discovered or learned in the "Powders" unit are based

Types of powders	Using the body senses for making observations about powders				Using other materials to make observations about powders			Logical operations
	Visual (Grain)	Touch	Taste	Smell	Water	Iodine	Vinegar	
1 Baking soda	Little crystals		Sour or bitter	None	Dissolves		Fizzes or bubbles	
2 Starch	Powdery			None	Does not dissolve all the way (gets sticky)	Turns dark		
3 Sugar	Crystals		Sweet	None	Dissolves			
4 Salt	Boxlike crystals		Salty	None	Dissolves			
Mixtures:								
5 Starch and soda					Some cloudiness	Dark	Fizzes	Dark → Starch† Fizz → Soda ∴ → Starch and soda
6 Starch and salt			Salty		Some cloudiness	Dark		Salty → Salt Dark → Starch ∴ → Salt and starch
7 Soda and sugar			Sweet*				Fizzes	Sweet → Sugar Fizz → Soda ∴ → Soda and sugar

*Sweet taste usually masks any bitter taste from the soda.

† → = implies.

Note: When a child has made the observations in lines 1 to 7, he has the necessary information to begin on the problem of identifying powders 5 and 6. In general, those observations filled in on the table are the key discriminations which are a prerequisite to identifying powders 5 and 6. Touch, smell, and to a lesser extent granularity provide no distinctive discrimination information for the set of four powders.

LESSON 1

Objectives:
1 Use touch, taste, sight, and smell to make observations about four powders.
2 Practice using senses to find the properties of other powders.

Task analysis for Lesson 1

Procedures	Observations	Concepts	Logical operations
Use touch, taste, seeing (size of grain), and smell to find the properties of four powders.	(Upper left segment of summary table.) The observations shown below (of the many that could be made) are the minimum that would be essential for the child to make in order to distinguish one powder from another.	1 All the powders are white, but they have other properties that are different.	Salty property implies salt.
		2 You can tell that one powder is different from another by comparing the properties of one with another. If the properties are the same, the powders are the same. If one or more properties are different, the powders may be different substances.	Strong sweet property implies sugar.

	Sight*	Touch*	Taste	Smell
Soda		Little crystals	Bitter	None
Starch		Powdery crystals		None
Sugar			Sweet	None
Salt		Boxlike crystals	Salty	None

LESSON 2

Objectives:
1 Identify the four powders: baking soda, starch, sugar, and salt.
2 Practice using the senses to find the properties of other powders.
3 Observe how the powders act in water.
4 Learn how to hand out, *clean,* and put away equipment. (See the comment at the beginning of the lesson analysis. *Clean* means to remove all traces of a contaminant.)
5 Use writing down of observations as a way of remembering them.

Task analysis for Lesson 2

Procedures	Observations	Concepts	Logical operations
Put water on each of the powders. *Skill:* Transfer liquids from large containers to very small containers.	(See column headed "Water" in summary table.) Soda dissolves. Starch gets sticky. Sugar dissolves. Salt dissolves.	1 The four powders act differently in water. *Note:* The idea of *dissolve* is not used as such. What is explicitly taught is "some things disappear in water."	Sweet taste implies things that are like sugar.
Compare the properties of powder 1 with the properties of each of the known powders (e.g., sugar). *Skill:* Write down observations.		2 Identify the powders by comparing their properties with properties of known powders.	

Note:
One concept taught is "things disappear in water." The task analysis suggests that the evaluator and curriculum writer may want to check up at some point on whether "disappears" means "gone" or "still there, but just not visible" to the child. Obviously the latter statement is a more generalized learning. It does not have to be taught now, but the analysis suggests that it be "tagged" and kept track of, so that the *disappear* concept will eventually be broadened to the *dissolve* concept. *Dissolves* = "disappears from view, but is still present." So, what has yet to be taught is: "If it disappeared, where did it go?"

*A whole range of descriptions will probably be offered. (See comment on summary table.)

LESSONS 3 and 4

Objectives:
1 Use *combinations* of properties to distinguish one powder from another (see summary table).
2 Practice using a known substance as a referent for comparison with unknowns.
3 Write down observations and try to arrange them in useful ways (i.e., "useful" means arrange the observations in such a way that you are helped to *compare combinations* of properties of two or more substances).

Task analysis for Lesson 3

Experimental operations	Observations	Concepts	Logical operations

Put water on each of the powders that have been identified.
 	
Powder 5 is a new powder. Observe its properties; put water on it.
	(See Lesson 2 and column headed "Water" in summary table.)
	
	Powder 5 partly makes the water milky. Part does not dissolve.
		1 Things disappear in water in different ways.
		  a Some powders disappear immediately; others disappear gradually.
		  b Some powders disappear partly but not entirely. Others disappear entirely.
		See note on *dissolve* in Lesson 2.
			Powder 5 does not disappear in the exact way any of powders 1–4 did, so it is probably a new powder.

Teacher or students or both put observations on the board or on paper or both.		2 Writing down observations saves time by helping one to remember. If you forget, you may have to repeat experiments.	In order for the observations to be a reason for telling the difference between powders, one has to compare the observations.

Task analysis for Lesson 4

Experimental operations	Observations	Concepts	Logical operations
Put the iodine on the five powders. Find powder 6. Do all the tests you did on the other powders on powder 6. Write down results.	Soda: light pink or lavendar purple Starch: blue Sugar: tan Salt: tan Powder 5: purple Powder 6: purple	The powders do not all act the same way when iodine is dropped on them.	Starch turns blue. If powder 5 and/or powder 6 turns blue, then they might have starch in them.

Note:

An objective of Lesson 2 was to have children learn to be responsible for their own equipment—getting it, cleaning it, and putting it away; but in Lesson 4 the teacher is directed to end the lesson by collecting the materials. This task analysis shows that a general objective was not practical because a pedagogical directive was given that got in its way. This small example illustrates why it is a good practice to leave the pedagogical directives out until the analysis is done. The analysis helps to suggest that pedagogical directions need to be given. One option suggests itself: if all eight powders were introduced in Lesson 1, there would have been more than one powder illustrating each of the "taste" properties.

Similarly, the directions tell the teacher to put the findings on the board. The question the analysis raises is the following: If *ordering* information is important, and if some orderings are more useful than others, then might a lesson be inserted in which children play with different models of ordering the data? (The task analysis points out that there are options. They need not be taken.)

LESSONS 5, 6, and 7

Objectives:

1 Practice objectives of Lesson 4.

2 Different opinions mean doing the experiments over to see if you get the same results. You might not get the same results if:

    a Some condition has changed (such as getting rid of the contaminants).

    b You made an error in remembering or recording.

    c You did something different from the way the other fellow did it.

Note:

Disagreement is supposed to occur over what happened to the various powders. The teacher tells the children that they have not been "careful." But "careful" does not mean anything operational, as the unit now stands. "Careful" in this context means: (1) They have forgotten what happened. (The recording of data is relevant to this point). (2) They used "unclean" powders. (See comments at the beginning of the unit concerning inadvertent mixtures.)

Task analysis for Lessons 5, 6, and 7

Experimental operations	Observations	Concepts	Logical operations
Skill: write down results and compare them with other members of the group.	Some results agree; others do not.	Objective 2, above.	If we agree, do nothing. If we disagree, repeat the experiments. Use *combinations* of properties to distinguish powders; e.g., powder 5 turns blue and fizzes, therefore it must be starch and soda.
Lessons 5 and 6: Repeat previous experiments on "clean" powders. (This means repeating about 30 tests.) Try vinegar on powders.			
Lesson 7: Repeat the previous tests on powder 6 (see summary table)	Two powders fizz or bubble, four do not (see summary table).	The powders do not all act the same way when vinegar is put on them.	

LESSON 8

Objectives:
Same as for preceding lessons (5, 6, and 7).
Note:
Lesson 8 introduces a new powder, powder 7, consisting of soda and sugar. It could very well be used as an assessment lesson by the teachers.

Task analysis for Lesson 8

Experimental operations	*Observations*	*Concepts*	*Logical operations*
Powder 7 (soda and sugar): Do all the previous tests and write observations down (seven tests).	(See summary table.)	You can find out what materials are in a new powder by comparing its properties with properties of other substances you already know.	
	a It tastes sweet like sugar. **b** It turns pinkish like soda with iodine. **c** It fizzes in vinegar.	Different *combinations* of properties mean different powders.	The combination of properties is not exactly like any so far. **a** Sugar **b** Soda **c** Soda, probably sugar and soda

Evaluation:
For the teacher: Lesson 8 serves as a natural test. The teacher can look for the plans children have for solving the problem. She can check whether they record results, etc.

For the unit evaluation:

1 Performance test
   a Set up eight capfuls (two cases per powder of the four referent powders) and label them: "Soda," "Starch," "Sugar," "Salt."
   b Have three containers and label them: "Water," "Iodine," "Vinegar."
   c Give the child two capfuls of a new powder mixture. The problem is to identify the new mixture.

2 Oral or written test item (mental experiment)
   Suppose you had three liquids that were slightly yellow or brown. How could you find out whether
   a They are all the same?
   b Two are the same, but one is different?
   c All three are different?

Note:
This item reverses the emphasis, shifting it from the *detection of types of powders* using the liquids to detection of types of liquids using the powders as detectors. It involves no new concepts but simply alters the sequence of thought. Even the operations performed do not change. Only the items which are unknown change.

CHAPTER 17

"She don't tell me nothin'. She just gimme back the paper."

—ANGRY FIFTH-GRADE BOY

"Well, our science teacher makes us think up our own answers. Then we try it. If it works, it's good enough."

"Yeah. If it doesn't, you try something else. And we argue, but you have to be able to show it. If you can't show it, then you shouldn't say it."

"I don't like the lab notes we have to make. I know its good and all, but I don't like it."

—COMMENTS BY STUDENTS ON A FIFTH-GRADE SCIENCE CLASS

EVALUATION

OBJECTIVES

At the conclusion of this chapter and its associated activities, you should be able to do the following:

1 Distinguish between norm-referenced and criterion-referenced testing.

2 Recognize that evaluation is a special form of investigation.

3 State some procedures for getting data on students' performance.

4 State some procedures for getting a coarse indication of emotional climate.

5 Identify the kind of information to be collected, before a test, that permits the teacher to infer which of many reasons could account for a student's failure to answer a question.

INTRODUCTION

In one way or another, all of this book is about evaluation —if by evaluation we mean the attempt to understand what makes things work as they do, or the inquiry that goes with trying to make things work in some new or more effective manner. Evaluation is subject to the same kinds of restrictions as any disciplined search in science; that is, it must have its roots in some kind of data. Just as in scientific research, the variables may be both quantitative and qualitative, measurable and not measurable; in education we collect both kinds of information and make judgments about their implication for decision making.

In a scientific investigation, people usually do not collect data at random. Instead, according to the intention of their inquiry, they pick and choose from a rich stimulus-filled world what they deem relevant and *ignore* the rest, at least for the moment. So too in evaluation, the questions to be answered require that some things be temporarily ignored while others receive detailed attention. Making decisions about what to ignore and what to include as relevant does not invalidate a scientific investigation. On the contrary, such decisions make progress possible, since the world is far too rich in possibilities to allow inclusion of them all. The same limitations apply to evaluation. Enough happens in just a few minutes of classroom discourse to keep a person who wishes to explore all its facets busy for several days. Most of us do not have that kind of time. We have to be selective.

Evaluation is part of the effort to reduce the number of decisions which people make that are based wholly on unsupported introspection and relatively untutored feelings about what is happening. It is a process in which values and knowledge become coupled. But you must be warned: data have a way of shattering fancies and dispersing illusions. Some people so harbor their fancies that they reject all attempts to evaluate. Part of that rejection probably has to do with trust: they suspect the way in which the judgment process might go on and see judgment in the context of "good" and "bad," instead of in a framework of inquiry. For them such information does not convey more insight into their own operations; it simply becomes a weapon in the hands of others. Such fears are not entirely without justification. Data are data and nothing more. What people make of them, however, is another matter.

What data people decide might be relevant depends

on what they intend to do with the information. All the latitude in selection and interpretation of data naturally makes for problems. Any successful evaluation process must have its origin in an atmosphere of trust. Students, who furnish information by taking tests, answering questions, and undergoing observation, must trust their teachers to use the information wisely. Sometimes students must help their teachers to do so. Teachers, for their part, must trust administrators, parents, and children to act sensibly about whatever data they think should be collected. And parents—they have to trust the whole system to work effectively for their children.

In science a theory can only encompass the available facts and suggest what to look for next. Investigations always proceed in a context of incomplete knowledge. The application of knowledge to particular settings must necessarily go on under conditions of even greater uncertainty, since each situation has some unique as well as nonunique characteristics. Before involving yourself in this chapter, you may find it useful to review Chapter 7, Conflict and Inquiry, and Chapter 9, Science and Soul: Some Musings on Fate Control, where the philosophy of dealing with uncertain systems is discussed. The burden of those discussions might be summarized in the following way: You learn to live with some level of uncertainty, which is partially related to the degree of knowledge you have about a system. When you have more knowledge, that means you know more about the relationships, and the system becomes potentially a little more predictable. When you know how the elements of the system are probably connected, you can plan in such a way that the system can be made to function for you. When you have less knowledge, you necessarily operate intuitively more of the time and are less certain about the outcomes.

Fear and anxiety are high in a random world. On the other hand, frustration and anger are high in a world that is too stable, too unresponsive to our needs. Evaluation helps you maintain some reasonable balance between these two extremes.

COLLECTING DATA THAT MEAN SOMETHING

In planning an evaluation program, you need to be certain that the devices you employ to collect data do, in fact, collect the data you intended to obtain. That means you must know what kind of information you want and approximately how long it will take to get it. If you know *why* you want it, so much the better. For any information you anticipate collecting, ask yourself two questions:

1 What would I or the student do with the data if we had them?
2 Given the answer to question 1, is the way in which I plan to collect the data appropriate to my intention?

If you cannot supply good answers to those questions, you should probably not bother to collect that category of information.

COLLECTING START-UP AND FEEDBACK DATA

By the time children arrive in your classroom or come to you for instruction, they are all operating with personal "thought systems." Children differ in the kind of information that attracts them. They share some values but do not act predictably in relation to those values. They can be unbelievably cruel or kind, depending on the whim of the moment. Some children like taking in information one way (e.g., orally), and some prefer getting their information another way (e.g., visually, through reading and movies). Children organize information according to both shared and unique sets of tenets. Their attempts to explain the world they experience are wonderful and fearful in their mixture of insight and illogic. They come from all kinds of homes, and there is no chance of starting their training over. Parents, teachers, and students alike must take what is given in themselves at any moment in time and work from there. Every day they change a little; but, for the most part, you are still the same. Experience does things to the way they deal with the world and the way they think about what happens to them. The change is gradual, barely detectable. That is what makes monitoring change so difficult. The problem is to make the process visible so that you can help students use the knowledge of it to improve the quality of their efforts.

By getting into the habit of collecting information and using it to plan the next steps in instruction, you increase the chance that the instruction will be appropriate to the state of skills and knowledge possessed by the students. Some of the suggestions that follow for collecting and using data are a little unorthodox, but the arguments in their favor are cogent. People do evaluation for three reasons: diagnosis and prescription; administrative decision making; and program evaluation. None of those cases really calls for rigorous research designs. The case in which we have particular interest—diagnosis and prescription—focuses sharply on individuals and their needs. Since that aspect of evaluation is not yet well developed, being unorthodox can only be an asset.

Start-up data include all the data that would be useful in planning a next phase of instruction. Such data are available under a great many guises. *Feedback* is all the data collected in the course of instruction that prompt modification of instruction and learning. The techniques for collecting data described below can apply to either start-up or feedback. These techniques are intended to supply data, so that diagnosis of learning and planning of instruction can proceed in a way that depends less on whims and magic and more on what actually happens in the system.

Listening and recording

When an anthropologist wants to study some segment of another culture, he often mingles with, listens to, and watches the activities of the people who interest him. Sometimes he becomes a *participant observer,* taking part in the activities of the culture as a new learner. This approach makes sense, since the new culture frequently differs radically from his own, so that taking part *without trying to direct or shape the activity* helps him learn the nature of it. The same approach may be useful in the classroom for teachers who want to appraise the processes going on around them. Just as the anthropologist may learn about people while they work and talk, so the teacher has a remarkably rich opportunity to learn about children while they work with scientific phenomena.

If they are permitted, children talk while they work. The talk is part of their effort to make their own kind of sense out of what they experience, and it tells something about the kind of progress they are making. For the teacher prepared to listen, the conversations of children supply at least the following kinds of information:

1 What they observe or are attending to
2 What they fail to observe or talk about
3 What sequences of events they thought happened

What can a teacher learn about students from interacting in the laboratory?

4 What puzzles them and what they do about it
5 What ideas they conjure up to explain events
6 How complete their explanations are

In addition, for teachers interested in language development, the dialogues prompted by engagement with scientific phenomena provide rich opportunities to study certain properties of language in use:

1 Vocabulary in use; i.e., active vocabulary
2 Sentence structure in use
3 Length of explanations
4 Coherence of discourse

By occasionally tape-recording samples of children's discourse, the teacher can make permanent dated records, useful for documentation, of what they said. These tape recordings are helpful for diagnosis and valuable for comparison with future samples of behavior. The tapes have at least two other uses. For students, they become sources for analyzing their own reasoning. When they hear a playback, students often go through a new clarification process, which helps them to learn to use language with increasing precision. They also come to find it valuable to listen to each other, so that during analysis their peers will not accuse them of unnecessary repeating. If they learn to use the tapes to analyze their own arguments, they will come more quickly to the distinctions between evidence and inference, and to the way in which a set of ideas is put together to form an explanation.

For parents, tape recordings can give a great deal of insight into the nature and quality of work going on in which their own children are directly involved. The tapes may also be useful in helping parents learn how to listen. The use of videotapes adds still another dimension of information for parents, since videotapes help them see what is going on as the children work. Information for, as well as from, parents is part of evaluation. The parent is one consumer of evaluation reports.

Example: Transcript 17-1. Examine Transcript 17-1, which was recorded while children worked with simple electric circuits that included batteries, bulbs, and two kinds of wires. Activities of this kind appear in one form or another in virtually all elementary science programs and so may be taken as representative. The conversation took place between two fourth-graders during the third classroom session on circuits. Previously they had connected lightbulbs to dry cells and used the appearance of light as evidence of interaction. Between experimenting and talking with the teacher, they had apparently learned that there would be no evidence of interaction unless they formed a completed circuit. By the time this conversation took place, all children in the class could complete a circuit—i.e., connect the lightbulb to the dry cell by means of wires in such a way that the bulb lit. The lighted bulb supplied the evidence for the existence of a complete circuit (see Figure 17-1). Consider what the conversation teaches us about the state of knowledge of the speakers.

Just before the conversation, the children received a piece of nichrome wire to put into the circuit in place of the bulb. Nichrome wire is a poor conductor of electricity. Its resistance is evidenced by the fact that the wire heats up. Putting it in the circuit is like creating a traffic jam on a major highway. Everything throughout the circuit heats up, rather like the heating up that happens in a traffic jam. Little flow of current occurs anywhere in the circuit. The wire becomes detectably warm.

From the talk of the children, you can infer what has already happened. Note that something failed to happen according to their expectations and that this failure provoked the conversation. As they try to rationalize the difference between what did happen and what they apparently thought should happen, you can tell what concepts they are employing and how they *use* those concepts as they hunt for meaning. At this juncture in the conversation, they have just connected both the bulb and the nichrome wire into the circuit, as shown in Figure 17-1.

In this short piece of interaction between two fourth-grade boys and a simple electric circuit, the teacher can learn a great deal about the knowledge the boys already possess relative to the problem in hand—*knowledge in use*. That is what a listener can assess in this bit of exchange. Here an observer can tell how previous experi-

Transcript 17-1

	Dialogue	*On-the-spot analysis*
First child	That's crazy. Why didn't that bulb light? If this is the positive end of the battery, it should go on. The electricity is going all the way around the circuit because everything is connected.	**Observation** made: the bulb did not light. Checks system and **states concept** governing the checking: circuits must be complete.
Second child	Maybe something's loose, or maybe this funny wire [pointing to the nichrome wire they had just put in the circuit] doesn't conduct. [Pause, about 5 seconds.] Hey—this [the nichrome] is getting hot. Wow. Feel it. It's pretty hot.	**Looks for some condition** that might mean the concept does not apply. **Observation** made: one wire is hot.
First child	[Feels wire.] That's proof it's electricity. It's going around the circuit or it wouldn't heat up if it wasn't. So why doesn't the bulb light? Its like this wire [the nichrome] is holding up the electricity. But nothing is supposed to happen if there isn't a circuit. We know that. So there is a circuit, but the bulb isn't going on.	Gives **evidence** for concept: there is interaction. **Identifies inconsistency. Suggests explanation.** There is **evidence** of interaction. Electricity is flowing, but the bulb does not light.
Second child	Maybe it just isn't enough electricity to light the bulb. Let's take it [the nichrome] out and put this in instead [a piece of aluminum foil used earlier]. If it lights again, then we know it's something to do with this wire [the nichrome].	Tries to put the inconsistent events into a rational context. **Designs experiment.**

ences governed expectations. In this case, when the boys completed a circuit, they expected a light. When those expectations were not met—that is, when the observations seemed to present an inconsistency—the teacher was able to see and hear how the children tried to incorporate their findings within the schema they already possessed. It is also possible in this bit of discourse to observe a very exciting event, *the birth of a new idea,* which will probably be the next concept to be incorporated within their schema: the nichrome wire might be "holding up" the electricity in some way.

These two children next hit on the idea that the nichrome wire might be using up electricity, so they tried putting the bulb in the circuit in different places to see if they could get it to light before the electricity was "used up." They went back and forth between a "holding up" and a "using up" explanation for what was going on. In any event, the presence of the materials and the problem created an occasion for their thought processes to become visible through the agency of conversation.

Small groups as an assessment technique

Thus, it may be a useful assessment technique to put children into small groups, present them with some stimulus or problem (or whatever you choose to call an event that provokes conversation), and then listen carefully to their conversation. Since this technique of presenting a stimulus, problem, or situation is intended to give you information about the learners, you must be careful not to intrude into the process. Your problem is to discover what their conceptual organization is like and how it is functioning, so you must be careful not to impress your own organization on them. Their problem is to engage in the structured experience you provide in such a way that they emerge having confirmed some ideas they already had, or having developed one or more new ideas and assimilated them.

You can observe closely only four or five pairs of children during the course of a 40-minute session. You sample the behavior of each pair for 2 or 3 minutes at a time, move on, and sometimes return to see what progress a pair has made. This means that any pair of children may be observed approximately every third or fourth day. But you can do something else. You can develop a set of structured experiences, which children completing some unit of activity can try. As some children feel they have mas-

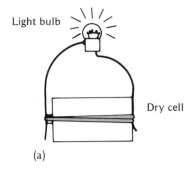

(a)

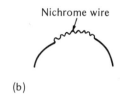

(b)

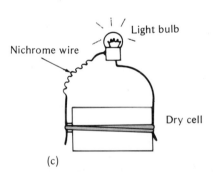

(c)

FIGURE 17-1
Batteries in circuits.

tered a topic, they can try out one of the investigations or structured experiences. (An example of such a problem is described later, in the discussion of performance testing.) You can listen in from time to time to observe how they are progressing. According to how the assessment experience is structured, the children may be called upon to use measurement skills previously learned, to use knowledge already acquired, to organize data, to draw inferences, and to design an experiment. What they have to do depends on what you are trying to assess. If you have previously done a task analysis (see Chapter 16) of each structured experience, you will be able to identify the points at which greatest difficulty seems to be occurring for a particular child or group, and you will then be able to provide help.

Using a number line to help in assessment

Sometimes it is useful to know how well children liked a particular kind of activity. It may also be useful to know when children feel very confident about what they are doing and when they feel less certain about what they know. Building interactions and confidence may be important objectives of instruction. On occasion it may also

FIGURE 17-2
Use of number lines.

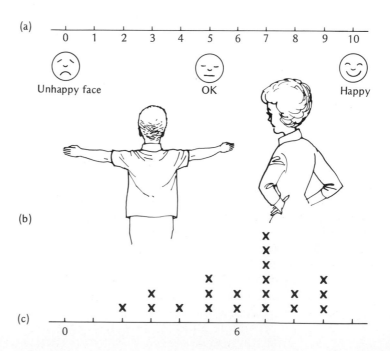

be helpful in planning to obtain an estimate from children of how hard they felt they worked on a particular task or how difficult they thought it was. A very simple technique for collecting such information is to use a number line as a measuring device (see Figure 17-2).

Make a long number line, perhaps as long as four feet, on a strip of paper and attach labels to it at intervals. Put it on a wall, easily accessible to the children. Suppose, for example, you want to know from a child how much he liked or disliked a particular activity. You ask him to show you by using the number line. He puts his two hands on the line and shows you how much he liked the activity by how far apart or close together he places his hands (Figure 17-2*a* and *b*). If he liked it only a little bit, then his hands will be close together on the line. If he liked it a lot, then his hands will be far apart on the line. You simply write down the distance between the two hands. If he did not like the activity at all, he puts both hands on top of each other right over the zero on the number line.

You can also get some indication of how confident children feel that they know how to do something, or how well they feel they have mastered a subject or topic, by using a number line. Suppose, for example, you presented a problem and the children worked out answers to it. Some students might feel sure of their results. Others might not. They can all indicate what they felt about how correct, complete, or sensible their answers were. They simply indicate this on the number line by the distance between their hands. The farther apart the hands, the surer they are about the correctness of their answers. It is useful to start with a ground rule that the left hand will always be placed on the zero as a starting point and the right hand moved out along the line as far as the child thinks appropriate.

Older children, those in third through eighth grade, can quickly learn to indicate the same information on a smaller number line by putting an X at the appropriate point on the line or drawing an arrow to that point. You can routinely place such number lines on tests or laboratory papers to get some feedback from students about how difficult they perceived something to be, how much they liked or disliked an activity, how much confidence they had in their answers, etc. (see Figure 17-2*c*).

I sometimes ask students to show how much more of a particular subject they think there might still be left to learn some day. A question you might pose using the number line, which can help you make decisions about moving students on to new subjects or about the level of sophistication of the materials that you should use next, is this: "How much more time do you think you need to learn or complete x?" Here, x stands for anything being studied at the time. If the students really feel the need for more time or more examples or more investigation, then they will indicate fairly large distances on the number line. If they want to move on or out of a topic, then they will show only small intervals on the number line.

Sometimes children work well but not as well as they might. The reasons can come from many directions: physical or emotional conditions on a particular day; the quality of interaction with their partners (psychosocial factors); confusion about what they are to do; insufficient knowledge; and low interest. The number-line technique allows the children to tell you, and themselves, how hard they felt they worked or how well they thought they worked. If they indicate a rather small spread between the hands as they place them on the number line, then it may be useful once in a while to find out what accounted for their estimates. It is equally useful to know what prompts them to work hard, to persist in the face of difficulties. Often they can tell you. The knowledge may help you improve the conditions for learning.

It is occasionally helpful to show a class how its members responded to some activity, and then to let the class discuss how the activity might be changed so that more students would give it a better rating. One group of children told me that my way of getting materials back in place at the end of a class not only rushed them but also made them turn in things before they were properly cleaned or stacked. As a result of that conversation, they devised their own system for restoring order to the room. It was better—and a lot less work for me. Once children grow accustomed to the idea of giving and receiving feedback, a great deal more information begins to flow between them and the teacher, especially when the teacher demonstrates that he or she has constructive responses to make. Feedback is one form of evaluation.

TESTS AND TESTING IN SCIENCE

Limitations

While the technology for standardized testing is well developed, the kinds of testing techniques that will produce information useful for guiding teachers and students are practically nonexistent. Standardized testing is mainly useful for institutional decision making and program evaluation. With its emphasis on end products, it leaves someone holding the bag. If some group fails to perform according to expectation, then the policy makers can only conclude that somewhere along the line something went wrong—and everybody is free to think up explanations. Only rarely does someone analyze the test items to discover what kinds of difficulties accounted for poor performance. Consequently, few of the people actually involved in the process of education, especially teachers and students, get helpful information. From the point of view of modern elementary science programs, with their emphasis on production, organization, and interpretation by students of data from experiments, standardized tests give little help to teachers who are trying to improve the way in which students go about that process.

Psychological theory is not of much help when it comes to understanding how students aggregate and reshuffle concepts in the course of generating and solving problems. Certainly the research on context learning suggests that the ways in which this process goes on may be as numerous as the students who are attacking a particular problem. It may well be that a student would learn more about himself by analyzing his own performance than by comparing his test scores with those of other students. In addition, some students take longer to work through certain problems than do others. What usually appears on a test paper is only the end product of certain very individualistic processes. That is one reason why ordinary tests do not function particularly well for diagnostic purposes. They do not yield information about the strategies students use when they confront a problematic situation, but it may be the strategies—the ways people develop of seeking solutions to difficulties—that have the greatest significance for later performance in occupational and social roles.

The ways in which an individual student reaches a solution are partly a function of the kinds of concepts, hypotheses, or ideas he holds about a situation, and partly a function of the *combinations* of ideas he tries out. If some good diagnostic techniques adopted to specific programs could be developed, we might begin to get a more precise idea of how an individual organizes and uses his knowledge. Techniques of organizing and applying knowledge are what will probably prove useful to the student in the long run.

Another limitation of standardized testing is that tests fail to model the "real" world. Normally a test specifies the boundaries of a problem. Often a test asks the student to choose between a fixed number of alternatives (for example, a multiple-choice test provides the list of alternatives from which the student chooses); but how often do real-life problems come along with a nice list of the possible solutions all drawn up? *Half the difficulty in real-life problem solving is finding out what such a list ought to include.* In modern science programs, part of the training focuses on developing many possible explanations and then finding ways to decide which of them make better choices. Can you model that kind of process on a test?

Whatever its difficulties in any other field, testing in science presents especially hazardous problems to anyone who cares about the quality of the values and thought a science program is supposed to generate. Scientific relationships form a web which both enmeshes and originates from a multitude of empirical events. To "understand" in science means to know how an idea or fact participates in that network. No concept can be grasped in isolation. That would be like dropping a stitch in knitting—it leaves an ugly hole in an otherwise beautiful pattern. A part of the diagnostic process may be to find a way to construct tests that show what kind of an "idea map" a student develops and how he uses it to get from one point to another in an investigation.

While the problems connected with testing are numerous and difficult, they are not insurmountable. Any inquiry into nature presents problems to the observer. Not only must he decide which variables are relevant and which may be ignored, but he must also find some way to detect and measure them. Testing is nothing more than this basic problem of investigation transferred to the classroom.

It is amazing with what vigor we go about the business of writing and administering tests when they contribute so little in the way of information that can be directly used to guide instruction and learning.

Factors affecting performance and interpretation

Conditions that exist before administration of a test frequently govern the interpretation or meaning that can be assigned to the results. Consider a few factors that relate to performance on tests and to decisions that depend on performance.

Time as a factor in interpretation of tests.   It makes a difference *when* in the course of events a student takes a test. If, as sometimes happens, he takes a test before he has completed the work of a unit, what does the test provide in the way of useful information? Furthermore, if he takes a test administered under strict time limits, will his performance be the same as it would be if there were no stringent time limits? These are not trivial questions, because the kind of answers you give partly determine how much helpful information tests will give you.

Suppose, as a case in point, that a student fails to answer certain questions. That constitutes information. How do you interpret it? What set of teaching decisions might you make on the basis of it? You could imagine that failure to respond might be accounted for by the fact that a child failed to finish the unit, that he did not have time to complete the test, that he completed the unit but did not understand the content, that he did not understand the question, that he cannot read well enough to know

FIGURE 17-3

Interpretation problem presented by a failure to respond to a test item.

Data	Possible inferences	Teaching decisions	Comments
No response.	Failed to finish the unit.	Get this information in the future. Wait for completion before retesting.	Use a number line or a check list preceding the test.
	Finished unit but did not understand it.	Check back over main ideas to find what is wrong.	
	Did not have enough time to finish the test.	Consider flexible time limits.	
	Simply did not remember the necessary information.	Consider letting him use his notes if he has any.	Examine cues to see if they are sufficient and in a *format* that is appropriate.
	Does not understand the question or item.	Find out what he thinks the statement asks him to do.	
	Cannot read well enough to know what the question or item asks him to do.	Make the items available on audiotapes or perhaps in figural form.	
	Has no interest in the unit or the test items.		Use a number line to get some indication of the degree of interest before the test.

what the question asked, or that he did not care about the unit or the question. (See Figure 17-3.)

What sense can you make out of failure to respond to a question? Unless you can specify for each student the conditions that accompany the test situation, the amount of useful diagnostic information you will get will be small in comparison with the effort that goes into preparing the test and evaluating it—and in comparison with the damage the test may do the self-concepts of students and teachers alike. (Of course, some teachers employ tests as a whip. In that case, a child's failure to respond will generally be the occasion for punishment rather than for diagnosis.

Suppose we stop for a moment to question the use of *time limits* on science tests—i.e., requiring students to write responses to items within some fixed time interval. The alternatives to time limits are unrestricted time to complete items and very flexible limits. What do time limits accomplish? If you can answer that, then you can decide how time limits should be set or when they should be abandoned. While many problems that scientists confront must be solved as rapidly as possible, only rarely can they count on pursuing an investigation on a fixed time schedule. Nature is too intractable; so are people. The notion of fixed time limits, then, fails to model what goes on in science, and certainly flexible limits ought to be experimented with, at least a little, in the classroom.

Think of a simple experiment that would produce some useful data on which to base an answer to the question, What are the effects of time limits on test performance? You might give some of your more interesting tests on a fixed-interval plan and others on an open-interval plan. Compare the results. If you see no difference in the kind and quality of performance exhibited by each student, then the fixed interval, being more efficient, would be the usual practice. In that case you have to estimate an average time for completion. If, on the other hand, you detect qualitative differences that give you more diagnostic information, then the flexible-interval plan may be desirable.

Reading as a factor in interpretation of tests.   Failure to respond on a test item could be construed as a reading problem. If some students read poorly, test items will give very little diagnostic information so far as science is concerned. An analogy in a scientific investigation would be the use of a thermometer calibrated for measurement of low temperature systems, say under 60 degrees, in a system where temperatures normally run much higher, say 200 degrees. The best the thermometer would ever show is 60 degrees, which would not be at all representative of the temperature conditions in the system. All you could say is that the temperature probably exceeds 60 degrees. Giving a test in written form to someone who has a reading problem is like using the wrong thermometer in a system—the test will simply not represent the conditions in the system.

One thing you can do when there are reading problems is to supply sound as well as printed text for the questions. Tape-record the questions so that students can hear as well as see them as often as they require and whenever they require. Tape recordings offer the advantage of supplying a uniform stimulus. That is, the questions can be repeated to each student as many times as necessary in exactly the same way. Thus you control for differences in wording and inflection that frequently accompany the repeating of questions or items.

Cues as a factor in interpretation of tests. From research on how people put things into memory and retrieve them, it seems clear there is a relationship between how information was stored in the first place and how it can be gotten out of memory later on. Most information that is retained over a span of time and is meant to be useful is learned and stored in some kind of context. (See Chapter 7.) That is especially the case with modern elementary science programs which deemphasize rote memory and mimicry as a way of learning. If you are to avoid underestimating what a student knows, a test item must either supply sufficient context to suggest what pieces of information probably are pertinent or present a problem stimulus which acts as a first-level organizer. Such a problem suggests to the student which sets of relationships probably apply. These contexts then provide the basis for deciding which pieces of information should be given. It all functions something like an index system in which you find broad topical ideas that subsume other topics, which in turn subsume others, and so on. The test items must somehow turn on that "looking up" facility in the brain—otherwise the test will tend to underestimate the state of knowledge. It will fail to get the information out of storage.

Tests as diagnostic instruments

If science is a kind of thinking and doing process that depends on possession of a growing network of relationships, you need some way of making the process visible so that you can study it to learn how to help it grow better. It will take great care to construct tests that will not do violence to the coherence of ideas and data which is the mark of science. The aesthetics of science lie in the appreciation of its patterns of concepts. It may be possible to construct a series of items which will show what in a situation arouses curiosity, how a student converts curiosity into a question that can be answered, how a student gathers and organizes inferences, and how a student connects the evidence together to form inferences. Then it may eventually be possible to determine in what forms learners organize their knowledge and what the content of their knowledge is.

Think back for a moment to the student who brought us into this discussion by failing to answer some test items. For each possible interpretation that you make of his situation, some corresponding instructional decision has to be made, as Figure 17-3, page 525, suggests. Tests are meant to be used, but they will be of little diagnostic help unless, as you construct items, you imagine how you would interpret various kinds of responses. Tests—in the sense in which they are referred to in this chapter, i.e., as diagnostic instruments—supply the base of evidence upon which to build some guesses about what might be reasonable next steps in instruction. Tests can supply helpful information to students as they analyze their own performance, provided they are used that way and provided that nobody takes them too seriously.

Performance tests. It would be perfectly appropriate in the context of modern elementary science programs to present problems which require students to design and perform simple experiments as one means of evaluating their knowledge of content and procedures. Performance tests present management problems, but their potential for studying how students elaborate and extend their thought patterns is tremendous.

To understand something of the information that can be acquired through performance testing, it is first necessary to make a brief digression to discuss the nature of concepts or definitions in science. Every definition and concept in science contains an implicit "do"—that is, an *operation* to perform. Sometimes the words used to state the definition or concept mask that fact. If a student fails to couple the content of the concept with the implicit operations, then the concept will be of little functional use to him. Consider the common example given here:

> *Concept: Like poles attract.*

What does it mean? What ideas must a student associate with the statement if its content is to be meaningfully available to him? As Figure 17-4 shows, the simple statement contains the notion of magnetic poles, the idea that there must be some way to distinguish two kinds of poles, and some sense of what the evidence is that gets tucked away under the word "attract." What the statement does not contain, except by implication, are the facts that to produce the phenomenon described—attraction of like poles—something has to be *moved,* and that then, to *detect the evidence,* some force has to be felt.

Performance tests provide a way of finding out how much of the concept the student actually has at his command. They can tell you and him whether he knows what operation to perform as well as what evidence to expect, since he actually does the operations and picks out the data. If the student fails to perform the operation or does not select relevant evidence, then you know how to proceed. You do not have to guess about the probable

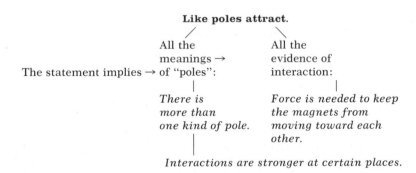

FIGURE 17-4

Illustrate the implicit content hidden in the statement of definitions. The statements develop relations between terms, and each term carries a set of meanings. The statements also carry an implicit operation.

causes. You can infer from observation what part of the network of relationships is apparently missing and can then design a bit of instruction that will add the missing part.

Performance tests have the added advantage of allowing you to make some accommodation to the differences in aptitude in the classroom. In contrast to more traditional test formats, performance tests allow students to encounter phenomena directly and then to organize them according to the means that best fit their own aptitudes. The difficulty with performance tests, however, is that they are time-consuming and that their results are sometimes difficult to interpret. Summarizing results with one number—i.e., giving a score—cannot be done so conveniently as with traditional test procedures. Performance tests require careful planning, usually involving a task analysis, if they are to be of most help in the appraisal of knowledge, skills, and reasoning. Often the tests must be administered individually or in small groups; consequently, they create some new management problems for certain kinds of classroom organizations.

Conflict of views on testing: Behaviorism and humanism. It may be well to digress for a moment to summarize two opposing views about the usefulness of evaluation. These views, in one form or another, insinuate themselves into the work of most educators. You probably can identify where you stand in relation to them. How a person approaches questions of evaluation will be determined by his membership in one camp or the other. A few eclectics borrow outrageously from both camps and probably learn a great deal. Members of the two camps will differ in the basic assumptions they make about what phenomena should be the focus of attention.

Beliefs of behaviorists:
Human behavior is lawful, predictable, and orderable.

This lawfulness makes it possible to state rules for controlling instruction.

Therefore, the sensible thing to do is to discover the laws and search for the rules.

There is a clear distinction between the knower and what is to be learned. Since the rules are known and the logic can be established, no importance is to be attached to feelings.

It follows that the curriculum should be prepared as a script which can be increasingly perfected. Evaluation is simply the business of measuring acquisition of the script.

Beliefs of humanists:
The search for rules is useless, since the world of man—i.e., social behavior—will not be well described by models or governed by rules.

Intellect, will, tastes, and passions condition the learner's reception of information. Making learning interesting is an important criterion. Ideas are complex and intertwined. They take years to develop, and piecemeal analysis makes a travesty of the pattern.

It follows that the curriculum should consist of loosely specified units. Evaluation involves the sensible appraisal of how children function in a great variety of circumstances and how they feel about what they are learning. Observation of students at work will give all the necessary information.

Science makes use of constructs embedded in networks of relationships. The humanists argue that the behaviorists make two mistakes. First, they break this network down to such minute elements that they end up with too many variables to be investigated. Second, no list of specific responses to situations, regardless of its extensiveness, can define a construct, since the construct is meant to apply to new situations which cannot even be specified at this point in time.

The behaviorists, for their part, say that the empirical evidence for the relation of interest to achievement is sketchy. Until they know more about that, they prefer to be able to make statements of the form suggested by Louis Guttman as well as by others:

Performance of student X (name) on an item presented in
(verbal)
(numerical) language (choose one)
(figural)

$$\text{and requiring} \begin{pmatrix} inference \\ application \end{pmatrix}$$

of a rule $\begin{pmatrix} choose \\ one \end{pmatrix}$ *(exactly like) (similar to) one taught* $\begin{pmatrix} choose \\ one \end{pmatrix}$
(unlike)

produced $\begin{matrix} (high) \\ (low) \end{matrix}$ *performance (choose one).*

The behaviorists argue that what one needs to know to think effectively in different fields tends to be specific to the field. What you should measure, according to this view, is achieved knowledge or specific skills, instead of general abilities such as critical thinking. Critical thinking is just the application of specific factual knowledge to specific problems. This group advocates working for mastery of specific content.

Actually, there are facets of both positions that can prove useful. If the humanists use the difficulty of the task as an excuse for sloppy thinking, then they deserve some prodding. If the behaviorists dissect the curriculum and responses of children into such tiny fragments that they destroy the entity—i.e., lose sight of the network—then they too must be prodded. For the classroom teacher, who must live day to day in the malestrom of behaviors that will not stay still long enough to be identified before they change again, the system is dynamic. Neither view really captures its essence. The teacher cannot wait; neither can the children. So they must dive in together to produce their own ways of monitoring development. The state of knowledge leaves them free to experiment—that is, to create the knowledge which is now missing.

Categorizing test items

With reference to verbal, numerical, and figural language, the reader should recall the research described in Chapter 7. Students who receive instruction that is cast primarily in formats matched to their patterns of aptitudes learn substantially more than do students who receive instruction in incompatible formats. Similarly, in test construction, the items may be presented in verbal, numerical, or figural language. The items may also be such as to elicit responses in any one of the formats. That is, there are two formats to consider: the format for asking the question and the format called for in the response. It is possible to construct a simple grid for categorizing the kinds of test items we might produce. By using a grid sheet designed like the one in Figure 17-5, or a similar design, you accomplish two ends:

1 As you enter items (actually item numbers) in the grid, you get a display that tells you what kinds of processes you are emphasizing, their relative

FIGURE 17-5

Grid for categorizing test items

Test for unit _____
Date constructed _____
Number of items _____

Processes	Format 1 Verbal	2 Numerical symbols	3 Figural	Novelty 4 Low (exactly like)	5 Moderate (similar to)	6 High (unlike)	Performance Low Sat. High
A Problem identification	Ex #1		Ex #1	Ex #1			
B Information, observation, data	Ex #2		Ex #2	Ex #2			
	Ex #3			Ex #3			
C Procedures, skills, design	D		C-6	C-6			
	E				E		
D Inference, empirical relationships	F		F_r			F	
			G			G	
	H		H_r			H	
E Explanation	Ex #4				Ex #4		
	H_2					H_2	
F Application	Ex #5		Ex #5		Ex #5		
	Ex #6a					Ex #6a	
	Ex #6b		Ex #6b			Ex #6b	
	I				I		

Items in the form "Ex #1" refer to examples in the text. Letters refer to items on the sample test. The subscript "r" refers to the response to an item.

For each item enter in the performance column the number of individuals whose performance was high, the number whose performance was satisfactory, and the number whose performance was low. By comparing data from several tests you can find out what categories of items require more practice.

Staple this sheet to one copy of the test.

novelty, and the language formats in which the items are being presented.

2 Examination of a series of grid sheets will show you what categories are being omitted or are getting very little use.

If we now modify Guttman's sentence, the relation between it and the grid in Figure 17-5 becomes apparent:

Performance of student X (name) on an item presented in

Question format
(verbal)
(numerical) language (choose one) and requiring
(figural)

Cognitive operation   **Novelty**

(problem identification)

(information, data, observation)

(inference, empirical relations) $\begin{pmatrix} choose \\ one \end{pmatrix}$ *(exactly like)*

(explanation)   *(similar to) one taught* $\begin{pmatrix} choose \\ one \end{pmatrix}$

(application)   *(unlike)*

                                              Response format

(high)   *(verbal)*

produced (satisfactory) performance $\begin{pmatrix} choose \\ one \end{pmatrix}$ *in a (numerical) format* $\begin{pmatrix} choose \\ one \end{pmatrix}$

(low)   *(figural)*

The difinitions of the five categories—problem identification, observation, inference, explanation, and application—need not be too rigorous. You can take the suggested meanings given below or modify them as you see fit, but once you select a definition try to be consistent in the way you apply it. If you fail to be consistent, then you may assign a question to a particular category one time, and a few days later assign it to a different category. That would make the data on the grid sheet practically useless for monitoring your own process of test construction. Your system would have little reliability.

A. Problem identification.   Concepts in science do not exist in isolation. Instead, they contain explicit and implicit components. (Refer again to Figure 17-4.) All concepts or ideas are tied together with other ideas. If a student has formed the connections among ideas and understands the hierarchy, he will be able to identify inconsistencies in an argument or in a description of experimental outcomes. If he has not formed key connections, then he will fail to find an inconsistency where one exists. Consider these sample test items constructed from the unit "Spinning Tables" of the Elementary Science Study. A section of this unit is analyzed in Chapter 16.

(You can make a simple spinning wheel by taking an ordinary lazy Susan and taping a piece of paper to it. A record player is somewhat better, but the lazy Susan will be good enough for you to examine the variables yourself.)

Example 1

Jim, Betty, and Lee each produced a pattern that looked like this [see top of opposite page]:

Jim said he got it by moving his pencil in a straight line fairly fast. Betty said she moved the wheel counterclockwise:

Lee said he did it by moving the wheel fast.

                                     X

1 *Are they all right?*   ————   ————
                                  Yes   *No*

2 *Explain your answer.*

Note that the format of this question is both figural and verbal. Novelty is low, since the pattern is exactly like one produced in class. To respond, the students have to recognize that Jim, Betty, and Lee all produced the same result and that they probably all did it in the same way. The reason they each give apparently different reports lies in the fact that they each reported only part of the whole process. The pattern could be produced by moving the wheel counterclockwise, moving the pencil in a straight line at a fairly fast speed, and then adjusting the speed of the wheel. The speed of the wheel and the speed of the pencil together determine the extent of curvature. The direction of curvature depends on whether the wheel is spun clockwise or counterclockwise. The student has to reconcile three different reports.

B. Information, observation, data. This category, which you will recognize from the task analysis, includes all questions calling for knowledge of facts, reports of observations or identification of observations, and all data in any form.

Example 2
Draw the three different patterns that you produced during the experiment.

Note that this item calls for reporting data that have low novelty, i.e., for exactly what was done during the experiment conducted earlier. The presentation format is verbal with a figural response.

Example 3

In the paragraph about Jim, Betty, and Lee, what are the data?

Note that this item calls for recognizing data and distinguishing data from procedures. Novelty is low. The format is verbal (with a figural response). The data consist of the drawings made by Jim, Betty, and Lee. The procedures are the ways they said they produced the figures.

C. Procedures, skills.   You will recognize this category also from the task analysis; it includes all descriptions, identifications of procedure, and design of experiments. It includes questions of procedure that attempt to get at sequence of procedures and all items that attempt to assess performance of some skill, such as measurement of temperature, use of a magnifier, or measurement of weight.

D. Inference, empirical relations. All attempts to relate one variable to another are included in this category. Hypotheses also fall into this category.

E. Explanation. This category includes those items that require students to put together concepts or inferences in order to show how they are related. It may involve both *analysis* and *synthesis.*

Analysis of elements is the use of concepts or variables and the specification of *relationships* as steps in the production of an explanation.

Synthesis is the process of combining variables or relationships or both, by means of logical connectors. It definitely involves arranging ideas in some kind of *order* or specifying the network of relations that is pertinent.

Example 4

Even though you moved the pencil along a straight line, the pattern produced on the spinning table was a curve. Explain why you think that happened.

Note that this is a question in verbal format. It has some novelty in that it refers to a supposedly familiar situation, but the question has not been asked. It calls for the statement of relationships between variables.

F. Application. This category encompasses the use of relationships in new or additional problems in order to achieve a solution.

Example 5

Here is a picture of a moving belt or band such as one you might find in a food market to carry groceries to the checkout counter. Suppose you tried to draw a line straight across the belt with a piece of chalk while the belt was moving. Show the pattern you would get.

If you draw a line with chalk while the belt is moving, what does the resulting line look like?

Note that this question is in a mixed format, verbal and figural. It has some novelty since it involves a straight rather than a spinning surface. (It would have novelty if the students had not worked with such belts prior to starting on the spinning table.) But it is similar to the work covered in the unit in that it calls for putting together two variables, the moving pencil and a moving belt, instead of a moving lazy Susan, to make a predication.

Example 6a

Suppose a boat started across a river that was running fairly fast in the direction shown by the arrow. Draw a picture of the path or course of the boat until it reaches the opposite side.

Example 6b (alternative)

Suppose a boat starts at the point on one side of the river marked "Start," and it heads across to the opposite side of the river. The river is moving in the direction shown by the arrow. Will the boat end up at point A, B, C, D, or E?

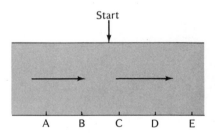

Note that the two forms ask for essentially the same information. The figural presentation in the alternative form would be helpful to some students. The item has high novelty in that the situation is unlike any previously encountered. The student has to see that the flow of the river may be thought of in the same way as the moving belt—i.e., the moving river corresponds to the moving belt. Thus he must analyze the situation to see whether it corresponds to one he already knows.

Novelty. Items that are high on novelty—i.e., that are unlike any presented during instruction—will help you distinguish children who are especially insightful relative to the content of the unit in question. In a new unit, different children may solve the most novel problems. In setting achievement criteria, I am inclined to consider these items as optional. It is delightful when some of the children do them successfully, but the expectation for good performance on them by a majority of the class members should not be a part of the criterion.

Difficulty.   It is often useful to predict performance on each of the items. Another way of saying the same thing is to rate each question according to its predicted difficulty. Assign a value to each item:

> Low difficulty, i.e., easy. Should be successfully done by nearly all the students (more than 90 percent). These items represent the minimum criteria. (Percentages are rough estimates made on the basis of your knowledge of the class.)

> Normal difficulty. These items usually will be successfully done by more than 75 percent of the class. They usually contain some novelty, or they require ideas to be analyzed, synthesized, or applied. The longer the chain of reasoning, the more difficult the item becomes.

> High difficulty. These items usually are highly novel. They often call for the statement of abstractions or the compounding of somewhat sophisticated explanations. They are not ordinarily part of the achievement criteria set for the class.

Once the students take the test, you can compare actual performance with predicted performance. The objective is for the children to be facile on all six processes, it is hoped at the first two levels of novelty—i.e., on items that are exactly like those encountered in the unit and items that are similar to those encountered but contain some new aspect.

Interest.   The number of children who try the optional problems becomes a rough indicator of level of interest. Students whose interest is high are more likely to try items that are voluntary. This information, coupled with information obtained by using a number line on which students give an indication of their level of interest in the unit, should enable you to distinguish students who are turned on and students who are turned off by the unit. Not only does that information help you decide which units to retain and which to drop, it sometimes suggests that the

Who listens and who asks?

method of presentation may need to be changed. If you keep track of the students who are turned on and turned off in each unit, you may be able to distinguish and give special assistance to those at either end of the spectrum, the persistently bored as well as the persistently excited. Remember, it is not in the nature of people to be equally interested in all things all the time.

Interest is a legitimate objective of instruction in science. The problem is to identify indicators of interest. I have suggested two: the number-line indicator and the voluntary performance of more difficult, optional problems. You will think of other indications if this objective has high priority for you. I have sometimes used task persistence—i.e., working a problem through to completion at some satisfactory level—as an indicator of interest. Such a judgment would be made during laboratory phases of instruction.

Constructed and structured responses. A sample test based on the section of task analysis of the "Spinning Table" unit appears on pages 540–541. The item numbers

Sample test for the portion of the unit "Spinning Tables" which was task analyzed in the preceding chapter.

Name _____

Date _____

A Did you complete this unit before today? _____ , _____
                                              Yes   No
  If the answer is no, how much more time do you think you would need? _____

B Show on the number line how you felt about the unit.

  0   1   2   3   4   5   6   7   8   9   10
Completely   Interesting   All of it
boring   exciting

C Here are some patterns students made during the experiments.

  A   B   C   D

  E   F   G   H

  1 Which pattern might have been drawn while the wheel was not moving? _____
  2 Which might have been drawn while the wheel moved clockwise? _____
  3 Which might have been drawn with the pencil left in one place? _____
  4 Which might have been drawn while the wheel moved rapidly? _____
  5 Which might have been drawn while the wheel moved slowly? _____
  6 Which might have been drawn while the wheel moved counterclockwise? _____

D What must you do to make a curve like the one above?

_____

_____

E If you want less of a curve, what must you do?

_____

_____

F (*Optional.*) In a way you can think of the earth as a spinning table. Suppose you fired a rocket out from the earth near the equator. What path do you think it would seem to follow? Draw the path on the diagram. (Neglect gravity for the time being.)

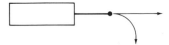

G Two boys pull on a wagon. One wants to go straight ahead, and one wants to run in a circle. On the diagram, show the path you think the wagon would follow.

H (*Optional.*) Suppose you fired the rocket out from the earth at the North Pole. What path do you think it would seem to follow? (Neglect gravity for the time being.)

   1 If you answered question F as well as question H, would the answers be the same?

                               _____   _____

                               Yes   No

   2 Explain how you made your decision.

    _____

    _____

    _____

I If you know you moved the pencil across the spinning table in a *straight* line, how do you explain the fact that the pencil mark is *curved*?

    _____

    _____

    _____

Note to the teacher: As a cuing device, you can furnish each student taking the test with a straight pin, a piece of cardboard, and a strip of paper so that he can set up a small model to help work out answers. Alternatively, students may use any records they made during the unit.

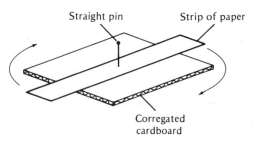

Straight pin   Strip of paper

Corregated
cardboard

Alternative versions for some of the questions on the sample test.

Alternative to item C

C Check all the statements that apply to each figure.

List of figures	Wheel not moving	Wheel moving slowly	Wheel moving fast	Wheel moving clockwise	Wheel moving counter-clockwise	Pencil moving straight	Pencil moving slowly	Pencil moving fast
A								
B								
C								
D								

Alternative to item F

F In a way you can think of the earth as a spinning table. Suppose you fired a rocket out from the earth at a point somewhere near the equator. Choose the figures which you think might show the path which the rocket seems to take.

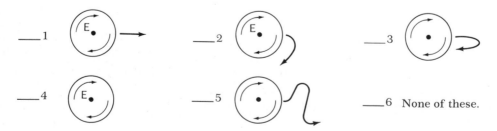

——6 None of these.

Alternative to item H

H If you fire a rocket straight out from the North Pole, which figure probably shows its path?

are categorized in the grid on page 533. Alternative forms of some of the questions appear on page 242. They show that information is collected using two response modes. The *constructed-response* mode requires the student to supply the answers: he constructs the responses (this is characteristic of most items on the sample test). In a *structured* item, on the other hand, you supply a list of possible answers (e.g., multiple-choice or true-false), and the student selects one or more answers from the list (the alternative forms shown on page 542 are of this nature). Each of types has some advantages and some disadvantages, which any standard text on tests and testing will describe. For the moment it is only necessary to say that free-response test items in science must be treated analytically. You should construct answers yourself in which you identify the variables and the relationships among them. A good practice, although one rarely followed, is to write your own skeleton response to each item, whether it is free-response or constructed-response. In that way you will be sure that the item can be answered and will supply a criterion to use for evaluating students' responses.

Performance tests to assess skills.   Most of the discussion on testing to this point applies to performance tests as well as to the more traditional paper-and-pencil tests. Assessment of skills in science usually requires a performance test. You want to know whether a child can use a microscope satisfactorily, for example; or perhaps you want to find out whether he can successfully measure variables such as distance, weight, time, and temperature. You give him some apparatus and an appropriate task. You set certain performance criteria which must be met before you and he can agree that he has acquired the skill. (Whether he uses the skill when he needs it is another question. One thing seems certain—he will not use the skill when it is necessary if he does not know how. Of course, he may interrupt his work on the problem he is pursuing and learn the necessary skill. In that event he will exit at the other end of the problem with a newly acquired skill.)

If you wanted to convert a test item like the one in example 5, in which the student predicts the pattern formed when a pencil moves straight across a moving belt, to a performance situation, you might build a piece of apparatus like the one shown in Figure 17-6. Pairs of students could examine the variables much as they did

FIGURE 17-6
Paper belt for studying tracks produced by a pencil. One student moves the belt, and a second student applies the pencil.

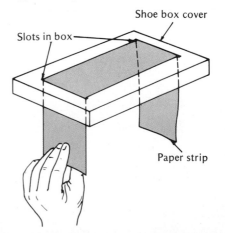

Shoe box cover

Slots in box

Paper strip

in the "Spinning Tables" unit. You could record their predictions, the variables they seek to identify, the patterns they produce, and the explanations they give.

Assessing the worth of content

As a part of evaluation we may want to question what worthwhile content the unit teaches or for what it develops some readiness. On the surface, what could be so valuable in the set of inferences or hypotheses students form about the shape of a path formed by moving a pencil across a spinning table? While the task may be fun, is it trivial? Probably not. Let us see why.

The unit starts students on the analysis of vectors (see section I). Vectors describe the path of moving objects and the directions along which forces act. The magnitude of the vectors, in addition to knowledge of the directions in which they act, allows scientists to make predictions about such diverse things as the trajectories of rockets, planets, and atomic particles in a force field, as well as the flight paths of airplanes. The items in examples 5 and 6 and in the sample test, items *F* and *G*, seek to find whether or not the student is developing a functional grasp of resultant forces. (When two or more forces act on an object, the resultant path of the object will be some kind of compromise between the competing forces. In this case, your hand supplies one of the forces, and the moving belt supplies the other. These act on the pencil point to produce the resultant line.) The "Spinning Tables" unit contains many other examples of interacting forces, so that students get plenty of practice in observing and predicting results in a variety of contexts. As a matter of fact, the directions suggest that you try the experiment using a moving band of paper, or some equivalent object that travels in a straight line, before experimenting with circular motion. (The directions suggest, for example, that you could pull a student along on roller skates while he tries to draw a line from the top of the chalk board to the bottom of it.)

Criterion-referenced evaluation

Evaluation, as discussed in this chapter, refers to those diagnostic and prescriptive techniques that are useful to teachers and students. The techniques are intended to provide data on which to base judgments about how teaching and learning are progressing. The use of judgments made by students as well as teachers about the meaning of accomplishments or the adequacy of performances is a rare occurrence in education at any level. Criterion-referenced testing makes possible joint decision making because it supplies a different kind of information about performance in relation to a specified criterion instead of in relation to all the other people in the class. When performance is related to a criterion, the student knows he has achieved the criterion or knows what he must do to achieve it. But in the more traditional norm-referenced testing, all the student knows is where he stands in comparison with other people. He may well have met or exceeded a criterion, but he will not get that information.

To help you distinguish between criterion- and norm-referenced testing, consider the following situation. Suppose you wanted to teach a group of children to swim. Criterion-referencing would work as follows: As a criterion for success you decide that a student will be judged, and judge himself, successful when he can swim four lengths of the pool in 5 minutes or less. Everybody who meets the criterion "passes" on that test item. But norm-referencing would work like this: You would record all the actual swimming times, group the scores into categories, and assign grades accordingly. Despite the fact that virtually all the students might have met or exceeded the criterion, some would get low grades, indicating poor performance in relation to others. Norm-referenced testing can tell you whom to put on the swimming team. Criterion-referenced testing tells you which children can take care of themselves in deep water.

At the close of any unit of instruction, it is desirable if all the students taking part exhibit proficiency on whatever measures reflect the objectives. In criterion-referenced testing, the intention of the test is to identify students who are ready to move on to the next stage of instruction and to find out what the nature of remedial instruction should be. In contrast to norm-referenced testing—which operates on the assumption that institutions, businesses, athletic teams, and so on can function best by choosing from the top of the heap—criterion-referenced testing assumes that there is no constraint on how many people may be competent in various areas. Consequently, more people actually meet certain criteria than the current norm-referenced procedures would indi-

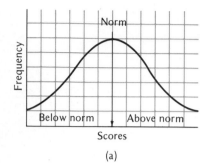

(a)

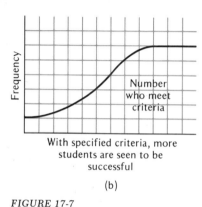

With specified criteria, more
students are seen to be
successful

(b)

FIGURE 17-7

a **Those falling below the norm may
in fact have achieved minimum
criteria, but compared with a whole
population they appear to be failures.** *b* **There is no norm in criterion-referenced testing.**

cate. While both kinds of testing have their uses, norm-
referenced testing is for competition leading to selection
and criterion-referenced testing is for educating (see
Figure 17-7).

Criterion-referenced testing jeopardizes traditional
grading systems. All students who meet or exceed the
criterion receive the same "pay." There is no normal
curve under this system.

The mental set for construction of test items differs
in the two cases. In norm-referenced testing you try to
write items so that the population ends up divided into
approximately two equal segments, those who succeed
and those who fail. For that reason you try to avoid items
which are too easy or too hard even though they may be
consistent with a criterion, because they fail to divide the
population into approximately equal segments. Items
which are ambiguous must also be discarded, because
too many people fail to answer them or answer them one
way at one time and another way a few days later. In
criterion-referenced testing, on the other hand, if the item
is a valid example of the objective, then the fact that virtually everybody succeeded on it or everybody failed on it
gives useful information about the state of the learners
in relation to the criterion. The fact that the item fails to
discriminate among people is irrelevant, since diagnosis
takes precedence over selection. *The norm-referenced
tester builds failure into his items. The criterion-referenced tester focuses on success.*

An invitation to inquiry

The economic model of scarce resources still dominates
the evaluation strategies of most of us. But there is another way to conduct evaluation. Diagnosis and prescription techniques are not well developed yet, but that very
fact offers an invitation to the curious and concerned.
Since there is no dogma, one can have a free hand to think
and experiment in new ways. The presence of physical
and biological systems for students to work with furnishes a new and exciting context for evaluation. People
learn in different ways, and some of the learning process
becomes highly visible as students work with natural
phenomena. If the research on learning profiles has any
meaning for instruction, it suggests that assessment
items need to be presented in a variety of formats. Coupled
with task analysis, careful observation of what students

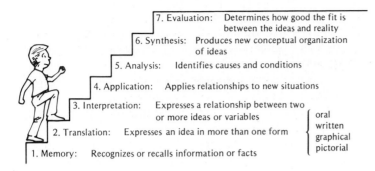

7. Evaluation: Determines how good the fit is between the ideas and reality

6. Synthesis: Produces new conceptual organization of ideas

5. Analysis: Identifies causes and conditions

4. Application: Applies relationships to new situations

3. Interpretation: Expresses a relationship between two or more ideas or variables

2. Translation: Expresses an idea in more than one form { oral, written, graphical, pictorial }

1. Memory: Recognizes or recalls information or facts

FIGURE 17-8
Levels of thought. Students need stimulation to climb to level 5 or beyond it. Provocative discussion, well-phrased questions, and numerous examples help them to climb.

do and say provides the context out of which to compound test items and to plan instruction in science. When a student demonstrates his ability to perform certain kinds of mental operations during a unit, he moves up the cognitive stairway (see Figure 17-8).

Note: For a lucid description of the differences between norm-referenced and criterion-referenced approaches to measurement, see J. James Popham and T. R. Husek, "Implications of Criterion-referenced Measurement," *Journal of Educational Measurement,* vol. 6, no. 1, Spring 1969, pp. 1–9. The authors discuss the implications of the two forms of measurement for (1) variability, (2) item construction, (3) reliability, (4) validity, (5) item analysis, (6) reporting, and (7) interpretation.

SUMMARY

1 As discussed in this chapter, evaluation is the attempt to understand what makes things work as they do. It includes inquiries attached to trying to make new things work or make old things work more effectively.

2 Investigations always proceed in the context of incomplete knowledge. So does evaluation.

3 In choosing to collect data during evaluation, you should be able to give yourself satisfactory answers to two questions:

  a What would I or the student, or both of us, *do* with the information?

  b Is the way in which I plan to collect data appropriate to my intentions?

4 People do evaluation for three purposes:

  a Diagnosis and prescription.

  b Administrative decision making.

    c Program evaluation.

5 Tape recordings of discussions among students give the following information about the work of students:

    a What observations they make.

    b What observations they miss.

    c What puzzles them, and what they do about it.

    d What explanations they make.

In addition, tape recordings give information concerning:

    e Vocabulary in use.

    f Completeness and coherence of explanations.

Tapes can also be used in these ways:

    g As feedback for students.

    h For education of parents.

Discussion in small groups is the technique to employ to obtain data on language and logic in use.

6 Concern for the quality of thought is only part of the educational package. Emotional conditions (atmosphere) have a great deal to do with learning. Number lines can be an indicator of the emotional climate.

7 Failure on the part of a student to answer a test question could be accounted for in the following ways:

    a He had not completed enough work before the test.

    b He did not have time enough to answer on the test.

    c He did not understand the content in the unit.

    d He did not understand the question.

    e He could not read or write well enough to make a response.

To interpret a wrong answer or a failure to respond, you must know which of these conditions apply. As part of test data, the teacher should collect information that would allow him to choose one or more of the above interpretations with a fairly good probability of being correct.

8 For students who have trouble reading, test questions can be tape recorded as well as printed so that the students can both hear and see the test items.

9 Tests tend to underestimate what a student knows.

10 Performance tests require students to demonstrate:

a Skills.

b The operation associated with a set of concepts.

11 Test items can be categorized according to the choices made in the following sentence:

Performance of student X (name) on an item presented in

Question format
(verbal)
(numerical) language (choose one) and requiring
(figural)

Cognitive operation **Novelty**
(problem identification)
(information, data, observation)
(inference, empirical relations) $\left(\begin{smallmatrix}choose\\one\end{smallmatrix}\right)$ *(exactly like)*
(similar to) one taught $\left(\begin{smallmatrix}choose\\one\end{smallmatrix}\right)$
(explanation) *(unlike)*
(application)

Response format
(high) *(verbal)*
produced (satisfactory) performance $\left(\begin{smallmatrix}choose\\one\end{smallmatrix}\right)$ *in a (numerical) format* $\left(\begin{smallmatrix}choose\\one\end{smallmatrix}\right)$
(low) *(figural)*

12 In criterion-referenced evaluation the student receives information about how his performance compared with a specified criterion (he either achieved the criterion or he did not, and he knows what he must do to reach the criterion). In the more traditional norm-referenced testing, the student receives information about how his performance compares with the performance of others (if he got an A, he did well in comparison with others; if he got an F, he did poorly). Criterion-referenced testing is useful for diagnosis and for self-appraisal. Norm-referenced testing is useful for selecting some students at the expense of others—i.e., for institutional decision making.

REFERENCE

Bloom, Benjamin S. (ed.): *Taxonomy of Educational Objectives,* David McKay Company, Inc., New York, 1956.

CHAPTER 18

"If science isn't certain, then what is certain in this world?

How do we decide? Who can we trust?"—SIXTH-GRADE TEACHER

WHICH KNOWERS ARE WE TO TRUST?

OBJECTIVES

On completion of this chapter, you should be able to do the following:

1 Recognize that although there may be different ideas of what kinds of emphasis are appropriate in education, there is general agreement that science education should be characterized by a "hands-on" approach.

2 Recognize that as scientific knowledge grows, so do the number and complexity of the choices we have to make.

3 Recognize that most modern elementary science programs, when properly taught, probably can contribute to the development of language, thought, sense of fate control, and a probabilistic view of nature.

INTRODUCTION

In a Baltimore hospital a newborn child was allowed to starve to death. At first the baby, a defective child diagnosed as a Mongoloid, was kept alive intravenously, while the doctors prepared to perform a routine operation to remove an intestinal blockage that prevented the child from digesting food taken by mouth. The parents, however, decided that it would not be fair to themselves or to their other children to accept the burden of such a child and so refused to give permission for the operation. Eleven days after their decision, the infant finally died. Legal, ethical, and moral considerations prevented everyone concerned from either saving the child's life or ending it any sooner. Not so long ago, no decision would have been necessary, for there would have been no way to detect the intestinal blockage. The child would still have died of starvation, but no one would have known why. There would have been no choice to make. The progress of science and technology confronts us with *choices*. Conflicts of values are inevitable.

The case history described above is one of many that eighty scientists, theologians, psychiatrists, lawyers, moral philosophers, and psychologists used as a basis for discussion during a weekend symposium sponsored in October of 1971 by the Joseph P. Kennedy, Jr., Foundation. The symposium, "Choices on Our Conscience," focused attention on the urgent issues that knowledge from the biological and behavioral sciences is forcing on us. Social, moral, legal, economic, and political decisions once undreamed of are now required of us by the growing capabilities that science gives us to shape our destiny. How are we to make those choices? Can we make them in time? Clearly, the decisions are no longer simply medical or scientific. Whatever gap once existed between science and the body politic is gone. It may be that only by convening people from backgrounds as diverse as those of the people who participated in the Kennedy Foundation conference will society finally find a means of making the more complex decisions that knowledge forces upon it. Meanwhile, the baby and its parents could not wait.

Nearly three hundred years ago researchers began to band together into professional societies and, in so doing, dropped a new force into the social system. This new force gradually changed the shape of economic and political affairs, altered the ethical structure of societies, created new freedoms, and sent social systems into dizzying rates of change. Today this force gives us power over life and death, health and sickness, eugenics and genetics, population and pollution. Suddenly we have to make decisions once reserved to the gods or to nature. That is frightening, especially when some of the decisions produce unanticipated consequences, as in the case of insecticides, detergents, and fertilizers. It is frightening, too, because our social system may not be geared to respond appropriately fast enough, as, for example, when air-pollution levels produced thousands of deaths in London, Pittsburgh, and Los Angeles. The baby in Baltimore could not wait, and the people with low tolerance for pollutants could not wait.

Science is the central enterprise of the societies which people the planet Earth during the twentieth century. Still, virtually anywhere in the world that you might stop to inquire, science means almost nothing to the man on the street. Yet its impact on him is growing. Although he may not know it, the man on the street cannot wait. He must find out how science is affecting him and what he can do about it.

What is this mysterious force which is of our own making and yet seems to be shaping our destinies in ways we cannot always control? How did it come to be? What are the people most allied with it like? What chance do we have to control it? What kinds of decisions is it forcing on us? How should we educate people about it?

In this chapter we will get a bare start on answering those questions. All kinds of groups are producing innovative science and social-studies programs. How many of those programs develop skills and attitudes that will help the future man on the street to cope with the kinds of ethical, economic, and political issues that he will have to face?

One question should be kept constantly before us: *Which knowers are we to trust?* To answer that question we must constantly demand to know what their ways of knowing are. Just as science grows and changes over time, so the programs of education that adults think will best ensure the future of the next generation change. Guided by the perspectives of a given era, curriculum writers choose content and problems most likely to equip the next generation appropriately. But of course they cannot know the future in all its detail, so each program is a kind of guess. Each year in which the child takes part in the educational enterprise, society, in the person of his teachers and parents, guides him according to the knowledge it has at the time. Whether he receives mental and spiritual nourishment of the sort that will help remains to be seen. Education of the young is a kind of experiment in which the results are not all realized at one point in time (see Figure 18-1).

Toward the end of the chapter, we will take part in a symposium in which the participants try to decide what science should be taught and how it should be taught in elementary schools. Facsimiles are given of discussions heard over the years within and between writing groups that were preparing new science programs for elementary schools. At all points of disagreement, the reader should try to imagine what kinds of experiments would produce evidence that could be used in resolving the conflicts. Some of these discussions will make the social and moral issues more salient. In such instances one has to examine carefully where empirical evidence can be most useful

FIGURE 18-1

Philosophical, sociological, and psychological components that are involved in welding together the institutions of science and education through curriculum and instruction.

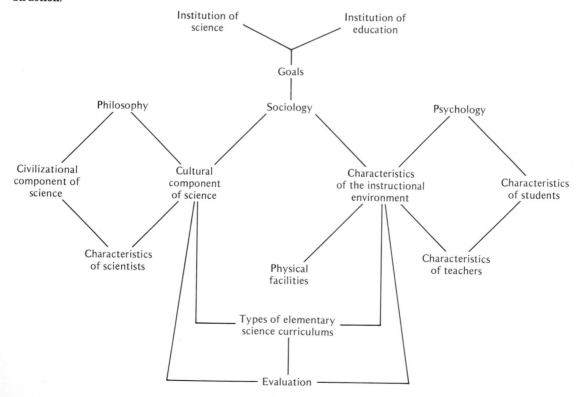

and where its usefulness is limited. Decisions as important as those mankind must make today are never simple. Each one has enormous ramifications, all of which must be reasoned through and evaluated against the social fabric of our times—and in the light of our imaginings about the kind of future we want for ourselves and for our children. One thing seems clear: the decisions we make now help to shape the kind of future we will have.

Very few major decisions are simple. Instead, they usually set off a chain of events, each of which must be evaluated to determine its effects. For instance, if you find ways to improve the general health of a population, you increase its life span. Out of some apparently simple decisions, such as to make a new kind of hybrid rice or corn available to some region and to provide a few medical services, can come just a small change in the level of health and fertility that eventually thrusts new problems on a people. More people survive longer. That means you must develop correspondingly larger systems for supplying food and removing wastes. Living space must be re-evaluated, as must the conditions for housing. The nature of health care changes, particularly as the population of older people increases. The kinds of illnesses that develop tend to be long-term rather than short-term; as a result, the hospital facilities must be altered. The number of individuals carrying defective genetic information who live to reproduce increases, and so eventually the frequency of defective genes in the population at large increases. That can mean that a whole chemical industry must be developed to supply the chemicals which defective human systems fail to manufacture. Of course, political and economic changes will also occur in the society, bringing new questions to the forefront. For instance, what proportion of the population in what age brackets will process resources and furnish necessary services?

The interface between knowledge and its application is not well understood. There is as yet no science of application. At the stage where men could put knowledge to use—that is, at the interfaces between science and society —each system falls apart or, rather, proves inadequate. Because we understand too little of the forces acting across that interface and even less about how to marshal the energy of the various sociopolitical systems to take proper advantage of technical knowledge, we risk riding away on a runaway horse.

SCIENCE AS A SOCIAL SYSTEM

The organization of scientists into professional societies

As part of coming to understand enough to take part in determining what our future will be like, we need to examine science as a social system. Recall that science was described earlier as a conflict-driven enterprise. Its strength lies in that. However, this was not always so. Long before scientists formed themselves into professional societies, individual researchers were often isolated from each other by distance and the absence of a good technology for communication. With limited communication, ideas developed relatively slowly. Without the stimulation that comes from different interpretations of phenomena, the body of knowledge grew sufficiently gradually to provide few social or ethical disruptions. Ideas did not reach a broad public rapidly. When one did —as, for example, the Copernican view (originally voiced by a few daring Greeks) that the sun, not the Earth, was the center of the universe—then furor of a kind that is common today but was rare then spread throughout Europe. In the instance noted, as in many others, it was a religious furor—theologians exploded. Today we move through such crises of beliefs frequently. Our crises are of a different sort—we do not know what to believe. Our knowledge is extensive, but incomplete where it most needs to be complete. We are busily trying to establish frameworks for making decisions.

Once the professional scientific societies formed, the whole character of science and its relation to the body politic changed. By bringing together men of different scientific persuasions to consider pieces of research and to argue over theories, and by providing journals in which to circulate descriptions and results of investigations, the whole scientific enterprise acquired a remarkable vigor. The level of critical response that the work of an investigator was likely to encounter in professional meetings meant that more thought went into investigations. Priority —being the first to produce a particular result or to report a particular finding—became important, because the scientific societies paid little attention to also-rans. This characteristic of the social system of science produced a paradox in the gradually emerging ethos of what has come to be called the *scientific community*. There existed an ethos connected with sharing ideas. That, after all, was a part of the motivation for forming the societies. But as the element of priority began to gain importance, it had some dampening effect on the open sharing of ideas. What a man was thinking about was less likely to be discussed than what he had finished thinking about.

Once the professional societies formed, governments had at their disposal a wealth of technical help. With the formation of professional societies, governments could have quick access to panels of scientists. The societies made it possible for governments to mobilize the kind of help needed, whether it concerned matters of health, agriculture, or making war. What is more, scientists who advised the governments knew they were accountable to their peers, so there were some checks and balances.

Governments had always sought the help of individual scientists, particularly in the matter of waging war. Examine, for example, the remarkable fortifications and instruments for the conduct of war designed by the artist-scientist Leonardo da Vinci. Today it often happens that scientists advising the government give conflicting suggestions. To a person familiar with how competing ideas in science drive inquiry along, these controversies are understandable. But to a person who does not understand that data may be subject to different interpretations and that the state of knowledge is such that most ideas have to be held with some degree of tentativeness, the controversies tend to produce dispair. Far more than just knowledge per se is involved when governments make decisions. Moral, political, economic, and spiritual values contend for attention. All kinds of questions arise: How should a people decide to invest its resources? Whose information can they trust? Can they distinguish arguments based on evidence from those based on innuendo? Scientists can supply technical knowledge and suggest what might be the consequences of its use, but the members of society at large must evaluate those consequences in terms of their current values.

From scientist to society

It is a matter of more than passing interest to know how ideas get out of a laboratory and into the economy or the government for consideration. Once, the people who made original discoveries believed that they had no responsibility for the ways in which segments of the society put them to use. That view is no longer tenable. In the first place, most of the research is paid for directly or indirectly by the public. In short, the public employs the scientists (including engineers) and has some right to expect help from them in interpreting probable consequences of their work once it is done.

Furthermore, private corporations employ large numbers of scientists and engineers. The corporations own the products of research. The use of the products depends on what management decides will benefit the company. Thus it is often the corporation, rather than the individual scientist, that influences the public, the government, or both.

It is a pity that most scientists must, of necessity, be rather specialized and so are unequipped with the social and economic perspective necessary to provide the kind of advisory help needed by our society today. Most managers and politicians with the political and economic perspective lack the knowledge necessary to evaluate the consequences of a technical idea put into use. When these different kinds of actors come together to work on the problem of making informed decisions, they frequently fail. In the first place, they do not know how to talk to each other, because each has a language full of special meanings not shared by the other. There is very little in the training of either group, but especially of the scientists, to teach them how to work in such settings. Even when scientists go to symposia where the aim is to bring together researchers from different scientific disciplines to examine one topic, many return home dissatisfied because the problems of bridging the gap between the disciplines are difficult to solve. Good will is not enough. For one thing, the language of each discipline becomes so specialized that the transmission of ideas from one group to another becomes a formidable task. Sometimes the conceptual organization of one field leads to deductions which directly oppose the deductions logically flowing from the conceptual organization of another field. Thus, for example, demographers and biologists frequently reach quite different conclusions about the possible consequences of population expansion.

It is a fact of modern science that it requires larger and more costly research instruments than it once did. The cost of these instruments places them beyond the means of private groups; only governments can marshal such resources. It is also a fact that in what is referred to as *basic research,* the investigators cannot tell in advance what they will find. If they could, there would be no necessity for the construction of expensive instruments. Because results, and their eventual usefulness, cannot usually be forecast, there is no accurate way of deciding what sort of planning the government ought to do and how much support it ought to give. To some extent, it is up to the professional societies and panels of scientists convened to give advice that will protect the government against sharp scientific salesmen.

Here is an important paradox that faces governments: if they commit huge sums to conduct research, they may reap great benefits; but what those benefits will be, or whether there will be any, must remain in the realm of the unknown for some indefinite period.

Recently some scientists and politicians have suggested that if, instead of gambling so much on basic research, more of the national resources were devoted to solving problems of social import, more problems would in fact be solved sooner. In the process basic knowledge would be generated. In the scientific community proponents of each view are trying to be heard. If the government puts most of our money into applied research, it may achieve solutions for the present but lack the reservoir of knowledge on which to draw for future emergencies.

The question is now raised whether there is a more efficient way to make scientific manpower more immediately available for meeting the needs of mankind. One segment of the scientific community says that it should be allowed to engage in the pursuit of knowledge for its own sake. Past experience justifies its faith in the ultimate usefulness of basic research. Another segment of the scientific community argues that more resources should be devoted to direct attacks on identified problems. It argues that the government has the right to support mission-oriented research and that in fact this kind of research frequently makes substantive contributions to basic knowledge. How, then, shall a people decide to spend its human and fiscal resources? At the time of this writing, there are many scientists out of work. It still remains to be seen whether they can make their knowledge and skills available to work on new problems, such as those having to do with the environment. Are scientists any more adaptable to major changes than other people are?

There is a view that the supply of basic knowledge is something like the fuel for a fire. The technology is using it up at a faster and faster rate. According to this view, most resources should go into basic research, which the government would fund. Then the pool of knowledge available to everybody would keep growing. Those who have particular problems may apply this knowledge. It is interesting to ask the proponents of this view in what sense knowledge is "used up" rather than simply "used." They have a cogent reply. Suppose, for example, there had not been all the research on the structure of atoms. All the uses that man presently makes of atomic energy would not be even imagined. That would mean that much of the work on production of hybrid plants and animals would have moved at a much slower pace or would not have occurred at all. It would mean no radiation treatment for cancer victims. It would mean no hope for new supplies of energy to operate machinery. In short, the imaginative capabilities of the users of basic knowledge will be limited in proportion as the supply of new basic research dwindles.

Some characteristics of scientists and their societies

Since scientists have been so involved in preparation of curriculums during the 1960s, it is worth finding out what scientists are like. Almost a quarter of a century ago Anne Roe, psychologist wife of the Harvard biologist George Gaylord Simpson, began a study of a group of eminent scientists. Being a clinical psychologist, she naturally employed the in-depth interview as her major vehicle for gathering data. She describes the results of her study of sixty-four scientists (including a sample of social scientists) in a highly readable book entitled *The Making of a Scientist*.[1] Beginning with a dedication of the book to "My Favorite Scientists: My Husband and My Subjects" and ending with a chapter called "What Does It Mean for You?" she describes the scientists' family backgrounds, how they became scientists, and how they think.

Roe says of her eminent scientists, "One thing seems clear. Scientists are people, not rational automatons" (p. 230). In relation to discussions of learning earlier in this book and to our own interest in education, some of her observations merit particular attention. Roe found among the scientists different styles of thinking about

[1]Anne Roe, *The Making of a Scientist*, Dodd, Mead & Company, Inc., New York, 1953.

problems. Some men drew elaborate diagrams, laid out visual representations of their ideas; others reported that they used no imagery at all; still others depended on auditory verbalization of formulae and ideas, i.e., they talked to themselves; some preferred to construct concrete, usually three-dimensional representations of relationships. These reports suggest that the scientists in this study exhibited distinctive profiles of mental ability. In fact, the data from Roe's study suggest that particular fields of investigation tend to attract people with certain kinds of "ability profiles." In her sample, for example, a substantial proportion of biologists (30 percent) and theoretical physicists (36 percent) used verbal imagery, but none of the experimental physicists reported using it (0 percent) (pp. 147–148).

Roe concludes that what was important in the background of her scientists was the value placed on learning for its own sake. If such a value were missing in the home, some teacher supplied it. She remarks that in general the scientists relied on their own resources early. Of the adult stage, she says that a large part of their time is spent ". . . in thinking about things, in a question-answering way" (p. 234). Roe remarks that many adults are unable to be curious to any great degree, and she notes that even some of the scientists she studied were curious only in some things. Most, however, exhibited a more general kind of curiosity. She hazards a guess, possibly on the basis on her work as a clinical psychologist, that the repression of curiosity in healthy, intelligent adults ". . . may result from repressive training, from discouragement of questioning by weary parents or teachers, from an adult know-it-all attitude, and insistence on a child's conformity" (p. 235).

Some of Roe's observations have implications for our discussions of fate control in Chapter 9. She notes that the scientists she studied exhibited a general need for independence, for personal mastery of the environment. She remarks that she thinks such needs are stronger in men than in women, but does not know whether to attribute this to biological or cultural factors. Perhaps girls do not receive the early independence that seemed so essential to the development of the scientists.

If we want to extrapolate Roe's findings into this era, we must do so with caution. Her work is, as has been noted, nearly a quarter of a century old. It is about eminent men whose average age was in the late forties. That means they fall into the category of children from World War I. They came up through the Depression, when scientific research could still be done by individuals operating on relatively small budgets.

In 1961 researchers at the Institute of Personality Assessment and Research at the University of California, Berkeley, published the results of a 5½-year intensive study of creativity, the creative person, and the creative process. Of special interest to us in the context of this book are those aspects of the study that relate to scientific research personnel.[2] Forty-five physicists, mathematicians, and electronics engineers, identified as working in laboratories requiring creative output and nominated by a director as creative, underwent three days of intensive assessment by the research team. One thousand and seven quantified variables, in addition to a great deal of qualitative and anecdotal material, were collected from each man as he took part in interviews, group tasks, informal discussions, standard tests, stress situations, laboratory and darkroom problems in thinking and perception, and other activities. The objective of the study was to describe the group in detail and to discover the factors that related to differences in creativity within the sample. The average age of this group was 35.7 years: these men were more than ten years younger than those in the group studied by Roe. Again, the sample was all male. (In the same conference, Helson reported a study of the results of an investigation of creativity in male and female mathematicians.)

All the men in the investigation ranked well on the Terman Concept Mastery Test, which suggests that they are bright. As in Roe's study the achievement drives of this group were strong, particularly as regards independent, autonomous effort (p. III-5). In general they exhibited an open, empathetic mode of sensing and perceiving others.

Imagine now that men such as these formed the backbone of the major nationally funded groups which set out to prepare new curriculums for the post-Sputnik period. Classroom teachers and psychologists were also

[2]Conference on The Creative Person, presented October 13–17 at the University of California Alumni Center, Lake Tahoe, California. The Institute of Personality Assessment and Research, University of California, University Extension, Liberal Arts Department, Berkeley. Researchers in the scientific research personnel phases of the study were John E. Arnold, Frank Barron, Richard S. Crutchfield, Harrison G. Gough, Ravenna Helson, Donald W. MacKinnon, Nevitt Sanford, and Donald W. Taylor.

included on these teams, but the values, emphases, choice of content, and methods of presentation came largely from the scientists. It is not surprising, therefore, that while the programs differ in conceptualization of content and in details of presentation, they all put considerable emphasis on developing independent thinking, multiple interpretations of data, and learning by doing and thinking about it. They all hold high expectations for children. The faith that characterized the scientists' belief that most difficulties or problems can be mastered must somehow be transferred to children. It is natural, then, that such groups would place emphasis on those elements of what they do and think that have seemed to them most valuable.

In a way, any curriculum reflects the consensus of the group, or the pattern of biases of the individual, it was produced by. Since we are all potential consumers of curriculums, we have a right to know what some of the points of view are.

CHOOSING A SCIENCE PROGRAM

Curriculum writers

Almost every commercial publisher who markets to elementary schools has some kind of science program to sell. Some of the programs began when the National Science Foundation made money available to certain groups for the express purpose of developing new curriculums. Other programs developed totally under private aegis. Virtually all of them, regardless of their initial source of support, were prepared by teams of people rather than by a single individual. To some extent, each program represents a kind of group consensus on what is important for children to read and to do in science. Almost without exception the writing groups included people with "direct knowledge" of children (whatever that means), science educators, and usually some scientists. In the case of the projects funded by the government, scientists constituted the bulk of the writing groups. These projects also included science educators and classroom teachers. All the government-funded projects went through some kind of field testing, a luxury not easily afforded by the privately operated groups.

As a social phenomenon, the decisions of such writing teams are of great interest. What kinds of ideas did they develop? What values did they push? In the remarks which follow, the basic conceptual arguments that emerged as the result of the work of the government-supported groups may be applied as well to the work of the private groups. In spite of the fundamental differences in approach propounded by the various groups, no coherent research program has been developed to start the process of converting the arguments into testable propositions. All we can do at this point is to analyze the arguments, see why they might have arisen, and consider how some experiments might be designed to help us obtain data for making decisions.

You have to be a little sympathetic about the deaf ear that the writing teams turned to people who seemed to disagree with their ideas. When you have struggled hard to produce a punchy lesson that meets everybody's approval and seems to be making it with the children, you just cannot hear anything critical. It is as though some stranger attacked your child. It takes a couple of years to get sufficiently beyond that state of strong feelings to be able to sensibly consider other alternatives. Some very amusing, and unscientific, conflict developed among the writing groups. Some people never got over it. Mixed in with all the activity were different conceptions of the child as a learner, different views on what science children needed to know, and different perceptions of the feelings, values, and ethical stances the programs were meant to convey.

Sometimes visitors from other countries ask me why the government supported so many different efforts; it sometimes seems wasteful to the outsider. I think it was not wasteful. All the variety increases the probability that we will ultimately find good solutions to the problem of how to bring the next generation into a fruitful relation with all the enterprises related to science. In the long run, it well may be that the major consequence of the science programs of the 1960s will be the changes wrought indirectly at the college level. A remarkable number of scientists began to take a serious interest in teaching as a result of their participation on a writing team. Others, recruited to help disseminate the new programs to communities near their colleges, began to revise their ideas about what should be the content and method of instruction in science courses for nonmajors. Most elementary teachers, they found, received their undergraduate science instruction in such courses. It seemed clear to those scientists that the college science courses failed, for the most part, to convey content and process, or to foster attitudes that were compatible with the new programs. College science courses turned a lot of people off. (See Figure 18-2.)

The problem

Science is something men and women *do*. It is also a *way of thinking,* which eventually results in some kind of product such as a research paper, an improved piece

of technology, or a set of recommendations for action of some kind. In the course of producing such products, researchers depend on an intricate network of relationships among concepts to give them guidance in reasoning about the phenomena in question. *Each idea has to be understood in its relationships to other ideas. Nothing stands in isolation.* The relationships have been constructed from a multitude of empirical events and suggest what additional information must still be discovered. All the members of the curriculum groups were people who traversed the network, or some substantial part of it. They possessed the gestalt. Their problem was to figure out what its key ingredients probably were and then to invent some way of transmitting its major aspects. Imagine the problem. Not only did everybody have different ideas about the nature of the conceptual structure that students should acquire, but there was also the problem of the children. What could one hope to expect from them in the way of interest and reasoning?

The different solutions developed by each of the writing groups tell us something about what men and women who work in some part of the scientific enterprise think is socially and spiritually valuable in what they do. Participation on a writing team meant that they stepped out for a while from their routines to reflect on the enterprise to which they were giving their lives, so that they could abstract what was important for the next generation to grasp. Having decided what was important, they had next to decide how to convert it into a program of instruction. The task of constructing and sequencing activities was something like trying to transfer an image of a map, piece by piece. Junctions on the map corresponded to points in development where certain combinations of facts, concepts, and principles had to occur almost simultaneously in order to be able to proceed to the next junctions.

The solutions

On the face of it, four distinct approaches to the problem of producing a suitable science curriculum emerged: (1) emphasis on process or intellectual skills, (2) the discovery approach, (3) problem solving, and (4) emphasis on content, or thematic emphasis. To explore the ramifications of these various positions, imagine that you are attending a symposium. Speakers for each kind of program try to represent the views of the program, and then discussion begins. First we shall hear four brief presentations. The discussions will follow. At a symposium anyone is free to take part, so you too will add your comments to the talk, as you see fit. You may be in a position to help reconcile differences and to suggest what investigations should be conducted to provide data for making decisions. After all, we can become the victims of our own prejudices and inferences, especially when they refer to events in the social domain. It is more difficult to unburden ourselves of false social or psychological inferences than of erroneous scientific inferences. Without a mental set that disposes us to obtain data when feasible, we can continue to cherish equally our misconceptions and our correct conceptions. Let the symposium begin.

Mr. Process: *Ladies and gentlemen, I speak for the process approach. When the members of my group came together, we sought to find out what we all shared in common. At first we were mightily discouraged because we found that since each of us worked in a different discipline, we had almost no shared content, if one speaks about content in its traditional meaning. Even our language separated us. I confess that although I am a pretty good physicist, I am an awful biologist and did not understand what it was important to know in biology. In spite of these differences we all identified ourselves as scientists. That set us to thinking that what we shared was a way of doing things. As we examined the characteristics of each of the disciplines, we found they had some elements in common. It seemed to us that if we could identify and teach those common elements, children would be able to progress in almost any of the separate disciplines.*

These basic knowledges or skills are a means to the practice and understanding of science. We identified the following processes as being generally applicable, even in the social sciences: observing; describing; classifying; measuring; recognizing and using spatial, temporal, and numerical relations; drawing inferences; experimenting; and speculating. In addition, children need to sense the limitations as well as the advantages that the practice of these processes offers as they try to do science. This is not a complete list, but it seemed enough to manage. Scientists learn how to use these processes by engaging in them, and we feel children should learn them in a similar way—namely, by doing them. Therefore our emphasis is on teaching children how to perform these key procedures. To accomplish that end we analyze each of the processes (which are in themselves rather complex) into components. Then we try to devise a training sequence that will teach competence in the desired areas. We require that the child demonstrate the subordinate behaviors that combine to produce competence for each process. To ensure maxiumum transfer of these skills from one discipline to another, we construct lessons using content from many disciplines. The content is subordinate to the process. That is to say, we choose the contents best suited to illustrating and teaching the processes.

In the early years the proportion of effort and time that goes directly into teaching skills is high. Although the skills cannot be taught without using content, content is deemphasized in favor of basic-skill teaching. In the later years of the program, this separation of content and process, which is after all somewhat artificial, progressively disappears. The processes become well enough established to function as we meant them to— that is, they become a powerful means for mastering content.

We have based our curriculum on our analysis of what scientists do. We admit, however, that we know more about the structure of the disciplines than about how people acquire the structure. We shall have to study how children operate with these processes.

Mr. Content: *Ladies and gentlemen, while I respect the views of Mr. Process, I think there is another way to think about what in science would have the widest applicability for students. Understanding in science presupposes a minimum level of cognitive maturity and sophistication in the subject matter. Without the knowledge, you simply cannot make valid inferences or design appropriate experiments to test the correctness of the inferences. Contrary to what you might think, the major organizing conceptions of modern science do not change very rapidly. As you know very well, science is a network of connected, mutually supporting propositions. While the facts trapped in the net may change, the structure of the net itself actually changes very gradually.*

The way in which we proceeded was to try to identify the major integrating principles that permeated all the areas of science. At this point we split into two groups, each with a somewhat different emphasis but both focusing on what children would need to know and do to qualify as scientifically literate. The first group agreed with the observations Mr. Process made concerning the failure in communication among scientists from different disciplines. That problem arose because the various sciences did not share a universal language. If I could use one phrase to describe the content this group thought was important, I would use the phrase "system approach."

The content which would have the greatest probability of transfer was that class of concepts which might be described as the "metalanguage" of science: objects have properties; properties, in turn, can be ordered serially, and sometimes quantified, to form variables; when variables interact there is evidence of some kind; systems are those sets of relationships that a person decides to investigate; systems are entities with properties that can be investigated. Finally, in the later stages of this program children learn to construct models of those aspects of systems that are not immediately available to their senses. Since energy relations are such an important organizing notion in science, the physical scientists used them frequently as a vehicle for conveying systems ideas. The life-science program follows a similar development with a strong emphasis on interactions in biological systems of increasing complexity: organisms; life cycles; populations; environments; communities; and finally ecosystems.

The second group took a somewhat different position. It said that there are certain major conceptions or organizing themes which pervade virtually all of science. These major ideas do not change in any substantial way for long periods of time. This group chose themes that seemed most likely to last and developed a program around five conceptual schemes. You will recognize that there are some similarities in thought between the two groups—as you might expect, since they both operate on the hypothesis that without knowledge, discovery is unlikely. Other schemes might have been chosen, but these seemed most powerful at the time: the structural units of the universe, the hierarchies of forms that include stars to atoms, animals to cells, etc.; interaction and change, which happens continually in the universe at all levels of organization; energy, its conservation and degradation, which helps to explain and eventually to control some of the changes; and finally, woven through it all, a statistical view of nature. This statistical view is seen as a major factor in prediction and control of phenomena. Nature becomes predictable only as one learns to let go of idiosyncratic events in favor of studying the properties of collections of events. This approach has great importance for how we function in the social as well as in the scientific domain. This group believes that most of what it is important to learn in elementary science is incorporated within the framework of these schemes. These schemes are characteristic of science as a whole and are not specific to or focused on particular disciplines (e.g., biology, chemistry, or physics) in the traditional sense.

Mr. Discovery: *My two colleagues have labored hard and long, but I think they have missed the most important goal of science instruction. Their programs produce a knowledge product. In the first case the students will have learned some pervasive processes, or so it is argued. In the second case the students will have learned some pervasive, relatively stable content. Ladies and gentlemen, the objective of the discovery approach is to change the relation in which the learner stands to the knowledge. Our effort is directed toward producing situations in which children find it rewarding to carry on investigations of phenomena. We are interested in developing an attitude of intellectual self-reliance. We have been developing, therefore, units of instruction which are likely to provoke inquiry because they have their bases in the natural curiosity which characterizes all human beings when they feel safe enough to explore. We try to choose materials and events that will provoke conjecture and then to nourish the impulse to discover on one's own. It would be too bad, in my opinion, to develop a generation of people who knew a great deal of science and hated it.*

Science is a dynamic, open-ended process of investigating, which we all enjoy. Just as we all come from disciplines chosen as our interests developed, so some units will attract certain of the students and other units will appeal to others. It was therefore necessary to prepare a large number of discrete units that supplied a great variety of contents which could be explored. All of them are meant to be engaged in within a framework of enjoyment, associative play if you like.

There are as many potential organizations of content in science as there are people. It is our idea that the schools can choose those combinations of units which they think would meet the objectives they most cherish. Our sources of puzzlement have been connected not with questions of what content is appropriate but rather with questions of how much and what kind of guidance to provide. Some of our members favor a kind of trial-and-error procedure where the instructional guides as well as teachers use provocative questions to move the investigations along. Others of us have pressed for careful sequencing of ideas and much more guidance. Until we know more about what should be the nature and degree of guidance given, we are inclined to trust the learners to make their own way from task to task. They will get practice looking for patterns of relationships. Self-confidence comes from interiorizing "discovered" rather than "copied" relationships. We hypothesize that students exposed to these units will develop the same kind of healthy attitude toward confrontation of felt difficulties and problems that typifies people who do science. They will come to believe that they can find solutions. After all, when any of us begins an investigation, does he not proceed as though he believed he could find answers? That is a very important kind of faith to transmit to the young.

Mr. Problem Solver: *Before the government paid so well for their attention to the problems of science instruction, very few scientists took any active part in curriculum construction. I say that not so much to indite the profession as to make it clear that the way in which scientists would go about responding to the need for new programs might lack social perspective. Indeed, I think that is the case. The members of the various writing groups are hardly representative of the membership in the scientific and technological enterprise—for I submit that Oppenheimer was correct when he said that science and technology are just two sides of the same coin. How well represented was applied science? How many elementary science writing teams included a substantial number of engineers or technicians, people who might have put more emphasis on how to use information to solve problems of social consequence?*

By the turn of the century, approximately half our population will be directly employed in technological phases of the economy. Even today, only about 10 percent of the manpower of science can be said to be doing basic research. The rest of the people are involved in mission-

oriented, problem-solving activities. By the twenty-first century the half of our populace involved in technology will, for the most part, have to function as facile problem solvers. We are facing today problems thrust on us by unanticipated consequences of an accelerated technology. This same driving force has put into our hands capabilities that we never had before, and we must think how to use them. When, for example, we can alter the sex of unborn children and when we make it possible through medical intervention for people who might otherwise have died before procreation to live and pass on genetic defects, we present all kinds of problems with consequences for generations yet unborn. We have problems to solve. What kind of a program will teach people to be effective problem solvers?

In the first place, we must choose to focus on problems that have some relevance for children. In the beginning the problems ought to be simple enough that the children can learn from them certain sequences of behavior useful in finding solutions: observing, describing, drawing inferences, and making hypotheses. Possibly this sounds like the approach that Mr. Process described; but it is very different, because we do not think that these processes can be separated from the problems and learned as things in themselves. The content of each problem is foremost.

What we try to do is to create situations in which intelligent questions are likely. We would like to see a greater participation of social scientists in our writing groups as well as applied scientists. Population and pollution, for example, are two major problems we are facing and expect the next generation to face also. The technological aspects of these problems are susceptible to solution far more easily than the economic, moral or ethical, and political conflicts that must also be confronted if the technical knowledge is to be put to use. We think children should not learn science apart from the social condition. To learn about pollution without doing something about it seems to be a vacuous exercise.

It is natural that our colleagues on the other writing teams might think that the way to present science is to try to teach children to function like miniature scientists. But very few of the students are going to be members of that elite group. Most of them are going to become very adroit problem solvers and good question askers. We are willing to sacrifice the beautiful con-

ceptual structure of science to that end. We opt for a problem-solving focus.

The Symposium Chairman: *You have heard the opening remarks. Comments will now be entertained from anyone present. We do not ordinarily settle our controversies in science by popular vote or by acceding to pressures from elite groups. Rather, we prefer to base our decisions on empirical investigations. Perhaps when these discussions are concluded, a plan for investigation might result. At least we should keep that objective in mind.*

Speaker from the floor: *I confess to being confused by the details of all these presentations. At least one point needs clarification. All the speakers and the programs that they represent stress the importance of direct involvement with materials. All the programs are activity-oriented. But I could not tell from what anybody said whether the activity was primarily for psychological reasons or whether it had its origin in the philosophy of science. Mr. Process talked about the activities in his program as important because they provided the means for teaching children how to do things. Mr. Discovery spoke about the motivational features of action which leads to discovery. The others seem to use activities for illustrating ideas.*

I think you have all missed the most important aspect of experiments. Experiments are questions one asks of nature. You cannot speak to nature directly, so you plan how you will get the information you seek. Usually the experiment is the end product of a chain of reasoning. You arrive at a place in that reasoning where you need to know something more, so that you can go on. That is when you plan how you will extract the information from nature. Somehow I have failed to hear this point of view expressed by any of the speakers. Experimenting is only one of a list of things a researcher does. He reads, he talks to other people who might have information that bears on his problem, and he goes to meetings to give and get ideas that might help him think how he should design his experiment and interpret the data he gets from it.

The implication of this point of view for some of the presentations is obvious. How can you expect children to make discoveries without substantial knowledge? They will not do much more than very trivial things, I think.

The power in science comes from the way in which ideas accumulate and fit together. It is this conceptual structure that dictates what to look for next. Experiments grow out of it. I think that the discovery and problem-solving approaches fractionate this vital property of knowledge.

Mr. Content: *I agree with the speaker from the floor in most respects. All the other programs have made decisions that seem to me to be subject to three criticisms. They depend on a narrow base of knowledge, so whatever children learn will have little generalizability. It is likely, furthermore, that there will be a tendency for children to retain facts rather than concepts or principles. Finally, these programs impose a logical structure or present a view of scientific method that children can copy but not necessarily interiorize.*

You all know that the way in which we actually do our research resembles only very remotely the published form which the research report finally takes. I am afraid children will get the idea that there is some kind of fixed form or set of procedures for generating knowledge or making discoveries or solving problems. Ladies and gentlemen, you know that is not true. On the contrary, half the game at least consists in thinking of new ways to look at knowledge you already had. Even Einstein did not do an experiment in the usual sense to produce his theory of relativity. He based his work on data and ideas that already existed. He organized them differently—dramatically so—and out of the reorganization emerged a whole new edifice of ideas. There is no prescription for that kind of thing.

Mr. Discovery: *One problem I see with the content approach is that it makes it too easy for teachers to transmit knowledge by simply reading, telling, or demonstrating. Since I hold that it is self-defeating to transmit knowledge in some way that makes students into excellent scientists but also teaches them to hate science, I would rather risk losing some sense of the beautiful conceptual patterns in favor of a better attitude. Anyhow, if a discovery unit works as it should, the children acquire depth of knowledge in one area. They find out what it means for ideas and relationships to be knit together. They learn a great deal about a very little piece of nature. My friends, I submit that this process not only resembles* *what we do as researchers but creates a basic metaphor. Having done it in one area, the children come to understand that in each new area of investigation the problem is to find the pattern of relationships. Our speaker from the floor is right in his remarks about the status of experiments. As a student does an in-depth investigation, the function of the experiment becomes obvious to him. He designs one when he needs it. At other times he gets information from books, from adults, and sometimes from films. You know very well that we are each specialists, not in one field but in some subsection of the field. I submit that we are all operating with a very narrow, specialized piece of the conceptual net people are so glibly discussing. The piece is important because it contains what is most relevant to a particular area of investigation. Children will build their own networks of relationships when they are stimulated by some incongruent, discrepant, or puzzling situation.*

I admit, however, that if children are to progress to any level of conceptual sophistication, they probably need teachers and resources that can help them pass beyond the phenomenological level. Many problems simply cannot be solved at that level. That is why we are still struggling with the problem of how to provide guidance that will help teachers become more sophisticated in their question asking and their thinking in general.

Chairman: *There are some things all these programs have in common. In fact, I suspect that if you visited a classroom, you might have a difficult time deciding just which one was being taught. The behavior of the students in any group would resemble that of students in the other groups in more ways than it would differ. I think all these programs urge teachers to give students the time they need to become actively involved in conducting their own investigations. They expect plenty of mistakes—indeed they accord the student the right to be wrong, to learn from mistakes by retracing one's steps or by reorganizing one's procedures. Suppose all students learned to ask the following questions routinely—*

Evidence:
1 *What do I know?*
2 *Why do I believe it?*
3 *What is the evidence? Do I have it all?*
4 *Where did the evidence come from? How good is it?*

Photograph courtesy of Phyllis Marcuccio.

Inference:

5 *What do I make of it? What are all the possible interpretations?*

Action:

6 *What must I do with what I know? What possible actions should I take?*

7 *Do I know how to take action?*

Evaluation:

8 *What does it all mean? Do I value some outcomes more than others? Why?*

If these programs help to develop a sense of fate control in students, if they develop a statistical view of nature and a willingness to tolerate some level of uncertainty and if they instill the belief that there are patterns of relationships among variables which when found can be put to use, then these programs and the people who teach them will have done a tremendous job. But curriculum is not a static thing. We change our conceptions of what content and emphasis should prevail as we accumulate experience and try to foresee the kinds of futures in which our students will have to operate. Will what we do develop sufficient flexibility and suf-

ficient mental and emotional fluency to put them in command of their fates rather than make them victims of circumstance?

SUMMARY

1 Growth in scientific knowledge means that we are confronted with the necessity of making decisions that have more and more social, economic, political, legal, ethical, and moral implications.

2 The social system of man, the devices by which he makes decisions, must be mobilized to work more rapidly. That may be made possible if more prople come to understand the relationships between science and society.

3 In choosing curriculums we are trying to guess how to educate people for a future whose characteristics we can only barely guess.

4 Most decisions set off a chain of concomitant changes. The problem in decision making is to reason forward in time to the likely consequences. Each alternative has to be evaluated for its possible effects.

5 The interface between knowledge and its application is not well understood.

6 Science curriculums seem to be organized according to one or more of the following emphases:
  a Emphasis on process of intellectual skills.
  b Emphasis on discovery.
  c Emphasis on problem solving.
  d Thematic emphasis, or emphasis on content.

7 Although modern elementary science programs differ in organization, they seem to have many properties in common.
  a Students encounter phenomena directly.
  b There is time and opportunity to investigate.
  c There is room to make mistakes and retrace steps.
  d Covering content is not quite so important as the process of interaction between students and materials.
  e Quantitative concepts are introduced; measurement and prediction are stressed.

8 All the programs, properly taught, should make a contribution to the development of language, logic, fate control, and hope.

ACTIVITY 18-1
A CASE STUDY

OBJECTIVES

1 To identify examples of ethical, political, religious, and scientific beliefs that influence thought
2 To infer what curriculum would emerge in each era

Researchers carry on their work while embedded in a cultural milieu that conditions how they think and what they do. What is taught in school reflects the prevailing beliefs of each era. Ethical, political, religious, and scientific beliefs intertwine, often making curriculum construction difficult.

What to do:

1 Read the case history below.
2 Identify the sources of conflict at each point in time.
3 Identify the ways in which people responded to differences in the point of view.
4 Write a series of short paragraphs telling what the content of a curriculum might be as suggested by each individual or group whose view is stated.
5 Examine a few current elementary science series to determine whether they convey the idea that researchers *know* how the earth is formed and shaped or whether they show the *tentative* nature of the idea.

Note: In *The Discovery of Time,* chapter 7, "The Earth Acquires a History," Stephen Toulmin and June Goodfield describe with great sensitivity the struggles men had with each other as some of them tried to replace the static Renaissance view of nature by a developmental one. Researchers Stephen Toulmin and June Goodfield, *The Discovery of Time,* Harper Torchbooks, The Science Library, TB 585, pp. 141–170.

Case history:

Imagine with what joy and anxiety geologists interested in the origin of the moon greeted the lunar samples. Five centuries ago their counterparts might have been curious about what the surface of the moon was like, but their interest would certainly not include speculations on how the formation of the moon might be related to the formation of mountains and valleys on the earth. Until about the fifteenth century, most Western men believed the earth was created by God in the form in which they saw it then. Only an unchanging earth could last into eternity. The idea that the earth might have developed to its current state in stages and might in fact still be undergoing changes would have contravened the religious conception of the world that held men's minds at the time.

When Count Buffon proposed that the world got to where it was in stages and that things were not then as they once were or would someday be, he got into a great deal of trouble with theologians who, in turn, got him into trouble with the public and his friends. Finally the social pressures forced him to recant, much as Galileo before him had. A century later Hutton, an erudite English geologist, blatantly proposed that the earth might once have been a hot, molten ball, which when it began to cool "wrinkled" its surface as it shrank and that is how mountains formed. Hutton, like Buffon a hundred years before, revived the beliefs of Plato. Poor Hutton not only brought down the theologians on himself, but even the great Goethe took up the cudgel against him expressing his outrage through the medium of Mephistopholes in *Faust*. Mephistopholes, the Prince of Darkness, spouted the evil, dynamic theory of a hot, fluid interior to the earth, while Faust who represented the struggle against evil, spoke eloquently for the instant earth conception in which mountains were part of the original creation.

It is no easy matter ever to discard a well-embedded theory either in science or religion. A theory is like a platform; it holds up so many other things that when it starts to crumble, sometimes whole mental worlds crumble with it. Man may be right to be cautious because the cost for such restructuring can be so great. In the fifteenth and sixteenth centuries men were not ready to exchange an "instant earth" model, i.e., one created by God in the state men saw it, for a "dynamic earth" model, i.e., one that pictured the earth as evolving in stages. Most geologists did not share Hutton's views. They, after all, grew up living and working under the umbrella of a static model so they quickly jumped to its defense. Geologic processes, they argued, go on so slowly that the earth could not possibly have developed mountains in the sixty centuries or so that it was supposed to have existed at that time. They fought eloquently for the divine-origin model, and they accepted without question that the age of the earth must be about sixty centuries. Hutton had to agree that volcanic action could not have accomplished the changes in that time interval. So the adherents to one model or another arrived at an impasse.

Either the magnitude of the forces that brought about the changes must have been very different in the early stages of the earth than they were at the time the argument commenced, or, the dynamicists argued, the basic assumption about the age of the earth must be incorrect. When men reach such impasses in science, they often use the competing models to reinterpret existing data. They challenge the assumptions of the competing models. What would happen, the dynamicists wondered, if they made new estimates of the earth's age? Suppose the earth were really much older than their opponents supposed it to be. Then there would be time for the forces to work on molding the earth's surface to bring it to the stage in which men saw it. Consider how time is the culprit in this conflict. If the time could be increased, then the forces might reasonably explain the dynamicists' model. The static earth proponents needed an earth that did not change once formed, because that was the only way to assure its existence throughout all time. Each side used its model to reinterpret existing data as well as to guide its search for more supporting evidence.

Men continue into this century to construct different models of how the earth developed mountains, but all the models today tend to be dynamic, i.e., to show how the earth progressed in stages from some earlier condition to its present condition. One view held that the moon was ripped out of the earth's surface at an early stage of the cooling and this resulting imbalance in the fractured crust greatly increased the movement of the crust on its liquid base, enhancing mountain growth. But in all models, that ubiquitous variable time creeps through the considerations and into the choice of systems. One of the more popular views among geologists today, a model that essentially portrays a hot earth which is shrinking as it cools, still faces challenges on occasion. What each group considers as important evidence depends on how they have defined their systems. The moon group includes the moon in its reckoning. The original static-model people could not have cared less about the moon. The shrinking-earth people focus on analyzing forces deep inside the earth.

Anybody who would tamper with the most strongly held views of the scientific community in each era will not escape without wounds, even today. To win objective appraisal of a new model when it confronts one generally held requires that the people who invested so much of themselves in the prevailing model must undergo a complete reorganization of thought and sometimes must see a portion of their life's work become irrelevant. In principle scientists know what vitality these changes may bring to a discipline, but major changes in thought must fit into many other interlocking ideas before they displace what exists.

In the March 3, 1962, issue of *Science*, for example, Ray Woodruff and Marjory Goering, a geology professor and his graduate assistant at the University of Montana, proposed that the mountains of the earth formed from interactions between the moon and the earth. The earth, they argued, billows and swells five to fifteen inches in response to the passage of the moon. These waves ". . . wrinkle the earth's surface, pile up rocks, and gradually build the mountains" (p. 43). The authors describe how this action makes the rocks creep into piles, but they admit that little research on rock creeping exists. More people, however, started studying the phenomenon after the Woodruff and Goering paper. What man looks for in the way of facts depends on what his theories guide him toward.

Of course, Woodruff and Goering, who argued against the shrinking-planet model currently in vogue, did not have the theologian to face as they attacked what might *now* be called the traditional position by showing that at least one deduction from the starting assumptions of that model does not seem to be supported by the facts. A cooling-earth model would suggest that the circumference of the earth should be decreasing 3½ inches a year, and no evidence of that has been reported. They add, "Such a shortage is entirely too great not to have been noticed."

The article, which the two writers obviously thought would bring a storm down upon them, has at its conclussion a brief statement of their credentials as reputable, professional geological researchers. It ends with a remarkable plea to their fellows, "Since geologists as a group tend to be bound rather tightly by tradition, conservatives among them probably will challenge the thesis. All that the article's senior author asks is that *the challenges rise from fact rather than habit*" (p. 46; italics mine).

ACTIVITY 18-2

There is no last chapter to this book. You have to write it. That last chapter has a title—"You and Science." It is meant to be about you, about the views, feelings, hopes, fears, and messages you will transmit in science. Try to write it now, at this point in your life history.

ACTIVITY 18-3

In the symposium there were speakers for different points of view. State your own position.

REFERENCES

Cailliet, G., P. Setzer, and M. Love: *Everyman's Guide to Ecological Living,* The Macmillan Company, New York, 1971. (Paperback.)

Terry, M.: *Teaching for Survival,* Ballantine Books, Inc., New York, 1971.

Toffler, Alvin.: *Future Shock,* Bantam Books, Inc., New York, 1970. (Paperback.)

GENERAL REFERENCES

Books

Berger, Melvin, and Frank Clark: *Science and Music.* Whittlesey House, New York, 1971.

Caillict, G., P. Setzer, and M. Love: *Everyman's Guide to Ecological Living,* The Macmillan Company, New York, 1971.

Cooper, Elizabeth K.: *Science on the Shores and Banks,* Harcourt Brace Jovanovich, New York, 1960; *Science in Your Own Back Yard,* Harcourt, Brace Jovanovich, New York, 1960.

De Vries, L.: *The Book of Experiments,* The Macmillan Company, New York, 1959.

Herbert, Don: *Mr. Wizard's Science Secrets,* Popular Mechanics, New York, 1953; *Mr. Wizard's Experiments for Young Scientists,* Random House, Inc. New York,

Kormondy, Edward: *Concepts in Ecology,* Prentice Hall, Englewood Cliffs, N.J., 1965.

Leavitt, Jerome, and John Juntsberber: *Fun-Time Terrariums and Aquariums,* Children's Press, Chicago, 1961.

Lynde, Carlton J.: *Science Experiences With Home Equipment* (1955); *Science Experiences with Inexpensive Equipment* (1956); *Science Experiments With Ten-Cent Store Equipment* (1955); D. Van Nostrand Co., Inc., New York.

Podendorf, Illa: *The True Book of Science Experiments* (1954); *Discovering Science on Your Own* (1962); *101 Science Experiments* (1960); Children's Press, Chicago.

Report of the International Clearinghouse on Science and Mathematics Curricular Developments, J. D. Lockard (ed.), Science Teaching Center, University of Maryland. (Updated every two years).

Tale, Larry L., and Ernest W. Lee: *Environmental Education in the Elementary School* (Holt, Rinehart & Winston, Inc., New York, 1972).

Terry, Mark: *Teaching for Survival,* Ballantine Books, Inc., New York, 1971.

UNESCO Source Book for Science Teaching, UNESCO Publications Center, 801 Third Avenue, New York, N.Y. (This is especially useful for work in settings where materials have to be constructed.)

Periodicals*

The Aquarium, Innes Publishing Co., Philadelphia, Pa. 19107. (Monthly; C and T.)

Cornell Rural School Leaflets, New York State College of Agriculture, Ithaca, N.Y. 14850. (Quarterly; T.)

Current Science and Aviation, American Education Publications, Education Center, Columbus, Ohio 43216. (Weekly during the school year; T and C.)

Environment Action Bulletin, Rodale Press, Inc., Emmaus, Pa. 18049.

Junior Natural History, American Museum of Natural History, New York, N.Y. 10024. (Monthly; C and T.)

My Weekly Reader, American Education Publications, Education Center, Columbus, Ohio 43216. (Weekly during the school year.)

National Geographic, National Geographic Society, 1146 Sixteenth St. N.W., Washington, D.C. (Monthly; C and T.)

Natural History, American Museum of Natural History, 79 St. and Central Park West, New York, N.Y. 10024. (Monthly; C and T.)

Newsletter Ecolog, Center for Environmental Education, 5400 Glenwood Ave., Minneapolis, Minn., 55422. (Free.)

Outdoors Illustrated, National Audubon Society, 1000 Fifth Ave., New York, N.Y. (Monthly; C and T.)

Science Newsletter, Science Service, Inc., 1719 N Street N.W., Washington, D.C. 20036. (Weekly; T.)

Science and Children, National Science Teachers Association, Washington, D.C. 20036. (Eight times a year; C and T.)

Scientific American, 415 Madison Ave., New York, N.Y. 10017. (Monthly; T.)

Technology for Children Project (T4CP), Division of Vocational Education, New Jersey Department of Education, 225 West State Street, Trenton, N. J. 08625. (Monthly newsletter.)

Space Science (formerly *Junior Astronomer*), Benjamin Adelman, 4211 Colie Dr., Silver Springs, Md. 20906 (Monthly during school year; C and T.)

Tomorrow's Scientists, National Science Teachers Association, Washington, D.C. 20036. (Eight issues a year; T.)

UNESCO Courier, The UNESCO Publications Center, 801 Third Ave., New York, N.Y. 10022. (Monthly; T.)

Weatherwise, American Meteorological Society, 3 Joy St., Boston, Mass. 02108. (Monthly; T.)

*C means "child-oriented"; T means "teacher-oriented." The publications listed are helpful in keeping abreast of changes in science.

ORGANIZATIONS CONCERNED WITH THE ENVIRONMENT

American Forestry Association
919 Seventeenth Street N.W.
Washington, D.C. 20006

Animal Welfare Institute
P.O. Box 3492
Grand Central Station
New York, New York 10017

Environmental Defense Fund
P.O. Drawer 740
Stony Brook, New York 11790

Friends of the Earth
30 East 42 Street
New York, New York 10017

Izaak Walton League
1326 Waukegan Road
Glenview, Illinois 60025

League of Women Voters
1730 M Street N.W.
Washington, D.D. 20036

National Audubon Society
1130 Fifth Avenue
New York, New York 10028

National Geographic Society
17 and M Streets N.W.
Washington, D.C. 20036

National Parks Association
Washington, D.C. 20009

National Wildlife Federation
1412 Sixteenth Street N.W.
Washington, D.C. 20036

The Nature Conservancy
1522 K Street N.W.
Washington, D.C. 20005

Planned Parenthood-World Population
515 Madison Avenue
New York, New York 10022

Population Reference Bureau
1755 Massachusetts Avenue, N.W.
Washington, D.C. 20036

Sierra Club
1050 Mills Tower
San Francisco, California 94104

The Wilderness Society
729 Fifteenth Street N.W.
Washington, D.C. 20005

Zero Population Growth
367 State Street
Los Altos, California 94022

Tuberculosis and Respiratory Disease Association
National Headquarters
1740 Broadway
New York, New York 10019

INDEX